A History of Eastern Michigan University
1849 – 1965

A History of
Eastern Michigan University
1849 – 1965

by Egbert R. Isbell

Eastern Michigan University Press 1971

CONTENTS

FOREWORD

The history of a university, like its mission, is never complete. The university's central purpose, the pursuit of knowledge, ideas and truth, is not a purpose easily measured and evaluated, nor captured in place and time. In essence, the inner life history of an institution, committed to teaching and learning, is an unending series of intellectual encounters among the members of the university community. The membership changes year-by-year, even day-by-day, but it is always united in a search for enlightenment. The fruits of this search are tested and assimilated through a process which takes unmeasured time. The results are often surmised rather than calculated. The influence of a great teacher, however, never ends and an illustrious university must be a great teacher.

Although our history is not easily captured, it is valuable to us as a measure of our successes and failures, a chronicle and evaluation of what has gone before. This history is of special interest and inspiration as it traces the story of one of the most significant chapters in the development of higher education in the United States. It is a sober, documented account of historical facts.

I find much of it quite moving. For example, there is the account of the work of Isaac Crary and John D. Pierce, in the early days of Michigan's statehood, when Michigan was for the most part a wilderness of forests and swamps that nearly concealed the small settlements. These young men saw that, if a tolerable life was to be made here and if a viable society was to arise, an effective educational system would be needed. They saw further that for the creation of a worthy educational system, a corps of educated teachers would be required. They concluded that the State must establish a school for that purpose. Against legislative skepticism, indifference, hostility and pleas of poverty, they waged an energetic and unremitting campaign for years until they won. So it was that Michigan State Normal School came into being.

vii

The little school went about its business quietly but with a sureness of purpose. It became a four-year Normal College, and soon was recognized as one of the premier institutions of its kind in the country. It survived a civil war, two world wars and the intervening depression, and now an Asian war.

This is the inspiring story that Dr. Isbell unfolds, with a skill and sensitivity that reveals both his high professional talent and an extraordinary devotion to this task. This was, for him, a labor of love. As professor of history at Eastern for 36 years and as Dean of Administration for 15 of those years, it might be said that the subject chose him as much as he chose the subject. In any event, they were clearly meant for each other.

Dr. Isbell, a native of Michigan, and having earned the AB, MA, LLB and PhD degrees from the University of Michigan, taught at Eastern from 1937 until his retirement. This manuscript was virtually completed at the time of his death in 1968.

He was a quiet and scholarly man, proud to be a part of this University because he believed (and rightly so, in my opinion) that it had made memorable contributions to the development of public education in the State and in the nation. Drawing upon his education, his wide experience, and his zealous devotion to the University, he would almost appear to have been destined to tell the story of the origin, struggles, and development of this university; to set forth its contributions to American education, and to define its relation to the history of America itself.

Professor Isbell unfolds an inspiring story. Thousands of graduates of Eastern Michigan University have carried into schools and colleges over the entire country the idea of their University. They have influenced the minds of legions of young people and their professional colleagues. Thus, much that has happened in the last 120 years is now playing a part in shaping the course of American education.

This book should interest and gratify all who have ties with Eastern and will be of value to all who have a professional interest in the development of education in America.

The portfolio of sketches of the presidents, executed by Professor Jane M. Dart of our Art Department, enhances the attractiveness of the book. For Professor Dart as well as for Professor Isbell, this was largely a labor of love. Her work is as excellent as his narrative.

Final editing and publication were completed in the absence of the author; some minor errors will doubtless appear. They are the responsibility of the University, not the author.

While Dr. Isbell is not here to express his gratitude to all those who helped him, I am sure that I speak for him when I say that the debt is large and the appreciation great. We cannot name all who assisted, but they will know, and they will find special pleasure in these pages.

Harold E. Sponberg, President
Eastern Michigan University
Ypsilanti, Michigan   1971

INTRODUCTION

Eastern Michigan University was established in 1849 as Michigan State Normal School to train teachers and mold good citizens. As an academic institution it was at first rated as a glorified academy (or "high school" of later date), but it also offered instruction in pedagogy (the art of teaching). It was a pioneer venture, the first west of the Allegheny mountains, sixth in the United States. There are now 385 institutions (public and private) in this country accredited for teacher training.

In its first half-century this school evolved into a four-year college, with a well-developed liberal arts program to supplement the teacher training. It was the second in the nation to achieve this status. During its second half-century it evolved further into a more broadly oriented liberal arts college, but with the emphasis still on teacher preparation; then, into the university that it is today.

In the course of its existence Eastern Michigan University ("Normal," as we shall for the most part refer to it) developed a nationwide reputation as a source of highly capable teachers. Its alumni include men and women who have won national and international recognition as leaders in education, science, and the professions. Among its faculty have been many exciting teachers, and a number who became eminent in their fields, both pedagogical and academic. Michigan Normal has been both a pioneer and an example of the best in teacher preparation.

The eleven and a-half decades treated in this history cover a period of sufficient length for some perspective on evolutionary processes, educational and social. Changing moods and modes, a radical transition from a primitive, provincial, rural to a sophisticated, worldly, urban society, an amazing development from a penurious to a highly affluent industrial economy marked these years.

These changes were accompanied by changes in viewpoint and modifications in objective. Progress in professional educational knowledge, information and techniques was steady. Growing demands of the communities of the State found a sensitive response. Indeed, that the status of Eastern Michigan University today derived from a simple normal school is impressive tribute to the wholesome and extensive development of the social consciousness of the people of Michigan.

A number of developments in this history deserve brief reference here.

As a state-supported institution, Eastern Michigan University was until recently under the authority of a state board of control and is of necessity greatly concerned with the attitude of the state legislators, source of financial support. Until recently the board in control was known as the State Board of Education.

It had four members, three elected and one *ex-officio* (the State Superintendent of Public Instruction). Its original function was to govern the Normal. But from about the turn of the century other responsibilities were added, including three other normal schools. This development created a new situation in which close attention to the affairs of any one institution became impossible.

With the new State Constitution of 1963, this was changed and Eastern was provided with its own governing body composed of eight members called Regents.

As for relations with the legislature, the story, until the post-World War 11 years (and for a few years after World War 1) was marked by denial and frustration. The enthusiasm displayed at the founding of the institution did not find expression in legislative appropriations. In the early years this was due in large part to the financial condition of a young state that had not yet developed its potential. Support for the Normal rested largely on land grants and the genuine enthusiasm of the citizens of Ypsilanti who, in the first instance, made a generous offer of cash and, through the ensuing years, made several gifts of land for campus expansion.

One president, in a despondent moment, commented that up to his time not a building had been constructed according to original plans. Each had been curtailed in dimensions or facilities to satisfy a limited appropriation. At another time, when additional normal schools were being proposed, faculty and administration united in opposition, fearful of even smaller budgets.

Proximity to the University of Michigan also played a role. The U-M at all times was given priority and the Normal suffered in consequence. Faculty salaries in Ypsilanti were small compared with those in Ann Arbor. Yet, during the Great Depression, the percentage cutbacks at the Normal were twice those imposed upon her larger neighbor.

(Relationships between the two schools shifted over the years. When the U-M established a chair for education in 1870, the Normal felt that its area was being invaded. A persistent effort in the face of lengthy resistance succeeded in gaining U-M recognition of credits earned at the Normal as equivalent in value to its own.

(In athletics, the proudest moment in football occurred when a Normal team *almost* defeated a Michigan team in a year when the latter won the Western Conference championship.

(The Graduate School of the U-M proved to be an excellent and readily available source for new Normal faculty. Aspirants for the doctoral degree could become members of the faculty and, on the side, pursue their studies. And when the State Board sought assistance from the U-M in establishing graduate work in the teachers colleges, a co-operative program was developed that paved the way for the present independent programs on the several campuses.)

Twice in Normal's history, there was threat of closing the institution, once as an economy measure during the depression, again on a demand for housing for factory workers in a neighboring war plant during World War II.

The spirit of the school was from the first marked by a strong sense of pride of mission. In the earlier years, this was colored by a moral and religious zest. As the curriculum grew and the social climate changed, the emphasis became more secular, the spirit of scientific inquiry more pronounced.

As one surveys the faculty scene, a significant fact stands out. Although the Normal was established to train teachers, liberal arts in time assumed a dominant role. Though the faculty aspired for years to make the institution a strictly professional school, as in law or medicine or engineering, and even persuaded the State Board to their point of view, the experiment failed, and the school developed a high-grade liberal arts curriculum that led to its becoming a college, and to a faculty of national prestige.

It is surprising to discover that, in this teachers college, the names that gave it national eminence came largely (though not exclusively) from the liberal arts rather than the professional education side. Such were McFarlane and Jefferson in geography, David Eugene

Smith and Lyman and Stone in mathematics, D'Ooge in the classical languages and Ford in the modern, Strong in the physical sciences and Sherzer in the biological, Harrold in English literature. At the same time it is noteworthy that these men were as fully imbued with the high importance of the role of the teacher as were those in the pedagogical area. Indeed, the school and college textbooks that flowed from the pens of McFarlane, Jefferson, Smith, Lyman, Stone and D'Ooge received nationwide acceptance.

At the same time, the professional side was also attracting attention. Wilbur Bowen contributed importantly to the field of physical education and health; his textbook in anatomy was revised repeatedly long after his death, and is still in use. Charles Hoyt contributed substantially to the history of education. And Charles Elliot established the first normal college program in the nation for the training of handicapped children.

A second noteworthy aspect of the Normal faculty was the role played by women. Free from the long-standing prejudice in major institutions of learning against women on the faculty, the Normal from the first benefited by this. Abigail Rogers, first Preceptress of the Normal School, was known as an ardent and determined pioneer in the movement to open the doors of higher education to women. Julia Anne King, as preceptress and later first head of the Department of History and Social Sciences, made a lasting impression on the campus and became recognized as one of the most effective educators in the state. Alma Blount, English scholar, was an early holder of the PhD degree, and became widely known for her textbooks.

Estelle Downing, also in English, was not only an excellent teacher but a crusader for peace and international understanding. Genevieve Walton, head librarian, made a lasting impression on the library profession of Michigan. Lucy Osband, in biology, frail but dynamic and with vision beyond her area of instruction, deserved the lion's share of credit for the creation of a department of physical education. The list could be greatly expanded.

As for the students, the doors of the Normal were from the first open to both men and women, and to all cultures and races. The image of "Ypsi" as a girls' school, fostered by the demand of society for women teachers and enlivened by the nocturnal influx of males from the nearby University of Michigan (an institution that did not admit women until 1870, and whose alumni for the next half century took pride in returning their sons to a "man's" school), became less and less true as the programs in industrial arts and physical education developed, and with the return to school of war veterans. The latter factor, not important after the Civil War because relatively few returned to the classroom, became important after the first World War and decisive after World War II.

For a century, the Normal served as an opportunity for young people to acquire a college education at minimal cost, and administrative policy was at great pains to retain this distinction. Tuition was kept relatively low and, as dormitories came into the picture, rates were kept to a minimum. This policy was without doubt inspired in large part because teachers for the public schools were drawn largely from the middle and lower economic classes.

The tremendous influx of students that has taken place since World War II has affected one institutional policy of considerable significance. The traditional view was one of sympathy and patience for the border-line student. Pressures of numbers and costs today have modified the practice and shortened the patience, but the philosophy persists.

A word should be added concerning the Purpose. The Normal became a nationally known and highly respected teacher-preparation institution. But the history of the institution reveals that its growth and expansion took place in response to the felt needs of the society it served. It has not been the product of formal planning in advance. Thus, with greatly increased demands of the post-war years, involving a great variety of student abilities and ambitions and a corresponding variety of social needs to be met, its early identity has merged with the broader purposes of a university.

CHAPTER ONE

THE FOUNDING OF
MICHIGAN NORMAL

Creation of a state-supported institution for the training of teachers in the young backwoods State of Michigan in 1849 was an extraordinary step forward in education. The very concept of a Normal School was, for America, new; her people had yet to be persuaded that to teach, one must have special preparation. Of the twenty-five states that preceded Michigan into the Union, only two—Massachusetts and New York—had taken such a step, and in both the venture had been recent, experimental and tentative. That twelve-year-old Michigan, rural and wooded and remote, with her population of just under 400,000 widely scattered over a vast area, should become the third state to establish an institution exclusively for the training of teachers must be attributed to her good fortune in having attracted a few exceptionally public-spirited citizens who were at the same time alert and well-informed as to what was taking place in the outside world.

A vivid picture of early Michigan and sense of its rapid development is provided by the following description by a former State Superintendent of Public Instruction:

> The first half century of state history has witnessed many wonderful changes. In 1837 the interior was sparsely settled, and the forests and prairies showed few signs of human industry. Wagon roads were scarce and poor, and there was no completed railroad. Postal arrangements were exceedingly inconvenient, and correspondence was an expensive luxury. The population of the state was 174,467. Cities there were none. Schools, churches and newspapers were few, and the privations of pioneer life were many and severe.[1]

1

When, in 1835, a convention met to form a state government for Michigan, the subject of elementary education was being pressed as of great importance. Population was increasing rapidly; more and more school districts were being formed; there were no uniform requirements as to courses of study or length of terms or qualification of teachers. There was no professional training for teachers. Judge Cooley, in his "Michigan, a History of Governments," remarked that there were as yet no professional teachers. Some farmer or mechanic, pérhaps a grown-up son or daughter, who had the advantage of the common schools of New York or New England, offered his or her services as teacher during the dull season of regular employment and consented to take as wages whatever the district could afford to pay.

By the fall of 1838 some 245 townships reported to the newly created office of State Superintendent of Public Instruction a total of 1509 school districts, and 34,000 pupils between the ages of 5 and 16.

In the East, particularly in Massachusetts, a new type of school was being considered as the answer to the problem of the untrained teacher. Known as the Normal School, this concept was supported by reports from educators who had traveled in Europe. Among these reports was that of the Rev. Charles Brooks of Hingham, Massachusetts. On a journey from Liverpool to New York in 1835 he was accompanied by Dr. H. Julius of Hamburg who had been commissioned by the King of Prussia to visit schools in America. Brooks became acquainted in detail with the Prussian system of elementary schools, and became an urgent advocate of the normal school idea. He spent much time in the next three years traveling throughout Massachusetts, explaining the Prussian system. Henry Barnard of Connecticut visited European schools in the years 1835–1837, and thereafter devoted his great editorial talents to the improvement of public education in this country, particularly through the *American Journal of Education* (which he founded).

Three reports in particular on European educational systems attracted major attention beyond the confines of Massachusetts and Connecticut, and were widely circulated. These were that of the Frenchman, Victor Cousin, made to his government in 1831; one by the Rev. Calvin E. Stowe of Ohio; and the 1843 report of Horace Mann. The Cousin Report included surveys of several European countries. The first half dealt with the Prussian system of public education, and was translated into English and reprinted in New York in 1835. It is described as the first document on the subject to make a deep impression in America. Two aspects of the report found acceptance here—the policy of centralized state control of education, and the concept of the normal school for the professional preparation of teachers.

The report by Stowe (husband of Harriet Beecher Stowe) came as the result of a visit he made to Europe in 1836 to buy a library for Lane Theological Seminary. He was at the same time commissioned by the Ohio Legislature to report on systems of elementary education there, and did so in his "Report on Elementary Education in Europe" of 1837. It was quoted extensively by educational journals and was read widely.

In 1843, Horace Mann, secretary of the Board of Education of Massachusetts, spent several months visiting schools in Britain, Holland, Belgium, German States, and France. From this came his "Seventh Report." This is held to be the most influential of all reports on European education. In it, Mann ranked the Prussian system first and the English last.

Thus, the educational pot was being brought to a boil at the time that the two founders of the Michigan system, Isaac Crary and the Rev. John D. Pierce, appeared on the scene. These men were friends. Crary, indeed, had lived in the Pierce home at Marshall, Michigan, for a time. Both were deeply interested in the problem of education.

Pierce had been sent to Michigan in 1831 by the Home Missionary Society. He settled in Marshall and organized the Congregational church there. He had been born in New Hampshire, educated in Massachusetts, and was a graduate of Brown University. While in Marshall, Pierce showed great interest in public education. He obtained a copy of the Cousin Report as published in the United States and discussed it at length with his friend, Crary. This occurred just when Michigan was organizing to become a state. Crary was a member of the Convention of 1835 that would draw up the Constitution.

On the urging of Crary, Michigan's first governor, Stevens T. Mason, appointed Pierce State Superintendent of Public Instruction, an office created by the new Constitution. Pierce served for five years, returning to the ministry in 1842. In 1847 he was elected to the State House of Representatives, and was re-elected in 1851. He was a member of the Constitutional Convention of 1850. During his incumbency as State Superintendent he founded and edited the *Journal of Education* (1838–1840), an official voice of the department and a means of communicating with township and district school officers throughout the State and securing their support for this program.

Crary (some seven years younger than Pierce) was a lawyer. He, too, was born in New England (at Preston, Connecticut). He graduated from Trinity College, Hartford, studied law, and commenced his practice in Marshall in 1833. As a delegate to the Constitutional Convention of 1835, he was made chairman of the Education Committee. He was elected as a Democrat to the 24th, 25th, and 26th Congresses, serving as Michigan's first Congressman from 1837 to 1841. He served as a Regent of the University of Michigan from 1837 to 1844, and was a member of the State Board of Education from 1850 to 1852. He served as a member of the State House of Representatives from 1842 to 1846, and as Speaker of the House in 1846.

Pierce and Crary held similar views as to what should be done in Michigan about education. To these two men Michigan owes her pioneer position in the history of public education in America. Crary was the creator by virtue of the fact that, as chairman of the Education Committee of the Constitutional Convention, he was the author of Article X which established the Michigan system. Its distinctive features were that education should be represented by a separate branch of the government, that there should be a state officer in charge of the whole system, and that lands granted by the federal government for school purposes should be granted to the State as trustee rather than, as had been the rule, to the townships.

With the creation of the office of State Superintendent of Public Instruction, Michigan became the first state to adopt the Prussian system of vesting the educational authority in a single individual.

Pierce was the organizer. As the first State Superintendent of Public Instruction, it was his responsibility to present to the legislature a system of common school and university education, and to administer the system as well as the more than a million acres of federal-grant lands. Of his part in the establishment of the public school system, he said:

> It is my pride to have been one to help lay the foundations of our present system, and I want no better monument to my name than this.[2]

Our interest in these two men lies in their basic concepts concerning public education. Both believed it to be a state, rather than local or private, function. Superintendent Pierce found opportunity in his annual reports to express his philosophy and outlook in some detail. He was so strongly in favor of free public education that he would have liked to make it compulsory and prohibit private academies.

With regard to teachers to conduct these schools, he did not doubt the necessity for professional training. But he did not, in fact, at this time propose a normal school. Rather, he would have used the proposed branches of the University of Michigan as teacher training institutions. He recommended that, in each county with a sufficient number of inhabitants, a school or branch of the U-M be established, with a department for the education of teachers for primary schools, and a three-year course of instruction.

But the U-M branches, designed to feed it with students prepared to undertake university-grade of work, failed to prosper. In 1839, five such branches were in existence in Pontiac, Monroe, Kalamazoo, Detroit, and Niles. Of a total of 161 students attending these branches, just 10 were planning to teach in the public schools. At no time were there more than 10 branches, and in August of 1848 only 4 were in existence. Furthermore, they proved to be a serious drain on the financial resources of the young and growing U-M. From this time, little is heard of the branches and no further appropriations were made for them. Their place, as far as preparatory schools for the U-M was concerned, was taken by the Union School system (parent of the high school), and unincorporated academies and seminaries, mostly with religious backing.

Superintendent Pierce's successor, Francis Sawyer jr., in his report for 1841, dwelt on the importance in a teacher of the ability to teach, and referred to examples in Holland, Prussia, and in Massachusetts where "*the art of teaching* is taught like any other art."

Oliver C. Comstock, successor to Sawyer, in his report for 1843, also urged the importance of knowing *how* to teach, and referred to practices elsewhere. He said:

> . . . it is plain that an acquaintance with general literature and science does not of necessity prepare one for the arduous, but delightful business of educating the undying mind. Such a preparation is chiefly derived from the study of the science and art of teaching. Firmly persuaded of this truth, many of the governments of the old world and some of our sister

states have instituted normal schools, in which the science and art of teaching are elucidated and enforced. Model schools are formed and taught in these institutions.[3]

Ira Mayhew, Comstock's successor, repeatedly asserted the importance of a normal school. But he seems to have felt that Michigan was not yet ready and urged the value of teachers associations and institutes. In his report for 1847 he became more definite:

> The interests of popular education require that something should be done for the improvement of the present generation of teachers. This, perhaps, can better be accomplished through the agency of Teachers' Institutes, than by any other instrumentality. There is, at present, a great lack of suitable persons to take charge of these institutes. This lack can be supplied only by the establishment of a Normal School for the professional training of teachers. Such an institution would be productive of incalculable good. In relation to the nature and advantages of both of these institutions the Superintendent is prepared to submit his views to the legislature in such form as they may direct.

In his report for 1848 Mayhew, while repeating his belief in the need for normal schools, added:

> I would not, however, at our age as a State, and the advancement we have made in the department of public instruction, recommend the establishment of a single Normal School; and especially when we consider our present necessities.

Meanwhile, in August, 1847, a significant report of the Board of Visitors of the U-M had been made to the Superintendent of Public Instruction. The chairman of the Board was the Rev. Mr. Pierce, and it is reasonable to assume that he wrote the report. After commenting vigorously on the need for good grammar schools, seminaries, or branches of the U-M "to fill the intervening space between the common school and the University," the report turned to the topic of a normal school:

> New York has for many years past emulated New England in its liberal and varied provisions for diffusing education and knowledge among the masses of her multitudinous population. She has also within a few years past established a State Normal School, which has excited the strongest

> interest . . . Michigan need not be far behind her elder and more advanced, but not more forward, sisters. She has accessible and quite within her reach, an ample fund . . . It is not by abstracting from either the common school or University funds . . . But we have certain Salt Spring lands . . . We propose that they should be appropriated to the support and assistance of a State Normal School, Branches of the University, Academies, High Schools and other Seminaries of learning of a high order, throughout the State.[4]

The center of interest in this report was unquestionably the U-M; the proposal for a normal school was merely a part of a wider proposal for a variety of intermediate institutions that would serve to feed the University. But there was here a practical suggestion for financing, and on this the Board of Visitors for the U-M took formal action, as follows:

> Resolved, That it is expedient that the Salt Spring Lands should be appropriated to the support and assistance of a State Normal School, branches of the University and other seminaries of learning . . . and that we recommend that the Legislature take immediate measures to appropriate the Salt Spring Lands to the purpose above contemplated.

The salt spring lands referred to were those granted to the State by an Act of Congress of July 25, 1838. Salt springs, not exceeding 12 in number, together with 6 sections of adjoining land each, were granted to the State for its use, but could not be sold or leased for a period longer than 10 years without the consent of Congress.

It should be noted that salt springs were held to be of great potential value as possible leads to salt sources that could be profitably mined. The first task that Douglass Houghton, first State Geologist, assigned to himself was the investigation of brine springs of the Lower Peninsula. By 1840, he had located more than half of the salt spring sections, but the manufacture of salt was not put on a commercial basis until 1859, when the Saginaw valley was found to be sufficiently productive.

There is little doubt that the consistent emphasis of the first four Superintendents of Public Instruction (Pierce, Sawyer, Comstock and Mayhew) on the importance of professional preparation for teachers of the common schools, the numerous references to the importance of Normal Schools and what must have been an increasing concern on the part of parents over the kind of education their children were getting, served to stimulate active interest in the state legislature.

In 1848, a resolution was offered in the House of Representatives as follows:

> That the committee on education be instructed to inquire into, and report
> to this House, the propriety of establishing by law a separate department
> in the university of this state, for the education of teachers, both male and
> female, and that they have leave to report by bill or otherwise.[5]

But no bill was reported in the House. A bill was introduced in the Senate to establish a branch of the U-M as a State Normal School. It failed to pass. Two petitions in the House requesting passage of a bill providing for a State Normal School were tabled.

In 1849, Superintendent Comstock was succeeded by Francis W. Shearman. Comstock was elected to the State House of Representatives and was made chairman of its Committe on Education. It was this committee that reported out a bill for the establishment of a normal school, and Comstock worked hard for its adoption. Success rewarded his efforts. On March 28, 1849, Act No. 138 was passed, entitled "An Act to establish a State Normal School."

The purpose for the new institution was stated as follows:

> Section 1. *Be it enacted by the Senate and House of Representatives of the
> State of Michigan,* That a State Normal School be established, the exclu-
> sive purposes of which shall be the instruction of persons both male and
> female in the art of teaching, and in all the various branches that pertain
> to a good common school education; also, to give instructions in the
> mechanic arts, and in the arts of husbandry and agricultural chemistry, in
> the fundamental laws of the United States.

The Normal School was placed under the authority of a Board of Education to be appointed by the Governor by and with the advice and consent of the Senate. This board was to consist of three members, with a term of three years, and two ex-officio members—the Lieutenant-Governor and the Superintendent of Public Instruction.

Provisions as to the powers and duties of the Board included the annual election of a president "who shall be empowered to visit the various villages and places of importance in the State, and obtain donations and receive propositions for the establishment of said normal school." The Board was also to appoint a principal, an assistant, and teachers, prescribe the textbooks to be used, make all the regulations and by-laws necessary "for the good government and management of said school." The Board was also to procure a site and erect buildings "in or near some village in this State, where it can most conveniently be done, and where in their judgment it will most subserve the best interests of the State." A model school in connection with the Normal School was to be established.

The Board was also to set the rules for admission of pupils, following these guidelines set forth in the Act:

> Every applicant for admission shall undergo an examination under the direction of the board, and if it shall appear that the applicant is not a person of good moral character, or will not make an apt and good teacher, such applicant shall be rejected.

Furthermore, each applicant could be required to sign a declaration "of intention to follow the business of teaching primary schools in this State." The Board was authorized to make exceptions, however.

The Act further provided that a student, after having attended the Normal School for 22 weeks, would, upon due examination and approval, be certified for teaching.

Ten sections of salt spring lands were set aside as the Normal School Building Fund. Fifteen sections were placed in a trust fund, the interest from which would be used for salaries. This was designated as the Normal School Endowment Fund. The 25 sections were not to be sold at less than $4 per acre. The State Treasurer was to be treasurer of the Board. Three days later a supplementary act was passed consolidating the two funds into a single permanent endowment fund, the proceeds to go to buildings and current expenses.[6] It is worth noting here that the land, 16,000 acres in all, was completely sold by 1868, the average price being $4.50 per acre. As of 1880, the endowment fund stood at $69,000, and produced an annual income of $4,300 (round figures).

On March 25, 1850, an "Act to consolidate and amend the Laws relative to the establishment of a State Normal School" was approved.[7] This ratified the two preceding acts, located the school at Ypsilanti, and included a number of other features. The three members of the Board of Education were to be appointed by the Governor "by and with the consent of the Senate and House of

Representatives in joint convention." The State Treasurer was to serve as an ex-officio member of the Board. A Board of Visitors was to be appointed by the State Board to report to the State Superintendent of Public Instruction. The superintendent himself was to visit the Normal once a year and make an annual report to the legislature.

Important financial provisions followed. The State Board was given authority to receive and spend sums donated by the citizens of Ypsilanti and vicinity. All lands granted to the State or the Board in trust for the support of the Normal were to be held in a perpetual fund for the use of the Normal School. The Board was incorporated.[8]

The decision to locate the Normal in Ypsilanti had been made by the Board more than six months earlier. This Board was composed of Samuel Barstow, Randolph Manning and the Rev. Samuel Newberry, with State Superintendent Francis Shearman and Lt.-Gov. William M. Fenton as ex-officio members. Newberry was elected president, and had set forth to find a site for the school.

His success may be measured by the fact that the Board was able, at its meeting in September, 1849, to consider five written offers. These came from Niles, Gull Prairie, Jackson, Marshall, and Ypsilanti. The last-named was supported by recommendations from Monroe, Adrian, Tecumseh and Detroit. After due deliberation, the Board unanimously decided to accept the offer of Ypsilanti.

Superintendent Shearman reported the decision in the following words:

> The location of the school has been a duty of great delicacy and no small difficulty. Each of the places mentioned proposed to furnish a site for the buildings, and tendered a large subscription in aid of the institution, to be paid in money. After a full investigation and examination of the various proposals, and taking into view all the objects to be attained by the location, the board finally fixed upon the village of Ypsilanti, which was conditionally designated as the location of the normal school . . . The advantage of this site in point of health, accessibility and locality, were deemed, under all circumstances, not second to any other, while the proposition to the board was by far the most liberal . . . Such a proposition was deemed by the board satisfactory evidence not only of the liberality and public spirit, but of the existence of interest in the general subject of education . . . which cannot be less important to the institution in the future, than the liberal offer which it induced.[9]

The Ypsilanti offer consisted of a site of four acres; a subscription of $13,500 "well secured," one-third payable September 1, 1850, and the rest within two years thereafter; the use of temporary buildings for the Normal and the Model School until suitable buildings could be erected, and the salary of the principal ($700.00) for five years.

By the revised Constitution of 1850, the composition and manner of selecting the Board of Education were changed. The three appointive members became elective, for a six-year term. The number of ex-officio members was reduced to one, the State Superintendent, who served also as secretary of the Board.

The first election, which took place in 1852, resulted in the following membership: Isaac E. Crary, president; Chauncey Joslin, Gideon O. Whittemore. Superintendent Shearman was named secretary. To this Board fell the responsibility for breathing life into the plan for the Normal.

To the four acres donated by Ypsilanti were added four acres by purchase. On this site was erected a three-story building which was described at the time as follows:

> The building is of brick, finished with stuccowork, three stories in height, with a basement for furnaces and is divided into a model school room, with entries, reception, library, and recitation rooms and entries; a Normal School room in the second story with similar arrangements, and a large and spacious hall in the upper story.[10]

Faculty positions and staff were determined as follows: Adonijah Strong Welch, Principal and Professor of Greek and Latin Languages; Miss Abigail C. Rogers, Preceptress and Teacher of Botany and Belles-Lettres; Orson Jackson, Professor of Intellectual Philosophy; and J. M. B. Sill, Teacher of English Grammar and Elocution. Four other positions were created but not filled, namely, Professor of Natural Sciences and Professor of Modern Languages, Teacher of Vocal Music and Drawing, and Principal of the Model School.

The Michigan State Normal School was the fifth such institution to be authorized by a state legislature, and the sixth to open its doors. It was the first institution west of the Allegheny Mountains. On the continent of North America, it was the ninth, Canada having previously established three.

CHAPTER TWO

FORMATIVE YEARS, 1853–1865

Dedicatory exercises for the Michigan Normal School were held in the auditorium of the new building on October 5, 1852. Hundreds of Michigan citizens, including the State Board of Education and "a large congregation of teachers," climbed the flights of stairs and crowded into the room. Those on the program were Superintendent of Public Instruction Shearman, the first Superintendent of Public Instruction (Mr. Pierce), Issac E. Crary, president of the State Board; Chauncy Joslin, member of the State Board; Divie Bethune Duffield, secretary of the Detroit Board of Education; Adonijah Strong Welch, the newly-appointed Principal; and a guest speaker, Federal Judge Ross Wilkins.

The sentiments expressed were optimistic. Pierce, in a long address, revealed that he looked upon a normal school as an intermediary step from the public schools to the U-M.

Crary, in a brief statement, dedicated the building "to the People of the State of Michigan, to promote the great cause of education—the cause of man—the cause of God." Joslin delivered the commission of office to the new Principal.

Judge Wilkens was concerned, not with the concept of an institution to prepare teachers for the public schools, but with that part of the statute establishing the Normal School which required that instruction be given in "the fundamental laws of the United States, and in what regards (concerns) the rights and duties of citizens."

It was Duffield who suffused the proceedings with poetic fancy and optimistic hope. He had written a hymn for the occasion, in

13

which he addressed the "spirit of immortal truth," in part as follows:

> To thy great purpose now we raise
> These noble walls, this song of praise.
>
> Here have we built a holy shrine,
> Where thy true worshippers may kneel,
> And seek to know the art divine,
> Of teaching what thy laws reveal;
> Pour then thy flood of golden light,
> And cheer the groping student's sight.

Thus, with modest concept and high hopes, Michigan took her place among the first states in the Union to recognize the need for professional training for teachers.

An early means of providing some training for those who were engaged in the teaching of children was the Teachers Institute, an approach first definitely organized in Connecticut in 1839 by Henry Barnard who defined the Teachers Institute as follows:

> A Teachers Institute, is . . . a gathering of teachers, old and young, experienced and inexperienced, of both sexes, and of schools of different grades;—in such number as will develop the sympathies and power of a common pursuit, and yet not so large as to exclude the freedom of individual action; for a period of time, long enough to admit of a systematic plan of operations, and yet not so protracted as to prove a burdensome expense, or an interruption to other engagements;—under the direction of men, whose only claim to respect and continued attention must be their experience and acknowledged success in the subjects assigned them—and in a course of instruction, at once theoretical and practical, combined with opportunities of inquiry, discussion and familiar conversation.[1]

In Michigan, establishment of a normal school was accompanied by organization of a teachers institute. This followed immediately after the dedication of the Normal building, and preceded the opening of the Normal. A circular from the Superintendent of Public Instruction, of July, 1852, contained the following announcement:

> The permanent opening of the Institution for the reception of pupils, will
> be preceded by the holding of a Teachers Institute, at the Normal School,

for four weeks successively after the dedication (5th of October) and while citizens, parents and friends of Education are invited to attend and participate, the Teachers of the Primary Schools of the State are specially expected to attend. The exercises at the Institute will be free of expense to the Teachers, and it is expected that arrangements will be made with the officers of the Central and Southern Railroads, to extend to them the advantages of reduced rates of fare.[2]

The Institute was under the direction of Principal Welch. Courses offered were a review of subjects taught in the Common Schools: English, arithmetic, natural science, anatomy and physiology. The time allotted was three weeks. Two hundred and fifty teachers were in attendance. In addition to the course work, evening lectures were delivered on such topics as "Responsibility of Teachers," "Physical Science," "Female Education," "Teachers' Mission," Natural Science," "Music," "Relation of the Normal School to Teachers," and "Teachers' Duties."

In 1855, the legislature passed a law providing for a limited number of teachers institutes annually, to be held under the general direction of the Superintendent of Public Instruction. During at least the remainder of the century, these institutes exerted a growing influence of public school teaching in Michigan.

One development of lasting importance, which occured during the holding of the first Institute, was the organization of the State Teachers' Association, parent of the present Michigan Education Association. This was done at the suggestion and mainly through the efforts of Principal Welch. Officers were elected on October 12, 1852, Welch being named president. A constitution was adopted the following year.

At the opening of the school (March 29, 1853), two programs of study were offered, a "Classical Course" and an "English Course." The first catalog of the school gave this explanation:

The Classical Course is designed to prepare teachers for our Union Schools (predecessor of the high school) which are rapidly increasing in number and importance. As these institutions supply the place of Academies in the State, they should be conducted by men of thorough classical and scientific attainments.

The English Course is composed of studies which all who intend to become teachers should understand.[3]

The age for admission was not less than 13 years for the Classical Course, and not less than 14 years for the English Course. The Board of Education authorized each member of the House of Representatives to appoint two pupils (a boy and a girl) from his district. These pupils could attend at the reduced fee of $1 per term for the English Course, $2 for the Classical. All others paid $3 and $4 respectively. A higher scale of fees was prescribed for pupils not intending to teach.

The school year was organized into two terms, one of 17 weeks, beginning the last Tuesday of March, the other of 23 weeks, beginning the first Tuesday of October. A Model School (primary and secondary) was to be opened with the first fall term, to be taught "by a Principal Teacher, assisted by the Senior Class of the State Normal School."[4]

The minimum length of the program of academic studies was to be two years, to which would be added the work of the Model School and the professional courses. But one need not complete even the two years to be qualified to teach. And the State Board soon imposed a requirement that all who entered the school must make a declaration of intent to teach. This requirement remained in force for more than three-quarters of a century.

Principal Welch reported that students who had completed certain listed courses were considered capable of conducting a primary school, and recommended to the Board that certificates be granted to this effect. On the list were arithmetic, geography, map drawing, orthography, English grammar, vocal music, and drawing. These would require about a year of study.

The suggestion by Welch that the State Board issue certificates to those held to be capable of conducting a primary school was not followed, but Superintendent Ira Mayhew, in his report for the following year (1858) did recommend granting a diploma to all Normal School graduates. He noted that under existing conditions all graduates must submit to an examination before a township board of school inspectors before they could be recognized as "qualified teachers."

In 1861, an additional stipulation for graduation required that every student should master the rudiments of two foreign languages, the comment being made that there was a demand for young men to teach the two "ancient classics" in the Union Schools, and that there was also a demand for young women who could teach French. It was further observed that the young men who graduated were being encouraged to complete their classical studies at the University of Michigan before entering permanently on the duties of teaching.[5]

Students were not enrolled as freshmen, sophomores, etc. but in classes designated as B, C, D, E, F, and Senior Class. Students were considered capable of teaching in the primary grades after completing classes B and C. Some difficulty had been experienced from the fact that students were inclined to go out and get a teaching position after having only the B term. As a result, the Normal School exacted a promise not to teach until at least two terms (B and C) had been completed. This meant a full forty weeks of work. The remaining classes (D, E, F, and Senior) averaged one and a half terms each. The total time for graduation as of 1861 thus appeared to be about four years (as compared with three years in 1856). Terms were numbered consecutively from the time of the school's opening. Thus, the term beginning in April of 1861 was designated as the "17 term."

The early influence of the Pestalozzian method of teaching was being felt. In his annual report for 1861, Principal Welch said:

> The objective methods of training the senses of the child and the more natural order of studies adopted here and recommended by those high in authority as educators, are gradually finding their way into the primary schools, and we are glad to know that our theories of education, in general, harmonize with those of prominent teachers in other institutions.[6]

In 1863, the course of study was reorganized to give all students instruction in the Pestalozzian system. This was reported by the State Board as follows:

> The Board of Education are now convinced that the time has come, when the school can render no greater service to the State, than to so modify its course of study that all its pupils may receive thorough instruction and practice in the Pestalozzian system of Primary Teaching.[7]

The courses of study were reorganized into two major programs— a Normal Training Course, for teachers of primary schools, and a Higher Normal Course, for teachers of Union and Graded Schools. One-third of the total time was to be given to strictly professional (education) courses.

Finally, the legislature of that year granted authority to issue a diploma to graduates. "This diploma," the Board commented, "supersedes the necessity of examination by the Township Inspectors of the State."[8]

A study of student enrollment during the Welch period (1853–1865) reveals an uneven growth. In general, the Fall (long) Term exceeded the Spring (short) Term in numbers. "Ladies" exceeded "Gentlemen" in all of the Fall Terms, and in all but three of the Spring Terms, (the exceptions being 1858, 1859, and 1860). In general, enrollment of men in the Spring Term ranged from 30 per cent (Civil War years) to approximately 50 per cent (in 1858). The low point for men was the fall of 1863 when only 48 enrolled, as compared to a high of 148 in 1858. Total enrollments for a single term ranged from 122 (the first year, 1853) to a high of 357 (1859).[9]

Enthusiasm as to the success of the new institution was more consistent. Reports of the State Superintendent, the State Board and the Board of Visitors, as well as of the Principal, all reveal pride in the work being done by the Normal School and confidence in its future.

In one respect only do we hear a negative voice, and that points out the serious lack of capacity of school to meet the needs of the State.

Michigan Normal's first graduation class—that of 1854—numbered three. For the next ten years no graduating class numbered more than twenty-four. Michigan contained several thousand school districts, so by no stretch of the imagination could Normal, even counting the relatively many who earned teaching certificates without graduation, begin to meet the State's need.

Statistics for the year of 1850 show the number of teachers in the public schools as 3,231. In his report for 1853, Superintendent Shearman noted a sharp rise in the reported number of children attending school. Superintendent Mayhew suggested that the small number of trained teachers would act as leaven "until the whole body of teachers and the whole community, is leavened."

In his report for 1859, Superintendent Gregory pointed up the problem:

> The question of the establishment of additional Normal Schools in this State has often arisen among those who know the utter inadequacy of this one school to supply the thousands of teachers needed yearly in the state.

He stated that in 1859 there were 7,504 teachers employed, of whom "probably not less than two thousand were without any previous experience in teaching, and it is safe to affirm that the ranks of our public school teachers must be reinforced each year with more than two thousand fresh recruits." He continued:

> To furnish these new teachers with professional training, would require twenty Normal Schools of the same capacity as that at Ypsilanti, costing an annual expenditure of nearly two hundred thousand dollars.

Gregory's solution to the problem was to organize teachers' classes in all the colleges, leading Union Schools, and academies in the State, under general supervision of the State Superintendent. He repeated this suggestion in 1860, 1861, and 1862.

In their report for 1859, the Board of Visitors of the Normal School made the following recommendation:

> . . . the accommodations in this school are far below the demands of the State. We would therefore respectfully urge upon your consideration, the organization of at least one other like School in some other convenient portion of the State . . .

Gregory, in his report for the same year, went on to make a suggestion that was receive serious consideration at a later date, namely, that the Normal School confine its work to professional instruction (courses in Education), thus increasing its teacher training capacity. He said:

> Could our present State Normal School be relieved, on the one hand, from some portion of the labor of merely academic instruction, and provided, on the other hand, with increased accommodations for students, it would probably be able to furnish professional training to all who wish to devote themselves somewhat permanently to the business of teaching, and who desire to pursue a full course of normal instruction.

Superintendent Hosford, his successor, referred to the shortage problem. He said:

> One of the most serious obstacles in the way of the complete success of the school system has been the difficulty of obtaining competent teachers for the district schools . . . much more remains to be done, before this sad want shall be fully supplied. The great demand was formerly for cheap schools; teachers must be obtained at very low wages—'the cheapest is the best' was the prevailing sentiment. Good schools are now called for, and competent teachers earnestly sought after.[10]

In a later report, Hosford stated that hundreds of teachers annually were getting their training in the Union Schools. He pointed out that nearly 10,000 teachers were now employed in the state, instructing some 338,000 children. Then he said:

> Although we have no definite statistics to determine the number of new teachers added to the list every year, we may safely write it in thousands. Whence do they come? The University, the colleges, and the Normal School furnish but a fraction of them. The Union Schools, in the aggregate, give them hundreds. The remainder are but graduates of the primary schools, and it is to be feared that many of these are from the shorter course.[11]

He urged that a Normal Department be formed in the colleges and in every Union School, under supervision of the State Board and State Superintendent. "This (he said) would be almost equivalent to creating a hundred normal schools at once." And again came the suggestion that the proper function of the Normal School was to give professional courses only:

> With this arrangement the Normal School could at once so arrange its course of study, as to attempt nothing but professional work. This is the legitimate sphere of this school. This is the kind of work which it was intended to do . . . The Normal School should be purely a training school. Its course should be confined to two years.[12]

A modified curriculum, eliminating academic courses, was attempted some ten years later but was never put into more than partial operation. Professor Putnam, writing in 1899, remembered the plan as having been adandoned after a trial of a couple years.

The only solution, of course, was the establishment of additional normal schools but that was still a long way off and the very idea was fought tooth-and-nail every step of the way by the faculty at Ypsilanti.

That the State Board had done well in the choice of a principal became increasingly evident in subsequent years. Welch's concept of the educational process was expressed early.

> No amount of text book knowledge as such, no memory of straggling undigested facts or details—no skimming of the area of knowledge of whatever sort, can make the genuine scholar or the independent thinker. It is rather by investigating the relations of *facts* and *things*—by a close

scrutiny of the reasons on which opinions are founded . . . that the student, at last, attains to a genuine cultivation of the intellect.

He emphasized the importance of a balanced education, insisting that the function of the true teacher is to educate the whole mind. He said:

By some, even the eccentricity of a distorted intellect is regarded as an index of genius. The nose of the antagonist of Sancho Panza, which hid all his other features, was not in more ghastly disproportion. Would we nourish an exuberance of limb or feature, until it amounts to a deformity? Would you fix the head of a giant upon the shoulders of a dwarf? . . .[13]

Welch was impressed with the educational philosophy of Pestalozzi who would make the child, rather than subject matter, the center of the educational process. In 1862, he published a book titled "Object Lessons Prepared for Teachers of the Primary Schools and Primary Classes." In the preface he wrote:

The first instruction given to a child in school should be based on the fact that his intellectual activity consists in seeing and hearing rather than in reasoning and reflection . . . equally natural, also, is his aversion to abstract thinking. Any mode of teaching, therefore, which thwarts the former while it seeks to overcome the latter, is false in its philosophy and bad in its results.

CHAPTER THREE

CERTIFICATES DIPLOMAS
DEGREES

The need for specific requirements for teachers has always been recognized. Questions have always arisen, however, concerning what those requirements should be, who should set them, and who should issue the certificates. In Michigan, nearly a century passed after statehood before a stable and satisfactory pattern was achieved. In the meantime, responsibility shifted from township to county, from the State Superintendent of Public Instruction to the State Board of Education to the faculty of the Normal; and at times, the University of Michigan, the Detroit Board of Education, and certain other schools issued certificates.

The problem antedates statehood. Election of township "inspectors of common schools" was provided for by the Territorial Laws of 1829. Five inspectors were to be elected at the annual township meeting.[1] This provision was later incorporated into state law. In the revised Michigan Constitution of 1850, the authority to examine persons who proposed to teach and to certify them was given to the principal of the Normal, acting with the State Superintendent of Public Instruction. Township officials, however, still had authority to examine, and Normal graduates were often required to submit to such an examination. In other words, the first certificates issued by the Normal were not recognized locally as legal qualification for teaching.

After a decade, the state legislature took action to end the confusion. A County Superintendent of Schools was provided for, and among his duties was that of issuing teaching certificates. A Third Grade Certificate licensed the holder to teach for six months in a specific township. The Second Grade Certificate was valid throughout the county for one year. The First Grade Certificate was available only after one year of teaching experience, and was valid for two years. Qualifications for these certificates were set by the County Superintendent. The State Superintendent was authorized at the same time to grant certificates valid in any schools in the State until revoked.

County Superintendents took their assignment seriously and made a concerted effort to raise the standards for certification. They raised requirements each year, and those who met them were increasingly qualified.

In 1875, the legislature reversed itself, passing a law abolishing the office of County Superintendent and revoking the authority of the State Superintendent to issue certificates. The authority reverted to townships. County boards were given the authority again in 1891.

In 1878, the State Superintendent noted that many township boards had expressed dissatisfaction with the examining system. They were too busy to give it adequate attention, and often found it embarrassing to decide on the qualifications of neighbors and friends. He recommended a state certificate, with authority vested in the State Board of Education. The legislature agreed and enacted a law giving the State Board authority to grant certificates valid for ten years in any school in the State. The Board was directed to prepare examinations for the various grades of local certificates, but the local authorities were not obliged to use them.

In 1889, the legislature gave the State Board authority to issue a Life Certificate, valid in any school. Requirements included two years of teaching experience and approval of the Normal. The latter required that the candidate complete the Normal's first two years (or graduate from a four-year high school) and two additional years of college-grade work there. It was also required that courses completed be listed on the certificate. This practice has been retained to the present time.

The State Board issued the certificate on the recommendation of the principal of the Normal and "a majority of the heads of departments of said school."[2] This served to improve the status of the certificate holder and make him more secure.

It was this Life Certificate which, in 1897, first listed Michigan Normal as College rather then School. Two years later, the legislature changed the name of the institution to Michigan State Normal College.

In 1927, the minimum requirement for a Life Certificate was

raised to four years of college-grade work. In 1936, the Provisional-Permanent Certificate now in use was established, and the Life Certificate was not issued after June, 1939.

The policy of issuing teaching certificates based on examinations was abandoned in 1921. Only professional training was considered a qualification from then on. Counties could still issue certificates, without examination, providing that one year of professional training was required for Third Grade Certificates, one and a third year for the Second Grade, and one and two-thirds for the First Grade.

Licensing of teachers for rural schools became a concern for the State Board within 15 years of the opening of the Normal. The Board, under authority granted by the legislature, issued a certificate after 1867 for teaching in rural schools only. The certificate was valid for three years and was renewable once upon a showing of teaching success. Further renewals required, in addition, that the applicant pass an examination in two advanced courses. The Normal's one-year English Common School course was required. The certificate was abandoned in 1882 when the Normal dropped that course.

Two years later, it was replaced by a five-year certificate which licensed the holder to teach both in rural and elementary graded schools. Requirements included completion of the Normal's new three-year English Course (which included two years of high school work). It was not renewable except upon a showing of the completion of advanced studies.

In 1897, the legislature authorized the State Board to issue a two-year certificate valid only for teaching in a one-room rural school. It was based on the training requirements for the Third Grade county certificate, plus professional training as might be prescribed by the Board.

In 1903, two three-year certificates were authorized by the Board. One, the Graded School Certificate, was valid for grades one through nine; the other, the Rural School Certificate, was valid in rural school with not more than two teachers. The Graded School Certificate was based on graduation from a good high school plus completion of a professional course at the Normal extending over 42 weeks. The Rural School Certificate required completion of a program at the Normal extending through seven terms of 12 weeks each. This time could be shortened to three terms by showing credits for corresponding studies completed in high school and experience in teaching. Both certificates were conferred by the Board on the recommendation of the principal of the Normal and a majority of department heads.

In 1927, the three-year Rural Certificate was revised to require more college-grade credit and a year and a summer of work at the Normal instead of one year. At the same time, the three-year Graded School Certificate appears to have been dropped in favor of the five-year certificate mentioned earlier. The five-year certificate was upgraded, requiring two years of college-level work rather than only one, and was valid for rural schools and graded schools through the eighth grade.

Specialized Life Certificates

In 1901, the State Superintendent was authorized to endorse state-wide certificates in certain specialized areas—kindergarten, music, and drawing. This was supplemented in 1905 to authorize the granting of special certificates for these areas, and enlarged in 1915 by the inclusion of domestic science, manual training, and physical training.

Beginning about 1917, and varying in number from year to year, other specialized forms of the certificate appeared. Thus, from 1917 to 1920, Life Certificates were issued in physical education, commercial work, kindergarten-primary (kindergarten and the first three grades), and supervision and critic teaching. To these were added primary grades (the first three grades), public school music and drawing, teaching in the intermediate grades (grammar grades) in the rural school, and in special education (the broad area of handicapped children). From 1920 to 1925 appeared additional certificates called high school and departmental, drawing, commercial art, fine arts, music and fine arts, early elementary, industrial arts, public school music and art. From 1925 to 1930 appeared public school piano, agriculture, junior high school, and later elementary (grades five through eight). One, titled "Supervision and Teacher Training," listed among desirable talents the "ability to drive a Ford car, operate a typewriter, and lead community singing." There was also a certificate in business administration. The years 1930 to 1936 saw the appearance of certificates for senior high school (grades ten through twelve), administrators and supervisors of schools, and administrators and supervisors of schools, rural communities.

A teacher certification code was at last adopted in 1936. Some fifteen different kinds of certificates were then in existence, including those issued by the University of Michigan and the Detroit Board of Education. The new code was to be administered by the State Superintendent of Public Instruction. It reduced the number of different certificates to three.

Two introduced the new provisional-permanent concept which provided that the candidate, upon qualifying for the certificate, could be granted a limited certificate good for five years. If, in that period, he could show at least three years of successful teaching and ten additional semester hours of college credit, he would be granted the permanent certificate. Upon receipt of the permanent certificate, he still had to teach at least 100 days in a five-year period or lose his license, which could be renewed only by an application showing that he had earned another ten hours of credit. One form of the provisional-permanent certificate was for elementary teachers, the other for secondary.

A third type of certificate was designated the State Limited Certificate. It required two years of college work, including a certain amount of professional training, and was valid for five years for teaching in rural schools. Renewals were based on additional college credit and were designed to lead ultimately to a college degree and a provisional-permanent certificate. This enabled many young people to teach for a living and, in summer sessions and off-campus classes, to complete their education and training. Need for this certificate diminished over the years and the State Limited Certificate was discontinued in 1960.

Thus, over a century and a third, authority for granting teaching certificates moved to a highly centralized authority and control. In that time, teacher preparation became an important function of universities and colleges, both public and private, and the Normal School evolved through college to university status. Conflicts of opinion over certification have advanced from questions of form and location of authority to questions of content.

Diplomas and Degrees

Until 1960, it was possible for a student to earn some kind of teaching certificate without graduating from college. Those who graduated from the Normal received special recognition in the form first of a certificate, then a diploma and, after 1889, a degree. After

1903, the degree became the Bachelor of Arts or Bachelor of Science in Education. The academic content was equivalent to that of the bachelor degree in the better colleges.

Course content and quality had varied over years. Deficient preparation in high schools had made it necessary to provide much of the instruction that should have been given before the student arrived at the Normal College. One comment on the quality of work was made by the Board of Visitors in 1878, when they observed that "the Normal School was more like an excellent academy, with some excellent instruction given in pedagogics and the science of education, than a Normal School proper."[3]

However, the Normal was by 1890 conferring its first degrees—Bachelor of Pedagogics (B.Pd.). Requirements were the holding of a Life Certificate plus two years of college work. Since the Life Certificate was granted on completion of a course that demanded two years of college work beyond a four-year high school, this was a four-year college degree. The only person to receive the degree in 1890 was William H. Brooks. Several faculty members received the degree in 1891 and 1892.[4] The Master of Pedagogics (M.Pd.) was also initiated and granted in 1890, and represented the Normal's first venture in graduate work.

Daniel Putnam, writing in 1899, commented on the degrees:

> The specific conditions upon which these degrees are given are not yet permanently settled, but are modified, from time to time, as experience suggests. It is intended, however, that the degree of Bachelor of Pedagogics shall indicate scholarship equal to that required for the degree of BA from a reputable college; and the degree of Master of Pedagogics shall indicate, in addition to the scholarship just mentioned, that the person receiving has been engaged in teaching or in school supervision continuously and with pronounced success for at least five years since receiving the Bachelor's degree; and has prepared and presented a thesis acceptable to the Faculty of the school upon some subject connected with the history, science, or art of education.[5]

In 1902, the degree of Bachelor of Arts in Pedagogy (later referred to as the Bachelor of Arts in Education) was adopted. This degree was described as requiring the B.Pd. plus one additional year of college work. This, in effect, transformed the B.Pd. to a three-year degree, based on what became known as the "junior degree course" and procurable for one year of college work beyond the Life Certificate.

In 1917, the degree of Bachelor of Science in Education was adopted. It applied to the specialized curriculum of Household Arts. In 1918, both degrees dropped the modifying "education" and became simply AB and BS degrees.

The M.Pd. degree was officially adopted as an honorary degree in 1920. The names of faculty members and others on the list of recipients would suggest, however, that from the first it had been used as an honorary as well as an earned degree. In 1922, the honorary degree was designated as Master of Education.

In 1941, the college presented a vocational curriculum known as Occupational Therapy, offering a certificate to accompany the BS degree. In 1949, a certificate for directors of Teachers of Recreation was also offered. In 1957, two undergraduate specialized degrees were offered—Bachelor of Science in Business Administration and Bachelor of Music Education.

* * *

The story of the teaching certificate in Michigan scarcely inspires enthusiasm. For nearly a third of a century the State's authority to certify teachers was delegated largely to local political bodies, oscillating between the township and the county. There were thus as many different standards for qualifying as there were townships and counties, and the judgment of the institution that prepared the candidates might or might not enter into the decision. A variety of state-wide certificates, most of which pertained to teaching in the rural schools, appeared. But nearly a century had passed before a state-wide authority was given exclusive control. When, in 1935, the State Board was given this responsibility, some fifteen varieties of local certification existed. To state it another way, not until 1935 were there educational vision and leadership, and climate, adequate to make an issue of a very bad situation and find a remedy. One naturally is inclined to raise the question as to why it took so long to accomplish the obvious; why a recommendation by the State Superintendent in 1878 was not fully implemented until 1936, some 58 years later. In the answer lies the story of the democratic process, beset by narrow interests and local prejudice, reaching an apogee of confusion, and, out of strong reaction to incompetence, rising at last to face the issue and resolve the problem.

The story of the degrees, on the other hand, portrays a trend that was consistent, and which led Normal from the status of school to college to university. This trend is the more noteworthy in that it occurred in the face of strong, sometimes bitter, opposition from those within its own ranks who wished to make the professional education program primary if not exclusive. Much of this development was due to the demands from the high schools, which grew rapidly both in quality and number. As early as 1889, a degree was offered which purported to be the equal of a degree from any reputable four-year college. From 1903, a degree from Normal was legally recognized as such.

The North Central Association

In 1928 Normal, along with the other three Michigan normal colleges, was finally included in the approved list of "Accredited Institutions of Higher Education" by the North Central Association of Colleges and Secondary Schools. The story behind this event is of particular interest in that Normal had played a role in the founding of North Central some 34 years earlier.

On December 1, 1894, the Michigan Schoolmasters Club (an organization representative of university and college presidents, school superintendents, high school principals and teachers, whose primary objective was "the establishment and perpetuation of cordial relationships among all educational forces within the commonwealth"), meeting at the Normal, adopted a resolution to ask the presidents of the University of Michigan, University of Wisconsin, Northwestern University, and the University of Chicago to unite with a committee of the Schoolmasters Club in calling a meeting to form an association that would represent the North Central States.

Action on this resolution was prompt, and within the month a letter was posted to representatives of colleges and secondary schools in 10 states inviting them to attend a meeting to be held in March at Northwestern University in Evanston, Illinois. The purpose would be "to organize, if deemed expedient, an association of colleges and secondary schools of the North-Central States, representative of universities, colleges, scientific schools, normal schools, high schools, and academies."

This letter was signed by the presidents of the four universities named above, the principal of Grand Rapids High School, by William Butts (with whom the idea had originated), Principal of the Michigan Military Academy, and by Richard G. Boone, Principal of Michigan State Normal School. The convention was held as planned. A constitution was drafted and membership defined as consisting of colleges, universities, and secondary schools (normal schools were looked upon as secondary schools), together with such individuals as might be nominated by the executive committee and elected by the Association. The first president was James B. Angell, President of the University of Michigan.

At this point a mystery takes shape. Boone was not present at the Evanston convention and Normal thus lost the opportunity to be designated as a charter member.[6] The first annual meeting, held in 1896, approved the first list of members, and on this list Normal appeared as a secondary school. It was so listed for the remaining years of Boone's administration (through 1899). From 1900 to 1915, however, which included the Leonard-Lyman and the Jones administrations, Normal was absent from the list. During the ten years of the Jones administration (1902–1912), he was listed as an individual member, and for the year 1905–1906 he was named as a vice-president from Michigan. But Normal did not hold an institutional membership, and Jones attended the annual meetings on only three occasions.[7] During these same years, as we have seen, he was active with the North Central Council of State Normal School Presidents.

This delay in recognition, extending as it did through four administrations, derived from the haughty attitude of the universities (who controlled North Central policy from the first) towards normal schools—an attitude less seemly in the University of Michigan which, by its close proximity, was in a position to know the developments at its sister institution in Ypsilanti and which, furthermore, had shown a pioneering concern for the training of teachers. The general mood of the universities of the time was, however, to prevent teachers colleges from training high school teachers.

By legislative authority of 1889, Normal had begun in 1890 to grant a bachelor's degree (Bachelor of Pedagogics) based on four years of college-grade work. In 1893, in a detailed brochure prepared for circulation at the Columbian Exposition of Chicago in that year, Normal had stated that its function was to prepare teachers both academically and professionally for both primary and secondary schools. It listed courses in the fields of mathematics, history, English, physical science, natural science, Latin and Greek, French and German, and psychology and pedagogics that were of college grade and would support a program typical of liberal arts colleges leading to the bachelor's degree.[8]

When, in 1913, the Association published its first list of accredited institutions of higher education, normal schools (and colleges) were designated as "unclassified institutions." The resulting dissatisfaction, however, prompted what proved to be a temporary concession. At the 1914 meeting of the Association action was taken to replace the title "Colleges and Universities" with "Higher Institutions", and include in this listing some normal schools and junior colleges. This was effective in 1915. Normal's McKenny acted promptly, and secured accreditation for Normal (which was tantamount to membership in the Association).

But this arrangement lasted only two years. In 1917, a new category was added, called "Institutions Primarily for the Training of Teachers," and here the name of Michigan State Normal College (together with the other three normal colleges of the State) went. The action that established this in-between category did not resolve the issue, however.

The dispute within the Association continued for another decade. Finally, in 1928, the Association acted to discontinue the in-between category. It decided to broaden the list of colleges and universities to include a variety of institutions of higher education. This was to become effective as of 1931, but the four Michigan Normals were made an exception and placed at once in the category of "Colleges and Universities."[9]

The record of Normal's membership in the North Central Association is thus a curious one. Normal was host to the Michigan Schoolmasters Club meeting from which came the initial impulse for the formation of such an organization. Normal's principal, Richard G. Boone, signed the letter sent to representative colleges and schools in the North Central states calling for an organization meeting to be held in Evanston.

Through the failure of Boone to attend the organization meeting at Evanston, Normal did not show as a charter member,[10] but it appeared in the first membership list (as a secondary school), and retained this membership through 1899 (i.e. through the Boone administration). From then it was not a member until McKenny restored it in 1915. For two years it was listed with the higher education institutions, then shunted to the in-between category where it remained until 1928. From that time, its true status has been recognized.

CHAPTER FOUR

THE TRAINING SCHOOL

As we saw earlier, practical experience in teaching was a vital part of the "Normal" concept. Although a large professional body of theory and knowledge has been since developed, "student teaching" is still held to be an essential part of the training of a teacher.

Limited provision for student teaching at Michigan Normal was made, beginning in the second term (fall, 1853), with the organization of a special school called "The Model." It occupied one room, enrolled 27 pupils, and was conducted by one teacher, Miss H. K. Clapp.[1] These facilities were too limited, however, to provide adequate opportunity for Normal students actually to do practice teaching, or even to observe. Hence, within two years, the State Board of Education approached the Union School Board of Ypsilanti for its consent to the use of the Ypsilanti school as a Model. This effort failed.

In consequence, the State Board decided to enlarge the Model, expand its curriculum, and bring in a principal to conduct its affairs. By 1856 the change was made and D. P. Mayhew, formerly Superintendent of Schools at Columbus, Ohio, (destined to succeed Adonijah Welch as principal of the Normal School) was hired. This arrangement made possible only a minimum of actual practice teaching for the highest Normal Department class (the E class). It was assumed that each member of this class (which numbered 20 at that time) could be required to teach one class in the Model each day for one term. In practice, however, very little teaching was done by the students.[2]

The curriculum consisted of the following, which covered the equivalent of about four elementary grades:

> First, object lessons and the elements of natural science, and afterwards arithmetic, grammar and elementary history, thorough training in read-

33

ing, penmanship, spelling, drawing, composition, singing and moral lessons . . .[3]

In 1863 the Model was enlarged further and organized into a
graded school. Thus, at the close of the administration of Adonijah
Welch (1865) we find the Model School consisting of a *primary
department* (three grades), *a grammar department* (three grades),
and a *high school* (three grades). Much of the instruction was given
by the staff; comparatively little by student teachers. Many years
were to elapse before a stable pattern was established.

Meanwhile, the Normal experimented in collaborating with the
city schools. In 1871 relations with the Ypsilanti school board were
particularly good. The new principal of the Normal School, Joseph
Estabrook, had been superintendent of Ypsilanti schools for many
years. Daniel Putnam had held the same position during the previous year, and upon returning to the Normal was made principal of
the Model (now referred to as the *Training School*). Furthermore,
facilities on the Normal campus had been expanded by the completion, in 1870, of the Conservatory Building, and the Training School
was placed there. It was, therefore, now possible to reach an agreement to discontinue the city high school and transfer its students to a
newly organized *preparatory department* in the Training School. At
the same time the elementary and grammar grades of the city Union
School were to become schools of observation and, to a limited
extent, of practice for the Normal students. The primary and grammar grades of the Training School were discontinued.

This experiment lasted only two years. Many objections arose,
especially from parents who felt that their children were not receiving adequate attention. Consequently in 1872 the primary department was re-activated; two years later the grammar department was
restored. A teacher was provided for each department, and the grading within the departments was made to conform to the public
schools.

In 1878, an important curricular development occurred. The training School (also referred to as the *School of Observation and Practice*) was re-organized and enlarged to constitute a graded school and
also to serve as a preparatory school (high school) for students
undertaking to qualify for admission to the Normal Department.
This move was prompted by the decision of the State Board to
reduce academic teaching in the Normal Department to a minimum.
Teaching in this preparatory division of the Training School was to

be done by students from the Normal Department, under the supervision of that department's faculty (each in their respective subject areas). Thus once more, this time at the high school level, the faculty of the Normal Department became involved in the practice teaching program. A particularly interesting innovation was the introduction of oral lessons in French and German in the third and fourth grades of the primary department, and reading in Latin, French, and German in the seventh and eighth grades of the grammar department. At the high school level Latin, German, Greek, and French were provided for consecutive years in the language course. Drawing and music were taught in all grades.

Malcolm Mac Vicar, who became principal in 1880, not taking kindly to the plan for abrupt abandonment of academic courses in the Normal Department, restored them promptly. Thus, the Normal staff taught the courses for students still in need of work preparatory to the professional curriculum. The high school department of the Training School was eliminated.

In his annual report to the State Board, Principal Mac Vicar placed special emphasis on the importance of the Training School, and outlined what he conceived to be its proper organization and function under the following major points: (1) management of the school should be placed in the hands of the director, subject only to the authority of the Principal; (2) specially-appointed critic teachers should be employed (teachers in the Normal should *not* be asked to function as critic teachers); (3) the critic teachers should visit, observe, and meet personally with their pupil-teachers, should see that defects were actually corrected, and should require written outlines of lessons; (4) each pupil-teacher should be required, at the end of a course, to give an accurate account (orally or in writing) of (a) the order in which each topic was discussed, (b) the illustrations and devices used, and (c) the method of drill pursued.

These proposals became the substantial guide for practice in subsequent years.

In 1882, the west-side addition to the main building was completed. At the same time the director of the school was given the status of a department head (which included the right to choose his own personnel). Austin George was made director, replacing Daniel Putnam who became Acting Principal of the Normal School. From this time regular and systematic practice teaching for all students in the senior class was required. The pattern of operation became stabilized, and it was possible to give extensive attention to problems of curriculum, of coordinating practice teaching with the academic program of the student teacher, of defining the duties of the critic teacher, and of the proper division of time of the student teacher between observation and teaching.

The addition of a north and a south wing to the Main Building in 1888 made possible another important step. In that year a kindergarten was added. This had been advocated as early as 1871 by State Superintendent Oramel Hosford, who argued at some length on the nature and advantages of the "Kindergarten system" of Friedrich Froebel, and its success in Germany.[4] Four years later, in his report as head of the Training School (now referred to also as the *Experimental* School), Putnam urged, not the establishment of a kindergarten, but the use of kindergarten materials and "plays." He said:

> The kindergarten, in its purely foreign form, will never, in my judgment, meet the wants or the requirements of American life and society, and consequently, outside of a few large cities, will not take deep root on American soil . . .

> But some of the kindergarten material and employments, or plays, can be introduced into our primary and common district schools, I am confident, to the very great advantage of all concerned. And more than this, and better than this, *the spirit and tone* of the kindergarten may be infused into and made to pervade the entire organization and working of these schools.

In his report for 1876, Putnam grew more enthusiastic. He recommended the employment, as an experiment for one year, of a trained kindergarten teacher.

The State Board did not give heed to this request, supported though it was by the State Superintendent, Daniel Briggs. With the completion of the addition to Old Main in 1888, however, the Board did give its approval for a kindergarten.

Putnam commented, years later:

> This unfortunate delay deprived the Normal School of the honor, which it should have secured, of leading the movement in Michigan for the establishment of free kindergartens in connection with the public schools.[5]

Along with the addition of a kindergarten, a *model first primary* department was organized, and both the kindergarten and the new department were provided with a special teacher. With reference to the former, Principal Sill said:

> We should have a competent kindergartner who, in my judgment, will be needed throughout the entire school year. She should look to the kindergarten, give instructions in its methods and supervise pupil teachers taking a special kindergarten course; and the entire training school corps should be active in finding out and practicing the best methods of adjusting kindergarten methods to the first four primary grades.[6]

It would appear, then, that the staffing of the Training School in 1888 through grade eight was as follows: a special teacher each for kindergarten and first grade, a teacher for the primary grades two, three, and four, and a teacher for the four grammar grades.

In 1892 the staff was enlarged by provision for a "competent model and critic" teacher for each of the eight grades, and the Experimental School was expanded by the addition of a ninth grade. The pupils of this grade, however, sat with the Normal students on the third floor of the main building (Old Main) and were taught by members of the senior class, under the supervision of a department head of the Normal Department.

Thus was made possible a much greater emphasis on both observation and practice for the student teacher.

At about the same time, a library was established composed of books selected for the use of pupils and for reading and other purposes in the various grades. Thus began the library of the Roosevelt Laboratory School.

From 1894 to the close of the decade, now that the question of administrative organization was fairly well settled, there was much experimentation with the organization of courses (under Principal-President Boone).

A new principle or organization of the curriculum was introduced by Boone. It was known as the "principle of concentration," and required that the various courses offered should, in greater or less degree, be correlated with a central subject. If one might apply a modern term, there was to be a "core" subject and a "core" program. The area decided upon to serve as the core was Nature Study. But along with this was an ultimate concern for man. To quote Putnam:

> History, literature, geography, and reading were correlated to some extent. Mathematical work was connected with science, with geography,

and with the affairs of everyday life. The facts and ideas derived from the
study of nature were treated in their relations to man, thus introducing
the humanistic element into the work. Drawing and writing were treated
largely as modes of expression.[7]

In the year 1895–96 this approach, which had been undertaken
for the first three primary grades only, was extended to all eight
grades. But a problem of a practical nature developed that is not
strange to the "core" program of our own day. A need was felt to
give more definite form to the courses of study. In 1896, therefore,
they were arranged into five distinct areas—science, history, geography, arithmetic, and language. The courses in science and history
were organized in consecutive steps through the eight grades. Geography also was made to follow this sequential pattern, and an effort
made to correlate it with history and science. A similar pattern was
followed, insofar as practicable, with regard to arithmetic, language,
reading, and literature.

The Boone experiment in the "principle of concentration" was a
pioneer effort in the direction later given prominence by John Dewey
and Abraham Flexner, and which, within the last three decades, has
flowered again as the *core curriculum*. The experiment appears to
have been abandoned after President Boone's resignation, though
the principle of selecting subject matter in accordance with the
child's natural interests persisted within well-defined course areas.

In the course of the development of the Model School into a well-
organized and well-staffed Training School *(School of Observation
and Practice)*, there were problems of emphasis and coordination
with the work of the Normal Department. For example, over many
years great concern was expressed over the lack of opportunity provided for actual practice in teaching. Then the question arose of how
much of the student's time should be devoted to observation and how
much to practice. And finally, there was lack of agreement as to how
the student's experience in the Training School could be coordinated
with his work as a student in the Normal Department.

In 1884, the plan was tried of limiting the practice teaching to a
single session each afternoon. This was found to be inadequate, and
from 1890 these sessions were held also in the morning. Then the
question arose as to how much of the student's time should be
devoted to teaching. Principal Sill gave particular attention to this
problem, and urged that the student teacher should be free to give
his *whole* attention to teaching during the allotted time for this part

of his training. He recommended that all academic work be completed before entering upon practice teaching.

He felt that this proposal provided the only true solution to the problem of time conflict between academic classes and practice teaching. It was not, however, adopted. The problem is still with us.

Another question of great importance was how much of the teaching should be done by the student teacher, how much by the critic teacher. Parents were loath to trust their children to student teachers. The Normal felt a responsibility for providing good instruction. Yet the reason for the existence of the Practice School was to provide experience for the student teachers. Obviously, there were just two ways in which this responsibility could be met: (1) by a close, expert supervision of the student teacher; (2) by assigning a definite share of the teaching to the critic teacher.

Putnam, who was Director of the Training School at the time, felt that in the first and second primary grades at least half of the teaching should be done by the student teachers; in the "highest grammar grade" (eighth) a third by the critic teacher would be desirable.

In the mid-nineties the Board of Visitors made a highly critical report in the following vein: the Training School is not a model . . . the work lacks system . . . the appearance of the rooms is generally unpleasant and in some instances repellent, untidy . . . blackboards are gaudily decorated . . . pupils are listless and inattentive . . . the manner of dismissing classes is awkward, producing confusion, not done alike in all the rooms . . . the giving of forenoon and afternoon recesses is not followed in what should be in the fullest sense a model . . . critic teachers do not give enough model lessons.

But the report concluded with a recommendation for "a new building, separate and apart from other buildings."[8]

The New Era

The new Training School building was given a site by the citizens of Ypsilanti.

Principal Boone said:

> In making the appropriation . . . it was understood by the legislature that the site should be otherwise provided. This was done. In keeping with the past generous attitude of the city, Ypsilanti came forward and offered a beautiful tract adjoining the old campus. Its acceptance puts the

school in possession of almost double the amount of land reported two
years ago.[9]

The original plans for the building called for more money than
the Legislature had appropriated. Hence, the building as completed
in 1897 was only the main structure of the plan, leaving the wings
for some future date. When the building was occupied,[10] seven
grades only were transferred to it, the kindergarten and first grade
being left in the old quarters in the Main Building. Just three years
later the two wings were completed, pursuant to the urgent request
of Principal Boone.

In 1908 the Legislature appropriated for a further addition to the
building. President Jones explained at the time:

> The large increase in the number of students needing practice in the train-
> ing school has cramped us very much for room in that department. The
> addition now being erected will not only give us additional class rooms,
> but will allow much more commodious accommodations for the depart-
> ments of manual training and domestic science and art.

In this same report, however, Jones included a significant comment:

> With the single exception of the little chapel which was the gift of Mrs.
> Starkweather . . . no building on this campus has been completed accord-
> ing to the plans or wishes of the educational authorities; but modifications
> have always been brought about on account of the small appropriations
> allowed by the legislature, so that in the end each building is more or less
> of an abortion, and not a single one of them is so perfectly adapted to its
> uses as should be the case of a state educational institution, standing, as
> this one does, for the giving of the right ideals of general public education
> to those who are to be teachers in the public schools of the state.[11]

Although the Training School Building was too small even when
first built, it did provide substantial relief. The director was given a
new title, "Superintendent of the Training School."

Austin George, upon assuming headship of the Practice School in
1882, had requested that the name of the school be changed to
"Training School." During his tenure the kindergarten was added,
and the school later organized into eight grades with a trained critic
teacher for each grade. George had also made a large contribution of
institution-wide importance. He is credited with having founded the

student paper *Normal News*. He was largely instrumental in establishing the oratorical contest, which became such an important feature of college life. He was chairman of the committee that secured a legislative appropriation for the gymnasium, erected in 1894, and gave the principal address at its dedication. It was George who wrote the vivid and moving account of the participation by Normal boys in the Civil War and preserved the record of their service.

The vacancy caused by his resignation in 1896 was, until 1900, filled by a succession of directors. Charles O. Hoyt held the title from 1896 to 1898. The Honorable James W. Simmons, resigning his post as State Superintendent of Public Instruction, accepted the position of Superintendent of the Training School, but remained only one year. He was succeeded by Charles T. Grawn who came from the superintendency of the Traverse City School. Grawn also remained just one year, leaving to become principal of Central State Normal School at Mount Pleasant.

During this period, in spite of the rapid succession of heads, some progress was made in raising standards. The relation between observation and practice teaching for student teachers was set at 12 weeks of observation, followed by 12 weeks of practice.

In 1900, Dimon Harrington Roberts succeeded Grawn. Roberts remained in this position until his death in 1928, meanwhile stamping his personality on the whole College. In his later years the students paid him the following tribute:

> Every student in this college comes in contact with Mr. Roberts before receiving a diploma of any size, kind, or description. He inspires, advises, and admonishes aspiring young teachers. His critic meetings are invigorating, to say the least. In saying a thing he remembers that the shortest distance between two points is a straight line. Mr. Roberts believes in young people, and heartily approves of bobbed hair. He is a cordial friend to all—even to the stray cats and dogs wandering about the Campus.[12]

In a resolution at the time of his death, the State Board said:

> Due to his unusual ability as an organizer the Training School has been developed into one of the very best institutions of this kind in the United States and Mr. Roberts won for himself an enviable reputation as a teacher and educator . . . He liked other people and was liked in return. He was not only a school man but active in the affairs of the city and interested himself in all projects that make for better community life.[13]

The Roberts period coincided with the presidencies of Lewis Jones and Charles McKenny. These were years of outstanding achievement on the part of individual members of the faculty (D'Ooge, Strong, Sherzer, Jefferson, Ford, Charles Elliot, Pittman, among others) and of a strong surge of institutional pride.

Roberts undertook at once to place greater emphasis on the importance of the training School, and to raise the standards of its work. In re-writing the statement of purpose he said:

> The leading purpose of this school is to afford an opportunity to the student for both observation and practical work in the school room. It is here that theory and practice meet, and consequently the work in this department should test in a very large measure the ability of the teacher to do successful work in the public schools of the state. As far as possible the aim is to make the school fulfill a double function in being both a model and a training school.[14]

One of the first steps was to add certain stipulations to qualifications for student teaching. Students were not to be permitted to take more than two subjects in college along with the work in the training school. In 1903 to meet a growing demand, a special course was announced for the training of critic teachers. Only students who had demonstrated ability to teach were eligible to enroll. In 1911, an incentive in the form of Honor Teacher was provided. The critic teacher of each grade would select her best student teacher of the term to serve as her assistant during the following term.

In 1903, Roberts established a new position, Principal of the High School. To this position he appointed Mary M. Steagall who had been Fifth Grade Critic Teacher, and had taken leave of absence for two years to attend the University of Chicago. Coincident with the arrival of Miss Steagall a tenth grade was organized. In 1904, an eleventh grade was added, and the four-year high school became a reality with the organization of a twelfth grade in 1905.[15]

The origin of the Roosevelt High School traces to President McKenny and Dimon Roberts. In his first full biennial report to the State Board (June 30, 1914), McKenny said:

> The attendance in the training school, which includes the kindergarten, eight elementary grades, and a four-year high school, has been all that our buildings could care for. It is hoped that in the near future a new high school building will be erected which will enable the College to extend its work and care for more students in that department, thus making more

efficient its training of high school teachers, for which there is a demand
far beyond the ability of the College to meet.

Earlier, McKenny has proposed that the Legislature undertake a
building program for the College that would extend over a period of
years. The Legislature responded to this approach, and in 1913
included in a list of specific projects $50,000 for a high school addi-
tion to the Training School. In 1915 this appropriation was raised
to $95,000. No action was taken, however, to construct such an
addition.

In fact, a whole series of construction projects took priority—an
addition to the old gymnasium (1913); a "plant house," and a
health cottage (1914); an administration building (1914); a magnificent auditorium and home for the Conservatory of Music (1914);
renovation of the old gymnasium (1916). Then the war in Europe
brought a halt in construction and the building program was not
resumed until the war ended.

By this time two forces were at work which greatly emphasized
the need for an enlarged training school. The running debate of the
previous two decades on the reorganization of the public school,
marked as early as 1908 by a report of a committee of the National
Education Association favoring a six-year elementary program and a
six-year secondary program (as opposed to the traditional 8–4 division), in the post-war period culminated in a wide acceptance of
what came to be known as the 6–3–3 plan. In this the seventh,
eighth, and ninth grades formed an intermediate grouping known as
the junior high school.[16]

The second force was rapidly expanding enrollment which jumped
from a low of 950 in the last year of the war to a new high of 2,640
in 1924. Thus a new area of specialization for which teachers must
be prepared (the junior high school) and presssure of numbers seeking admission to the teaching field combined to present overwhelming evidence that a new Training School building was a necessity.
Added to this was the expansion of the Training School program,
begun in 1922, to include provision for handicapped children.

The Legislature made an appropriation and on May 5, 1924,
ground was broken for a new building that would cost $500,000 to
build and equip.[17]

With the opening of this building in the fall of 1925 the long-
familiar name of Normal High was changed to honor Theodore
Roosevelt and it became known as Roosevelt High School.

Burns Fuller, principal at the time of old Normal High, became the first principal of Roosevelt High.

The building was designed for 420 pupils. The old quarters of Normal High on the third floor of Old Main (since 1922 known as Pierce Hall) had been crowded with 150. The move included the seventh and eighth grades from the Training School. The plan of the building provided for a Home Economics Department, cafeteria, and science laboratories on the ground floor. The senior high school (grades ten, eleven, twelve) was given the second floor, and the junior high school the third. The rooms were arranged according to the "unit plan," each department of subject area having a grouping of three rooms (a large and two small recitation rooms, interconnected.)

The pupils were impressed:

> Although looking forward to the new building, we had become such good friends with the old one that it was a bit sad at parting. But when, after climbing a notch higher to the tenth grade, we found ourselves in new surroundings, we promptly fell in love with the new building—not that it is proper to fall in love with a building, especially a school, but we couldn't help ourselves.[18]

But the road ahead for the new school was to provide some very rough going.

In November of 1929, McKenny proposed that the senior high school be discontinued. He was moved to make this request as the result of discussions with the State Board beginning the previous year. The problem was simply one of inadequate space, and had been precipitated by plans for a new library building, for which the Legislature had provided and which would be ready for use in January, 1930. The location of this building, just west of Pierce Hall, would require the razing of the west wing of Pierce. That wing, however, housed on its second floor the history and English departments, and on its main floor the Department of Special Education. What to do with these departments was the problem. McKenny came to the conclusion that adequate space could be found if the elementary school were moved to the Roosevelt School building, thus making the Training School building (Welch Hall) available.

Appropriate action was taken by the State Board, and the announcement made in *The Ypsilanti Daily Press*. A form letter, signed by McKenny, was sent to each member of the senior high school staff. It read in part as follows:

My dear Mr. ———:

    As you have known from discussions on the campus, the State Board of Education has had under consideration the discontinuing of the senior high school at Roosevelt. Final action has been taken in the matter. The reasons for this action are that the unit is not needed for practice purposes and that the crowded condition of the campus, owing to the wrecking of the rear wing of the Main Building, makes it necessary to get additional classrooms.

    I am sorry to say that because of the discontinuance of the senior high school the college will not need your services next year . . .

Immediately there was a strong protest on the part of parents and friends of the Roosevelt School. McKenny promptly called an open meeting and answered the protests by making the following points: The College now had more high school facilities than it needed. This situation arose because, after the construction of Roosevelt had begun, the Lincoln proposition (for a consolidated rural school in the vicinity) became a reality, and the outcome was not one high school but two. Since the College was committed by a long-term contract to the Lincoln School to supply its teachers, there was only one alternative and that was to close the senior high school at Roosevelt. He reminded the citizens that "the primary purpose of the Roosevelt High School is not to educate pupils but to train teachers." "The entire State," he said, "is taxed for that purpose alone." And he informed them that, in a survey made during the previous year (1927), it was found that the combined capacity of Lincoln and Roosevelt Schools greatly exceeded the demand. He further stated that throughout the State the supply of teachers exceeded the demand, and in consequence it was to be expected that a decrease in enrollments at the College would occur.

His second point was the urgent need for space for the college departments, as mentioned above, in connection with which he said that it would be at least five years before any relief could be expected by way of legislative appropriation.

These arguments, however, did not appeal to the patrons of Roosevelt. A committee was formed to meet with the State Board. Petitions were circulated. The high school paper lamented:

> The entire student body of Roosevelt has expressed a sincere regret. Every
> student feels the loss of Roosevelt as a tragedy in his or her life.[19]

On December 31, a citizens' committee met with the Board in
special session and succeeded in getting the decision tabled.
McKenny, protesting that he still felt the Roosevelt Senior High
School should be discontinued, made the following statement to the
Board:

> In view of plans that are under consideration by certain citizens of Ypsi-
> lanti for the relief of congestion in the special education and other depart-
> ments at the Michigan State Normal College, I recommend that my
> request for a discontinuance of the Roosevelt Senior High School be laid
> on the table.[20]

Citizens, patrons, and students of Roosevelt were jubilant over
this victory. Reaction of the Roosevelt pupils was exuberant. They
exclaimed:

> What does this mean? Just this, we must now justify this victory. Every
> student in Roosevelt must do his level best to impress those that hold our
> fate, so that they will never again attempt to discontinue this high
> school.[21]

The letter to the teachers was forgotten (though never formally
withdrawn).

The final adjustment was worked out by a college committee consisting of the President and faculty members Pittman, Elliot, Tape,
Misner and Fuller. As finally approved by the State Board on
March 31, the "solution" was to crowd the elementary training
school into the Roosevelt building regardless of consequences, and to
place the elementary school and junior and senior high schools under
one principal. At the same time the class hour was to be reduced
from 55 to 45 minutes, and the class-load of the critic teacher raised
from four to five classes per day. The whole arrangement would also
make possible a reduction in staff of three teachers, and would take
effect in the fall term of 1930.

McKenny, overlooking the fact that the Roosevelt building had
been originally designed for 420 pupils, asserted that with this
arrangement the building should easily accommodate between 500
and 600. The recommendation of the committee contained, however,
the following significant request:

It is recommended that an adequate type of building be secured for special education and for a few additional rooms for the training school. This building should provide for a pre-school unit. This building should be located near Roosevelt or be an addition to Roosevelt, as the present day view of workers in the special education field is that children in such departments should mingle as much as possible with normal children.

Relief for Special Education came a decade later through the initiative of its head, Charles Elliot, and a private gift rather than legislative grant, and in 1939 the splendid Rackham building was dedicated.

The hoped-for elementary school was never built and Roosevelt Laboratory School, as it was now known, settled into a routine which remained unchanged.

In 1933, pressed by the full impact of the Great Depression, the College administration was forced by lack of legislative appropriation to take drastic measures to cut costs, functions were performed on a minimal basis. With an enrollment in 1930–1931 of 567, and with elementary, junior high and senior high crowded together in one inadequate building under a single supervision, the junior high school concept (which is of such great national importance today) was never given a chance to develop. Roosevelt became strictly a teacher-training institution, and lost its other function of presenting a model school.

But depression injury was to be compounded. Drastic cuts in state appropriations called for drastic cuts in staff. Upon the retirement of McKenny in 1933, the State Board looked for a successor who might have the courage to economize wherever necessary and at the same time maintain the institution as an effective, going concern. They found him in John M. Munson, President of Northern State Teachers' College at Marquette, Michigan. Munson had built a reputation as a strong administrator with, at the same time, a meticulous concern for educational standards. He was, in fact, typical of the old school of college presidents, who assumed total personal responsibility for every phase of institutional operation. Hiring of staff, for example, was his responsibility and his prerogative, and decisions were usually made without consultation with subordinate officers.

Under this style of administration, and in those particular times, the door became tightly closed against individual initiative, at times even normal performance, in any direction. A static condition set in which reduced the institution to routine operation.

Some thirty years later a second effort was made to close the Roosevelt High School, again on grounds of economy. But the conditions were very different. The College (now Eastern Michigan University) needed much more than the combined facilities of the Lincoln and Roosevelt schools for its student teachers in the secondary field. Now, however, the public schools of the State were staffed with well-prepared teachers, large numbers of whom possessed training and experience which equalled that of the critic teacher. Many schools were equipped with facilities which far surpassed those of the teacher-training institution. The University could send its student teachers into the public schools of the area for their practical experience confident that they could witness good schools operating in a life situation, and receive a fair-to-good experience in practice teaching at much less cost. The original concept of a campus school that would serve as a model for the schools of the State (and for the student teacher who would soon be staffing them) had long since faded.

Nevertheless, in the spring of 1961 citizens of Ypsilanti again intervened on behalf of Roosevelt. Excited meetings were held. The teaching staff, with the vaguest of assurance concerning their future, spent agonizing days and nights developing a campaign to combat the threat to their future. This time no one knew for certain whether the threat pertained only to the senior high school, though this seemed at the moment to be its objective.

The public meetings brought forth a multitude of arguments both of sentimental and personal character. The threat had been launched precipitately, sparked by a continuing financial crisis in Michigan higher education. The conclusion was reached speedily. On May 4, a delegation of citizens took their protest to the State capital;[22] on May 20, a second delegation met with the State Board. And on that day the Board voted to continue the Roosevelt school. A rise in tuition, still a modest figure, was prescribed. Once again the Ypsilanti citizens, this time with the frantic help of the teaching staff, had won. Again, the role of the Training School had not been debated.

However, the State Board of Education asked Elliot to determine some longterm goals for the school, and a committee of 17 was appointed to work on the problem.[23] The activities of the committee, extending over a period of eight months, included surveys of local opinion and exploration of state and national policies and trends concerning laboratory schools. The final report, submitted in July, 1962, concluded that Roosevelt's key role in the area of teacher training should henceforth take the direction of experimentation and research. The underlying considerations that would justify abandonment of the old objective of practice teaching were the tremendous increase in the number of student teachers to be served, the existence of public schools of such quality that students could gain satisfactory teaching experience and guidance by being assigned to them, and the relatively low cost of providing for student teaching in this manner.[24]

The proposal caused fear and consternation among a staff whose tradition and habit had been the training of student teachers. The transition would have to be accomplished with skill, patience, and appropriate staffing. The Legislature would have to be convinced.

In 1967, a resolution by that body required that the entire school be phased out by the fall of 1969.

CHAPTER FIVE

PROFESSIONAL INSTRUCTION

Since the *raison d'etre* of Normal was the education and training of teachers, the professional side of Normal's curriculum is of particular interest. Indeed, as was noted earlier, for many years academic courses were included only because it was felt that the students admitted to Normal were seriously lacking in the subject matter of the courses they would have to teach. By 1878 the general concensus, both at the faculty and State Board levels, was that the Normal should henceforth confine its work to the professional side of teacher preparation. This policy was soon abandoned, but this singleness of purpose was to control the thinking and guide the development of the institution until the retirement of President Munson in the middle of the next century.

Curriculum

From the earliest time the approach to the professional training of teachers took the form of instruction in psychology, history, and philosophy of education, in the legal basis and structure of the public school system of Michigan, and in observation and practice.

When, in the spring of 1853, Normal opened its doors to students, the Rev. J. M. Wilson, A.M., gave lectures in Intellectual Philosophy, and a principal of the Model School was yet to be named. The Model School would open in the fall. This was the extent of the *professional* offerings. Two curricula were available—one for teachers in the primary schools (the *English Course*) and one for teachers in the union schools (the *Classical Course*).

But soon the curriculum was to be shaken by a force from Switzerland. Johann Heinrich Pestalozzi (1746–1827) had succeeded in

51

breaking away from the current teaching method of repeating words and memorization, as well as from the brutality that characterized the learning process. School must be a place where children were loved, and thus innate powers developed. Three quarters of a century later (in 1890) a great American educator, William T. Harris, would comment: "The name of Pestalozzi is forever dear to the hearts of all men. For he is the first teacher to announce convincingly the doctrine that all people should be educated—that, in fact, education is the one good gift to give to all, whether rich or poor."

Principal Welch, an enthusiast for the Pestalozzian idea and method, published in 1862 an instruction book for primary teachers. The following year the State Board gave its sanction. State Superintendent Gregory, in his report for 1863, said:

> The Board of Education is now convinced that the time has come when the school can render no greater service to the State, than to so modify its course of study that all its pupils may receive thorough instruction and practice in the Pestalozzian system of Primary Teaching.

Thus, the way was prepared for a new emphasis in teaching on observation and inquiry, rather than in the mere acquisition of knowledge.

In adopting this philosophy, Normal was neither ahead of nor behind the times. Pestalozzi's work had been known here and there in the United States for some time. It had been given strong support and wide publicity in Horace Mann's Seventh Report (1843). But Pestalozzian methods did not gain a strong foothold until after 1860. Indeed, major credit for the effective introduction of Pestalozzian ideas and methods goes to Edward A. Sheldon of Oswego, New York, who, through his missionary zeal and program of teacher training, was responsible for the development known as "The Oswego Movement," which took its rise at about this time.[1]

Normal, in pursuance of this new policy, reorganized its two programs of study. The First Course, called the Normal Training Course, prepared teachers for the primary school. The Second Course, called the Higher Normal Course, prepared for the union or graded school.

The State Board, in an official circular, explained this new step as follows:

> Prominent Educators of the West are aware that a radical change is taking place in the methods of Primary Education. In our best schools there

is a growing conviction that the old routine of early studies, and old methods of teaching, are out of harmony with the wants and instincts of childhood. Many parents are beginning to inquire, why is it that their little
ones, though kept faithfully at school most of the year, make no satisfactory intellectual progress . . .

Within fifteen years (by 1868) the professional work could be
described as consisting of formal courses in Mental Philosophy, the
Philosophy of Education, Professional Ethics,[2] lectures on topics of
professional concern, and methods of teaching.[3]

The formula for the teaching process was labeled "The Educational Principle," and described thus:

Thorough knowledge of subject; presentation in logical order; the Pupil's
degree of Maturity; the Pupil's self-activity; the Pupil's progress from the
Known to the Unknown, from Easy to Difficult, from Simple to Complex,
from Single to Combines, from the Concrete to Abstract, from the Empiri-
cal to Rational . . .[4]

The professional curriculum was explained as placing the emphasis on teaching method, and differentiated from the academic curriculum. It is well stated in the following excerpt from the 1868–69
catalog:

. . . generally whatever subject is taught in classes is given with reference
to the best methods of teaching it, together with the pedagogic axioms
applicable to each step . . . differing in this respect from mere *Academic
Instruction,* the chief aim of which is attainment of *knowledge concerning
the subject of Study* only with an incidental, often uncertain aim at what
is called 'Mental Discipline.'

The policy statement concluded in a sweeping vein:

Indeed everything in and about the Normal School,—its course of study,
discipline, movements, arrangements, surroundings and moral influence,
its very spirit and atmosphere, is intended to have an important and direct
bearing upon the professional training of the students.

Some twenty years later (in 1888, under Principal Sill) the Pestalozzian emphasis on the psychology of the child (with its obverse side
of de-emphasis on the acquisition of facts, of the mere hearing of
recitations by the teacher) had developed into a major emphasis on

psychology in the professional curriculum. The two professional courses were again reorganized, this time consolidated into one inclusive program called *General Instruction in the Science and Art of Teaching.* Twenty weeks were now to be devoted to Psychology as a subject of study, followed by consideration of applications to the theory and art of teaching, the order in which both physical and mental powers are developed, and the "harmonious" development of the child.[5]

Graduate Programs

Another development was the beginning of a short-lived venture into graduate work at Normal. Two programs of this character were initiated. One was the offering of the degree of Master of Pedagogics. This was to be conferred upon holders of the Bachelor of Pedagogics degree who could show five years of successful teaching and present a thesis acceptable to the faculty on some educational problem. The new degree was first granted in 1890. The other program was entitled "Professional Course for Graduates of Colleges." This was designed for "graduates in the Literary and Scientific Courses of the University and incorporated Michigan Colleges." It was a strictly professional course, and led to a life certificate and degree of Bachelor of Pedagogics. Its program included applied psychology ("mental science applied to teaching"), methods of teaching, the history of education, and practice teaching.

Graduate work was resumed after many years when, in 1938, a joint program under the auspices of the University of Michigan was inaugurated. In late 1952 it became an independent department of the Normal.

From the mid-nineties the influence of Johann Friedrich Herbart (1776-1841) of Germany and of America's G. Stanley Hall made a visible impact on Normal's curriculum. Psychology was becoming a science, and much more attention was given to it. The thinking of Herbart showed in the gradual abandonment of the Pestalozzian view that mind consists of distinct capacities or "faculties," in favor of the Herbartian view of mind as a unity.

Herbart's further insistence that the aim of education is broadly social rather than personal found recognition in such new education courses as Sociology (1898), Social Education (1913), Social Psychology (1914) and Socialized Curriculum (1919). Hall's emphasis on child study was first formally reflected in a course in Child Study (1900).

The appearance of two new areas of teacher preparation, Special Education and Rural Education, brought some expansion of curriculum, particularly in the application of existing principles to those specialties. Special Education (the preparation of teachers of handicapped children) became a department in 1924, but work was first offered in 1915 in a course called Psychology of Exceptional Children. A Department of Rural Education, for the preparation of teachers for rural schools, was organized in 1919 and brought in special courses in Rural Education (1921) and Rural Research (1925).

Proliferation of courses in the several areas now well established was conservative during the first decade of the present century (the Jones era), extensive during the second and third decades (the McKenny era). By 1931 they were being arranged under eight headings: General and Educational Psychology; Principles, History and Philosophy of Education; Tests, Measurements and Research; Administration and Supervision; Philosophy; Rural Education; Social Aspects of Education; and Special Education.

During the period of the Great Depression and World War II (the Munson era), expansion slowed to a walk, but was not to be entirely denied. Courses were added to the Special Education Department, a course in audio-visual aids to teaching was offered (1937), a graduate program in Education and Special Education was initiated in 1938, and in 1941 a program in Occupational Therapy was adopted. In 1953 a course called Core Curriculum was introduced which became a staple in the professional offerings.

An unfortunate casualty of this period was the offering in philosophy. Begun in 1905, under Professor Charles Hoyt, as "Degree Courses," two courses in this academic field were presented. The education staff thence provided the work in philosophy for thirty-three years. It was terminated by the death of Professor O. O. Norris in 1938. When revived, with the coming of Professor Manuel Bilsky in 1960, it was placed with the Department of History and Social Sciences, and at the present time has expanded to offer both major and minor concentrations.

Course work in Philosophy of Education was also initiated in 1905, and terminated by the death of Professor Norris. Twelve years later (1950) a course in History and Philosophy of Education was offered by Professor Carl Hood, and although Professor Hood died in 1958 the course continues.

Today, courses offered by the College of Education total 164, of which 42 are undergraduate offerings and 122 are at the graduate level. To these must be added 28 undergraduate methods courses, given by the several liberal arts and specialty departments (music, industrial arts, etc) to inform students how to teach the subject matter of their major areas.

A Department of Education

In 1893, (under Principal Boone) the work in professional education was organized as a department, with Daniel Putnam as its head. It was called the *Department of Mental and Moral Science and Theory and Art of Teaching;* its more convenient label, the *Pedagogical Department.* In 1897 the name was altered to *Department of Psychology and Pedagogy.* With the arrival of President Jones in 1902 it became *Department of Psychology and Education.* And from 1916 it was the *Education Department* until absorbed into the *College of Education* when, in 1959, the institution changed from college to university.

Professor Putnam, the department's first head, died in 1906. For a decade and a half thereafter a three-headed arrangement prevailed. Professor Samuel Laird represented Psychology, Professor Nathan Harvey Pedagogy, and Professor Charles Hoyt the Science and History of Education. By 1921, however, Hoyt appeared clearly as Chairman of the Department of Education. In the same year a new division was created within the department, called Rural Education. Professor Marvin Pittman was placed in charge.

The long career at Normal (thirty-two years) of Charles Oliver Hoyt deserves special attention. He was, in early training and experience, a Michigan, even a local area, product. His story up to the time of arrival at Normal reveals much about the status of public education at the time. Attending high school at the nearby village of Saline, he first taught in a rural school, became principal of a small-town high school (Blissfield), then was superintendent of schools successively at Wyandotte, Grass Lake, Jackson, and Lansing. It was not until he had held these positions that he received his AB degree from Albion College. He immediately (1896) joined the staff at Normal as Director of the Training School. What is exceptional in this story (though fairly typical of the colleagues with whom he was associated—D'Ooge, Ford, Sherzer, Gorton) is that he took a leave of absence from Normal and went to Germany where he earned the PhD degree from the University of Jena, center for the Herbartian movement (1903). His position as head of the department, subsequent writings, and the publication of his book, *Studies in the History of Modern Education* (1908), made him a figure of national interest.

Professor Hoyt died in 1928, and was succeeded in 1930 by Charles Leroy Anspach, Registrar and Dean of Ashland College, Ohio. Anspach headed the Education Department at Normal for four years, served as Dean of Administration for one, returned to Ashland as its president, and concluded his career as President of Central Michigan College (now Central Michigan University) over which he presided with marked success for a period of twenty years. He returned to Normal, now Eastern Michigan University, in 1961 as a Regent appointed by the Governor of the State.

In 1935, Noble Lee Garrison became head of the department. Garrison had been with the Normal since 1925, had published papers on coordination between college and training school, on teaching and on democratic participation in administration, and a book on *The Technique and Administration of Teaching*.

Retiring in 1953 (during the Elliott administration), Garrison was replaced by R. Stanley Gex, of the staff of Teachers' College, University of Cincinnati. The following year saw the several professional areas and departments of instruction grouped under the general direction of a Dean of Professional Education. The function of the dean was to coordinate the work of the departments of Education, Special Education, Extension Education (shortly to become designated as Field Services), the Laboratory Schools, and the methods courses. Earl Mosier, a member of President Elliott's staff when he was State Superintendent of Public Instruction, was named by Elliott to fill the new position. In 1956 Dean Mosier resigned, and two years later was replaced by Gex. The replacement for Gex as head of the Education Department was Kenneth H. Cleeton, a member of the Education staff at William and Mary College. In 1960, in line with the institutional change of name to Eastern Michigan University, the *College of Education* was organized and Gex was named Dean. The departments assigned to this college were Education; Library Science; Special Education and Occupational Therapy; Physical Education, Health, Recreation and Athletics; and the Laboratory Schools.

Under President Sponberg, whose administration began in 1965, some further adjustments were made. A new *Center for International Studies* was created and Dean Gex, whose interest had developed strongly in this direction, was placed in charge. His position as Dean of the College of Education went to Allen Myers, then head of the Special Education Department. Cleeton was placed in charge of the *Special Projects and Research Development*—a new agency prompted by the numerous opportunities that had developed in the post-World War 11 years for obtaining grants (federal and other) for fellowships and research projects at the faculty level.

The purpose for which Normal was founded was religiously and exclusively adhered to for nearly a century—and effectively served throughout its existence. The teachers who went forth from its halls became noted from coast to coast for their sound preparation and dedication to their calling. They brought national distinction to their alma mater.

It is noteworthy that those faculty who attracted national and international attention and respect came very largely from the liberal arts side of the curriculum. The stone that once was rejected became the cornerstone of a proud edifice.

CHAPTER SIX

TEACHERS FOR RURAL SCHOOLS

In considering the matter of teachers for rural schools it is well to remember that at the time Normal was founded the one-room rural school represented public education in Michigan. The graded, or union, school (forerunner of the public high school) was in its infancy; the one public institution of higher education (the University of Michigan) was in its early childhood and finding it very difficult to secure students who were adequately prepared for admission. Ninety-seven per cent of the population of Michigan was rural. Normal's function, therefore, was to train teachers for rural schools. One may well observe, at this point, the significant fact that the growth of this vital institution for public improvement and welfare came, as it were, from the bottom upwards, not from the top downwards. And as it grew, the Normal grew; as the demands of the society it served increased, the Normal responded—becoming in time a four-year college, and later the university that it is today.

Our concern here, however, is with the question of *when* Normal became conscious that it was no longer serving the rural school; *when* did the preparation of teachers for the rural school appear as a special function which called for a special curriculum?

By 1890, the rural population of Michigan had diminished to 65 per cent of the total. Normal's attention had been drawn to the preparation of teachers for the better-paid, more attractive positions in the urban areas serving the remaining 35 per cent of the population. In that same year Principal Sill included in his annual report a plea for the rural school.

In the ensuing years the Legislature took a series of steps to meet this need. In 1895 (two years after Sill's retirement), after much urging, it voted to acquire the private teacher-training school at Mt. Pleasant. The act provided

> That a normal school for the preparation and training of persons for teaching in the rural district schools, and the primary departments of the graded schools of the State, to be known as "Central Michigan Normal School," be established . . .[1]

This limited beginning has evolved into the Central Michigan University of today.

In 1899, a normal school was provided for Michigan's Upper Peninsula. The act stated

> That a normal school shall be located at Marquette, to be known as the Northern State Normal School, for the purpose of instructing persons in the several branches pertaining to a public school education, and in the science and art of teaching the same.[2]

This institution has become the present-day Northern Michigan University.

In 1903, a normal school was established for the western part of the State. In that year the Legislature voted that

> A State normal school shall be located, established, and maintained in the western part of the state at such place as the State Board of Education shall designate, to be known as the Western State Normal School for the preparation and training of persons for teaching in the rural district schools, and in the primary departments of the graded schools of the state.[3]

Today we have in Kalamazoo the large and thriving Western Michigan University.

In the same year the Legislature authorized county training classes, not more than one to a county, to be organized under the direction of a county normal board, for teachers of rural schools. By 1912 there were some 50 county normals, admitting young people from 18 years of age who had completed the tenth grade in high school or had two years of successful teaching.

At Normal, under President Jones, a special short course for rural teachers was first offered in 1902.[4]

When President McKenny arrived (in 1912), his first annual report to the State Board gave considerable attention to the rural problem. The course being offered, he said, was not very successful, the reason being that the Normal did not have sufficient funds to develop a rural school department. Such a department should be organized and placed under the direction of a person who understood rural school conditions and the kind of training necessary for rural school teachers. He asserted that the boys and girls on the farm were not getting a "square deal." There was no response.

Six years later, noting that a department of rural education had already been established at the Western and the Central Normal Schools, McKenny renewed his plea with increased vigor, saying:

> I believe the time is now here when the legislature should establish a rural school department with a recognized leader as its head. This department should establish practice schools in the rural districts near the college where teachers in training for country school teaching could learn the art of managing and teaching a country school under practical conditions . . .

The following year (1919), twenty-nine years and four presidents after Principal Sill's urgent plea, such a department was formed, and Ella Smith, at the time State Supervisor of the county normal training classes, became the acting head, serving while McKenny searched the nation for a director. Two curricula were offered—a year-and-one-summer program which led to a three-year rural certificate, and a two-year-and-a-summer program leading to a rural life certificate.[5] Practice teaching was provided by a one-teacher rural school, the Stone School, located six miles from the campus, reached by the electric railway.

In 1921, McKenny found his man in Marvin Summers Pittman. Pittman had been Director of Rural Education at the Oregon State Normal School since 1912, and had just completed his doctorate at Columbia University. For vision, energy, and dynamic personality a better choice could scarcely have been made. Indeed, during his thirteen years of service at Normal Pittman established a national and international reputation in rural education.

In the best tradition of the Normal faculty, he went abroad in 1928 to study rural education in France, Spain, Germany, Denmark and England. In 1929, McKenny placed him in charge of all teacher training at Normal. In the summer of that year, at the invitation of the University of Mexico and the Mexican government, he held a series of conferences with federal directors and inspectors of schools. In 1932, he was asked by the Cuban government to make a study of Cuban schools and teacher training. In 1934, he resigned his position to accept the presidency of Georgia State Teachers College.

The Lincoln Consolidated School

Pittman's lasting contribution at the Michigan State Normal College was the creation of the Lincoln Consolidated Rural School. His achievement was noteworthy because it meant the self-effacement of thirteen small primary school districts whose autonomy was long-standing. It was almost as if thirteen independent nations were to give up voluntarily their sovereignty.

The achievement draws attention to the means. When Pittman arrived at Ypsilanti in 1921 he at once acted to enlarge the training facility. In 1923, the Denton and Carpenter schools were added to the Stone School, and in 1924, the Begole school joined the list.[6] Pittman founded a Rural Education Club of a dozen members, gave it a new name, and boosted its membership almost overnight to 600 rural teachers, with a campus membership of some 30 student teachers. The campus group met bi-weekly in the home of either Pittman or Professor Hover. The nature of this organization was described thus:

> The name, "The Michigan Trailblazers," was adopted as symbolizing the broader vision and task of this earnest group. Trailblazer enthusiasm was felt in every corner of the campus. Members in every county of Michigan, in five other states, and in Canada have carried the Trailblazer spirit with them into their work this year. In May they will return to the Normal College for a reunion known as the "Hatchet Sharpener," and here make their hatchets keen to blaze new trails into regions of great need.[7]

But the step which led to Lincoln was the inauguration of the Zone School plan. This was a plan of supervision for rural schools. It appears to have been developed on a fairly large scale first by the Oregon State Normal School. At least this is where Pittman first saw it.

The plan was to divide a supervisory district into zones small enough to enable a supervisor to make the rounds of visitation and to conduct zone meetings for teachers. It was these meetings that led first to mutual acquaintance, then to cooperative effort.

Pittman, in inaugurating the zone idea, involved the local Kiwanis Club. His project was to give a dinner for the 40 teachers of the 40 one-room schools and the 120 officers in the Ypsilanti area. Thirty-seven accepted the invitation and the dinner was held in April of 1922. This first "County Club Dinner" (it became an annual affair) provided the occasion for adoption of a plan for the future.

Each school (teacher and school board) was to state in writing a desire for affiliation with the Normal. To defray expenses, each would pay a small fee. In return, the College would visit the school at least once a month, hold a monthly meeting for the teachers, publish a small paper for the pupils "that would boost them in their work," and in general render "whatever service possible to the school and the school neighborhood." The Kiwanis Club, too, was to play a continuing role. Each member would become an Honorary Patron of a school.

In the course of time, many found opportunities to contribute to their respective schools—the job printer printed school stationery; the music specialists gave music scholarships; the electrician wired his school; the historian conducted a contest and told stories; the photographer donated pictures, etc., etc. The club as a whole also found opportunities to be of service. At the annual meetings of the Hatchet Sharpener, it provided entertainment and organized sight-seeing trips; it organized the annual Country Club Dinner; it provided for medical examinations for pupils in special need. It was a beautiful demonstration of how, lighted with imagination and warmed with enthusiasm, Town and Gown could be brought together in an undertaking of great importance, serving a vital interest of both.

Ten of the 13 school districts that were soon to form the consolidated Lincoln School District were involved in this zone pattern. And when Pittman happened to mention (in October of 1922) to two leading citizens of the area, Willits Derbyshire and Henry Champion, that the College was contemplating the construction of a training school for rural teachers somewhere in the Ypsilanti area, the response was electric.

The matter was promptly brought up at a meeting of Fraternity Grange and a mass meeting of the citizens of the area planned. This meeting took place in the Willis Methodist Church on November 22, 1922 (seven months after the first Country Club Dinner), and there McKenny and Pittman outlined their project. A committee was formed which, with McKenny, met with the State Board of Education in December. From this meeting came the following resolution (freely rendered):

> In order to prepare teachers for the rural schools of the State, said Board agrees to designate a rural agricultural school, accessible to the Michigan State Normal College at Ypsilanti, provided a schoolhouse is suitably constructed for such purpose, as a part of the training school system of said College; and upon a cooperative agreement between the State Board and the School District, the State Board of Education shall employ and pay all teachers and janitors necessary for said school, and shall pay one-half the cost of transportation of pupils who are required by law to be transported to said school.

A vote on consolidation was held by 12 school districts on May 2, 1923. By a narrow margin (279 to 210) consolidation was approved. The favorable vote on the bond issue to finance construction of the new school was closer (212 to 196). On July 23, a thirteenth school district petitioned to be included, District No. 2 (the Vedder School) of Augusta Township.

Thus the new school district was formed, a site in Augusta Township was purchased (the Island School site), an architect (Warren S. Holmes of Lansing) employed, contracts were let, the cornerstone laid (April 16, 1924) and on October 31, 1924, the Lincoln School opened its doors.[8] Thirteen school districts had joined to make this possible; thirteen one-room schools went out of existence.

At least one was older than the Normal College itself, Model, whose existing site had been purchased in 1844. Another one, Lowden, dated from the year Normal opened its doors (1853). Each of them represented strong community loyalties of long standing (the youngest dated 1876). Nearly all held a reunion at some time during the summer of 1924. As recently as 1937 the Morgan School was still holding an annual Memorial Day reunion.

Nor should it be overlooked that, in the campaign for consolidation, the 13 rural teachers (not one of whom could qualify for a place on the staff of the new school) stood as one in favor of the change.

The original name of this new school district, "Agricultural Rural Training School No. 1 of Ypsilanti and Augusta Townships" was soon changed to "Lincoln Consolidated School" because, as its historian, Clara Smith, says:

> They (the School Board) felt it was the fulfillment of the ideals for which Abraham Lincoln stood—equal educational opportunity for rural as well as urban students.[9]

The people of the District had wanted to name it after Pittman but yielded to his dissent. Henry A. Tape became its first principal.

A year later (December 5, 1925), the worst that could happen happened—fire, of undetermined origin, destroyed the building. Stronger evidence of the increasing enthusiasm of the Lincoln community for their school could scarcely be found than the resulting vote on an additional bond issue, not only to rebuild but to enlarge the structure. It was 225 to 143 in favor. The re-dedication took place on Lincoln's birthday, 1927.

Through the ensuing years the story of the Lincoln School District was one of continuing enlargement of the school, increase and change in character of population, and sustained enthusiasm. Additions were made to the original building until it was nearly doubled in size. These included an industrial arts shop and a garage for the 13 school buses (1928); a cafeteria, girls' gymnasium, and industrial arts room (1936); a new and larger garage, and transformation of the old garage into classrooms (1948); a north wing to house more classrooms, a large cafeteria, and some specialized vocational training rooms (1951). A separate elementary school building (ten rooms) was constructed (1956). Six rooms were added to it and a 40-acre site for a new high school building purchased (1959). A new $2,100,000 high school building was constructed, with the most modern swimming pool (1961).

The original four-fold objective was faithfully adhered to: greater educational opportunity for the children; a practice school for Normal; inclusion of the practical arts of agriculture, home economics, and industrial arts; and a community center for adult groups.

The community-center objective was met by the use of the school as a meeting place for the various organizations within the district, the organization of evening class programs, evening church services during the summer, an annual fair, baseball games, community suppers, and numerous other activities.

The relation of Lincoln to the Normal College was beneficial to both.

When the twenty-fifth anniversary of Lincoln was celebrated in 1949, it was noted that some 6,000 student teachers had gained experience there. Ten years later, the figure was 10,000. Originally, only students intending to teach in rural schools were accepted; later, as the pressure on Normal for practice teaching facilities increased and Lincoln became larger, this restriction was lifted.

In the course of time, great change had taken place in the character of the Lincoln district. World War II spawned the great bomber plant at Willow Run. In the postwar years this was replaced by the Kaiser-Fraser automobile venture, then not only replaced but added to by General Motors which located its Hydra-Matic operation there and also its Corvair plant. And in 1957 the Ford Motor Company opened a large plant at nearby Rawsonville. Farmers were replaced by industrial workers. Enrollments in the Lincoln schools skyrocketed from the original 595 (in 1925) to more than 1,900 (in 1968).[10] By 1951 less than 12 per cent of the pupils enrolled in the vocational agriculture classes were from the homes of full-time farmers.

Administratively, important changes took place almost from the beginning. In 1929, Pittman's title was changed from Director of Rural Education to Director of Teaching Training (a title that was modified two years later to Director of Laboratory Schools). At about this time too, Pittman's attention was drawn to foreign projects, first Mexico, then Cuba. But he brought in Harvey Turner as Director of Rural Education and Francis Lord as Supervisor of Zone Schools.

Turner came to Normal from Arkansas State Teachers College where he had been, in turn, Professor of Rural Education and Head of the Education Department. Lord came from the Oregon Normal School of Pittman's early experience. When Pittman resigned in 1934, Turner was given his post as Director of Laboratory Schools. Lord was shifted to the Education Department where he served under Charles Elliot in the growing area of Special Education. He succeeded Elliot in 1941.

In 1941, the man who had headed the Lincoln School from its beginning, Henry A. Tape, resigned to become president of Northern State Normal School at Marquette. He was replaced by the head of Normal's city-oriented Roosevelt Laboratory School, Ben H. VandenBelt. During VandenBelt's administration the original contract between the Normal College and the Lincoln School District (which ran for 25 years) expired (1949). It was replaced by a similar contract for 15 years.

VandenBelt retired in 1954 and was replaced by Bruce K. Nelson, a native of Marquette, Michigan, and at the time Assistant Superintendent of Schools at Loraine, Ohio. Under Nelson's administration at Lincoln the six-room elementary school building was successfully financed. In January, 1956, Nelson was transferred to the College as Dean of Instruction. Two years later he was elevated to the status of Vice President for Instruction.

George Ruwitch replaced Nelson. Ruwitch was brought to Lincoln from Escanaba, Michigan, where he was Assistant Superintendent of Schools. During his administration the Lincoln School complex was expanded by the construction of the impressive new high school building.

Ruwitch resigned in 1961 to accept the superintendency of the East Grand Rapids schools, and was replaced by a member of the Lincoln faculty, at the time principal of the Lincoln Elementary School, Vernon H. Jones. During his administration the 15-year contract expired (1964). A petition against renewal was signed by more than 50 electors of the district but the Board, sensing the will of the district as a whole, voted to renew the contract for another 15 years.

This contract, like the previous one, had a provision for modification by mutual consent. In 1967, the University approached the Lincoln board on the matter of implementing this provision. The proposal was that the Lincoln faculty no longer be selected and appointed by the University but by the Lincoln board instead, thus severing the direct tie which had existed since the district was formed. This was approved by the school board and the Board of Regents (June 26, 1968) and became effective in September, 1969.

Lincoln continued to provide facilities for the University's student teachers, however, and the University paid a lump sum annually for this service. The agreement was for a five-year period running through 1973.

The Lincoln School District had been organized by rural people in the high hope that it would provide a much better quality of education for their children (equal to that made available to city children), a broader curriculum (including vocational skills that would be of particular value in rural areas); and that it would serve as a cultural stimulus and a community center for the adults. That it served these ends well is shown by the consistent financial support that was given and increased as needs grew. The story of a prosperous citizen of the area, Charles Eli Alban, is symbolic. He had strongly opposed the campaign for consolidation on the ground that too heavy a tax burden would result. He became a thorough convert. At his death in 1929 it was found that he had left his entire estate to the school district, to be used to help pay off the bonds.

From the standpoint of the College the aim was not only to provide a facility for the training of rural teachers and administrators, but also to promote and provide a model of school district consolidation.

If Lincoln attracted special attention it was largely because of three factors: its size, the extent to which it met the goals of the consolidation movement, and the fact that it was affiliated with the oldest teacher-training institution in the "West," which made it of national interest. Lincoln School was visited for many years by leaders in education, school superintendents and teachers, and members of Grange chapters. The United States Office of Education sent many foreign visitors, especially from countries in which rural education was still a problem. In 1931 the National Education Association held its annual meeting in Detroit, and many educators traveled out to Ypsilanti to see the Lincoln School.

CHAPTER SEVEN

FINE ARTS AND VOCATIONAL

Art

Instruction in art at the Normal was included from the beginning. One of the original staff positions was designated as *Vocal Music and Drawing.* These subjects were taught at first only in the Model or Training School. The work in drawing was given in connection with instruction in local geography which was taught with the aid of outline maps and requirements in map drawing.

In 1859, a senior student, John Goodison, taught a course in *Geography and Drawing,* and upon graduation was engaged as a regular member of the faculty to teach geography, drawing, and arithmetic.

Within a decade the importance of drawing as an aid to the teacher became recognized for other subjects as well as geography, particularly where the object method of teaching was employed. The school catalog soon carried the following statement:

> The limited time (one term) does not permit the acquisition of great manual skill in the art, but pupils receive a thorough grounding in principles. Real objects and not copies form the subjects of the lessons, and the laws of Perspective are learned by observation. The lessons include drawing the geometrical solids and objects of similar form, construction of shadows and reflections, leaf and flower forms and the elements of Linear Perspective. In addition a drill in printing on the blackboard and in drawing lines, angles and plane figures, is given.[1]

In 1871, a broadening trend was evident. This led in due time to a well-rounded, extensive curriculum in art. The purpose of the course in drawing was described as that of developing "an apprehension of

69

the utility of Drawing as a means of education, and as an acquisition bearing upon the industries or practical pursuits of life."

The outstanding name in art at Normal is Goodison, father and daughter. John Goodison ('59) taught geography and drawing, and at times arithmetic, from 1860 to 1869. He left to try his hand at the publishing business but returned in 1883 to teach until his death in 1892. Bertha, his daughter and also a graduate of Normal ('94), joined the staff in 1900 and headed the work in art until her death in 1937. Thus, the Goodisons were responsible for art at the Normal for more than half a century.

After John Goodison's death, Charles T. McFarlane taught geography and drawing. At a later time he was to achieve national eminence in the field of geography. At Normal he emphasized the general importance of drawing for effective teaching.

McFarlane acquired an able assistant, Hilda Lodeman, daughter of the head of the Modern Languages Department. A course in *Sketching from Life* was added. In 1901 he resigned, and was succeeded by Mark Jefferson who was to become eminent in the field of Geography.[2] In accepting the position at the Normal College, Jefferson insisted that geography be separated from drawing. His arrival thus signified the establishment of a Geography Department and a Drawing Department. Bertha Goodison, who had been teaching during the previous year in the Training School, gave the instruction in drawing. In 1912 the title Drawing Department was changed to Art Department. Miss Goodison's name headed the list of those giving the course work but it was not until 1919 that she was given the title of Professor of Art and Head of the Fine Arts Department. Bertha Goodison thus was the first to head a separate department in this area.

The trend during the Bertha Goodison era was toward greater breadth of offerings, service courses for other departments, and a more conscious cultural objective. New courses included *Applied Design* (1909); a program for *Specialized Students, History of Painting, Art and Manual Training* (1913); combined programs in Music and Fine Arts (1922); *Stage Decoration, Sculpture,* a program in *Commercial Art* (1927); and *Etching* and *Art Appreciation* (1933).

Miss Goodison was an artist of considerable merit. Her drawings, landscapes and still-lifes are still treasured in a number of Ypsilanti homes. Eastern Michigan University today possesses portraits painted by her of two outstanding member of the faculty of her time, Professors D'Ooge and Sherzer. Her death in 1937 left the headship of the department vacant until the appointment or Orlo Gill in 1940, a sensitive artist whose specialities were etching and drawing.

During the Gill period considerable attention was given to conferences and workshops for in-service teachers. Gill died in 1953 and Jane McAllister Dart served as acting head until the following year when August Freundlich was appointed. Freundlich resigned after four years and was replaced by a member of the staff, King Calkins, the incumbent, who had won considerable acclaim for his paintings. During the Freundlich-Calkins era, emphasis was placed on current trends in art, and on public exhibits. In 1965 the department moved into a spacious new building which it shared with the Industrial Arts Department. The plan of the building facilitated contact with large numbers of students and with the general public.

Thus the simple objective of instruction in art to meet the needs of the teacher was broadened in time by a growing awareness of opportunities for practical application as well as a desire to exploit the cultural values inherent in the subject. The art curriculum developed a program leading to a four-year degree of Bachelor of Art Education, and included the areas of history of art, design, drawing, graphics, sculpture, painting, ceramics, and jewelry.

The story of art instruction at Normal not only traces the increasing attention to art being given in the public schools but provides a significant example to evolution from a simple pedagogical role to practical application, and to a broad cultural purpose.

The Commercial Course

That the curricular development of the Normal College rested primarily on the demands of the public schools is again demonstrated in the establishment of a commercial course. The announcement of the course (1913) was accompanied by the following explanation:

> The chief vocational course given by high schools is the commercial course. Most high schools in towns of two thousand and above offer such a course. The value of the commercial course depends upon the efficiency of the teacher. Successful teachers of commercial branches are scarce for the reason that too few schools are training them.[3]

It was then explained that arrangments had been made with the Cleary Business College of Ypsilanti, Ferris Institute of Big Rapids, the Detroit Business Institute, and the Detroit Business University to provide the commercial training (penmanship, spelling, English, business correspondence, business arithmetic, shorthand, typewriting, commercial law, bookkeeping, accounting and auditing, office practice, teaching method and observation and practice teaching), while the Normal would add work in psychology, pedagogy, geography, commercial geography, political economy, English and civics. The two-year course would lead to a special life certificate.

This program was continued until the fall of 1925 when the course was lengthened to three years, the Normal College carefully explaining each year that none of the commercial work was taught at the Normal.

In the same year, however, a special arrangement with Cleary College led to the organization of a four-year commercial curriculum leading to the Bachelor of Science degree and Life Certificate.

In the fall of 1929, the Normal College added a major in Business Administration leading to the bachelor's degree (with teaching certificate). This program consisted of courses in accounting and business. It was assigned to the History and Social Sciences department, and a visiting professor, Frederick Juckhoff, was employed. Later Juckhoff was made a full-time member of the staff. The courses were described as follows:

> The courses in accountancy covering two full years' work are designed to meet the needs of three distinct groups of persons, i.e. (1) those who desire a knowledge of accountancy for cultural purposes, (2) persons who need a knowledge of the subject as an aid in the management of a private or public business, (3) those who expect to teach accountancy in the junior colleges and other institutions in the State. The course as outlined is believed to offer the necessary training for those who desire to take the Michigan C.P.A. examination.[4]

Two things in this announcement are noteworthy: that the Normal College was taking a first step in the direction of training teachers for junior colleges; that a beginning was made in the direction of training for a non-teaching vocation.

With the coming of President Munson in 1933 the courses in business administration, along with their professor, were eliminated. But the four-year curriculum for teachers of commercial subjects was retained. Normal still refrained, however, from offering commercial courses; these were to be taken, as before, in the affiliated private business colleges.

The next step was the discontinuance of the policy of affiliation. This became effective July 1, 1938.[5]

From this time change and expansion became the rule. In January of 1939, the school paper announced the addition to the winter schedule of four courses in the commercial field: typewriting, elementary accounting, commercial teaching methods and commercial law. Cleary College would have the same status as any other college insofar as transfer of credits was concerned. And it was intimated that a department would be developed which would make it unnecessary for prospective commercial teachers to take work in any other institution.

In announcing this step, President Munson said that it was taken as the result of continued requests, and complaints that other state colleges offered complete programs. "Several students," the announcement read, "protested having to pay tuitions at two institutions for a course offered at one place in other schools."

A new department, to be known as the Commercial Department, was established in the fall of 1939, with John C. Springman, a Normal alumnus, as its head and Nora Beth Wharton as instructor. Springman retired at the close of the school year, 1946–47.

The name of the department was changed to *Business Education,* and Julius M. Robinson was brought from Western Illinois State Teachers' College to head it. The story from this time was one of change of direction. The non-teaching, vocational objective was reintroduced, and, step by step, emphasized until it became dominant.

The very next year (1948–1949) the name was again changed, this time to Business Education and Business Administration. The explanatory statement read:

> The business Department includes two major professional areas. They are: I. The Business Teacher Training Curriculum which is referred to under the heading of Business Education . . . II. The Business Administration Curriculum . . . a four-year training program in business subjects for various positions in business and industry.[6]

Both were four-year programs leading to the Bachelor of Science degree.

In 1949 a special degree was adopted for those on the non-teaching program called *Bachelor of Science in Business Administration*. In 1952, the name of the department was changed once again, this time to Business Studies. In 1955, a two-year program was offered, called Business Technicians. This led to a *Certificate of Achievement*. Credit earned on this terminal program could be applied on the four-year degree program.

In 1956, the hoary, pedagogical name "Normal" was dropped, and Michigan State Normal College became Eastern Michigan College. A new curriculum was added to Business Studies called Business Management, leading to the degree of *Bachelor of Science in Business Administration*.

The name of the College was changed again in 1959, this time to Eastern Michigan University. In pursuance of the connotations of the new name the administration organized the several departments of instruction into two colleges (the College of Arts and Sciences and the College of Education) and an area designated as "Departments Not Assigned." The Department of Business Studies fell in the last-named category, with the tacit understanding that it was to become a College of Business in due time. This occurred in 1964. Business Education (the preparation of commercial teachers) had become definitely of minor importance.

In the fall of 1961 Robinson resigned to become Director of the Summer Session and was succeeded by Earl A. Roth, a member of the department since 1954.

The department increased rapidly in size and enrollment. In the year 1961–1962 the number of students majoring was 472. By 1965–1966 it was nearly 900. To carry this load, staff increased from 11 members to 30. The training of commercial teachers was provided by just one of five instructional departments—the others being Accounting and Finance, General Business, Management, and Marketing. The College of Business had achieved major status in the University.

Penmanship

Handwriting, offered under the name of *Penmanship*, had been taught at Normal from the first. It was generally taught as part of the work in drawing. Attention was also given to printing on the blackboard. In 1885, P. Roger Cleary, recent founder of a private school in Ypsilanti that soon became known as Cleary Business College (1883),[7] was appointed instructor in Penmanship. Cleary continued to teach Penmanship at the Normal for 14 years. The objective of the course was "to train students to express thought in plain rapid handwriting without conscious physical effort."

Also offered was an advanced course for those desiring to supervise writing, to be taken by the student before he entered upon his work in practice teaching. The catalog for this year explicitly required that all candidates for graduation must have credit in Penmanship. Those preparing to teach in the grades below the high school must also take a course in methods of teaching handwriting. With the development of a commercial curriculum, Penmanship was added to that program. By 1934 the name of the course had been changed to *Handwriting*. Although in this year the requirement that to attend Normal one must promise to become a teacher was dropped, all students still had to take it before the third year in college. Failure to meet this requirement meant no graduation.

In 1948, with the retirement of President Munson, followed by the increased voice of the faculty in curricular matters, provision was made for students to "test out" of this requirement. Many a valiant attempt met with disaster. Students in the elementary programs, however, were required to take work in *Handwriting Methods*.

In the fall of 1953 the performance requirement was dropped. The methods course was continued until the fall of 1962 when it, too, was abandoned.

Thus ended the sage of the flourishing pen. Useful enough in its earlier life, it became in the course of its long and exacting rule the vermiform appendix of the teachers' college curriculum. In an era of mechanical precision and speed, when costly typewriters were being sold to school children as a sure device for improving their grades, it lingered on beyond its time, supported by an aura of validity and the tenacious hold of institutional habit. The cause of many a headache, its elimination was deemed a blessing—perhaps not an unmixed one, however, for faculties who yet must wrestle with the untutored hand.

Home Economics

Once the manual arts had been accepted as having a proper place in an educational program, it was not difficult to expand this area of instruction. At Normal, *Manual Training* (later known as *Industrial Arts*) broke the barrier. It was soon followed by a program for the home-makers, called *Domestic Science*. This program was begun in the Training School in the fall of 1903 (in the College a year later as a two-year course) with the following announcement:

> Recognizing the fact that domestic science and art are becoming an important factor in the educational system of our state, the Normal College will offer during the school year of 1904–05 a specializing course for the training of teachers in these lines of work. . . . The work will include much practical work in bacteriology, cookery, dietetics, serving, marketing, household economics and art—including drawing, designing, hand sewing, drafting, machine sewing, and hand work for the primary grades. The hand work will include weaving, basketry, and designing similar to that which is done in the last year of the specializing course in Manual Training.[8]

The choice of a teacher for this area was a wise one. Annette F. Chase, former student at the New England Conservatory of Music, was a graduate of Pratt Institute in Brooklyn. This school had been established in 1887 "to promote industrial education, to inculcate habits of industry and thrift, to foster all that makes for better living."

As originally organized in the Training School, instruction in "Cookery" was provided in the seventh, eighth, and ninth grades, and made elective to Normal women.

Miss Chase, aware of existing prejudice against manual arts in higher education, took pains to argue the importance of her subject. She promptly made use of the college paper to explain that domestic science involved more than cooking and sewing, that it possessed also an intellectual side. She pointed out that those taking her course would be required to read in history, nature study, chemistry, bacteriology, physiology, and hygiene.

"One of the primary objects of the work," she said, "is to bring the home and school life into closer relation, and to awaken enthusiasm for the common duties of life, and a respect for self activity and the workingman and his tools. Like manual training, domestic science trains the whole body."

In a lighter vein, she quoted from an Englishman of literary fame, Lord Lytton:

> We may live without poetry,
>   Music, and Art,
> We may live without conscience
>   and live without heart;
> We may live without friends,
>   We may live without books,
> But civilized man cannot
>   live without cooks.

The course became very popular.

In 1905 Grace Fuller succeeded Annette Chase, and remained with Normal until 1914, having been given the added position of Dean of Women in 1909. Her tenure was marked by the establishment of a three-year course (1907), leading to the Bachelor of Pedagogics degree. It was this program that prompted an appropriation by the legislature of $30,000 for an addition to the Training School building (the present Welch Hall), to house both *Manual Training and Domestic Science*. The course was at first optional, but from 1912 was required of all student entering the program. Courses in *Millinery, Sanitation,* and *Decoration* were offered.

Miss Fuller won the affection of the women students to an unusual degree. One alumna, writing some fifty years later, said of her, "She gave me what I needed most, confidence in myself. Indeed she had a dedicated interest in all of her students and was generosity itself in every way to them." Toward the close of her stay at Normal, the college annual commented: ". . . her home has come to be a social center of great attraction for the girls, who find in her a faithful friend and judicious adviser."

In 1911, the name of the department was changed from Domestic Science to Household Arts. Two three-year programs were offered: *Food and Cookery,* and *Clothing and Textiles.*

During the year 1914–15, the department, without a head, was under the general direction of Dimon H. Roberts, head of the Training School. From 1915 to 1921, Martha French headed the staff. Mrs. French was a graduate of the Krauss Kindergarten Seminary of New York City and of the Oread Institute of Domestic Science and Art. She had studied at Teachers College, Columbia University, and was an alumna of Normal. Her administration was marked by the addition of a third program called *Household Arts*, the placing of all three programs on a four-year basis leading to the Bachelor of Science degree (1916), and the addition of a practice house where students could live for a semester and apply their acquired skills.

In 1918, Mrs. French, while retaining her position as head of Normal's Department of Household Arts, was named by the State Industrial Board to supervise all domestic science schools receiving federal subsidy under the Smith-Hughes Act. Normal was designated under this act as one of two colleges to receive federal funds for training domestic science teachers, the other being the Michigan Agricultural College at East Lansing.

In the fall of 1918, the curriculum in the Household Arts Department was again modified, this time to show just one broad program, called *Household Arts*. Within this, provision was made for concentration. The first two years were devoted exclusively to Foods and Clothing; the last two continued this program but permitted sufficient lattitude for a choice as to area of concentration.

In the fall of 1919, the name of the department was once again changed. It became Home Economics. Cooperation with the Fine Arts Department was undertaken, that department providing courses in *Home Economics Design, Costume Design,* and *Home Decoration.*

A year later, the curriculum was expanded to include, among others, courses in *Child Care and Child Welfare, Home Economics for Special Students* (teachers in rural schools or in special rooms), and in *Cafeteria Management.*

Jessie E. Richardson headed the department during 1921–1922, S. Deborah Harmes in 1922–1923, Florence Lytle from 1923–1925, and Sara T. Murray from 1925–1928.

In the fall of 1928, Lucy Aiken (later to become Mrs. Charles Elliot) was named Head. Miss Aiken came with bachelor and master's degrees from Teachers College, Columbia, and had done graduate work at the University of Chicago. She had taught at the Friends' Central School in Philadelphia, and the State Teachers College at St. Cloud, Minnesota. In 1933, she resigned and was replaced by Estelle Bauch.

Miss Bauch had earned a diploma in Home Economics from Nebraska State Normal College and, like Miss Aiken, the bachelor and Master's degrees at Teachers College. Her experience had been in rural and high school teaching, and in managing a large department store cafeteria.

Miss Bauch retired in 1953 and was replaced by Susan M. Burson, a graduate of the University of Georgia, with a master's degree from Columbia. Her background was unusually extensive. She had recently returned from Germany where she had been on a consultative assignment with the Department of the Army and the Department of State. Her experience had included surveys of college programs in home economics, organizing and directing of regional conferences, the position of State Supervisor of Home Economics for North Carolina, agent of the United States Office of Education for Special Groups, and Pacific Regional Agent in Home Economics.

At the time of Miss Burson's arrival Normal was experiencing the stimulating influence of veterans returning from wars, and particularly the presence of student married couples and families. She made a particular effort to meet the needs of these young people, on the one hand by offering a new course designed for them, called *Homemaking for Young Moderns;* on the other, making a point of the fact that courses should stress the family theme. Course work was developed under titles of *Children and Adults in the Home; Family Health; Housing the Family; Furnishing the Home; Parent Education.*

The department cooperated with the Fine Arts and Industrial Arts departments in the joint program of Integrated Arts, designed as a unit in the General Education program of the College, a course which it entered into experimentally in 1953, and listed as a regular offering in 1956.

Miss Burson retired in 1962 and was succeeded by Mrs. Gordon Fielder. The latter was a product of the graduate school of the University of Illinois.

The broadening of the curriculum, with its emphasis on preparation for marriage and family life, begun under Miss Burson, was continued. In the year 1962-1963, a two-year program was offered which would give full credit on a degree program if the student decided to continue in the field. The appeal for students was broadened by offering elective courses to all students, provided that prerequisites were met. The next step was to remove the word "provided." An announcement was made that chemistry, which had deterred so many young women from entering the program, would no longer be required as a prerequisite for those minoring in Home Economics, or enrolling in electives.

At the same time (1966–1967), emphasis was placed on Home Economics as providing for a wide variety of professional opportunities, and a new curriculum, *Home Economics for Business,* was introduced. An extensive offering of courses at the graduate level had begun in 1964–1965.

Industrial Arts

Eastern Michigan University takes some satisfaction in being the first collegiate institution in Michigan to offer work in Industrial Arts. This occured in 1901.

The question of such training appears first to have been raised at Normal in 1888 by Principal Sill. In his annual report for that year he said:

> It is also worth while to notice that the subject of instruction in manual training in the schools is at present occupying the attention not only of educators, but of a multitude of thinking people outside the schools. If I am not mistaken in the signs of the times, there will soon be a demand for teachers able to supervise and intelligently direct this coming branch of school instruction. This demand, when it comes, will insist upon recognition in our training school.

Twelve years later, State Superintendent Jason Hammond, in his report to the legislature, made an extended plea. He pointed out that the question had been vigorously debated at the Saratoga meeting of the National Education Association in 1882 and a resolution passed which supported manual training.

Hammond noted that, in spite of opposition, some 95 cities in the United States had adopted manual training by 1896, and that Massachusetts by law now required it in every city of 20,000 inhabitants.

In that same year (1900) Albert Leonard, President of the Normal School System of Michigan, in his annual report to the State Board of Education made a similar plea:

> After all these years of study and investigation the truth is being established that the education of a child that goes on in a strictly bookish way

develops the child imperfectly, making him less useful than he would otherwise be . . . Education may be defined as well-ordered self-activity, and a good school is one which succeeds in directing and utilizing the activity of children . . .

He asked for $2,000 to introduce the subject into the Training School, noting that until additional room could be provided in the College it would not be possible to undertake the training of teachers in this field.

The outcome was the employment of Alice Boardman, a graduate of Mt. Holyoke College and the Larsson Normal Training School, as Supervisor of Manual Training in the fall of 1901, and the organization of a program of instruction for each grade in the Training School, from the first through the ninth. The statement of purpose read as follows:

The aim of Manual Training is to aid in the development of observation, attention, accuracy, neatness, perseverance, independence and self-reliance, of sense perception and of muscular activity. . . . Whenever it seems practical the manual training is correlated with other subjects, such as reading, nature work, etc.[9]

The very next year, however, a course was announced for prospective teachers. It consisted of the following activities: wood-work, handwork for lower grades (venetian bent iron work, cardboard construction, weaving, raffia work, and clay modeling). This was known as the *Specializing Course.* In 1903, another college course was added. Its purpose was to familiarize non-specializing students with handwork for the primary grades.

By 1908, three college courses were being offered: the *Specializing Course,* a course in *Arts and Crafts,* and a course in *Supplementary Handwork,* followed soon by a combined course in *Manual Training and Drawing.* The contribution from the Drawing Department included work in life sketching and the history of painting. This combined program was continued for nearly two decades.

In 1914, Manual Training became a Department. Two new courses were added: *Arts and Crafts* (metal work in copper and silver; etching; repoussé, enameling and work in silver jewelry); and *Pottery* (both hand built and cast with design application, glazing and firing).

In 1915, the name of the department was changed to Industrial Arts. Two new courses were added, one in *Mechanical Drawing,* and one called *Industrial Hand Work* (a vocational emphasis in such skills as book-binding, chair-caning, etc.) aimed to show the relation between forms of handwork taught in schools and vocational training.

In the next few years courses in *Printing* (described as the correlation of printing with general English subjects), and *Household Mechanics* (concerned with repair work around the home, soldering, re-finishing furniture, electric wiring, etc.) were introduced. The explanation for the latter was that such a course was being given in many schools in the State. Courses were also offered in *Cement Handicraft* and *Industrial Arts for Elementary Grades* (describing industrial processes and their historical development).

In 1927, two more courses were organized, Woodwork or Machine Work, for men (concerned with furniture making, house construction, advanced joinery or machine shop work) and *Machine Shop*.

In 1929, after 28 years of pioneering, Miss Boardman gave the reins over to George Willoughby, a graduate electrical engineer and at the time head of the Industrial Arts Department at Ball State Normal School in Indiana. With the advent of Willoughby, the department enlarged its scope. Many new courses were added, and the combined program of the Industrial Arts Department became concerned with industrial and farm processes and methods, and with the problem of organizing industrial arts shops in the schools.

The basic educational objectives of work in Industrial Arts were retained in such courses as *Introduction to Industrial Arts, The General Shop,* and *Content, Organization and Supervision.* The aim at all times was to give broad training and experience in many areas, with the emphasis on principles and standards of workmanship rather than preparation for specific jobs in industry. Courses were organized in *Furniture and Cabinet Construction, Elementary Practical Electricity, General Metalwork, Practical Mechanics* (farm mechanics), *Toy Making.* Particular emphasis was placed on industrial drawing with courses in *Architectural Drawing, Industrial Arts Design, Machine Drawing, Advanced Drafting.*

In the 1940's new courses in *Weaving and Needlecraft, Plastics,* and *Descriptive Geometry* (described as a drawing course in technical and engineering work) were added. In 1955, in deference to pressures favoring the current concept and movement of general education, the department cooperated with the Fine Arts and Home Economics departments to offer a course called Integrated Arts (a revival of sorts of the "concentration" philosophy of the early 1900's).

In 1956, any pretense of teacher training as the sole function of the department was abandoned. The name of the department was changed to Industrial Education and Applied Arts. Programs were offered leading not only to teacher certification but also to a Bachelor of Science degree without teaching certificate, terminal technical work in drawing and design occupations, and technical industrial and building occupations.

In 1961, Raymond A. LaBounty, a member of the staff since 1945, succeeded Willoughby. Under his direction the department continued to broaden its offerings.

In the fall of 1965, the old basement quarters in what had been the administration building (now known as Boone Hall) were abandoned and the department moved into the spacious, even palatial, quarters of the new Sill Hall where it continued its neighborly relation with the Fine Arts department.

The rapidly expanding scope of the curriculum in the post-World War II years was reflected in the name of the department, and in its major programs. The time-honored title, Industrial Arts, that had stood since 1915, was replaced 40 years later (1956–1957), by the name Industrial Education and Applied Arts. This, in turn, was shorted a decade later (1967–1968) to Industrial Education. Under this abreviated title, two major degree programs stood forth—one called *Industrial Technology,* and the other *Education* (the preparation of teachers). The latter would have startled and mystified the teacher of the *Manual Training* era, with its major areas of *graphics, power, electricity-electronics,* and *materials processing.* And in addition there was a plethora of two-year vocational programs, under such titles as *Industrial Technicians, Drafting, Electronics, Graphic Arts, Materials Processing,* and *Power Technology.*

Music

Instruction in music began in Normal's second year. In the spring of 1854, Albert Miller was secured to fill a position provided for in the original plan of instruction, listed as *Teacher of Vocal Music and Drawing.* The man chosen to fill this position was born in Sonderhausen, in the Principality of Schwartzberg, Germany, and educated at the University of Jena. Upon coming to Normal, however, he taught, not music and drawing but music and German, and gymnastics and fencing!

The inclusion of music in the curriculum reveals the alertness of Principal Welch and his associates. For it was only as recently as 1848 that instruction in music in the public school had begun to find favor in some eastern cities.

As of 1968, music instruction at Normal had been under the direction of eight men—Albert Miller, Ezra Meade Foote, Frederic H. Pease, Frederick Alexander, Hayden Morgan, Warren Joseph, and Howard Rarig. Of the 115 years of music taught at Normal, 70 belonged to just two men. Pease was in charge of music and, from the time it was organized in 1881, of the Conservatory of Music for 45 years; Alexander for 32.

Albert Miller described his function as follows:

> My directions from the State Board of Education were very meager; the only one I remember was to the effect that every student should be taught music and no one should be allowed to graduate who could not pass a satisfactory examination, even where it should be found that he had very inferior, or no singing qualifications at all.[10]

After four years Miller left, and the position was filled by Ezra Meade Foote who taught music and elocution. The coming of Foote changed the emphasis in music from the classical to the more popular. Pease, of later time, made this comment:

> He was one of that famous class of convention leaders who did so much to arouse an interest in music throughout our land. He possessed a fine, ringing voice, commanding presence. . . . The change from the classical and somewhat severe work which had been done, to this light and pleasing study of songs of the day, was highly appreciated by the students and citizens, and proved conclusively that the first had been of too high an order, and was too far above the heads of the people. The music sung was descriptive, sentimental, patriotic, and told sweet tales of love and home. All this could not last, but it served its purpose of leading to better things. . . .[11]

Foote organized the first Normal Choir, which became known for interspersing patriotic and descriptive songs with oratorios and choruses from the best known operas.[12] Foote left after five years, but returned to Ypsilanti later to take charge of music in the public school.

His successor was Pease, a young man of twenty-four. Pease was the son of Peter P. and Ruth Crocker Pease whose name is associated with that of the Reverend John J. Shepherd, a co-founder of Oberlin College. Frederic, at the age of 18, had left his studies at Oberlin and traveled for two years with Foote, who was holding musical conventions. It was Foote, apparently, who influenced Pease to come to Ypsilanti where he attended the Normal, taught piano, and gave some assistance to the professor.

The career of Pease at Normal continued until his death in 1909. At first the offerings of the department were described as *Vocal Music and Reading*. Instruction in piano would be given "at the option of the student." By 1868, the program was described as *Vocal and Instrumental*. Vocal music consisted of training for teaching music in the grammar and high school grades, experience in the Model School, and membership in the choir. Instrumental music consisted of private instruction in *Piano-Forte, Organ and Melodeon,* and *Harmony* (procurable at the option of the student). Ten years later an *Advanced Professional Course* was offered which included voice cultivation, methods of teaching music in graded and district schools, and lectures and essays on professional topics.

In 1880, a step was taken, through the initiative of Principal Mac Vicar, that was to enhance immeasurably the character and reputation of the department. The establishment of a Conservatory of Music was authorized by the State Board. The object was to provide advanced instruction both for students and others *without expense to the State.*

Advantages advertised at the time included opportunities for students to play at recitals and attend and participate in concerts. As for the concerts, much was made of the nearness of Ypsilanti to Ann Arbor. "A motor line connecting Ypsilanti with Ann Arbor, gives Conservatory students an opportunity to attend all the concerts and lectures at University Hall." So read a statement in the catalog.

The Conservatory was to support itself by the fees charged.

To prepare himself for this added responsibility, Pease was granted a year's leave of absence to travel abroad and acquaint himself with the best European practices. This he did in 1881, visiting Italy, Germany, Switzerland, and England. He visited schools, attended opera in Naples, Rome, Florence, Venice, and took some instruction under such then well-known names as San Giovanni and Madame Filippi in Milan, and Gustave Scharfe and Johnssen (piano and organ), and Pohl (composition and counterpoint), at Kings' Conservatory in Dresden.

From 1882 four-year courses were offered. For many years the departments of the Conservatory were listed as *Piano, Vocal, Violin, Harmony,* and *Pipe Organ.* The addition of a pipe organ, installed in Normal Hall (on the third floor of Old Main), took place in 1886. The organ, referred to as the "Grand Organ," was described as "A fine two manual Church Organ, with full complement of pedals, one of the largest and best in Michigan, built by Johnson and Son, Westfield, Massachusetts."

As anticipated, the existence of the Conservatory stimulated many activities that were of cultural advantage both to the Normal School and the community: public recitals by Conservatory students, "The Wednesday Four O'Clocks" (informal recitals given by students), a Normal Lecture and Entertainment Course, begun in 1895 and extending over many years (in which the Normal Choir provided at least one annual concert), private lessons offered to Ypsilanti citizens as well as students, the inclusion of Ypsilanti talent in chorus and orchestra.

Over the years, Pease broadened his background and vision by visits and study abroad, edited and composed extensively, and established an excellent reputation for the Conservatory. He presided over the Michigan Music Teachers' Association repeatedly; taught culture and singing over a period of nine years in the Detroit Conservatory of Music; was organist in churches in Detroit, Jackson, and Ypsilanti; was in charge of music at Bay View; conducted at the National Summer School in Chicago. In 1870 he organized the Ypsilanti Musical Union (years later absorbed in the Normal Choir.)

In securing a successor to Pease, Normal was again fortunate. Frederick Alexander, a Michigan native son (Fenton and Detroit), had graduated from the University of Michigan (1894). He had studied under Professor Albert A. Stanley, a man who, as director of the University Men's Glee Club in the early 1890's, first brought it to national acclaim and who was a major factor in the organization of the University School of Music in 1892.

Alexander came to the Normal College at the age of 38 and remained in charge of the department and the Conservatory until his retirement in 1941. He established his reputation in the area of choral work, becoming a national figure with his choirs. His purpose in developing choral work was to foster community singing. Expressed in his own words, it was "the best music nobly sung by forces near at hand."

Within a few years Alexander was taking his choir to Detroit to sing in the Little Theatre at the Society of Arts and Crafts. A comment in the Detroit paper by an internationally-known music critic, Cyril Arthur Player, described vividly the impression and atmosphere created by an Alexander choir:

> The choir of Women from Michigan State Normal School at Ypsilanti came with a fine reputation to uphold, vindicated tradition, and almost set a new model in concert programs. . . . There was a dim religious glow to the program, as well as a cathedral calm. As for the technical part of the performance, it needs hardly to be said that the choir lived well up to its reputation and a little beyond; precise in attack, clear in delivery and enunciation, well poised, careful in phrasing, with well developed dramatic taste and a sense of values, a buoyant sustained quality and exquisite refinement of expression, these may be placed to the credit of Frederick Alexander's choir.[13]

Before leaving the subject of the Alexander choirs (which in time became an organization of some 200 mixed voices) the philosophy on which they were based is worth noting. In view of their reputation for performance, it is a surprising emphasis. It is expressed in the following formal statement:

> Voices are tested (for admission to the Choir) for quality and range. Musicianship and taste are not expected: the purpose of the choir being to stimulate and develop these assets through the sympathetic interpretation of masterpieces in choral literature. . . . Our object: to know intimately great literature—not to sing in public. . . . The choir always sings from memory.

Then a note of sternness: "Tardiness at rehearsal constitutes an absence."[14]

In 1929 and 1930, Alexander conducted the Massed Chorus Festival in Washington, D. C. In 1932 he was honored by being invited to take charge of the music for the dedication of the Folger Shakespeare Library in Washington, under the sponsorship of the Elizabeth Sprague Coolidge Foundation. Alexander, John Challis[15] (with harpsichord and recorder), and the Alexander Madrigal Club (consisting of faculty, alumni, and students) presented a program of Shakespearean music. The next year he took the group to Amherst College.

In 1931, note was taken of a new emphasis in the public schools, to include orchestra and band instruments. Courses were accordingly organized.

Alexander retired in 1941. He had been fortunate in his formal training, and in being able to build on the accomplishments of an able predecessor. He was also fortunate in that the long-delayed construction of a new Conservatory building (Pease Auditorium) took place in the early years of his tenure (1915). Upon completion of the new quarters the State Board had passed a resolution prescribing that henceforth the Music Department should be know as the Normal College Conservatory of Music.

Upon his death, in 1955, Alexander's will was found to provide a sum of nearly $90,000 for the purchase and installation of a pipe organ in Pease Auditorium. The will also requested that Earl V. Moore, Director of the School of Music of the University of Michigan and successor to Professor Stanley, serve as chairman of a committee to select an organ and builder. The instrument, designed and voiced by Erich Goldschmidt, a member of Normal's music faculty, was built by the Aeolian-Skinner Company of Boston.

The old "Grand Organ" silent for many years, was sold to a Dr. Parker of neighboring Wayne, whose hobby was the maintenance and repair of church organs. So, if a Normalite drops in on a Sunday service anywhere in Southeastern Michigan, he should listen with particular reverence; that special charm or moving note hidden in the outpouring of celestial music may be "Old Grand" speaking to him from an earlier time.

The new organ was dedicated October 16, 1960. Professor Russell Gee of Western Reserve University, an alumnus, was designated by the will to play the dedication concert.

In conjunction with this major event, the nearby Health Residence building (now replaced by a new and much larger facility), which had been transformed and enlarged to provide practice rooms and offices, was dedicated as the Frederick M. Alexander Music Building.

Alexander's successor was Hayden Morgan who took charge in

the fall of 1941. Morgan came with an extensive background in public school music, having been director of music in Grand Rapids, Findlay, Ohio, and Newton, Massachusetts. He had been guest summer school instructor in music at the University of Southern California and Harvard University, and had taught at the New England Conservatory of Music and Boston University.

Unlike his predecessor but more like Pease, Morgan was a composer, primarily of church music. His special contributions were the broadening of the music curriculum requirement and the development of a curriculum leading to a degree in music. In 1947, the curriculum was modified to require, of all students preparing to become supervisors of music, training in both vocal and instrumental music. Hitherto the two programs had been to a large degree mutually exclusive, with the emphasis always on voice and enrollments therein correspondingly large. In 1950, the degree of *Bachelor of Music Education* was authorized. This involved a further increase in the requirement for applied (instrumental) music. In 1955, the statement of purpose of the department was broadened to include non-teaching vocational objectives. In 1961, the emphasis on performance was greatly increased in both the vocal and instrumental areas, requirements being made for rather extensive experience in a wide variety of activities and standards of performance being more clearly defined.

In 1955, the historic name "Conservatory of Music," with its rich association with names of performers and its tradition of combining theory and practice at the level of advanced training, was retired. Henceforth, reference was made simply to "the Music Department."

In addition to its three distinguished directors, Pease, Alexander, and Morgan, many names come to mind. Among others, in voice it was Annis Dexter Gray and Carl Lindegren; in piano, Russell Gee, Clara Brabb (Mrs. Atwood) McAndrew, James Breakey (later to have outstanding career as Circuit Judge for Washtenaw County) and Mrs. Marguerite Breakey;[16] in violin, Emily Mutter Adams; in woodwinds, Marius Fossenkemper; in Public School Music, Lillian Ashby; in theory, Dorothy James.[17]

Morgan was succeeded by Warren Joseph in 1963, who in turn was succeeded by Howard R. Rarig, a graduate of the University of Michigan, in 1965.

As one contemplates the history of this department, noteworthy

are the widespread recognition and appreciation accorded to its
work and staff through the years; its tradition of including the
Ypsilanti community in its activities; and its longstanding informal
and mutually appreciative relationship with the School of Music
of the University of Michigan. Its emphasis on the preparation of
music teachers precluded, until recent years, a corresponding
interest in the development of the performing artist. Today the
schools of the State of Michigan give notable evidence of interest
and accomplishment in music, both vocal and instrumental. The
influence of Normal's Conservatory of Music in bringing this about
is immeasurable.

CHAPTER EIGHT

PHYSICAL EDUCATION

Concern for the physical well-being of the students developed within a few years after the opening of the school. Agitation for a gymnasium began in 1859. In its report for that year the Board of Visitors recommended that a gymnasium be provided. After praising the institution highly, the Board said:

> But we beg leave to suggest one modification, or rather addition to what facilities are now afforded. We think . . . that some provision should be made by the State for a *Gymnasium*. If we mistake not, there is a decided want of appropriate physical exercise among the pupils, and we would call your attention particularly to the question whether the frequent cases of mortality among students soon after graduating, may not arise from a like cause, and whether, even if, in the case of this single School, the evil results are not so serious as this question contemplates, they are not sufficiently so to make a small outlay in furnishing a suitable place for physical exercise, a measure of practical wisdom and sound economy.

Principal Welch, in his report for the following year, discussed the matter at some length. Noting that the subject of physical education was receiving nation-wide attention, he said:

> It is difficult to overestimate the importance of this movement. Thousands of valuable lives have been sacrificed, and scarcely any one has passed uninjured through the terrible ordeal of close and crowded rooms, long sittings, excessive mental effort and deficient exercise. Most of the graduates of our High Schools and Colleges carry with them as mementos of their School days, disordered stomachs, curved spines, enfeebled bodies or some nervous weakness, to embitter their lives and to rob education itself of much of its value. Nor can study be prosecuted with due success while the health and vigor of the body are so little cared for. Hour after hour is daily wasted in our Schools, in listless and futile efforts at study,

when, through mere weariness of the body, the sympathizing mind has lost its power of steady application. A skillful gymnastic drill of a few minutes would awaken the energies, quicken the sluggish circulation, and lend a new life and interest to the whole mental action. We owe it to our children, to the cause of popular education, and the humane spirit of our Christian civilization to remedy this too long neglected defect in our educational institutions.

Welch added that "more than a hundred teachers go forth annually from Normal. If these were thoroughly trained in the art of physical education, they in turn would 'diffuse the art' to all of the teachers in this State." Asserting that if it had not been for the disastrous fire of October, 1859, which destroyed the Normal building, the Board could have provided a gymnasium building, Welch requested an appropriation of $1,000. There was no response.

Because of the failure of the State to provide for this need, self-help was resorted to. Welch painted a graphic picture:

Early in the last spring term an appeal was made to the young men of the school for aid in putting up suitable apparatus. In response, those who were accustomed to the use of carpenter's tools came cheerfully forward and we soon had a horizontal bar and ladders erected in the open air. The young men were then divided into three classes, which were placed, respectively, under Messrs. Sill (English Grammar and Analysis), Miller (Modern Language) and Welch (Principal), for daily gymnastic instruction. In the meantime, Mrs. Aldrich (Preceptress) took advantage of the short recesses which occur between recitations, to give the young ladies systematic manual exercises. These exercises were taken simultaneously, by the entire department, the pupils standing by their desks and imitating, in concert, the movements of the teacher.

And he added:

A marked improvement in recitations, in order and quiet, as well as in alertness of step and erectness of figure, were among the benefits which the students derived from these simple lessons.

But Normal was intent on having a physical education building, and in 1863 a building there was. The report of the State Board for that year reads:

. . . an additional building was erected, the upper story of which affords a spacious and convenient gymnasium, while the lower part gives a large and secure woodroom and two sets of privy closets. The cost of this building was $1,250.00, and the entire expense of its erection has been met without asking of the State one dollar of extra appropriation.[1]

It was this building that provided the fuel for the second fire on the Normal campus, August 1, 1873. But for ten years Normal enjoyed a gymnasium.

The following years saw intermittent attempts to carry on a program of physical exercise. It was done in the study halls and the larger classrooms. In the late 1880's a room in the basement of the south wing of Old Main was outfitted with some apparatus, and voluntary activity carried on. With the coming of Principal Sill (1886), however, a serious effort was made to secure a new gymnasium building.

In his report for 1892, Sill stated that Normal had no suitable facilities either for exercise or for instruction in physical training, and he pointed out that the demand for trained teachers in this area was growing more urgent. "We need," he said, "a special instructor in physical training and we also need more play and exercise grounds and a suitable gymnasium." He added:

> The meeting of these wants is urged upon purely pedagogical grounds. No education can be deemed complete whose course of training has neglected the body and concerned itself only with the mental and moral development of the pupil . . . But, in addition to its pedagogical aspects there is another and immediately practical view. Our pupils are largely the sons and daughters of farmers. They are accustomed to vigorous exercise and plenty of it. They are remarkably earnest, faithful and laborious students. The new conditions of sedentary life tell most unfortunately upon the health and strength of many.

The Board of Visitors of the following year (1893) gave it support:

> It would seem to your committee that the great need of the State Normal school of the great educational State of Michigan, is a physical training department . . . The arguments in favor of this department are so many and so obvious that your committee would be trespassing upon common intelligence to herein state them. Let our great Normal school, whose roots are watered by the life of the State, have a physical training department, that the teachers coming from its portals may go forth truly and healthfully educated.

The Legislature was not to be easily persuaded, however, and much credit is due that remarkable woman, Mrs. Lucy Osband, head of the Natural Science Department, for playing a decisive role. The story is graphically told by her daughter, Marna:

> . . . a mass meeting of the students was held in the chapel when the legislature spent the evening here after visiting the University. The principal (Mr. Sill) appointed Professor George and Professor Barbour to speak in behalf of the building. Mrs. Osband knew enough of legislators to know that speeches would have no effect and prepared a dozen exceptionally skilled girls directed by Miss Grace Hall to put on a sample of what the actual classwork was. Professor Sill, always upset by anything unusual, refused to allow them to show because it would cause so much confusion to get the visitors off the stage and into the front seats . . . Then, for one of the few times in her life, Mrs. Osband resorted to woman's weapon—she cried. So Professor Sill relented. The speeches, as she knew would happen, proved ineffective. Members of the legislature spoke in turn and told how they got exercise by sawing wood for their board, etc. (although coal had taken the place of wood). The affair fell flat until the dozen pretty girls, graded as to height, came on the stage. At their superb military marching, the legislature pricked up their ears and showed interest. The Indian Club drill had them stirred and the dumbbell drill made them enthusiastic. "If that is what you mean by physical education—well, that was something worth while.' Professor Sill and the state board president came to Mrs. Osband later and told her that her girls had almost surely won the building.[2]

Mrs. Osband proceeded to correspond with Dr. Sargeant at Harvard and Dr. Luther Gulick at Springfield, Massachusetts, regarding building plans. Dr. Gulick sent her the detailed plans for his physical education building at Springfield, just completed, and considered the finest in the country.

Normal's gymnasium was dedicated May 18, 1894, and her protege, Wilbur Bowen, made head of the new department. The Board of Visitors expressed its satisfaction:

> The gymnasium . . . is a magnificent testimonial of educational progress in our own beloved State and a necessary addition to the school essentials . . . the sons and daughters of Michigan may with pardonable pride gaze upon the institution so well equipped, so ably managed, and so well attended, and exclaim "Behold the beauty and the strength of our State!"

This building (with an addition in 1914) served the institution for 71 years. The Legislative appropriation was for $20,000; the site was donated by the citizens of Ypsilanti. Thus the Department of Physical Education came into being.

Credit should also go to Austin George, Director of the Training School, whose efforts were recognized by the assignment to give the dedication address. In a letter to Governor Rich thanking him for signing the appropriation bill, George made a revealing comment when he said, "we do not desire a 'gym' in the ordinary sense of the term, but in a broader, higher and pedagogical sense. If the pedagogical aspects of the case had not been paramount, we should not have asked for the appropriation—much as we value the mere gymnastic or athletic features, and their applications to the present needs of our students."[3]

Principal Boone, who had taken over the reins in the fall of 1893, noted another unique feature, namely, a policy of making baths and other privileges of the gymnasium free, "a novel one," he said, "among school gymnasiums." He stated a new policy, that a minimum amount of practice was to be required of all students at some time during their course.

Sixteen years later the Board of Visitors of 1910 complained that the existing gymnasium was entirely too small, that it afforded opportunity for less than two-thirds of the student body to receive its benefits. In 1912, President Charles McKenny, in his first annual report, requested $35,000 for an addition. The following year the Legislature accepted McKenny's proposal for a building program to extend over a period of seven or eight years, one of the first items of which was an addition to the gymnasium. This was completed on 1914.

The first head of the Physical Education Department was Wilbur P. Bowen. From 1886, when he graduated from Normal in the shorter Latin course, until 1891 Bowen had assisted Professor Bellows in mathematics. Influenced by Mrs. Osband, he became interested in the potentialities of physical education and accepted an offer from the University of Nebraska to become Director of Gymnasium. In 1894, he returned to Normal to head the new department. From 1901 to 1903, on leave, he studied in the Medical School at Ann Arbor, earned the degree of master of science and taught physiology at U-M. He returned to Normal in 1903 to continue as head of the department, and remained in this position until his death in 1928.

Bowen's interest in the field of physical education took a scientific turn. His first book, published in 1898, was titled *A Teachers Course in Physical Training.* From 1909 he wrote prolifically. *Mechanics of Bodily Exercise, Action of the Muscles,* and *The Theory and Practice of Organized Play* (with Elmer Mitchell), were three of his books. His outstanding work, however, first published in 1919, was a textbook in *Applied Anatomy and Kinesiology.* This book went through many editions and was used in colleges and universities from coast to coast. Long after his death it continued to be used. In 1934, a fifth edition, revised by his erstwhile colleagues, Ruth and Elton Rynearson, was published and went through several reprintings. In 1949, a sixth edition, revised by Henry A. Stone of the University of California at Berkeley, appeared, followed in 1953 by a seventh edition.

The offerings of the new department included two years of practice and one term of theory. In the words of the announcement, the program was designed "to improve the physical condition of students, and prepare them to carry on the various lines of Physical Education in the public schools." In addition, students desiring to become special teachers in this area could get advanced work in theory, practice, and teaching. One semester was devoted to the Swedish system (a graduated program of formal drills), one to German exercises (emphasis on individual exercises on apparatus). A course was devoted to *Method in Physical Training* ("the history and leading features of the principal systems of Physical Training, application of educational principles to the teaching of the subject, and school Hygiene"). Another course was given in *Applied Anatomy.*

In 1921, a four-year program for specializing students was first offered. It led to the bachelor of science degree. Activity courses for men and women were provided. Those for women included gymnastics, school games, dancing, swimming, and tennis; for men, track and field sports, basketball, cross country running, and football. The academic courses for both men and women came under two general headings: *Human Anatomy and Physiology,* and *Physical Education* (courses in theory of the several sports, methods of instruction, planning of programs of work in physical education). Included in the latter category was a course in the *History and Literature of Physical Education,* one dealing with the Boy Scout movement, and one in practice teaching.

The department was also responsible for competitive athletics. An official statement of long-standing was still being used in 1960. It read: The department of physical education conducts athletic sports for students along three lines: (1) intercollegiate, (2) intramural and (3) recreational. The scope was broad enough to include all able-bodied students. It appears to represent the natural evolution of the original concept of an annual Field Day which provided intercollegiate competition in a variety of track and field sports, sports which were based on individual competition. The first of these had been held in 1890 and the idea was carried over into the Michigan Intercollegiate Athletic Association, which Normal joined in 1892 (along with Albion, Olivet, Hillsdale, and Michigan Agricultural Colleges).[4]

During most of the Bowen regime, the women's program had been under the direction of a woman member of the staff. Mrs. Fannie Cheever Burton held this position from the first year of the department. In 1914, she organized the Physical Education Club (co-educational). In 1923, she resigned to become Assistant to the Dean of Women, remaining in this post until the last year of her life (1935). Mrs. Burton was a native of Ypsilanti and a graduate of Normal ('83, honorary M.Pd. '04).

The position of director of the women's division remained open until the appointment of Ruth L. Boughner in 1941.

Miss Boughner, a member of the department since 1920, had been active in camping and Red Cross work, and taught with marked success courses in *Applied Anatomy, Kinesiology,* and *Physiology of Nutrition.* In 1959, Miss Boughner was honored by the Michigan Association of Health, Physical Education, and Recreation. Upon her retirement in 1952, Augusta M. Harris was appointed.

Miss Harris was a Normal alumna and had been a member of the department since 1928. She was instrumental in expanding the curriculum to include courses in recreation (1950). She became an acknowledged authority in the area of social dancing, served as president of the Michigan Association of Health, Physical Education, Recreation and Athletics, and in 1961 was given the honor award by that body for outstanding service to the field of physical education.

For 20 years after Bowen's death (1928) the curriculum had remained static. Along side it, however, since 1927 a small area of academic-type course work had existed as the Department of Health Education. This comprised courses in personal health and in the promotion and teaching of health in the public schools. It was headed, and largely taught, by the Director of the Student Health Service

(Dr. Glenadine Snow, the college physician). In 1948, this department was assimilated into the Department of Physical Education
and Health. Two years later, upon the adoption of the program in
recreation, it became the Department of Physical Education, Health,
and Recreation.

But another area of responsibility had always been a part of the
work of the department, namely, competitive athletics. This was
recognized in the departmental name in 1959, at the cost of a truly
cumbersome title—Department of Physical Education, Health, Recreation, and Athletics.

In 1966, the title was shortened to its present form—Health,
Physical Education and Recreation. At the same time, a position
that had earlier existed for a time was revived, that of Athletic
Director and Professor of Health, Physical Education and Recreation. The responsibility, however, included intramural sports as well
as intercollegiate athletics.

In 1960, consequent on the designation of Normal as a university,
the department was placed within the newly-formed College of
Education, where it functions at the present time.

In 1945, President Munson secured approval by the State Board
for plans for a Woman's Gymnasium, to cost $350,000. Greatly
increased enrollments after the second World War finally pursuaded
the Legislature to act, and architects were named to draw plans for
the proposed "Health, Physical Education, Recreation and Athletic
Plant." A decade later (December, 1955) the first unit of this plan
was completed, a magnificent field house containing facilities for
indoor track and basketball, practice facilities for football, baseball,
golf, and a spectator seating capacity of more than 3,700. It was
named, fittingly, Bowen Field House.

In 1965, the remainder of the plan moved the department entirely
out of its aging quarters. The Warner Gymnasium, with modern
equipment and provisions for flexibility of use, included a vast
assembly room which could be readily partitioned into several activity rooms. A magnificent swimming pool, now called a natatorium,
was provided with ample spectator facilities. Classrooms helped to
relieve the current acute shortage.

Wilbur Bowen died in 1928. His standing in the world of physical
education was well stated by R. Tait McKenzie, Director of the
Department of Physical Education at the University of Pennsylvania, when he said:

Dr. Bowen possessed the advantage of a practical knowledge of his work, with a gift of stating it in lucid English and with unbounded enthusiasm and industry. His earliest work on Blood Pressure demonstrated the scientific trend of his mind and his classic work on Kinesiology . . . must always remain the authority on the subject.[5]

In 1931, Bowen's successor was chosen from the staff of the department. Joseph H. McCulloch had come to Normal in 1918 as coach of football, basketball, baseball, track and tennis. He was a graduate of the Springfield College of Physical Education, the University of Michigan and Columbia. During his tenure as head of Normal's Department of Physical Education, he had the satisfaction of seeing many of his graduates serve in important positions of leadership. In World War II, he was eagerly sought by the military services to head programs of physical fitness.

Upon McCulloch's retirement in 1956, another replacement from the staff was made. Lloyd W. Olds, a native of Ypsilanti and a Normal graduate ('16), had been with the department since 1921. His first major contribution was the organization of an intramural athletic program to include every student. Dynamic, enthusiastic, impetuous, Olds pursued a career filled with action, achievement, and an ever-widening field of interest. Thanks to Olds, track and field became so successful that it stamped Normal as a national power in small college intercollegiate competition, and in occasional individual national champions. Cross-country running was elevated to the status of a major sport. The public schools of Michigan felt his influence in the organizing of state meets. He was instrumental in organizing the first state basketball tournament. At the national level he proved to be much in demand as a track coach, assisting with the American Olympic teams of 1932 and 1936, coaching an American-Scandinavian team in its tour of Europe (1935), serving as chairman of the Pan-American Track and Field committee of the Pan-American Athletic Association (1937), manager of the Pan-American team that competed in Mexico (1957). During World War II he had served as a lieutenant commander, in charge of the Navy's physical fitness program, 11th Naval District. Shortly after becoming head of Normal's department, he was called by the State Department to serve as consultant and lecturer for American forces of occupation, first in Europe, then in the Far East.

At Normal, upon returning from World War II service, he withdrew from coaching to give his full attention to the revival and expansion of the intramural program—an exphasis that he had become converted to in his apprenticeship days under Wilbur Bowen.

Retiring in 1963, Olds was succeeded by another Bowen (unrelated, however, to the earlier head). Keith C. Bowen, a doctoral product of the University of Indiana, was brought to Eastern from Montana State College at Bozeman. In 1967 Bowen resigned.

A clear-cut division of functions was made with the establishment of a Department of Intercollegiate Athletics. This was headed by F. L. (Frosty) Ferzacca, who came to Eastern from Northern Michigan University. The Department of Health, Physical Education and Recreation was headed by Patric (cq) L. Cavanaugh, who held a similar post at the University of Detroit.

The distinguished record in physical training and athletics that this department achieved owes much to the wise and able leadership of its first head, Wilbur P. Bowen. His emphasis on health, on physical activity and competition for all as well as on intercollegiate competition, and his scientific approach to problems in his field have characterized the department through the years. His contributions to physical education in anatomy and kinesiology were outstanding. In athletic prowess, credit must go to Lloyd Olds for making Normal nationally known and respected as a track power. Recognition by the State Legislature of the important role that physical education at Normal played in the life of the State came, belatedly but amply, in appropriations of the 1960's for the splendid facilities now standing on the campus.

CHAPTER NINE

SPECIAL EDUCATION AND OCCUPATIONAL THERAPY

The area of special education is one of particular interest and pride at Eastern because of the pioneering work done here in the training of teachers for handicapped children, and the study of their problems. Prior to 1920 most of the work with these exceptional children was conducted in residential schools. The democratic ideal of equal opportunity for all, however, found a growing response among educators in the second decade of our century. To this was coupled a stimulus in the public schools toward the improvement of teaching by recognition of individual differences in the pupils. The Progressive Education movement (after World War I) in its emphasis on the study of the child (all kinds of children) was especially open-minded to possible transfer values for the teaching of normal children from experiments with atypical children.

The term "special education" connotes, to the educator in this field, a program which provides special facilities and treatment for special needs. It involves a special corps of teachers with special methodology, and special equipment such as buses with lifts instead of steps, buildings without stairs, hearing aids, embossed globes of the world, equipment for braille reading, audiometers, crutches, braces, wheelchairs.

The story of the training of teachers for handicapped children began in Michigan with the work of two men, Charles Scott Berry and Charles Morris Elliot. It culminated in the first teachers college program in the United States for the training of teachers in Special Education.[1]

Professor Berry came to the neighboring University of Michigan in 1908 from a position as Traveling Fellow for Harvard University.

101

His interest in exceptional children became evident at the time in the course work that he gave in *School Hygiene,* found expression a couple of years later in a seminar in *The Study of Individual Differences,* and the next year in *The Psychology and Education of Exceptional Children.*

In the summer of 1914, under the authority of the State Board of Education, Berry organized a small class for teachers of the mentally retarded at the Michigan Home and Training School for the Feeble-Minded at Lapeer. The next year, with the consent of the school, the State Board transferred the course to the Normal College at Ypsilanti, where the basic offerings were given for teacher preparation. Here, under the direction of Berry, the course was given in the summer sessions of 1915 and 1916.

Born in Perth, Ontario, Elliot's parents brought him to this country at a very early age. To prepare for college he attended Michigan's famous preparatory school, Ferris Institute, from which he emerged with an idealism and sincerity of purpose that was strikingly characteristic of Ferris graduates. His college degree was earned at the Normal, where he made his career. As a student and young instructor, he embodied the sentiment and enthusiasm that the Normal inspired in those days by composing the words for three of the college songs that have been preserved.[2] He was a charter member of the college scholastic honorary society, Stoics.

Elliot, teaching psychology at Normal, was an admirer of Berry and had taken some work under him. Elliot took over the course for the summer session of 1917 and in 1918 organized, as part of the Training School program, the first laboratory class for feeble-minded children, placing Miss Blanche Towne in charge.

From 1920 to 1924, Elliot was loaned to the Detroit Board of Education where, at the Detroit City Normal School, he directed this work for a school system that had long shown an interest in its handicapped children. The Normal College continued to give the necessary preliminary work, and also maintained a room for subnormal children.

In 1923, the State Legislature took an action that greatly stimulated the public school demand for trained teachers of special classes. The act provided financial aid for school districts wishing to organize classes for blind and deaf children. Whereupon, the State Board designed the Normal College as the place where such teachers should be trained, and in 1924 Elliot was transferred back to Ypsilanti, given the responsibility for developing appropriate curricula for all branches, and made head of a Department of Special Education.[3]

The department was established on the basis of Elliot's recommendation, in which he urged, among other things, that a survey be made of the schools of Ypsilanti and neighboring Ann Arbor to determine the number of deaf, blind, and crippled children, that classes for these children be established in Ypsilanti, and that no teacher be deemed qualified to teach such special classes in the State of Michigan who had not had at least a year of successful teaching experience with normal children, a state life certificate (based on a two-year course at this time) and a year of special training in one of the special education areas.

A department was established, but no funds were appropriated. However, a way was found to ameliorate this hardship. The classes were organized under the auspices of the Ypsilanti School District, making them eligible to share in State aid. These funds, added to the college budget, made it possible to employ the teachers needed.

The establishment of a Department of Special Education involved the development of new and highly specialized courses, for which there was no precedent. Such, for example, were *Pathology of the Cripped Child: The Mechanism of the Ear; The Science of Elements of Speech; Blindness—Its Causes and Prevention; Stammering and Cognate Defects; Defective Speech; Phonetics and Voice.* The materials for these courses were drawn from every available source.

In the fall of 1926, consequent upon a suggestion from Professor Jacob Reighard, chairman of the Department of Zoology at the University of Michigan, who suffered from deafness, a class in lip-reading was organized for adults, its purpose "to strenghten the social and communicative abilities of deafened adults, and thus aid their life adjustment." It was one of the first of its kind in America.[4] The following January Elliot secured a gift of $15,000 in support of the training of teachers for lip-reading from Walter O. Smith of Flint, Michigan.[5]

In 1930, having moved from cramped quarters in the west wing of old Pierce Hall to more adequate quarters in the Training School Building (Welch Hall), the "open window" or "health" class for children of low vitality, long a part of the elementary training school, was absorbed by the department.

In 1938, an event occurred that was to facilitate the work of the department for all future time. Elliot had, from the first, envisioned a separate building for special education, planned definitely for this purpose, with all the special facilities required. In 1937, he approached the Board of Trustees of the Horace H. Rackham and Mary A. Rackham Fund of Detroit for assistance. This Fund had been established for "benevolent, charitable, educational, scientific, religious and public purposes" such as would "promote the health, welfare, happiness, education, training and development of men, women and children, particularly the sick, aged, young, erring, poor, crippled, helpless, handicapped, unfortunate and underprivileged, regardless of race, color, religion or station . . ."

The Trustees lent a ready ear, and in December an announcement was made of the gift of $250,000 for a building for special education at the Michigan State Normal College. In an explanatory statement, they said:

> Professor Elliot's dream of twenty years was an adequate modern building in which to house his department. It was because of his successful efforts with crippled children that the Michigan State Board of Education, eighteen years before, had designated the Michigan State Normal College as the one teacher—training institution in the State to investigate the needs of and to train teachers for the education of handicapped children . . . Professor Elliot's enthusiasm impressed the Trustees of the Rackham Fund with the value of such a project . . .

The grant carried two stipulations: one, that the work of the school would correlate but not duplicate the work of The Institute for Human Adjustment of the University of Michigan (subsidized in 1936 by the Rackham Fund); two, that the State Board would provide continued and permanent support.

The building was planned with a dormitory wing to house 24 children, which would make it possible to serve more distant communities. Facilities were included for physical therapy. Equipment included special desks, books, mechanical aids of various sorts, and provision for avoiding glare and preserving vision of the partially-sighted. For the completion of the therapeutic pool (standing above floor level to enable an attendant to accompany the child from outside; warmed as needed) and the dormitory, an additional $30,000 was granted. The building, described as the best facility of its kind in the world, was opened for use in the fall of 1939, dedicated June 27, 1940.

At the ceremony of dedication Berry suggested two inscriptions for the building—for those who enter, "Enter to Understand Those Who are Different" and, as they leave, "Depart to Serve Mankind Better."

Michigan Normal was hailed as the first in the nation to construct a special building for teacher-training in the field of special education and Elliot was henceforth to carry the title of Director of the Horace H. Rackham School of Special Education.

Elliot noted that since the Michigan State Normal College was the first teacher-training institution to organize a Department of Special Education, the department had become widely known in this and other countries, and students were coming from practically every state in the Union and from Canada. Also, visitors were arriving from other countries.

Expansion of the work of the department was inevitable. In 1938, a graduate program was initiated in collaboration with the University of Michigan, leading to the master of arts degree.

In 1946, subsidized by the Bell Telephone Company and in cooperation with the University of Michigan, a research project in "visible speech" was undertaken. The telephone company provided an elaborate instrument called a "cathode ray translator" which visualized on a screen the modulations of speech sounds and thus enabled an analysis which could be used to correct faulty speech and to teach the totally deaf to speak. It also, when connected to a radio, enabled the deaf person to "listen."

Elliot died in 1941, at age 70. He could leave this world in the full knowledge that the movement which he had pioneered had "taken," and had spread with great rapidity over the nation. By 1929, 43 institutions in the United States (and 2 in Canada) reported offering courses for teachers of exceptional children. By 1931, the number was 71; by 1936, 118.

His efforts were directed to the formulation and creation of a curriculum, the planning and obtaining of a suitable home for his program, one that would satisfy its unique needs, and the promotion of organizations to further the cause to which he was dedicated. He was a founder of the Michigan Society for Crippled Children and of the International Council for the Education of Exceptional Children. In 1928, he served as president of this organization, presiding over its sixth annual meeting, held at Toronto.

Elliot was succeeded by his assistant, Francis Lord. Lord's

administration was particularly noteworthy for its summer programs which drew students from all over the United States and Canada and, in cooperation with the University of Michigan, provided as lecturers distinguished authorities in specialized fields.[6] One summer featured the first collegiate course in the nation for children who were both deaf and blind. In 1949, 1950, and 1951 a program was organized for home teachers of the blind by the American Foundation for the Blind, sponsored by the Perkins Institution of Massachusetts. Lay readers from the Ypsilanti community supplied with enthusiasm an urgent need.

In 1949, a course in the education and treatment of the cerebral palsied child was organized, in cooperation with the National Society for Crippled Children and the Michigan Society for Crippled Children. The following year the program was extended to include the nursery school, and a parent institute for the mothers (a feature that was repeated in 1951, 1952, and 1953). In 1952, a special course in *Parent Education* was offered. In 1953, a special institute was held for parents and friends of retarded children. In that year Lord resigned to become Coordinator of Special Education at the Los Angeles State College of Applied Arts and Science. He was succeeded by Vivian Harway as Acting Director (1953–1954), followed by Morvin A. Wirtz (1954–1958), then by Allen Myers. In 1967, Myers was made Dean of the College of Education, and Frank Wawrzaszek, a member of the staff since 1957, became acting head of the department. (He was named head of the department in 1969. —Editor)

With the passage of time, as must always be the case, changes occurred. The adult lip-reading program was discontinued with the resignation of its very capable instructor, Miss Ann Bunger. It was felt that such a program, subsidized for a limited time as it had been with the gift from Walter Smith, could not be justified in the college budget. It was a rehabilitation program for adults, not a program for the training of teachers of handicapped children. The visual speech analysis program proved not as promising as had been hoped. Children found too much difficulty in associating wavy lines on a screen with specific sounds. The dormitory was discontinued in 1965 and the area turned into office space for a growing faculty. Developments in ease of transportation made it possible for children at a distance to live at home and attend the school, and there was no question of a dearth of children. The therapeutic pool, once such an important and unique feature of the building, now was used for physical exercise and recreation only. Hydo-therapy had been replaced by more effective methods.

Perhaps most significant, however, was the change in the demands made on the school. Until after World War II, the number of college students enrolling in any one year in the teacher-training curriculum had hovered around 60. Now it had risen to nearly 700. An awakened public conscience, expressed in legislative acts encouraging and appropriating for special class work in the public schools, had created a vastly increased demand for special teachers. In consequence, the character and responsibilities of the faculty had changed. No longer were the teachers of the special rooms (the faculty of the Rackham School) required also to conduct the college training classes. They were now able to devote their full time to the work with the children. At the same time, a professional teaching staff for the students in training in the Department of Special Education was developed that equaled if it did not surpass in size the faculty of the School.

The developing program was but symbolic of a national phenomenon; fruition of a single pioneering venture that was initiated only half a century ago.

A training program for therapists for the rehabilitation of the disabled (mentally, emotionally, physically) was, with the encouragement of the Medical Superintendent of the Ypsilanti State Hospital, Dr. Inch, initiated at Normal in the very year that America was plunged into World War II.

Affiliation of such a program with a state-supported college or university was a pioneering venture. Records of the American Occupational Therapy Association show that Western State Teachers' College (now Western Michigan University), which in 1936 took over the program that had been developed by the Kalamazoo State Hospital since 1922, was the first in the nation to obtain the necessary approval of this Association's Council on Medical Education and Hospitals. This was given in 1938.

Normal's program, initiated in 1941, secured the necessary approvals in 1944. At the same time, programs at Ohio State University (initiated in 1942), the University of Illinois and San Jose State College (initiated in 1943) were approved. Today all schools of occupational therapy are affiliated with a college or university— some 32 in all.

At Normal, the program was placed with the Special Education Department which from 1944 became known as the Department of Special Education and Occupational Therapy. At first the curriculum included the requirements for a teaching certificate. Should the O. T. graduate not find ready employment, she would be eligible for a teaching position in the public schools. The tremendous demands arising from the great war, however, obviated all doubt on this score, and the certification requirement was soon dropped. Beatrice Wade, O.T.R., was placed in charge. After two years she was succeeded by Gladys Tmey, and in 1950 Frances E. Herrick succeeded Miss Tmey. The enrollment grew from well below 100 students to the present (1968) high of 142.

The program of training led to the bachelor of science degree and registration (by examination) with the national association. It required four years of formal courses and an additional nine months of clinical experience in a variety of types of hospitals. Since the therapeutic approach employed the light crafts, considerable attention was given to courses in *ceramics, design, art, woodwork, art metalwork, needlework, stenciling, basketry, weaving.* The problem of deciding which activity would best serve the particular disablement, the degree of activity, and the results obtainable required of the therapist considerable knowledge in the areas of anatomy, physiology, medicine, surgery, psychiatry and psychology. Affiliations for clinical training were established with a score of State institutions and agencies.

* * *

It is a fact worthy of note that some people have both the native capacity and the interest to devote their lives to assisting the handicapped or the disabled. In addition to good intelligence, this calls for qualities of human empathy, patience, and creative imagination. The challenge is to young people who are possessed of these qualities, who see the human condition and are fired by a desire to contribute to its amelioration. Eastern has had the inspiring experience of enrolling ever increasing numbers who are attracted by this challenge.

CHAPTER TEN

ADONIJAH STRONG WELCH

1851–1865

The State Board of Education (of which Isaac E. Crary was president at the time) was fortunate in its first appointment of a principal for the Normal School.

Adonijah Strong Welch was 31 years of age, small and frail in stature but possessed of abundant and restless energy. Born in East Hampton, Connecticut, he had come to Michigan at age eighteen with his parents who settled in Jonesville. He entered the sophomore class at the University of Michigan in 1843, was appointed the following year as the first principal of the Preparatory Department of the U-M, and graduated with the class of 1846.[1] He went at once to Detroit where he studied law in the office of Lothrop and Duffield and was admitted to the bar. Instead of practicing law, however, he returned to Jonesville and organized a Union School. This school was one of the first of its kind on Michigan. In 1848, he joined a group of men from Jonesville and set forth for the west—a '49er. Upon his early return, he became active up and down the State in pleading the need for a normal school.

The problems that faced this first administration were many: the assembling of a faculty, organization of a curriculum, adoption of policies that would shape the character of the young school for generations to come. Just two years after its opening, the function of providing instruction in agriculture and the mechanic arts was taken from the Normal and assigned to the new Michigan Agricultural College. Six years after its opening, Normal lost its building by fire (1859). In its eighth year, the Civil War burst upon the nation.

The eagerness with which the new principal approached his assignment was evident in his inaugural address. He said:

109

It may savor somewhat of enthusiasm, yet in my humble judgment, this day's work will form a prominent item in the history of western progress. This side of the Empire State it is the first experiment of a similar character made under the auspices of legislative enactment. Who will venture to predict the influence which its success will exert upon the educational interests of the entire Northwest?

His attitude was both scholarly and infused with concern for the effectiveness of the educational process. In his address before the Teachers' Institute, held at Normal just prior to its opening, he said:

No amount of text book knowledge, as such—no memory of straggling undigested facts or details—no skimming of the area of knowledge of whatever, can make the scholar or the independent thinker. It is rather by investigating the relations of *facts* and *things*—by a close scrutiny of the reasons on which opinions are founded—by a right analysis of every subject brought before his attention—that the student, at last, attains a genuine cultivation of the intellect.

With obvious horror, he described his own early school days:

I trammeled my memory with a multitude of words, of whose significance I knew little and cared less. I sang with perfect readiness, a host of numbered rules, whose principles were a profound secret, and of whose application, I had not the remotest suspicion. And it was not until years afterward that I knew a preposition from a pronoun.[2]

That he was serious in his pedagogical concern is evident by the fact that during his incumbency he produced two books: "An Analysis of the English Sentence" and "Treatise on Object Lessons."[3]

Two who were students at Normal in the Welch era, and later became outstanding members of the Normal faculty, have left their impressions for posterity to read: C. F. R. Bellows, mathematician and for a year Acting Principal, has given us a rather grim view of the administrative atmosphere.

My recollections of the work of the school concern rather the strict discipline that was maintained by the Principal, than the excellence of teaching. Professor Welch's idea of a school was one in which first of all existed a condition of perfect system and order. He was the most rigid disciplinarian in the school room that I ever knew. His compressed and quivering lip was to the luckless transgressor an omen of impending calamity not to

be mistaken or misunderstood. It was a fearful foreboding of vigorous
corrective treatment.[4]

This picture is supported by the story that went the rounds that,
when Normal's janitor rang the bell calling classes to order for the
day much longer that the prescribed five minutes (out of sympathy
for certain laggard students), Welch suddenly appeared and hurled a
book at his head, thus terminating abruptly that gentleman's service
to the school.

Austin George, later to become head of the Training School,
commented on Welch as a teacher, as well as administrator:

> As a teacher he was . . . deliberate yet intense in thought, measured and
> careful in speech, he held the wrapt and undivided attention of all who
> were before him . . . His power to develop and help young men and
> women was remarkable . . . and he was so just and wise that his deci-
> sions and acts received the approval of those affected by them . . . He was
> a man of dauntless courage and immovable firmness. He had keen insight
> as to men and affairs . . . He had a great executive ability, and was a
> disciplinarian of phenomenal power.[5]

As mentioned earlier, twice during his incumbency Welch suffered
failing health. The first time, in 1859, he was restored by a leave of
absence while he toured Europe. The second, in 1865, was given as
the reason for his decision to resign. The State Board, in accepting
his resignation with regret, said:

> Your intercourse with the Board of Education, has ever been of the pleas-
> antest character. Although questions of the gravest moment relative to the
> interests of the Normal School have often arisen, and questions at once
> revealing the fact that there were decided differences of opinion, yet their
> discussion has been conducted with great candor, and the conclusions
> reached have been most satisfactory to all.

Welch thereupon became a carpet-bagger in Florida, staying for a
short time in Pensacola, then moving to Jacksonville where he
engaged, with a brother-in-law, in the lumbering and orange-grow-
ing business. He also taught in a Negro school.

He assumed an active roll in the Republican party and was made
State chairman. In June, 1868, the Florida legislature elected him to
the short term in the United State Senate. Just prior to this action he

had received an offer of the presidency of the newly-authorized Iowa State Agricultural College (now Iowa State University) at Ames. Since the short term would end the following March, Welch was able to come to an understanding with the governing board.

It should be noted here that the governing board, in electing Adonijah Welch president of the college, secured also an important bonus in Mrs. Welch, a woman of strong personality and wide culture, who from the first gave instruction in home economics, and in 1875 was appointed teacher of composition and domestic economy.[6]

As might well have been expected, however, of a man of strong conviction and dauntless courage, Welch was in the course of time caught up in a heated controversy among alumni, faculty, and farmers' organizations over the function of the college. Through a decade, the argument grew more and more heated and finally, in 1883, by the narrow margin of 3 to 2, the Board—in the face of protest by the entire faculty—removed him. He remained on the faculty, however, until his death in 1889.

The historian of Iowa State University, Professor Earl D. Ross, describes Welch as the strong executive type, "every inch a president within and without the institution . . . engaged in a great work, and he knew it and did not propose to have it interrupted by dissentiate or distracting counsels and projects."

In Ypsilanti, it was noted that "Professor Welch had the distinguished privilege of starting three educational institutions which were new in their states, namely, the Union School at Jonesville, the Michigan State Normal School, and the Iowa Agricultural College; and the great success of each is a triple monument to his transcendent ability."[7]

CHAPTER ELEVEN

MAYHEW, BELLOWS, ESTABROOK

1865–1880

David Porter Mayhew, 1865–1870

Upon the resignation of Principal Welch, administrative duties were distributed among the faculty, with the professor of natural sciences, D. P. Mayhew, acting head of the school. The following June (at age 48) he was made principal and served in this capacity until his retirement in 1871.

David Porter Mayhew came to Normal in 1856 to replace Professor Fiske who, upon the opening of the new Michigan Agricultural College at East Lansing, had accepted a position there as professor of chemistry. Mayhew, born in New York, was a graduate of Union College, having been prepared for college by the well-known divine, David Porter.[1] He had been head of the Lowville Academy at Lowville, New York, taught for a year in the Cleveland public schools, and served for a year as superintendent of the Columbus, Ohio, schools, resigning to take the position at Normal in January 1856.[2]

The *Detroit Daily Post* expressed the general approval:

> This is, in all respects, a fit appointment. Prof. Mayhew has been connected with the Normal School for a number of years, is an enthusiast in his work, and in every respect capable. The State is to be congratulated on having this important institution under such excellent management.

Principal Mayhew's chief contribution lay in his strong appeal as a Christian gentleman, a gentle, earnest personality, and his skill as a teacher. To the students his was a "cheerful and hopeful disposition. He was always the same. He made no one his enemy; everyone his friend. New students, appearing lonely or discouraged, became the objects of his thoughtful care. He loved children, and understood and sympathized with child nature. The children of the Practice School always greeted his entrance with demonstrations of pleasure . . ."[3]

Upon retiring in 1871, he moved to Detroit. He was appointed by Governor Bagley in 1874 for the few months remaining in a term on the State Board of Education. In Detroit, he interested himself in the problem of rehabilitating criminals, giving a series of lectures in psychology to the inmates of the Detroit Reformatory, also for a reformatory in Elmira, New York.

Upon his death in 1887, he was eulogized for his personal character and his superior ability as a teacher. The student paper spoke of him as a teacher who loved his work and was strongly attached to his students. According to his dying request, his pallbearers were selected from them. J. M. B. Sill, on the staff at the time and later to become principal, spoke of Mayhew as "a Christian gentleman, full of the child-like spirit."

Charles Fitz Roy Bellows, 1870–1871

Upon the retirement of Mayhew the State Board bought time for the decision on a successor by appointing C. F. R. Bellows, a member of the faculty, as acting principal.

Bellows, who came to Normal first as a student, witnessed the inauguration of Principal Welch, and graduated with the second class ('55). Born in New Hampshire, he came to Michigan at a very early age, his parents settling in Kalamazoo county. He spent several years in public school work, organizing the graded schools at Constantine, Michigan, teaching in Mashawanka, Indiana, and superintending the schools of Decatur, Michigan. He became the first County Superintendent of Van Buren County. Entering the Engineering School of the University of Michigan, he graduated in Civil Engineering in 1865. In 1867, he came to Normal to teach mathematics, and remained 24 years.

In the course of his years at Normal he published a dozen textbooks on mathematics, including a manual on surveying. He also published a journal called *The School,* whose life extended from 1872 to at least 1876.

A single year as acting principal would hardly be expected to produce developments of lasting importance. It was during this year, however, that the position of Director of the School of Observation and Practice was created, and Daniel Putnam appointed. This year also saw a lively discussion of the criticism that Normal was failing to give its students adequate professional training and experience. The discussion culminated, in the following year (under Principal Estabrook), in an arrangement with the Ypsilanti School Board whereby grades below high school were made available to Normal students for observation and practice.

Interest in Bellows' career at Normal centers about his emphasis on professional training. Dissatisfaction of the faculty (and a sore point with critics of Normal) over the time and energy devoted to instruction in academic areas, to the exclusion of professional training, culminated in the experiment of 1878 whereby an effort was made to exclude all academic work from the Normal and make it a strictly professional school. The experiment was abandoned within two years, but Bellows continued to fight for a strong professional emphasis. While acting principal, he had made a formal charge. He asserted:

> The people of Michigan, in their collective capacity, imagine that their Normal School is an institution for the specific purpose of teaching young men and women *the art of teaching.* If they knew that its pupils were merely or chiefly taught the things which can be just as well learned in any public high school in the state, they might not feel willing to spend $10,000 a year upon something that has no real existence.[4]

In the years following, Bellows appears to have become fanatical in his devotion to the cause, and after the rejection of the experiment in 1880 he insisted on conducting his classes in mathematics as courses in methods rather than subject matter. He described his method of teaching as follows:

> The work was carried on by lecture, the students taking notes. The manner of it was very much after the usual form of institute work. Day by day

review was had of the work of the previous day and, from time to time, of
larger parts of the ground gone over. No particular textbook was used, but
reference was had to any arithmetic the student might have.

Bellows helped to form a faculty club called the Pedagogical Society, "with a view," he said, "to promoting professional enthusiasm
in the faculty as a whole, and thereby conserving the professional
enthusiasm in the faculty as a whole, and thereby conserving the
professional welfare of the school at large." This organization was
particularly active in the years 1890–1895. Serious discussions and
carefully prepared papers, many published, marked its existence.[5]

With the arrival of Principal Sill in 1866, Bellows experienced
definite administrative opposition to his emphasis on professional
training in academic courses. In 1890, the State Board became sufficiently concerned to send a committee of two of its members (Samuel
S. Babcock and James M. Ballou) to Ypsilanti to discuss the matter
with him. Subsequently, in response to his own request for criticism,
Bellows received the following statement signed by Ballou:

> In regard to teachers' academic reviews, the committee on courses of study
> understand it to mean the assignment of lessons to the class and a recita-
> tion by the class of the lessons assigned. I call the work you were doing
> purely professional work. No lessons assigned, no recitations. All the
> work done by the teacher with now and then a drawing out question of
> the class . . . We desire to have the academic work the sharpest kind of a
> review of what is in arithmetic. Not original methods, devices or solutions.

The Board requested Bellows to adopt a textbook or resign. He
did neither. In 1891, he was dismissed.

The exit of Bellows from Normal led to developments that were
certainly unanticipated by either Bellows or the Board. By sheer
coincidence citizens of Mount Pleasant, Michigan, were at this time
organizing an "Improvement" association. They learned that Bellows had gone to Marquette in Michigan's Upper Peninsula in the
summer of 1891 hoping to organize a movement for a normal school
there. The citizens, now organized as the Mount Pleasant Improvement Company, decided that a normal school would be an excellent
project for Mount Pleasant. They approached Bellows and, in 1892,
he came to Mount Pleasant as Principal and Surveyor for the
Company. It was Bellows who, in the summer of that year, surveyed
the land for the original campus and, in the fall, presided at the

opening of the school. He brought in as his vice-principal a young graduate of Normal, Stratton D. Brooks, who would eventually achieve national recognition as, in succession, Superintendent of Schools in Cleveland and in Boston; President of the University of Oklahoma, and President of the University of Missouri.

Three years later the State was persuaded to take over this school.[6] Bellows stayed on, becoming thereby the first principal of the Central State Normal School (now Central Michigan University). At this point the State Board found itself in the position of having to support as principal of one of its two normal schools a man whom they had fired as professor. Furthermore, he remained resolutely loyal to his concept of what a normal school should be.

Bellows resigned at the end of the year. He apparently engaged in a number of educational activities during the next few years. In 1902, under President Jones, he returned to Normal (now a college) as a teacher of mathematics. A year later he was paralyzed by a stroke; in 1907 he died.

The story of Professor-Principal Bellows epitomized the battle that was waged with so much feeling for so many years over the question of whether Normal should become an exclusively professional institution. Time alone could bring the decisive answer. As we look back, it becomes clear that the cause that Bellows championed must fail—that even while he fought, forces were gathering that must prevail. With the rapid development of the high school the academic needs of the high school teacher had to be met. He needed to be well grounded in the subject matter that he would teach, and at the high school level this meant knowledge of one's subject beyond that which the pupils would acquire. If Bellows had seen the developing situation in its broader aspect he might well have avoided the trap which caused him so much unhappiness. It was this pressure, and Normal's response to it, that led to Normal's status as a four-year college, and paved the way for the outstanding work of her liberal arts faculty in the years that followed.

Joseph Estabrook, 1871–1880

The agitation for making Normal into an exclusively professional training institution came to a head under the principalship of Joseph Estabrook.[7]

Involved in the argument was the generally-recognized fact that the demand for trained teachers far outran Normal's capacity to meet it. To relieve the student of all academic work and use the whole time for professional training would enable him to complete the course in a considerably shorter time, and thus serve to increase Normal's output. Another means of increasing teacher output would be to establish more normal schools in the State. Thus the Estabrook decade was confronted with two major questions—one relating to the true function of the school, the other to its monoply in teacher training.

Joseph Estabrook became principal of Normal at the age of 51. A descendant and namesake of a very early settler from Middlessex County, England, and well-known preacher in Concord, Massachusetts, he was born in Bath, New Hampshire. He came with his parents to Clinton, Michigan, when he was 18 and prepared for college at the Tecumseh branch of the University of Michigan. Oberlin College was his choice, where he earned the degree of Bachelor of Arts in Science. This same institution conferred upon him the honorary Doctor of Divinity degree toward the close of his life.

Prior to coming to Normal he had held several administrative positions: principal of the Union School in Ypsilanti (1852), superintendent of the Ypsilanti Public Schools (1853–1866), and superintendent of schools at East Saginaw (1866–1871) where he organized the first public schools. The year prior to his selection as Normal's principal he had been elected to the Board of Regents of the University of Michigan, which office he retained until 1878. In 1880, he resigned from Normal and accepted an offer as principal of the Normal Department at Olivet College. In 1886, he was elected State Superintendent of Public Instruction, a post that he occupied for the next four years. Returning to Olivet in 1890, he devoted the brief four years left him to the College and the Congregational Church, serving as a delegate to the latter's National Council in 1892.

We are fortunate in the possession an an intimate description of Normal during the early years of Estabrook's principalship, written by an Englishman, Bernard Bigsby, who spent some time on the campus, visited classes, and made detailed notes of his impressions.[8] Speaking of Ypsilanti, he said:

> Peeping out among the wooded slopes of the picturesque banks of the Huron—more than half hid in the delicious groves of fruit trees, whose

white blossoms contrast pleasantly with the deep green of the spring-born foliage, nestles the little rustic town—I beg pardon, city—of Ypsilanti.

After highly complimentary remarks concerning classroom instruction in the several areas of learning, he touched upon what he termed Normal's Achilles heel, which was a distortion in the spelling of words that was "shocking." Bigsby continued:

> I called the Principal's attention to this, and he very candidly confessed the weakness, but attributed it to the lack of soundness in the teaching of the elementary schools. He also declared himself determined to stop the evil . . .

But he closed his article on a highly sympathic note:

> . . . wherever in after years I may be tossing about the world, the sunny recollections of those bright, earnest faces, the freshness of that little Western school-world, the openhanded American hospitality of the people, and the geniality of the professors, will write in 'letters of white' on the tables of my memory the unforgotten name of Ypsilanti.

The era of Principal Estabrook may be summarized by saying that, in the face of urgent need for more trained teachers as well as for improved quality of training, proposals for meeting the former were, on understandable grounds, resisted; for the latter, encouraged. That the quality of professional training was improved should not be overlooked in evaluating the period.

The other positive contribution of Joseph Estabrook lay in a character and personality that made a strong appeal to the public of his time. His colleague, Daniel Putnam, spoke of him thus:

> The most potent element of his power in the school was his own personality . . . First of all he was blessed with abounding physical vitality . . . Next, with a well-developed intellect, he was blessed with unusual depth and strength of emotional nature . . . Beyond these qualities he had an abiding faith in goodness and in God; and a profound spiritual apprehension and experience which enabled him to lay fast hold upon the unseen and eternal, and to make them real in his daily life . . . No teacher ever connected with the school was more loved, was remembered with kindlier feelings, or greeted wherever he went, with warmer or more sincere words of personal regard.

Joseph Estabrook died in September of 1894, in Olivet where the last fourteen years of his life were spent. Teacher, preacher (it was said that few pulpits in southern Michigan had not heard his voice), Superintendent of Public Instruction, and Regent of the University of Michigan, his influence in his own state had been widely felt. In a memorial service in Ypsilanti, held in the Methodist church, "every seat and every standing-space was occupied, and many who came later could not get inside the doors."

CHAPTER TWELVE

MAC VICAR, PUTNAM, WILLITS

1880–1885

Malcolm Mac Vicar, 1880–1881

When Principal Estabrook resigned in May of 1880, the State Board felt that special conditions made the selection of a successor one of exceptional importance.

"The school was to a certain extent in a transition state," they said, "and it needed most of all one who could bring to its administration large experience, great executive ability, high scholarship, and honest sympathy with the progressive spirit of the institution."[1]

They chose Malcolm Mac Vicar, principal of the Normal School at Potsdam, New York,[2] who took over the reins on November 12.

Malcolm Mac Vicar was unique among the heads of Normal; he was the only one to be foreign-born. He came with his family at the age of six from Argylshire, Scotland, to a farm near Chatham, Ontario, Canada. He entered Knox College, in Toronto, to study for the Presbyterian ministery but within a short time was ordained in the Baptist ministry. He transferred to the University of Rochester, New York, where he earned the baccalaureate and master's degrees.

At the time that Normal offered him its headship he had gained considerable administrative experience. As principal of the Brockport Collegiate Institute (1863–1867) in Brockport, New York, he became the first principal of the Brockport State Normal School when the Collegiate Institute was transformed (1867). Earlier, he had attracted the attention of the Regents of the University of the State of New York and at their invitation had read a paper at their convocation of 1865 which proved to be a first step towards the adoption of "Regents' Examinations" in the academies. He proposed to the New York Legislature (with the support of the State Superintendent of Public Instruction) a bill for the establishment of a Normal and Training School at Brockport. That bill was modified in passage to provide four normal schools instead of one, and these, in substantial accord with a plan drafted by Mac Vicar, were located at Brockport (1867), Cortland (1868), Potsdam (1869), and Geneseo (1871).

While serving as principal at Brockport Normal, Mac Vicar's health posed a problem and he was granted a year's leave of absence. Traveling in the West, he visited Leavenworth, Kansas, where he was urged to propose a reorganization of the Leavenworth schools. Attracted by the problem, he undertook the task. This led to his appointment as superintendent of the Leavenworth schools, and his resignation from Brockport.

After a single year, however, he resigned and returned to New York where he was received with enthusiasm. The Regents of the University of the State of New York conferred on him an honorary PhD degree (1869), and a year later his alma mater, Rochester University, conferred an LLD degree. In 1869, he accepted the principalship of the newly-organized Potsdam Normal School.

When, therefore, in 1880 the State Board of Education of Michigan offered their school to him, they were choosing a man of eminence in the field of public education and of proven interest in teacher training. His acceptance was based on the appealing fact that Normal was the only school of its kind in the State, and that there appeared to be no conflict of interest in its management (contrary to New York State). The fact that he remained at Normal only one year must have been a keen disappointment to the State Board. His biographer states that in one year he was "thoroughly worn out with hard work."

When Mac Vicar (age 51) arrived at Normal, he found in operation the experimental curriculum that undertook to make of Normal an exclusively professional school. Academic subjects were placed in a definitely subordinate position, pursued only as reviews of subject matter that the budding teacher must teach, taught only by upperclass students. Considerable unfavorable reaction had developed to this program, and the school had experienced a severe setback in student enrollment.

Mac Vicar's major task and his most important achievement, in the short year that he gave to Normal, was the restoration of balance in the curriculum, and the abandonment of the experiment. By shifting the emphasis from quantity production of teachers to quality of teachers produced, he persuaded the faculty to make a study of the needs of teachers on the job. And from this came a new approach to curriculum-making. The result was the abandonment of the attempt to restrict Normal's curriculum to professional courses in *Education* and a strong emphasis on academic preparation.

Insistance that *all* programs should include required courses in English was Normal's first step in the direction of what much later became known in higher education as "General Education." And the "special prominence" to be given to a particular area was the initiation of what later developed into required areas of concentration, known as "majors" and "minors." All of this led to the emphasis on academic courses in the preparation of teachers that brought high distinction to Normal.

Next in importance was Mac Vicar's emphasis on the fundamental importance of practice teaching. Observing that at Normal the Practice School had occupied a very subordinate place, he asserted that this was just the reverse of what should be. He said:

> In making provision for the education of teachers it must not be forgotten that teaching, organizing, or managing a school is essentially an art, and that the power to do work well must be acquired, like all other arts, by doing the work rather than by 'talking' about it.[3]

In this connection, he made a significant recommendation as to the role of the critic teacher. Criticism of the student in practice teaching, he said, should be performed by competent and experienced teachers, and no part of their time should be used as regular teachers of classes. The critic teachers should be required not only to visit and observe the work done by the practice teachers, but also to meet them personally at regular intervals to point out their defects and to see that these defects are corrected. (In our present era, when the traditional on-campus laboratory school is being eliminated and the practice teaching is being done in the public schools, such a procedure, faithfully followed, might have special pertinence.)

In the last months of his administration, Mac Vicar took one other innovating step, to the particular satisfaction of the students. This concerned required study hours, a practice that had been followed from the time Normal first opened its doors. Beginning with the fall semester of 1881, study hours were abolished.

"These," said the student periodical, *The Normal News*, "have of necessity been a source of annoyance to those students who were men and women and who had regulated their own movements for years."

The subsequent career of Malcolm Mac Vicar was characterized by a return to the Baptist church. From Ypsilanti he went back to Toronto where he occupied the chair of *Christian Apologetics and Biblical Interpretation in English* in McMaster Hall (the Toronto Baptist College). He was deeply concerned over the growing impact of science on the Christian religion. When Senator McMaster founded and endowed McMaster University of Hamilton, Ontario, in 1887, he made his close friend and adviser, Mac Vicar, chancellor, although during his incumbency only the theological department existed. In 1890, he left McMaster to become Superintendent of Education of the American Baptist Home Mission Society for the Colored People of the South, for the Indians, Chinese, and Mexicans. In this position he presided over a theological seminary, seven colleges, and twenty-four academies. His last four years (he died in 1904) were spent as president of Richmond Union University, Richmond, Virginia.

A restless, energetic, creative man, Mac Vicar had managed in the course of his busy and varied life to produce a number of texts and handbooks on arithmetic, and to write a manual on *Principles of Education*. His educational philosophy held that mental discipline alone was not an adequate preparation for life, but must rest on the building of a strong, reliable character.

In the training of teachers, he stressed the belief that no amount of book study can replace actual experience with children. The student teacher must, under the guidance of experienced teachers, "study the actual infant, child, youth and man under normal conditions and amid the various changes through which each passes in the process of development." He was known, too, as a very resourceful teacher in his own right, especially as an ingenious inventor of teaching aids for arithmetic, geography, and astronomy. The outstanding example of this was his globe of the earth, together with a handbook of instructions for its use, which found wide acceptance (Mac Vicar's Tellurian Globe).[4]

Daniel Putnam
1880; 1881–1883; 1885–1886

Principal Estabrook's resignation in the spring of 1880 was followed by an interval of several months before a successor could be found and placed in the job. Daniel Putnam served as acting principal during this time.

When Principal Mac Vicar submitted his unexpected resignation after one year, an emergency was created, recovery from which proved to require a good two years. Daniel Putnam again served as acting principal.

The successor to Principal Mac Vicar finally was found in 1883, but Edwin Willits, the man selected, was called to the presidency of the Michigan Agricultural College at East Lansing in 1885. Again to meet an emergency, Putnam was placed in charge, this time with the title of vice-principal (a title that he retained thereafter).

Putnam's career and service to Michigan Normal does not, however, rest on these administrative interludes. Brought to Normal in 1868 to occupy the chair of Natural Science (teaching theoretical and applied psychology); resigning shortly because of the small salary but returning after a year; first head of the Training School; organizer and first head of the Library; first head of the Education Department (organized as a separate department some 25 years later), author of books and many articles and papers, and of the early "History of the Michigan State Normal School"—his 38 years at Normal and in Ypsilanti represent an impressive contribution.

New England was once again the early environment of a Normal head. Putnam was born (1824) in Lynderboro, New Hampshire. With very little education before his twentieth year, he entered the academy at New Hampton, New Hampshire, and prepared for Dartmouth College, from which he graduated in 1851. He then did some postgraduate work at Amherst College.

In 1854, he came to Michigan to accept a professorship of Latin Language and Literature at Kalamazoo College where, at a later date and for a single year, he was acting head. For years thereafter he served as a trustee of the college. In Kalamazoo he also held the positions of superintendent of the Kalamazoo public schools[5] and superintendent of the Kalamazoo County schools.

While there, he became interested in the inmates of the Michigan Asylum for the Insane in Kalamazoo and served as their chaplain, maintaining this connection long after he came to Ypsilanti. Two books grew out of this interest, and these reveal both the compassionate and the deeply religious character of the man as well as a lively and genuine professional interest. The earlier one was a book of readings and prayers for daily use, entitled "Sunbeams Through the Clouds." "This little volume," he said, "owes its existence, not to the desire to make a book, but to a want of which long experience among a most unfortunate class of the suffering and afflicted has made me painfully conscious. The second book, "Twenty-five years with the Insane," was written as be brought this service to a close.

At Ypsilanti, the broad scope of Putnam's interests was again revealed. He served the community as alderman and mayor, and was ever a ready fill-in for the Baptist pulpit. During a brief one-year interval he held the position of superintendent of the Ypsilanti Public Schools (1870–1871).

With reference to community service, Sarah Putnam also deserves attention. Mrs. Putnam, although blinded by lightning (four of her five children she never saw), was also very active, and is credited with founding the Ladies Literary Club—an organization that boasts of being one of the ten oldest women's clubs in Michigan.

At the Normal his services were of a pioneering nature. As director of the School of Observation and Practice, a position that he held for 10 years, he was the first formal head of the Training School (1871). In 1873, under Principal Estabrook, the position of Librarian was established. Putnam was appointed. Julia Ann King, a colleague for many years, in eulogizing Putnam after 30 years of service at Normal[7] said that when he came in 1868 the library was merely a collection of books in an out-of-the-way room. Putnam had the books moved to a "suitable" room, and developed a card catalog system.

In 1875, as head of the School of Observation and Practice, he began to urge establishment of a kindergarten. In his report of that year to Principal Mayhew he said:

> Kindergartens are being established in many of our larger cities and villages . . . I rejoice in the experiments and efforts which are being made. Out of these . . . I have no doubt, will come valuable results. One of these results, and perhaps the most important and desirable one, will be, I trust, the essential modification of the employments, studies, teaching and

training of our primary schools . . . The Normal Schools of the country
should lead in this good work, and should by carefully conducted experiments determine how much and what of the kindergarten material, work
and methods can be made useful in the schools referred to.

The State Board was slow to move on this recommendation, and
although Putnam repeated his urging from time to time, no kindergarten was established at Normal until 1888, when an enlargment of
Old Main made possible the expansion of the Training School.

In 1893, the work in professional education was organized as a
separate department called the Department of Mental and Moral
Science and Theory and Art of Teaching—referred to commonly as
the Pedagogical Department. Putnam was placed in charge, and
retained this position until his death in 1906.

Along with his varied formal responsibilities, in the course of his
38 years with Normal, Putnam wrote and published rather extensively in the areas of history of education and teaching. Among his
major efforts were: a textbook in *Elementary Psychology* (1889); a
Manual of Pedagogics (1895); *A History of the Michigan State
Normal College* (1899); and a history of *The Development of Primary and Secondary Public Education in Michigan* (1904). Papers
and addresses would form a lengthy list. In 1897, Putnam was recognized by the University of Michigan with an honorary LLD
degree.

He would probably like to be remembered also as a teacher of
teachers. One of his colleagues said of him, "He seeks to make of his
pupils men and women of the best kind rather than simply scholars
and teachers." Another colleague, Professor Edwin Strong, once said
of him that "no man ever lost faith or heart or hope as a result of his
teaching; rather, for many was his class room a fountain of inspiration to firmer faith and higher service."

Edwin Willits
1883–1885

The vacancy left by the resignation of Mac Vicar was filled in
1883 by the appointment of Edwin Willits (age 53). Editor, lawyer,
public official, congressman, Willits was not the type to which
Normal had become accustomed. He was neither a protestant minis-

ter nor a professional educator. The State Board, in making the appointment, felt called upon to explain its decision. They said:

> In appointing to so important a position as the Principalship of the Normal School, one whose life-work had been in other callings than the profession of teaching, one who had not through experience and study a systematic course of pedagogy behind him, the Board were mindful that they were departing from the ordinary course of procedure; but they desired especially to emphasize that clause in the legislative action of this State, which, in instituting a Normal School for the preparation of teachers, required that the State Board of Education should also provide for the instruction of its pupils *'in the fundamental laws of the United States, and in what regards the rights and duties of citizens.'* With this in view, no one seemed to the Board to combine, as Mr. Willits does, so many of the requisites necessary to lead the Normal School on to that great future which its founders confidently expected for it.[8]

The Board praised the record of Putnam as acting principal, saying that he had served to their entire satisfaction, as also to that of the faculty and students. "Under this administration," they said, "the work of the school became more and more systematic, the interest of the students steadily increased, and the attendance was over twenty per cent larger than that of the previous year." But they stressed the very important position that Putnam would occupy in the "Chair of Moral and Mental Philosophy, and the Science and Art of Teaching."

The student paper expressed surprise that the mantle had not fallen on Putnam.[9]

A clue to why Putnam was not chosen lies in his attitude toward the question of the true function of a normal school. He had apparently taken a position in support of the experiment of 1878, whereby academic courses were to be eliminated and Normal would become strictly a professional school of education. This experiment was, as we have seen, abandoned with the Board's reversal of its stand, and its appointment of Principal Mac Vicar.

The attitude of Willits was expressed in his first annual report to the Board:

> I am not prepared at this time to solve the "Normal School" problem . . . I shall note only the most obvious points that have impressed themselves upon me during the year I have given to this work . . . Theoretically, it has been claimed that each should be strictly confined to its sphere

—that the academy, high school, or college should have the sole supervision of the subject matter and the Normal School of the methods. Like all theories, this one fails in its extremes.

By calling attention to the broader scope of the legislative intent for Normal, and implementing its position by the appointment of a man whose background was not that of the professional educationist, the State Board would appear to be insisting that the experiment of 1878 was not to be revived.

Thus, the very appointment of Edwin Willits was of fundamental significance to Normal. He remained with Normal only two years, resigning in 1885 to accept the presidency of the Michigan Agricultural College at East Lansing. In this connection it should be noted that Willits is credited with proposing the plan by which the Michigan Agricultural College was removed from the jurisdiction of the State Board of Education and placed under a State Board of Agriculture.[10]

But his influence was out of all proportion to the time-span and, indeed, had been previously felt by Normal over a period of a dozen years when he had served as a member of the State Board (1861–1873). Putnam commented at a much later time that when Willits became a member of the Board, Normal was but eight years of age; that it was during his incumbency that the character of the school became established; and that he exercised a strong influence on the selection of faculty. Putnam also asserted that Willits had the confidence of the school, the faculty, and successive legislators.

"The teachers who remained for any length of time in the school came to know him," Putnam said, "not only as an official of the governing body, but also as a personal friend and a wise adviser." He had, indeed, exercised a strong influence on the selection of the faculty. Six became potent factors in Normal's history: two (Bellows and Putnam) served as acting principal, and two (Mayhew and Estabrook) as principal. The other two (McLouth and Lodeman) were outstanding in their respective fields of physical sciences and modern languages.

The career of Edwin Willits parallels to a degree that of Normal's first Principal, Adonijah Welch. Both came from the East (Willits was born in Cattaraugus County, New York); both were graduates of the University of Michigan; both began as lawyers (Willits prepared for the bar by study in the law office of United States Senator Christiancy in Monroe, Michigan). Both were officially connected with the Michigan Agricultural College at East Lansing; both were members of Congress (Willits as a Republican in the 45th, 46th, and 47th Congresses); both were appointed to the Department of Agriculture.

Willits' experience as a lawyer was more extensive. He practiced in Monroe, was prosecuting attorney for Monroe County. In Congress he was a member of the Judiciary Committee and the Committee on Patents, and spent his last years in law practice in Washington, D.C. Other interests and occupations included journalism (assistant editor of the *Monroe Commercial* for several years), trustee and director of the Monroe High School (18 years), postmaster at Monroe. In 1873, Governor Bagley appointed him to a commission to propose a revision of the State Constitution and he was made chairman of the Committee on Education.

Willits' attitude concerning education was expressed in his inaugural address when he said:

> The time is coming when we must choose between the policeman and the moral sense. In all ages the best policeman has been a well-regulated conscience—with moral sense . . . An education that includes only intelligence may foster crime . . . The education we want must include the moral sentiments as well.

During his brief administration at Normal he dealt vigorously with two problems of considerable consequence. One was an attempt by the University of Michigan to secure passage of a bill by the State Legislature giving it the same authority to grant teaching certificates as that possessed by Normal. The historian of the School of Education of the U-M, Dean Allen S. Whitney, makes this brief comment

> A bill to this effect was presented to the Legislature at its session of 1884–1885, but it was defeated by the forces of the Normal School which felt that this action would be an interference with their own private domain.[11]

The other problem was one of classroom space. In 1882, Old Main had been enlarged by construction of a rear addition. Just two years later, Willits made an urgent request for further enlargement. He repeated this in more urgent language the following year. The Legislature finally, in 1887, responded and by 1888 a north wing and south wing had been added.

His stay at the Agricultural College, too, was short. After four years, he left to accept an appointment by President Harrison to the newly-created post of Assistant Secretary of Agriculture. Five years in this position, and he retired to practice law in the city of Washington, but only for two years. He died in 1896.[12]

CHAPTER THIRTEEN

JOHN MAHELM BERRY SILL

(1886–1893)

In September of 1887, the local newspaper, describing the fall opening of Normal, presented a graphic picture:

> The preliminary work of entrance was attended to with the precision and regularity of clockwork, and with more than the normal dispatch. Professor Sill, quick, nervous and administrative, was everywhere seen. Professor Putnam, calm, dignified and superb . . . Professor Lodeman, silent, knightly, a type of soldierly grace . . . Professor D'Ooge, brilliant, energetic, the hero of many languages . . . Professor George, active and businesslike . . . Strong, cultured and scientific . . . Bellows, tall and rhetorical . . . Miss King, fierce and resolute . . . At 1:30 the entrance examinations began with geography under Professor Goodison, who knows the earth as the hunter knows the trails of the forest . . . Wednesday morning the pupils filed in to their accustomed places. Professor Pease, ever graceful and chivalric, turned his back to us at the organ, and brought down the first crash of music. All sang two verses of 'Nearer My God to Thee,' after which Professor Putnam offered prayer . . . Wednesday evening the Students' Christian Association met under the leadership of President W. D. Hill. The hall was nearly filled and the meeting most earnest and enthusiastic; a propitious opening for the new year.[1]

The brief glimpse of Principal Sill here afforded does not, of course, give an adequate picture. It does name some of the leaders of a faculty of exceptional quality that he inherited. J. M. B. Sill had, at an earlier time, been a member of this faculty. Indeed, his connection began with the very opening of Normal in 1853 when he enrolled as a student. He constituted a full third of Normal's first graduating class (1854).

Sill was another in the list of early principals of Normal whose origin was in the east, having been born in Black Rock, Erie County, New York. His parents were caught up in the Westward-moving tide and, at the age of five, young Sill was one of the coming generation in Jonesville, Michigan. His Jonesville schooling led him to the new Union School, probably first of its kind in Michigan to open its doors, founded and presided over by Adonijah Welch. He spent a year in Kalamazoo studying dentistry, then returned to Jonesville as Welch's assistant in the Union School. When Welch was called to Ypsilanti to head the new Normal School, he brought young Sill with him. For a year Sill taught Latin and English in Ypsilanti's new Union Seminary; then, upon the opening of Normal, enrolled. As a member of Normal's first graduating class he earned not only this distinction but also stood alone as the first male graduate. The State Board immediately appointed him to the dual posts of Director of the Model Department and Professor of English Language and Literature.

He left in 1863 to accept an offer to become the second head of the Detroit schools. He remained there, alternating as Superintendent of Detroit schools, head and proprietor of the Detroit Female Seminary, and again as Superintendent of Detroit Schools until called back to Normal by the State Board in 1886.

This Detroit interval saw important beginnings. He filled a position that had been vacant for some years. He held the position when it was finally given the legislative authority that is associated with the administrative power of a modern superintendency (as contrasted with the supervisory function). He is credited with humanizing public education in Detroit; with overcoming the opposition to high schools and starting the high school system; and is looked upon as the founder of Wayne State University's College of Education, having organized the Normal class (1881) that became known as the Martindale Normal Training School (1914), then the Detroit Teachers' College (1920), and finally the College of Education.[2] Sill's recommendation to the Detroit Board of Education concerning teacher training was supported by a committee report that contained the following interesting line of reasoning:

> Your committee are well aware that the State Normal School is engaged in the work of training teachers and doing it well, and we have no doubt but that this Board could secure well-trained teachers by requiring every

inexperienced appointee to hold the diploma of this excellent institution; but such a requirement would practically exclude from our corps of teachers all graduates of our own schools who are unable to expend several hundred dollars in an effort to meet this condition. The drawing of such a line between the rich and poor could be justified only by a necessity which does not exist . . .[3]

Sill had to defend this step the rest of his days. As late as 1899, near the very close of his life, he was still justifying the Detroit Normal against the criticism that it was an unnecessary duplication of the work of the Ypsilanti Normal.

It was during the Detroit years that Sill was made a member of the Board of Regents of the University of Michigan. Though a Democrat, he was appointed to fill a vacancy by Republican Governor Henry H. Crapo.[4] While serving in this capacity he was made chairman of the Committee on the Scientific Course and the Chemical Laboratory, and had the distinction of putting the motion supporting the request of two professors to establish a course in mechanical engineering. He was also a member of the committee of three that journeyed east to make inquiries concerning James B. Angell, and made the original reporting favoring Angell for President of the U-M.

As Principal (at age 55) of Ypsilanti Normal for seven years, Sill made a significant and lasting contribution. With regard to the curriculum, he took the baton from the hands of Mac Vicar and widened the distance from the old Bellows-McLouth formula that called for elimination of the academics. He established a four-year program at the college level (over and above the traditional two-years of high school level and review). Thus he definitely broadened the concept of the school's function. Also he encouraged the upgrading of the three and four-year programs to the status of college-level work, thus eliminating the college preparatory courses.

In 1889, the State Legislature passed an important act revising and consolidating the laws governing the State Board of Education.[5] Section 5 gave the Board authority to grant "such diploma as it may deem best—

and such diploma when granted shall carry with it such honors as the extent of the course for which the diploma is given may warrant and said board of education may direct."

Under this authority, and based on the expanded curriculum which now provided four years of work at the college level, the Board established its first college degree, the Bachelor of Pedagogics. It was awarded for the first time in 1890. Of this degree, Putnam said:

> It is . . . intended that the degree of Bachelor of Pedagogics shall indicate scholarship equal to that required for the degree of B.A. from a reputable college . . .

At the same time a graduate degree of Master of Pedagogics was adopted. This degree was to be based on five years of teaching experience and the presentation of a thesis "acceptable to the faculty of the school upon some subject connected with the history, science, or art of education."

In the area of professional education, Sill introduced courses in advanced psychology, comparison of educational systems, advanced practice teaching, and methods in the teaching of history, science, and the ancient and modern languages. He also upgraded the work of the Training School by providing a supervising ("critic") for each of the grades, adding a ninth grade, and, at long last, establishing a kindergarten (1888). Later, there was a course in kindergarten methods applicable not only to the kindergarten but also the work of the first four grades.

At about this time, too, Sill undertook to introduce into the curriculum both "general education" and flexibility. He complained that the trend of Normal had been in the direction of more and more specialization, that a student was offered only a choice between specializations.

> This ought (he said) to be corrected, and to this end I recommend that the courses be arranged with certain necessary Normal School work common to all the courses required; and that there be freedom of choice in enough complementary studies to fill up the requirements for a four years' course.

In short, Sill's emphasis was on expanding and upgrading the curriculum and, at the same time, relying on the high schools for college preparatory work. By 1891, he could say that this had been accomplished.[6] He also urged that some provision be made for teachers in service so that, by offering brief professional courses, they might have the benefit of further training—a prophetic glance in the direction of a later day when, by means of summer school, extension courses and evening classes, this need was recognized. Also he made proposals for the inclusion of work in manual training and in physical education.

But Sill, having been so instrumental in developing a college-level curriculum, was not in sympathy with adopting the name "College." He looked at the matter from the standpoint of maintaining student discipline, asserting that the younger students at Normal would be encouraged to think of themselves as college students and "to ape college tricks and manners and to duplicate college noise and disorder." And he inveighed against "a tendency on the part of some teachers to promote the idea that a normal school should consider and call itself a college . . . some, whose ambition outruns their judgment . . ."

> A Normal School (he added) differs most essentially from a college. Its students come from schools of all kinds and conditions. Many of them have never seen a well-ordered school. Their idea of proper discipline and order will come of their own experience in this school . . . My experience teaches me that the propagation of the college idea makes against such proper order and piles up difficulties in the way of the executive. I believe that the best interests of the Normal School demand that you, as the controlling board, set your faces seriously against this particularly injurious manifestation of ambitious folly.[7]

Only six years later, under another principal, this "ambitious folly" was committed. But not for three-quarters of a century, under the impact of a world in turmoil, would the full fury of his prediction be realized.

Something should also be said with reference to the physical expansion of Normal during Sill's administration. In his final report to the State Board he stated it in percentage terms: library volumes up 70 per cent; school apparatus, including musical instruments, 83 per cent; value of furniture, 32 per cent; additions to buildings, 84 per cent of value in 1887.

The expansion in buildings included the appropriation of 1887 which Sill's predecessor, Willits, had vigorously urged upon the Legislature, and which resulted in the erection of the north and south wings of the main building. In the north wing were placed the library, four student society meeting rooms, and a "gentleman's study hall." The south wing contained several classrooms, a "ladies'

study hall," and a room for the "Drawing Department." Reporting
a year later Sill said:

> We are now well equipped with a capacious and beautiful hall for morn-
> ing exercises, lectures, etc.; adequate study halls for our students; conven-
> ient recitation and lecture rooms; a fine library and reading room; and
> excellent facilities for progressive instruction in Natural and Physical sci-
> ences, Geography, Drawing, Mathematics and History.

Sill's percentage statement also included a legislative appropriation, passed in the very year of his retirement, for a gymnasium, yet
to be constructed. It was built the following year.

Student enrollments in the Normal department had, during these
seven years, risen from 675 to 922, a 37 per cent increase.[8]

In this connection it should also be noted that Sill persuaded the
State Board to furnish free textbooks. Commenting on this move, he
made a broad statement of principle that our present age has translated into scholarships:

> Our students are working young men and women who earn their little
> money by the hardest toil. The cost of books is often "the last straw that
> breaks the camel's back." I shall be glad to see them relieved to this
> extent. I also believe that the State will find it to its advantage to make the
> way as easy as is possible for those who are preparing for public service in
> the schools. Many other states go still further in this direction, even to the
> extent of furnishing free transportation to the students of their normal
> schools.

Sill retired (at age 62) as principal of Normal in 1893, and moved
to Ann Arbor. He gave no reason, saying only that it was a personal
matter and involved no conflict with the State Board. His final
report to the Board indicated, however, that his move was made at
their suggestion.[9]

Whatever the Board's motivation, Sill left accompanied by sentiments of great respect and affection. Henry R. Pattengill, always
open and outspoken wherever criticism was involved, expressed the
general feeling well in his *Michigan School Moderator* when he
commented:

> . . . his kindness of heart, and genial manners have endeared him to all
> who have become acquainted with him. Mr. Sill's administration has been

one of comparatively little friction, and without detracting in the least from the good work of previous administrations, it is safe to say that the Normal is today doing the best work it has ever done.[10]

President Grover Cleveland had plans for him, however, and promptly appointed him Minister Resident and Consul-General to Korea. He served from 1894 to 1897, then retired, in poor health, to spend his last few years in Detroit.

As minister to Korea, he found difficulty in disassociating his strongly sympathetic feelings for the Koreans from the objective attitude that the State Department required of his official position. He found the country in the midst of a rebellion which was quickly followed by a war between China (Korea's suzerain) and Japan. On one occasion Secretary Olney cabled him: "Intervening in political concerns of Korea not among your functions and is forbidden."

J. M. B. Sill was a man of great personal charm and broad human interest. As superintendent of the Detroit schools, one of his early efforts was to bring about a better relationship between teachers and pupils, especially with reference to school discipline. He was popular with his fellow citizens in Detroit, becoming a well-liked member of the exclusive Prismatic Club. One of the records of this fun-loving organization shows a crude drawing of a cornucopia and pictures him entering the large end carrying a book entitled "The Story of the Three Scavengers." He will emerge from the small end. The accompanying ditty, in the vein of Old Mother Hubbard, ran:

> The gallant Professor he went to the dresser
> And brought to the Club a new tale.
> When he got there, he was filled with despair,
> For he found that his story was stale.

A contemporary said of him that "he read and recited beautifully and sang many songs, comic and otherwise, to the delight of all who heard him." A song that was published, written to his small daughter, Allie, ran in part as follows:

> Would that I thy coming fears,
>   From thy life could borrow;
> Would that I could weep thy tears,
>   Carry all thy sorrow.

> Come, come, sit upon my knee,
> Brown-eyed laughing baby;
> And I will ask of the Fates for thee,
> What thy future may be.

Sill was the author of two textbooks on English grammar, one written shortly after his graduation from Normal and while a member of the faculty, the other during the Detroit interlude.[12] Though he possessed no earned degree, he was the recipient of two honorary degrees, an MA from the University of Michigan in 1871 and an MPd from Normal in 1890. In the latter year he was ordained a Deacon in the Episcopal Church, and thenceforth exhibited considerable missionary zeal.[13]

When he died in 1901, at the age of three score and ten, it was said of him at Normal:

> He was an educator of the older school, and his pupils, going out into the primary, grammar and high schools of the state, carried with them the ideals and aspirations that he had imparted to them. In consequence there is hardly a city or village of the state that has not felt Mr. Sill's influence, exerted through the media of its schools.[14]

CHAPTER FOURTEEN

RICHARD GAUSE BOONE

1893–1899

The announcement by the State Board of Sill's successor gave promise of a yet bigger and better future for Normal. It read:

> Dr. Boone has already attained national prominence as an educator and author of educational works, and comes to our State and to the Normal School splendidly equipped for the services required of him. . . .

The equipment referred to was noteworthy in two respects: (1) it included teaching experience at every level of the educational scene, from rural district school to university; (2) it did not include a single earned degree from a college or university but it did boast two honorary degrees—an MA from DePauw University, and a PhD from Ohio University.[1]

It also included rather extensive research done in residence at Johns Hopkins University, and the publication of two books on American education, one of which was described by William T. Harris, United States Commissioner of Education, as "the first noteworthy attempt at a general history of education in the United States."[2] This became a standard textbook in colleges throughout the nation for many years.

Boone served for a year as superintendent of schools at Frankfort, Indiana, and in 1886 was called to Indiana University by President David Starr Jordan to organize a Department of Pedagogy. He remained there until called to Ypsilanti in 1893.

The six-year period of Boone's administration proved to be of great significance. It saw a professional course developed for college and university graduates; a still greater reliance on the high schools

141

for the academic work of that level; the expansion of physical facilities; important curricular development, and the Normal legally recognized as a four-year college. In 1897, the State Legislature authorized a change of name with respect to the four-year courses leading to a degree; in 1899 it changed the name from "School" to "College" and Richard Gause Boone became the first to hold the title President of Michigan State Normal College. It was the second normal school in the nation to become a four-year college-grade institution, the first being that at Albany, New York (in 1890).[3]

In another respect, too, Boone's coming was of exceptional importance. He represented the professional educator. Of his eight predecessors, five had been men of orthodox religious beliefs and strong missionary zeal. They were missionary-educators. Of the three exceptions (Welch, Bellows, Willits) the terms of office of two had been exceedingly brief. Richard Boone, despite a Quaker background (he had graduated from the Spiceland Academy of Spiceland, Indiana) presented the image of the educator rather than the preacher. In this respect, he picked up the lines of Normal's first principal, Adonijah Welch. Boone was primarily a student of the educational process.

Boone had noted in his writings the appearance of an educational development of "grave importance" namely, greater attention to psychological principles and "systematic observation and patient, scientific study of child-mind." But, along with his scientific emphasis Boone held as equally important knowledge of the historical antecedents. He stated:

> . . . so vitally is every present related to its past, that the study of contemporary institutions can be made intelligent only in the light of their origin. To know along what lines in educational experience have been the great changes, and why, and so what is new and what old, in current doctrine and practice, serves to temper undue enthusiasm over real or supposed new departures, and saves from condemning the worthy only because it chances to be old.[4]

Boone was at pains to distinguish between training and education, and in consequence was considered unfriendly to vocational and physical training, a judgment that failed to do him justice. What he was insisting upon was that, to be educational, an activity must have an impact on the mental life. He said:

I shall not disparage any form of physical culture when I say that neither strength of body, nor grace of carriage, nor agility, nor attractive presence, nor health, nor endurance, can for the moment be considered as an end of training. Here as elsewhere the essential fact is the amount and quality of the mental life that goes into the process, and the reaction of the process upon the mental life . . . The skill—the finger skill—incident to a course in shorthand or piano, or sewing, or cooking, or painting may be a means of livelihood. . . . But the educational value of such acquisition may be next to nothing because of the absence of this mental reaction. For this reason certain of the so-called practical subjects are the most unpractical often. . . .

Pursuing this theme, he doubtless shocked most of his faculty when he brought religion and the Bible into his discussion.

The mistake of the schools seems to me to be far less that moral and aesthetic and religious instincts have been ignored, than that the intellectual faculties and activities are not recognized as a great natural gateway and highway to these qualities of a noble life, not less than to scholarship. . . . It would seem to be a less serious alternative that the Bible be thrown out of the schools, than that the teacher should lack in the endowment of wisdom and right motives and humane interest, and faith in human instincts.[5]

With this brief glimpse of Boone's educational thinking, let us turn to his impact on the curriculum, the first area that engaged his attention.

In December of his first year he presented a paper before the Normal School Pedagogical Society entitled "Education as a Dialectic Process." Defining "dialectics of the mind" as a process of experience, the process by which mind seeks to achieve truth, he said that "the current of the mind . . . is on the side of total, not partial effects." The tendency of the mind, he said, is to want to unify its experiences, and the teacher should serve to help this along. From this premise he undertook to persuade his faculty that the public school curriculum should be organized around a central subject, based on a principle of concentration.

The teacher should, therefore, select "such thinking and other activities as most easily combine into one whole; and to effect this activity through the employment of properly coordinated subjects; this gives also the ground for the concentration of studies." He

referred to the humanities (history, literature), language study and
science as subjects that coordinate well with other subjects to form a
natural center of concentration.

Boone's presentation to his faculty stimulated formal papers by
the heads of the Departments of Modern Languges, History, Physical Sciences, and Education, and the five presentations were
promptly set in print and bound into a volume titled "A Study in
Unification of School Work."[6] They formed a symposium that
exemplified a seriousness of interest in the essential function of education that is impressive. But they revealed, too, a feeble hold by the
department heads on the "concentration" concept; a determination
to force it into the traditional mold.

Boone's proposal is of particular interest as a forerunner of the
present-day "core curriculum" concept that has found wide acceptance in the public schools. The "core" people of today look back
largely to Abraham Flexner and the Lincoln School of Columbia
University's Teachers College. Flexner's widely-read essay, "A
Modern School," appeared in 1916 and the Lincoln School experiment was undertaken a year later. Thus a pioneering concept that
might have developed into one of major significance lay dormant
until picked up again some two decades later and developed by the
more perceptive mind and persistent effort of Flexner, and the added
prestige and resources of a more alert board of control, the General
Education Board of New York.

Boone's influence on the curriculum at the Normal, however, was
significant. Two major policies were adopted: (1) the grouping of
courses that related to each other; (2) the expansion of the area of
free electives by the student but at the same time the requirement
that the student elect groups, not individual courses. In his 1895
report to the State Board, Boone was able to say:

> A continuous line of electives covering from three to five years each, may
> be had in any one of the following departments: history, music, mathe-
> matics, English, German, French, Latin, Greek, physics and chemistry,
> biology, and geography and drawing . . . Disconnected and aimless selec-
> tion of studies is discouraged or prohibited.

But attention was also given to other aspects of the curriculum:
the relative amount of the curriculum devoted to professional work;
the upgrading of courses by the improvement of entrance examina-

tions and encouragement of high school graduates to enroll at the Normal; expansion of the professional program for graduates from liberal arts colleges.

In 1898, Boone drew up a detailed report of Normal's progress during the past decade, a report that showed not only the developments that had occured under his own administration but gave due credit to his predecessor, Sill. Boone acknowledged indebtedness, for example, for a Training School that was staffed with a teacher for each elementary grade and had added a ninth grade. Sill's policy of recognition of the high school diploma for admission bore fruit in Boone's time. By 1896, Boone could show that two-thirds of the student body had been admitted on this basis. Sill's one and two-year certificate courses for high school graduates had contributed greatly to this development. The appropriation which Sill succeeded in getting for a gymnasium made possible, the following year under Boone, a new building and the organization of the new Department of Physical Training. Sill's emphasis on more flexibility in the student's program was given greater importance by Boone's insistence on a higher percentage of free electives.

Sill's policy of expanding course offerings and at the same time increasing the relative amount of professional work bore fruit under Boone to the extent that, in his review of the decade ending in 1898, he could report that the list of classes had almost trebled, and the amount of professional work relative to the whole had increased from 12 to 21 per cent. Moreover, he was able to show that class attendance relative to enrollment had substantially increased. He pointed out that class attendance at the Normal had long been much better than at seven large normal schools in seven other States. The current attendance at the Normal was 93 per cent of enrollment; for the other schools, 60 per cent.

In 1895, Boone had reported that the four-year "full diploma" (two preparatory and two college years) students could now elect a third of their courses and the "advanced" students (those enrolled in the four-year college-grade program that led to the bachelor of pedagogy degree) could in their last two years elect all of their courses. As for the course provided for graduates of liberal arts colleges, Boone had expanded it from the half-year under Sill to a full year. College graduates were now being admitted from the University of Michigan, Michigan Agricultural College, Michigan School of Mines, and the following private colleges: Adrian, Albion, Alma,

Detroit, Hillsdale, Hope, Kalamazoo, and Olivet.

The Boone administration was soon faced with a problem of major import. A development took place that had been long in the making, the occurrence of which had been delayed largely because of the resistance of Normal's faculty and administration—the establishment of additional normal schools in Michigan. Factors of prestige, and a deep-seated fear, born of long experience, that the Legislature, which had often been penurious with Normal, would find it much more difficult to support two Normals, were responsible for this attitude. The Board of Visitors for Normal had supported this stand in its report for 1889.

But agitation for additional normal schools persisted, and by 1895 the barrier was threatened. Two bills were proposed, one for a State Normal at Mount Pleasant, the other for one at Marquette in the Upper Peninsula.

Boone acted promptly. In a letter to Governor John T. Rich, dated May 25, 1895, he expessed, on behalf of himself and his faculty, great concern over the possibility of establishing other normal schools of equal rank with that at Ypsilanti. He said:

> With the present Board of Education there would doubtless be no difficulty, but the Board of Education is a changing body, and a new set of members might immediately present a bill to establish another or two more schools of exactly equal rank with our own. This . . . opens up opportunity of competition between different sections of the state for support at every session of the legislature.[7]

The Mount Pleasant bill represented an effort by local citizens to get the Legislature to adopt an existing private school. In 1891, a group of leading citizens had become interested and, on September 13, 1892, had opened a normal school in that city. C. F. R. Bellows (erstwhile of the Ypsilanti Normal) had been made principal. The hope was that the State could be persuaded to take it over. An effort to this end was made in the same year, secured the approval of the Senate, but failed in the House. In 1895, a second attempt was made and this time was successful, though failing to secure an appropriation. The Act authorized the institution to prepare teachers for the rural district schools (the one-room schools) and the primary departments of the graded schools of the State.[8]

At this point the role played by Boone was quite the opposite to that of his predecessors. Mindful of the jealousy of his staff and of the financial hazard, he yet saw and was concerned about the broader aspects of the problem. He undertook, therefore, simply to secure legal recognition of the pre-eminent position of the Ypsilanti school. He was eminently successful. Not only did the Act adopting the Mount Pleasant Normal limit the school to the preparation of teachers below the high school level, but in 1897 the Legislature enacted a statute confirming this status. At the same time it not only confirmed the Ypsilanti institution in issuing teaching certificates at all levels, but also authorized it, in certain instances, to use the title of "The Michigan State Normal College."[9]

As to the movement for a normal school in the Upper Peninsula— frustrated first in 1875 by faculty and friends of the Ypsilanti Normal and again in 1895 by proponents for the Mount Pleasant Normal—Boone was active in its support.

In 1899, a statute was finally enacted "to provide for the location, establishment and conduct of a Normal School at Marquette, in the Upper Peninsula of this State, and to make an appropriation for the same." As to the status of the school, the Act included the provisions of the Act of 1897 which defined the status of the Central Normal at Mount Pleasant.[10]

The Act of 1897 which empowered the State Board to designate the Ypsilanti Normal as Michigan State Normal College with regard to life-certificate and degree courses was accepted as changing the name of the school. Boone thenceforth signed himself as "President of Michigan State Normal College;" the annual catalog appeared under the new name; the school periodical changed its name from the *Normal News* to *Normal College News;* and the *Michigan School Moderator* commented that "Michigan State Normal School is now no more; 'tis now Michigan State Normal College."

Thus when, in 1899, the legislature passed the bill formally changing the name of the school (coincident with the establishment of a third normal, Northern, at Marquette) this was merely a legal confirmation of the step taken in 1897, and of the superior status of the Ypsilanti institution relative to other Michigan Normals.[11]

The proposal to hold a summer session was first made by President Boone. In his report of 1896 to the State Board, he stated that for several years there had been a demand for a summer session, and that occasionally short terms had been held, directed by someone not connected in an official or professional way with the Normal. He recommended that for the summer of 1897 the Normal hold a session of not less than eight weeks, whose offerings and conditions would be the same as during regular year.

The Board failed to act, and we find him repeating his recommendation two years later, with added arguments. A similar request, strongly supported by facts, was made at the same time by Charles McKenny, then principal of the Central State Normal School at Mount Pleasant. This time the State Board acted.

Superintendent of Public Instruction Jason E. Hammond, "impressed with the desire on the part of progressive school superintendents working in the smaller towns of the state, to avail themselves during the summer vacations of the advantages offered by the Normal College," presented to the Board a motion that reorganized the academic calendar so as to make this possible. Thus, the first regular summer session was held in 1899, coincident with the abandonment of the semester system and the organization of the academic year into four quarters.

When Boone came to the Normal, the Training School occupied the lower floor of the west addition to the Main Building. Adequate when first occupied, the area had become seriously inadequate. Just prior to Boone's arrival, the School had been reorganized to provide a critic teacher for each grade. This and the growing enrollments presented an urgent need for more rooms and more space. In his first year, therefore, Boone recommended that a separate building be erected for the Training School. At the same time he secured the backing of the Board of Visitors.

The appeal was successful. The Legislature of 1895 appropriated the sum of $25,000 for a building, to be ready for occupancy early in 1897. The sum appropriated, however, was inadequate to implement the plans drawn. On the completion of the building, Boone complained:

> The new training school building . . . is left unfortunately with the two end wings having foundations only. The original plan contemplated nine rooms, one for each of the eight elementary grades and the kindergarten, and a number of classrooms in which student teachers might have opportunity for their own teaching and practice in handling classes.[12]

Two years later Boone made another urgent appeal. The legislature responded, and by 1900 the two wings were constructed.

It should be noted, in passing, that the land on which the Training School building was constructed was part of a parcel of 3.99 acres, known as the Rorison site, donated to the Normal by the citizens of Ypsilanti in 1896, and dedicated by the State Board to provide a site for the erection of a building to house the Student Christian Association. Mrs. Mary A. Starkweather had just announced her gift that would make such a building possible, and that structure, occupying only a portion of the area donated, was dedicated in March of 1897.

At a much later time, Normal's Alumni Association was given the western part of this land as the site for a Union building.

Boone's deep interest in the history of education and his belief that no sound educational progress could be made in ignorance of the past led him to a keen appreciation of the significance of the history of his own institution at Ypsilanti. In his second annual report to the State Board, he sketched a brief history of the Normal and announced that a holiday had been declared for the school "to commemorate its founding in an appropriate way, and to make deserved and public acknowledgment of its generous service." The day set aside was the 28th of March, 1895 (commemorating the signing of the "Act to establish a State Normal School," on March 28, 1849), and was devoted to history and reminiscence. Boone said in part:

> It is earnestly hoped and recommended that, as the year 28th of March recurs in each succeeding year, it may be appropriately observed and bring with it some worthy contribution to the history and achievements and influences of the State Normal School. Much of its best history is yet little more than tradition. The occasion may serve at least as an incentive to gather up, as the years go on, the dropped strands of its life. Whatever was really worth incorporating into the school or, being incorporated, influenced its work or usefulness, is equally worth preserving.

This day was observed thereafter for many years.

In the spring of 1899, just as the Normal School had become legally designated as the Normal College, the *Detroit Free Press* revealed that all was not well between President Boone and his faculty. Within the next few days and weeks much of the story appeared in the Detroit, Ypsilanti and Ann Arbor newspapers.[13]

Boone had asked the State Board for the removal of the head of the Training School, James W. Simmons, and two critic teachers.

The *Free Press* article said that Boone was admitted to be a good educator and possessed of good executive ability but that he was alleged to have permitted personal animosities to dominate his judgment.

Pandora's box was opened. The *Detroit Evening News* dwelt on attitudes in the faculty, indicating that the row with the president had been going on for some years. The article said that the trouble arose "over the question of fads and as to whether President R. G. Boone should rule the faculty, or the old instructors whose influence dominated the school for half a century or more, should rule." He was called the "Miss Coffin of the Normal," a reference to an assistant superintendent of the Detroit schools who had earned a reputation as an extremely arbitrary, but able, administrator. The article went on to explain:

> The fad that President Boone first sprung at the Normal was the system of teaching by correlation. Correlation hypnotized H. R. Pattengill who was then State Superintendent of Public Instruction and ex-officio a member of the State Board of Education, at the very beginning. He agreed with President Boone that it was just what the Normal needed to make it the first institution of the kind in the United States. The older and more influential members of the faculty didn't approve of the system. Correlation, it may be said for the enlightenment of the common people, is a system of teaching a given thing and then dragging in everything that can be associated in any way with the subject.

The *Evening News* continued:

> There are members of the faculty who did much, long before Michigan heard of President Boone, to build up the Normal and place it in the front rank. They think they know as much as the president how to educate young men and women for teachers. There is a difference of opinion among disinterested citizens of Ypsilanti as to whether the burden of censure should be placed on President Boone or on the faculty.[14]

The controversy split the State Board two and two. The hold-over members (State Superintendent Hammond and Perry F. Powers) opposed Boone, the two new members hesitated to vote for his dismissal, but all agreed to re-hire the teachers. An article in the *Free Press* quoted Superintendent Hammond as follows:

> President Boone is a very able man, and a fine talker, but to the few per-
> sons who know what his methods are he is not the man the general public
> believe him to be. . . . He is a man who looks upon teachers and mem-
> bers of the faculty as he does upon the trees and walks in the college
> grounds. If any one offends him, he casts them out with the same hard-
> hearted purpose that he would order the removal of dead trees or any
> other offensive object.[15]

The unrest, unfortunately but inevitably, reached the student
body. A mass meeting was held, viewpoints were presented, a rising
vote was held (it was Boone vs. Simmons), and the Boone supporters
overwhelmed their opponents 449 to 28, with many abstaining. Two
seniors featured the close of the meeting by coming to blows.[16]

Beyond the borders of the State notice was also taken of the dispute. The *New York School Journal* expressed the hope that Governor Pingree would intervene to save Boone, saying: "Dr. Boone is
widely known and recognized as a leader among normal school men.
If the three most efficient workers in this important field were to be
mentioned, his name would be one of the three. Michigan ought not
to let him go."

But feelings on the Normal campus and at Lansing were running
too high. Boone resigned on September 1.[17] Editor Henry R. Pattengill of the *Michigan School Moderator* commented:

> Dr. Boone's administration has been a vigorous and successful one. The
> school has very materially improved under his regime, and the Board will
> find it no easy matter to secure a successor in every way as able as Mr.
> Boone. The Doctor is a fine speaker and well known in educational circles
> all over the United States. He is a man of untiring energy, and of inex-
> haustible capacity for work.

Names of possible successors to Boone soon appeared in the press,
and they made a very impressive list. Included, among others, were
Burke A. Hinsdale, incumbent of the Chair of the Science and Art of
Teaching at the University of Michigan; David Eugene Smith,
former head of the Mathematics Department at the Normal, then
president of the Brockport State Normal School in New York; David
McKenzie, superindendent of schools at Muskegon, Michigan (later
to become the first Dean of Wayne State University's College of
Liberal Arts); A. S. Whitney (later to become Dean of the School of

Education at the University of Michigan); Superintendent Lewis H. Jones of the Cleveland Schools (destined to accept the offer when renewed at a later time); and Albert Leonard, Dean of the College of Liberal Arts at Syracuse University.

The position appears to have been offered informally to Smith, who was not interested. Hinsdale, Jones, and Whitney were satisfied in their positions. McKenzie had doubts as to the progressive spirit of the Normal faculty and, on their side, the faculty felt that he was not well-enough informed as to the training of teachers. The choice finally went to Leonard, who accepted.[18]

Boone accepted an offer as superintendent of the Cincinnati public schools. There he found a school system in great need of being updated. In a centennial edition of the *Cincinnati Times-Star,* the article on the public schools had this to say:

> The close of the century finds the school system in a condition of reaction and decadence. An order of things which had undergone no essential change in half a century was visibly approaching the climax of its obsolescence. Regeneration was at hand. Superintendent Morgan was followed by Dr. Richard C. Boone . . . former president of the State Normal College, Ypsilanti, Michigan. Teachers were charmed by his cheerful smile, the effect of which was aided by a flowing mustache . . . amused at the opulence of his well-nourished frame and amazed at his facile fecundity of speech. They misunderstood his significance. For . . . Dr. Boone brought the earliest message of the new education which was destined to overturn an outworn system and remains dominant today.[19]

Shortly after Boone's arrival in Cincinnati, the *Cincinnati Enquirer* ran an article stating that the new superintendent of schools shocked the members of the Board of Education by rejecting all the changes recommended by the Board's committee on salaries. The article continued: "As Dr. Boone is on record as holding his independence higher than his position, the Board of Education will probably be treated to more shocks of this kind from time to time."

The statement was prophetic. After three years, Boone left the Cincinnati system.

For a number of years he edited F. H. Palmer's periodical, *Education,* and lectured on education. In 1913, he accepted an appointment as Professor of Education at the University of California at Berkely, serving also for a year as acting head of the School of Education there. When he died, in 1923, Normal and Michigan had almost forgotten him. Only in the educational periodical then published by Normal's faculty was mention made, and this in the form of a quotation from the journal of the California Teachers' Association. It was unaccompanied by comment of any kind.[20]

The administration of Richard Gause Boone at Normal was epoch-making. Not only did the Normal become the second in the nation to achieve legal status as a four-year degree-granting college (with Boone as its first president), but its national status was greatly enhanced. His up-to-date and forward-looking philosophy of education was revealed by papers read at national meetings, a full dozen in number by the time he left Ypsilanti. He was the first of Normal's administrators to bring its name vigorously to the national attention. On his own campus he played the stimulating role of iconoclast, and proved to be the first of a line of presidents whose professional approach represented a new emerging era in teacher preparation.

CHAPTER FIFTEEN

THE LYMAN-LEONARD
INTERLUDE

As the nineteenth century bowed out, the State of Michigan presented a far different picture from that which obtained when Normal first opened its doors. The scene has been graphically described:

> Fifty years have changed the wilderness into more than a hundred thousand cultivated farms. Eight thousand miles of railroads afford good market and travelling facilities to the people of almost every county in the state. The census reports show a population of nearly two and one-half million people. *Twelve thousand schools afford instruction to six hundred thousand pupils.* Postal facilities have improved a hundred fold.[1] (emphasis added)

We have seen that the establishment of a second normal school (at Mount Pleasant in 1895) created a new problem, that of coordinating the work of two schools. With the creation of a third (at Marquette in 1899), the problem assumed a more complicated form, and the State Board felt moved to try a novel experiment. They decided to place all three schools under a single head, to be given the title "President of the Normal Schools of Michigan." Subordinate to him would be a principal for each of the institutions.

In addition to general supervisory control and direct responsibility to the Board, the President would be required to give one or more courses of instruction in each of the schools each year upon the general subjects of philosophy, theory and art of teaching, and the history of education. His general supervisory function was described in such manner as to emphasize curriculum and instruction: "to so arrange, subordinate, and co-ordinate the courses of instruction in

155

each of the various Normal Schools of the State, that there shall be an interchange of credits between all of the said schools."[2]

The Board acted at once to appoint a principal to succeed President Boone, and began looking for a president for the Normal School System. The choice for principal fell on a recently arrived member of the faculty, Elmer A. Lyman, head of the Mathematics Department, to serve under the as-yet unnamed President of the Normal School System of the State.

Lyman was born in Manchester, Vermont, but came at an early age with his parents to Indiana. He attended the University of Michigan, graduating in 1886, and for the next four years gained administrative and teaching experience in the public schools in Kansas and Ohio. He then returned to the U-M as instructor in mathematics, where he served for eight years. He came to Normal in 1898.

Soon thereafter, the Board found the man they were looking for as president in Albert Leonard, Dean of the College of Liberal Arts of Syracuse University.

Leonard was born near Logan, Ohio, attended the Ohio Central Normal School, and graduated and took a master's degree from Ohio University. He came to Normal with an honorary PhD from Hamilton College at Clinton, New York, conferred in 1894 while he was principal of the Central High School at Binghamton, New York. In 1897, he joined the staff of Syracuse University as professor of pedagogy and Dean of the College of Liberal Arts. He had been on the staff of the *Journal of Pedagogy* since 1887 and, since 1891, its editor.

Leonard assumed his new duties July 1, 1900. A year later, in his first annual report, he noted that the Massachusetts Board of Education had just recommended a single supervising officer for the normal schools of that state. Also, in the first issue of the *Journal of Pedagogy* after his arrival in Ypsilanti he editorialized:

> While there is an impression in other states that neither the new (Michigan) plan nor any similar plan can be successfully and harmoniously carried out in Michigan owing to political and other complications, we are inclined to the opinion that the hindrances to the successful administration of the normal school system have been exaggerated.[4]

This was to be the one and only report by President Leonard. By the close of the next biennium the State Board had changed its mind about their Normal School System. In relieving Leonard of his duties, the Board said:

> The Board desires to place on record this belief, that the officer (the President) strove with all his power to successfully solve the inconsistencies, ambiguities, and anomalies of the new position, and the present Board put forth their most vigorous efforts to carry out the scheme devised by their predecessors . . .[5]

The startling reversal of its position by the State Board occurred before the second year of the experiment had been completed. In its biennial report for 1902 to the Legislature, the Board said:

> It is probable that the experiment should have been given more time, but by an opinion arrived at during the early spring of last year, which was concurred in by all the parties concerned, it was finally concluded that a compromise between the old and the new methods would bring about a happy solution of the matter of proper supervision and correlation of the then existing normal schools.[6]

The compromise referred to was the creation of a Normal Executive Council, composed of the president of Michigan State Normal College and the principals of the other State Normals, to be presided over by the Ypsilanti school's president, and to meet at least once each quarter at the same time and place as that scheduled for the regular meeting of the State Board. The duties of this Council would be

> to discuss all questions relating to the general educational policy of said Normal Schools and report to the State Board of Education for its consideration the result of their deliberations, and when said report has been officially approved by said board the same shall become binding upon and operative in all the Normal Schools of the State.

Not only was the president of the Ypsilanti Normal to preside over the meetings of the Council but to call them as needed, and he was further instructed to "counsel and advise" with the principals and faculties of the several normal schools.

This arrangement proved to be reasonably satisfactory, and continued in existence until, under the new State Constitution of 1963, effective January 1, 1964, each school was provided with its own board of control.

Lyman returned to his position as head of the Mathematics Department, which he filled with distinction until his death in 1936. Through the years he published a number of widely-used textbooks for high schools in arithmetic, algebra, trigonometry, and geometry, some in collaboration with such well-known names in the teaching profession in Michigan as Albertus Darnell (later to become Dean of the College of Liberal Arts at Wayne State University) and Edwin C. Goddard (later to become Professor of Law, and a national authority on Bailments and Carriers at the University of Michigan). He served as trustee for Alma College (Michigan) and Berea College (Kentucky), the latter conferring on him the honorary degree of LLD. As a teacher and colleague he was held both in esteem and affection. He died in his seventy-third year, active until within a few months of the end.

Leonard, who had maintained his residence in Ypsilanti, moved to Boston where he served in the Educational Department of Houghton, Mifflin and Co. for several years. In 1907, he became Superintendent of Schools at New Rochelle, New York, in which position he remained until his death in 1931. His alma mater conferred on him the honorary degrees of Doctor of Literature in 1909, and Doctor of Education in 1928. His city of New Rochelle honored him by giving his name to a junior high school, and the teachers of the State of New York made him president of their association.

CHAPTER SIXTEEN

LEWIS HENRY JONES

1902 – 1912

With the arrival of Lewis Henry Jones as president in 1902, Normal entered upon a period of cooperative, constructive effort that was to last for nearly a third of a century. In Jones and his successor (Charles McKenny) the college possessed a highly capable leadership that inspired both enthusiasm and affection.

Jones was born in Indiana of Welsh Quaker parents, grandson of an anti-slavery agitator who had been driven out of Tennessee. Like his predecessor, Boone, he attended Spiceland Academy. He graduated from the Oswego Normal School at Oswego, New York, a strong admirer of its head and founder, Edward Austin Sheldon. He took work at Harvard under Professor Agassiz who made a lasting contribution to his interests. It was Agassiz who secured for him his first teaching position, instructor in natural science, at the Indiana State Normal School at Terre Haute. This was in 1872. By 1876, he was assistant superintendent of the Indianapolis public schools and eight years later became superintendent. He was awarded an honorary MA in 1888 by DePauw University, and another the following year by Wabash College. He remained in Indianapolis until 1894.

Meanwhile, he was elected to the National Council of Education (1888), a small body of the older and more deeply interested members of the National Education Association, organized to give more serious consideration to fundamental questions of education, and to direct research and investigations. In 1893, he was appointed to the Committee of Fifteen on Elementary Education of the Department of Superintendence of the National Education Association. One of the reports made by this committee presented a set of principles for the organization of large city schools systems designed to take them

159

out of politics, to vest great authority in the chief school officer, and
to protect him in the performance of his duties. A fellow-member of
that committee, James M. Greenwood, Superintendent of Schools at
Kansas City, Missouri, later characterized Jones as follows:

> Superintendent Jones was rather conciliatory, and he did more than any
> other member of the sub-committee to pull us together when we would get
> far apart . . . (His) mind is acute, penetrating, and acts quickly and
> readily . . . When pressed too closely, he is dangerous . . . He is too
> gentlemanly to be a rough-and-tumble debater . . . he always prefers to
> be impersonal.[1]

Two years later, when the Cleveland school system was seeking a
new superintendent, the choice fell on Lewis Jones.

Jones remained at Cleveland until he accepted the call to Ypsilanti
in 1902. Those eight years were memorable. Favoring him were
laws passed by the Ohio Legislature reducing the size of the board of
education of the large city from 21 ward-elected members to 7
elected at large; conferring upon the superintendent the legal authority to hire, promote, and dismiss teachers; and protecting him with
life tenure. His use of the powers vested in him was judicious and
firm. It was later said that the Jones era saw one of the greatest
experiments in school administration, and its success in Cleveland
bore fruit in not less than a score of the greatest American cities.

His contacts with his teaching staffs were inspiring. At the time of
his resignation the people of Cleveland presented him with a black
leather chair and a loving cup. On the cup were inscribed these
words:

> Recognizing the services rendered the cause of public education by Lewis
> H. Jones, the people of Cleveland present this loving cup as a token of
> their personal esteem and appreciation.[2]

Jones came to the Normal at age 58. Less than a year earlier his
wife, Sarah Ellen Good, had died, leaving a 16-year old daughter,
Edith, to his care.

In Ypsilanti he purchased the spacious Samuel Post mansion, then
in rundown condition, which he repaired. Its gently sloping shaded
lawns stretched invitingly towards the campus; its hovering twin
Camperdown elms made intriguing contrast to the stately trees that

provided the setting. Edith, who in time became Mrs. Harry Shaefer and made her permanent residence in Ypsilanti, always felt that one of the reasons why her father was willing to leave his life-time position in Cleveland and come to this small community was his concern for her.

Before accepting the call to Ypsilanti, Jones laid down a strict condition. The authority to hire and dismiss faculty must be in the president, also the initiative in determining institutional policy. His intent on coming to Normal was to remain for ten years, then retire. He was hired for five, but when the five were up was re-employed for another five, and when those years were over he carried out his original intention, against the fervent protests of his faculty, students and alumni—and the State Board. Edwin A. Strong, revered head of the Physics Department who had been at Normal since 1885, commented in later years:

> Mr. Jones came to this school endowed with the greatest amount of power ever conferred upon any head of the institution. . . . no one ever used this power more sparingly, more justly or more graciously. This fixed policy gave us something upon which we could rely, and so the institution had rest after the turmoil of changing policies and administration.[3]

The ten years of the Jones administration at Normal were marked by a rapid increase in enrollments, with all the attendant problems of adequate facilities and staff, a reluctant and slow-moving State Legislature, further expansion of curricular offerings. Jones could scarcely have encountered a more difficult period from the standpoint of financial support, or a more enthusiastically receptive professional environment. At an interstate level he was active as a member of the North Central Council of State Normal School Presidents (an organization that later merged with the American Association of Teachers Colleges), serving as its president in 1911.

The problem with the legislature was out of a nature that quite justified the apprehension of the school in earlier years over the creation of more Normals in Michigan. The legislature was faced with the obligation to construct facilities and finance operations of two new normal schools when Jones arrived and, a year later, of a third, the Western State at Kalamazoo. In his first biennial report to the State Board, he noted that many of the departments were inadequately staffed, some classes numbering 60 to 70. He said:

The Legislature should . . . supply enough teachers so that no class in the institution should go beyond twenty-five of thirty members. It is a false economy in an institution of this kind to carry classes beyond that size.

He referred to the new science building that was under construction and complained that there had been considerable delay and the building was not yet under cover. He asked for ventilation for the main building, saying:

The ill effects of this condition are noticeable in the classes in the presence of headaches and in the lack of power to concentrate attention through the entire period of the recitation hour.

In 1906, he asked for an addition to the Training School building to relieve the cramped conditions that had developed there, and to give more room to the departments of Domestic Science and Art, and Manual Training (then housed in the basement). He asked for an auditorium that would hold 2,500 people and also provide rooms for the Conservatory of Music. As for the auditorium he said:

There are many things which can be taught to students only under the influence of that united fellowship which comes from seeing the entire school together in one body. Such an auditorium would simplify administration greatly by developing a sense of unity and responsibility among the students and increasing their love for the institution as a whole.

The legislature honored the request for enlargement of the Training School, and provided in niggardly manner for ventilation for the main building. As for the auditorium, authorization was given for drawing plans. Jones expanded his request here to include provision for a men's gymnasium under the auditorium, so that the present gymnasium could be given over entirely to the women. As for the structure, he urged (with a note of bitterness)

that this new building be made of some architectural value rather than a mere makeshift, as have heretofore been all the buildings erected on the campus. With the single exception of the little chapel which was the gift of Mrs. Starkweather . . . no building on the campus has been completed according to the plans or wishes of the educational authorities; but modifications have always been brought about on account of the small appropriations allowed by the legislature . . .

The report of the Board of Visitors for 1907, noting that more than 1,300 students were then in attendance, said: "The equipment, apparatus and books for illustrative purposes are entirely inadequate to the needs of the various departments of the school." They proceeded to ask also for a "central power, heating, lighting and ventilating plant, such as is found at the University at Ann Arbor."

Eight years after Jones' arrival at Ypsilanti he was still asking for the auditorium, and still complaining about inadequacy of staff and equipment. After mentioning the fact that members of the faculty and citizens of Ypsilanti had recently purchased 20 acres of land as a gift for the college, and had subscribed money for the improvement of the property so that it could be laid out for tennis, hockey, football and baseball, but with no bleachers or fencing, he stated:

> Appropriations for current expenses have been so meager for the college during the last few years that we have been obliged to purchase as few books as possible for our reference library. We are now far behind the times . . .[4]

At the same time the Board of Visitors carried on the tenor of complaint in some detail. They underlined the need for an auditorium, renovation of the main building, and enlarged facilities for physical education. The legislature made an appropriation for the auditorium, but it was vetoed by Governor Osborn.[5]

On the educational front the story was very different. One of the first matters that received attention was the relationship between the College and the high schools. With authorization by the State Board, Jones inaugurated what he termed "an important change of policy of a higher state institution toward the public high school." All graduates of four-year high schools who met certain standards would be admitted to Normal on the two-year (college grade) life certificate course without examination. All pupils from such high schools who had completed only two years of high school work would be admitted to the four-year (two preparatory and two college grade) life certificate course without examination. Students at Normal who failed to achieve a satisfactory standing in the first term could be either dropped from College or required to repeat the work, and in each case a report would be made back to the student's high school "to the end that superintendents and principals of high schools throughout the state may learn what our standard of requirement is and take measures to prevent pupils from coming to us without due preparation."[6]

With regard to curricular offerings, Jones gave immediate attention to expanding the work in domestic science and manual training. In 1904, he installed a course for rural school teachers. Encouragement and emphasis were given to the professional offerings in psychology, pedagogy, kindergarten, and the philosophy and history of education.

In 1903, the Legislature had been persuaded to vest sole certification authority with regard to graduates of the several normal schools in the State Board of Education, thus taking an important step in expanding the authority of the Board.[7] This aided the move to regularize and develop course programs.

In 1906, the summer school was enlarged by provision that its program should include the summer institute work of Washtenaw and the six adjoining counties. To enrich the summer's experience, a series of lectures was scheduled that brought national leaders in education to the campus, including John Dewey (of Columbia), George H. Palmer (of Harvard), Richard T. Wyche (of New York City), and Colonel C. H. French (of Miami). The enrollment jumped from about 600 in 1902 to more than 1,400 in 1906.

When Jones came to Normal in 1902 he found an exceptionally capable and relatively young staff awaiting him. One, Geographer Mark Jefferson, was to achieve an outstanding international reputation. Three had already achieved national stature (Frederic Pease in music, Benjamin L. D'Ooge in ancient languages, and William Hittell Sherzer in natural science), and five were to earn like distinction in the coming years (Wilbur Pardon Bowen in physical education, Charles Oliver Hoyt in pedagogy, Elmer Adelbert Lyman and John Charles Stone in mathematics, and Edwin A. Strong in the physical sciences). Besides these there were at least a dozen who had made or were to make a strong impression at the State level and contribute much to the spirit and tone of the institution.[8]

In raising the question as to how this came to be, proximity looms large in the answer. Strong came to Ypsilanti from Grand Rapids, Michigan, where he had been high school principal and Superintendent of Schools, D'Ooge was a gift from the Netherlands by way of Grand Rapids, his parents having emigrated from the village of Zonnemaire, Province of Zeeland. Both he and his brother, Martin Luther (older by 21 years), were trained at the University of Michigan. Sherzer married a Saginaw, Michigan, girl and served as high school principal both in Saginaw and Houghton. He, too, was a product of the University of Michigan. Bowen was born within 20 miles of Ypsilanti (at Lima, near Chelsea), was educated at the University of Michigan and taught physiology there for a short time. Hoyt graduated from Saline, Michigan, high school (ten miles from Ypsilanti) and from Albion College. He held administrative positions in public schools geographically nearly encircling Ypsilanti before being drawn to the epicenter. Lyman graduated from the University of Michigan and taught there for some years.

One might also assume that some already on the Normal staff may, by their contributions and growing reputations, have attracted others of outstanding caliber. Frederic Pease had drawn wide attention for his choral work and compositions, stamping the institution with the mark of superiority, by the time that any of those mentioned above arrived. Strong replaced Lewis McLouth, a man of exceptional competence in the physical sciences. David Eugene Smith, himself successor to a University of Michigan product, the outstanding Charles Bellows, left a challenging vacancy in mathematics for Lyman to fill. Sherzer could only be strongly impressed by the work in the biological sciences of that remarkable woman, Lucy Osband, and Jefferson could look upon his predecessor in geography, Charles T. McFarlane, with very high regard.

One cannot but speculate that the attraction which led Jones to accept the Ypsilanti offer may have been heightened by the promise of Normal's faculty.

During the period of his administration, Jones added to his staff names that were to become widely known: Clyde Ford in modern languages (1903) and Charles C. Colby in geography (1906). Others whom he brought to Normal lent great strength to the professional side of the College: Nathan Harvey in pedagogy (1904); H. Z. Wilber, pioneer in off-campus teaching (1908); Webster Pearce, mathematics, who became State Superintendent and college president (1909); and Charles M. Elliot, pioneer in the training of teachers for handicapped children (1910).

It would be stating the situation mildly to say that Jones commanded the respect and whole-hearted cooperation of his faculty. In his written notices to them he frequently signed himself "Respectfully, L. H. Jones, President." They responded to his leadership with enthusiasm, and in their personal relationships developed a strong

affection for him. Midway in his years at Ypsilanti he reported to
the State Board his feeling about the faculty:

> At no time during my administration of the State Normal College have
> the internal affairs of the institution been in a more satisfactory condition
> than they have been during the year just closed. The unity of purpose,
> enthusiasm in the work of training teachers, thorough devotion to even the
> details of work required—all these qualities of successful teaching have
> been signally illustrated in the work of the various members of the facul-
> ty.[9]

Two years later the Board of Visitors, in its report, noted the tone
and atmosphere of the school in these words:

> An uplifting atmosphere pervades the entire institution. One cannot but
> be greatly impressed with the spirit of unity and harmony existing
> between President Jones, his able and efficient faculty, and the student
> body.

A close relationship between faculty and students is one of the
great merits of a smaller college. At Normal, the president could
generally be included. Jones made a particularly lasting impression
on the students. The chapel hour, for instance, though attendance
was not required, became a strong attraction. "Through the stimulating influence of President Jones," said the college annual, "the
hour has become the nucleus about which all the student life seems
to center."[10]

Clarke Davis, loyal and active alumnus throughout the years,
recipient of the Distinguished Alumni Award, and one-time president of the Alumni Association, has given this account of his first
contact with Jones:

> One week before college opened I came to the campus and, not knowing
> any better, I made my first call upon the man to whom I had been writing
> —namely, President Jones. He treated me cordially and courteously,
> received me at his home, took me to his office, and walked over some of
> the city streets to show me rooming houses and boarding houses. Little did
> I realize that I was imposing on his time and that not all freshmen entered
> college in this manner.[11]

A year before his retirement, Jones bought some acres on the far
side of the Huron River (in whose valley Eastern lies), bounded on

the west by the river and on the northeast by a tributary stream. Here he built a rustic summer cottage with a fieldstone fireplace, and planted his favorite trees and shrubs and flowers. Until the ruthless invasion of apartment house owners, mute reminders of his stay were the hedge of black locust trees; the wild plum, red-bud, lilacs, syringa and honeysuckle growing along the drives; the bridge (student-built) over the creek; the great bed of lilies of the valley. He called it Riverbrink,[12] and shared it generously in the years of life that were left to him. Students strolling by on a chilly Sunday afternoon in the fall would be hailed in for a cup of tea before the fire.[13] Here he would retire for meditation and reading, and quiet conversation with colleagues and friends.

At the fall gathering of the Alumni Association, in the year of his retirement, Jones gave a short farewell talk in which he said:

> I have been assisted by what seems to me to be the best and most loyal faculty I have ever known. I have been supported by a loyal band of graduates of this institution . . . Of course I cannot but admit some of my visions have failed and many of my dreams are not yet actualized. There have been some short-sighted policies of legislators and state officers who ought to have known better and could have known better, but who had other interests to serve which seemed at the time dominant. So we have been compelled to wait for some things, but I am more than ever convinced that our day has now come, that the sentiment has now changed with respect to the financial support of the institution . . . It would be impossible to return adequate thanks to the students of this institution and the alumni who have so magnificently supported us in our efforts.

The five short years left to him after retirement were spent in Ypsilanti. In community activities he helped to write a new city charter and was active in the matter of improving county roads. He collaborated in writing the creed for the local Congregational church and opened Riverbrink to the public. He was at home to his friends on a portion of every pleasant day.

When reflecting on the past, he had much to remember. In addition to his work as administrator he had done some publishing of practical books for the teacher—a set of readers for the grades, a book on "Education as Growth."[14] He had been the recipient of four honorary degrees. He had founded for Normal an educational periodical, *The Western Journal of Education,* later changed to *The American Schoolmaster* and to continue publication until 1933 when the stringencies of the Great Depression forced its abandonment. To initiate this project, he had contributed generously from his own pocket.[15]

Upon his death (at the home of his daughter) in Ypsilanti in 1917, Edwin Strong, filling the front page of the college paper with review of his life, commented: "Few events of recent years have moved the whole community so deeply."

The administration of Lewis H. Jones was undisturbed either by invention or innovation. Rather, it was a time of expansion and constructive support for trends and purposes already in motion. He was unfortunate in his appeals to the legislature; fortunate in falling heir to a faculty of great promise, stimulated by the newly-acquired status of College. The College was most fortunate in a president who recognized and placed supreme value on this fact, and possessed the personality and judgment that could lead towards fulfillment.[16]

CHAPTER SEVENTEEN

CHARLES MCKENNY

1912–1933

I could not bend the bow Ulysses bore
Nor pose King Arthur's mighty blade . . .
And yet my soul will thrill at noble deeds,
And I may light my lamp at heavenly fire.
—Charles McKenny

This bit of poetic fancy does only partial justice to its author. In the league to which he belonged he bent a strong bow and wielded a heavy sword. But it does reveal an important side of Charles McKenny. Normal was fortunate indeed in securing the services of a man who would carry on for a score of years the spirit of his predecessor—a spirit now to be illumined by the inspiration and insight of the poet.

For the first time in her history Michigan Normal was placed in the charge of a native son. McKenny was born in a log cabin on a farm near Dimondale. He earned a bachelor of science degree at the Michigan Agricultural College, and at Olivet (Michigan) earned both the bachelor of arts and the master of arts degrees. His career was that of the teacher and educational administrator at both the public school and college levels. In the former, he taught for a time in the Charlotte schools, then became principal of the Vermontville high school. At the higher level he was professor of English and History at Olivet College until the State Board took him to head its newly-acquired Central Normal School at Mt. Pleasant. Four years later, he left to accept the presidency of Wisconsin State Normal at Milwaukee. In 1912, the Michigan Board brought him back to preside at Ypsilanti.

He returned to Michigan to guide the destinies of Normal not

169

only over a lengthy period (the longest, to date, of any of Normal's presiding officers) but through years that witnessed events which changed the very character of America—war, post-war, devastating depression. He came to Normal at age 52, vigorous, eager, experienced in college administration, with clear ideas as to Normal's needs. He was inaugurated in a large tent, erected on the north side of the campus. When he retired, at age 73, he was tired, ill, and inclined to be despondent, yet he had ample reason for satisfaction in what he had been able to accomplish, and in the expressions of respect and gratitude from those for whom Normal had deep meaning.

The first problem that he tackled was that of the physical campus. In his first report to the State Board, made within a few months after taking office, he boldly asked for a college hospital ("health cottage"), a building to house the Domestic Science Department, a men's gymnasium, an addition to the library, and an auditorium which would also house the Conservatory of Music. He described the existing plant as run-down, pointing especially to the gymnasium:

> During the twenty-five years the floors have become broken and have been repeatedly patched, as have also the linings of the pools. The pine partitions of the showers have rotted, and most of the showers are out of commission.[1]

His appeal led some 25 or 30 legislators to visit the campus the next year. But he followed this up with a novel request. He did not ask for an all-out, immediate appropriation for everything, but rather for a commitment of $100,000 a year for the next seven years. The legislature granted his request.

The local paper records the enthusiastic response in Ypsilanti to the news of the legislature's action:

> Whistles and bells will announce the gathering of Normal students and citizens in the natural amphitheater at Owen's field to celebrate the recent million dollar appropriations granted to the college by the legislature.[2]

There would be music by the college band, and speeches by the local legislators, President McKenny, President-emeritus Jones, outstanding members of the faculty, including Lathers, Strong, Ford, Barbour, Julia Anne King, and student leaders.

The outcome was a men's gymnasium (as an addition to the existing gymnasium; completed in 1913); a nursery ("plant house") for work in the natural sciences, a health cottage (1914); the auditorium-conservatory that President Jones had repeatedly requested, but smaller (1914); a building intended for domestic science but devoted instead to industrial arts, art, and administrative offices and known as the Administration Building (constructed on the site of the old Conservatory building) (1914); and the renovation of the old gymnasium (1916).

In later years, but not directly related to the program, several other notable projects were accomplished—the rural consolidated Lincoln School (1924); and the alumni-student-faculty social center, McKenny Hall, financed by private contribution (1931).

In 1927, McKenny inaugurated a second building program, this one to extend for six years. His approach to the legislature this time was based on a comparative showing of legislative favor for the other State institutions of higher education, in which Normal stood next to the lowest. One building only was constructed under this program, the library (1929). The Great Depression had struck, and an ambitious but much-needed building program became a casualty.

However, with the sole exception of the Elementary Training School building, this program, expanded and modified to meet the needs of a growing institution, provided the pattern for the building achievements of the next two administrations (the 35 years of Presidents Munson and Elliott).

It is reported that McKenny had one other thought for his campus, an air strip and a plane to carry faculty and athletic teams on their several more distant missions.

Nothing was more evident of the values held by McKenny than his belief in the greatness and high importance of the role of the teacher. This belief had the quality of a religious faith, and shone in his numerous addresses before professional groups, in his enthusiasm for his work, and in things that he did to promote and inspire better teaching.

"As a stream cannot rise higher than its source," he said, "so no educational system can rise higher than the character and qualification of its teachers."[3]

The critical importance he attached to public education is perhaps most pointedly shown in his comment, prompted by the Great War that occurred during his administration:

> War is no longer a contest between men on the battlefield but a struggle between the inventive, constructive, administrative, and moral capacities and forces of nations. Victory will finally come to the side in which these capacities and forces are strongest, and while it is not so evident it is just as certain that peaceful contests between nations for leadership in the world will be determined by the same factors. The world will appreciate education and schools as it has never appreciated them before and the nations after this war will make one of their first considerations the reconstruction, where necessary, and up-building everywhere of public education.

It took another great war, and the launching of the first Sputnik to demonstrate the full force of this prophecy.

His attention to the character, quality, and growth of the teacher was noteworthy. Two years before coming to Normal he had published a small book titled "The Personality of the Teacher," the outgrowth of a lecture that had proved popular at many a teachers institute. In it he discussed such topics as the tone of the school, sympathy, sincerity, good breeding, growth in personality, the joy of living.

"Its matter," he explained, "is old; so is the multiplication table. But there are always the young among us to whom the common wisdom of the world is new."

To provide stimulus, inspiration, and direction for his school and its alumni and the teaching profession in Michigan, McKenny initiated the Mid-Year Conference, bringing speakers of national importance and providing opportunity for intimate group discussions in departmental programs. The occasion for the first such conference was the cancellation of the annual meeting of the State Teachers Association and most of the Institute dates in 1918 because of the devastating influenza epidemic of that year. The response was so enthusiastic that the Mid-Year Conference became a tradition. It was held for 15 consecutive years, beginning with January, 1919. Its final program took place in the year of McKenny's death.

The pattern was simple—two days (Friday and Saturday), three or four main speakers of national repute, and discussion groups organized by the several departments of instruction. The invitation was broad—to teachers and educators throughout the State. The attendance was consistently large, taxing railroad and street car transportation and hotel facilities beyond their capacities. Along the way, the Conference became a convenient occasion for special observances—the dedication of the Lincoln Laboratory School in 1924, of the Roosevelt Laboratory School in 1925, Normal's Seventy-Fifth Anniversary in 1927, the laying of the cornerstone of the Union building (McKenny Hall) in 1931.

Speakers were brought from far and near, and included such names as Dean William C. Bagley, Teachers College, Columbia; Vihljalmar Stefansson, arctic explorer; Charles H. Judd, head of the Department of Education of the University of Chicago; John Grier Hibben, president-emeritus of Princeton University, and such outstanding Normal alumni as Charles E. St. John ('76), astronomer at the Mt. Wilson Observatory in California; William McAndrew ('81), superintendent of the Chicago schools; Stratton D. Brooks ('90, '92), president of the University of Missouri; Isaiah Bowman ('02), president of the American Geographic Society; Dean Benjamin F. Pittinger ('06) of the University of Texas.[4] For two decades after their demise these meetings, often referred to as the Midwinter Conference, were recalled wistfully by the faculty.

As with Lewis Jones, his predecessor, McKenny held his faculty in high regard. In one of his first reports to the State Board, he commented:

> Before coming to the Normal College I frequently heard it remarked by educators that in respect of the scholarship and productive activity of its faculty, and the general character of its courses, the Michigan State Normal College was unsurpassed by any institution of its kind in the United States . . . On coming to know the faculty and institution as only the executive head can know them, I am pleased to say that it is my conviction that the reputation of the College is well merited.[5]

His concept of what made a good faculty member in a teachers college included the belief that he should have had some teaching experience in the public school, for "no man can function as he should who does not know the public school problem." At another time he exclaimed that the president of a teachers college would give much to be assured of a teaching staff with scholarship, teaching insight, stimulating personalities "and the divine gift of being ever young in heart."

In working with the faculty the President at first operated through an administrative council which had been in informal existence since 1880, and informally recognized since 1902. During the administration of President Jones this body had tended to lose its distinctive character of department head membership by including all members of the faculty of the rank of associate professor or higher. This trend continued under McKenny until, by 1915, it had lost all character and included all members of the faculty above the rank of instructor (and there were very few indeed of the latter). At this point the faculty in organized form seems to have faded from view. The President looked formally to his administrative staff for counsel and recommendation, informally to individual heads of departments.

Several whom McKenny added to his staff made important contributions to the life and tone and intellectual standards of the college. Such, for example, were Dean of Women Lydia Jones; outstanding classroom teachers Ruth Barnes (Children's Literature); Jennings Hickman (Natural Sciences), and Carl Pray (American History); Gerald Sanders (widely-known for his textbooks on literature and English composition); and scholar of international repute Charles Frederick Harrold (Carlyle and Newman).

In general, McKenny's relation to his staff was comradely rather than authoritarian. He expressed his sense of fellow-feeling in a poem entitled "The Sabbatical." It read in part as follows:

> I've studied and lectured and quizzed
> Read blue books till I was blue
> But now I'll junk my work for awhile
> As a wise man ought to do.
> I'll leave this terrible clime
> Of winter and rain and snow
> And go for a rest to the golden west
> Where the roses forever blow . . .
> Like the Lotus Eaters of old
> I'll dream of the ghostly past
> Till a western quake shall shake me awake
> To the rude old world at last.[6]

McKenny had a close feeling for students. Professor D'Ooge, commenting on this aspect of the man at the time of his death, spoke of "his love for young people, his sympathy for them and his ability to understand their problems."

"This was largely due," D'Ooge continued, "to his own extraordinary youthfulness which he maintained to the end of his life. He . . . loved all kinds of sports and was no mean contender himself.

Less than a year ago I saw him play a hot game of tennis. On the golf links, too, he made an excellent score. Needless to say he was present at every athletic event on our campus and the boys and girls felt that he was with them in their struggles."

He felt also a deep concern for transforming them into teachers who would be not only capable but acceptable to a conservative midwestern public. In his first report to the State Board, he revealed a lively interest in both the health of the students and the regulating of their conduct.

He sought to aid the Dean of Women in the discharge of her responsibilities. He secured the services of a trained nurse, and created a Women's Council to advise the Dean on housing and social problems. The trained nurse idea proved to be the germ of the present-day health service for students. The Council was composed of members of the faculty and representative women from the city. Rules governing rooming houses were drawn up and published in the college catalog. They appear to have been satisfactorily effective with one major exception, the rule against smoking.

In the spring of 1922, a rumor appeared in the newspapers that seventeen coeds had been dismissed from college for smoking. A furor of national proportions ensued, and before it was over the Governor of the State, the State Board of Education, the State Superintendent of Public Instruction, and even the courts became involved. Actually, the number of girls dismissed for smoking was only four. But one of the four (Alice Tanton) sued in the Washtenaw Circuit Court asking for a writ of mandamus to compel the Normal to readmit her. Failing here, she appealed to the Michigan Supreme Court, where again her request was denied. A unanimous Court said:

> As is well known, the Michigan State Normal College is maintained at the expense of the taxpayers to prepare teachers for our public schools . . . Inherently, the managing officers have the power to maintain such discipline as will effectuate the purposes of the institution . . . Mrs. Priddy (Dean of Women) . . . should be commended for upholding some old-fashioned ideals of young womanhood.[7]

McKenny fully supported the dismissals, basing his position on the public attitude toward teachers. The College, he said,

believes that few, if any, school boards in Michigan would elect to a teaching position a woman who smoked. Since the college is to furnish teachers
to meet the standards of Michigan, it has taken the position that girls who
smoke are not suitable candidates and consequently should not remain in
college.[8]

McKenny did not misinterpret the attitude of the times. Resolution of support came from student, teacher, and women's organizations. The State Board upheld him. Nine years later this ghostly
problem was to rise again, prompted by the formulating of regulations for use of the new Union building. This time a nation-wide
reaction submitted the President to both praise and ridicule, the latter spurring him to defend his position in the *Baltimore Sun*. In the
course of his statement he said: "I suppose that, second to the
United States Senate, I am just now the biggest joke in America.
The newspaper boys are having a lot of fun with me . . ."[9]

Fortunately for McKenny, and the College that he served, his
devotion to the teaching profession and his deep feeling of responsibility were mellowed by the vision of the poet and lighted by a sense
of humor. One of the perennial problems that came to his desk,
occasioned by his own insistence on clarifying and then enforcing
housing regulations for women, was the Matron's Association of
Ypsilanti. His presence at one of the meetings of this Association
was reported in the local paper as follows:

> Whether or not the President of Michigan State Normal College winked
> at someone in the audience while a matron was explaining her position in
> the organization, is a new issue today in the controversy between the
> Matron's Association and College Administration. The President is in
> Detroit, so there is no official word available as to whether the alleged
> wink was really a wink or just a blink, and no other member of the facul-
> ty, or other person present at the meeting, has been found who wishes to
> assume responsibility for explaining the president's action or state of
> mind.[10]

McKenny was equally solicitous to keep the cost of a college education as low as possible. Noting that in large part the students who
aspired to be teachers came from the homes of the common people
and the great need of the State for their services, he placed heavy
emphasis on the importance of low-cost education. He pointed out

that the cost of an education at the Normal School was about 60 per cent of that at a university.

In the first year of his administration McKenny initiated a health service for women, and a program of off-campus instruction. As to the former, he pointed out to the State Board:

> Ypsilanti has no hospital. With relatively few exceptions, students room two in a room or two in a suite of rooms. The sickness of a student consequently means discomfort and perhaps danger to her roommate . . . Should a contagious disease break out among the students, the situation would be serious. The college should follow the custom of the better class of educational institutions and have a health cottage or hospital under its own control.

Step by step the goal was reached, first a trained nurse, then a room for headquarters, then a residence equipped as a "Health Cottage" and the service of interns from the Medical School of the University of Michigan, then (by 1917) a full-time physician to serve as Director of the Health Service.

As for off-campus instruction, time and patience were again required. McKenny requested a special appropriation for this work, saying: "Not only is it necessary to train teachers for their profession, but it is necessary to keep them growing after they enter the profession." His plea was not granted. But the work was continued as a self-liquidating proposition, and in 1921 an Extension Department was organized which rapidly expanded off-campus services.

In 1914, preparation of teachers for handicapped children was undertaken in a tentative manner. Professor Charles Elliot of the Normal Education staff, working with Professor Walter Scott Berry of the Education Department of the University of Michigan, received encouragement to try out a program in the summer session of that year. The program was transferred to the Detroit Teachers College for a time; then, in 1923, brought back to Normal's campus and organized as a separate Department of Special Education.

In 1924, a project to consolidate 13 rural school districts south of Ypsilanti, initiated by Marvin S. Pittman, head of the Rural Education Department, was consummated with completion of the Lincoln Consolidated School, which would also be used as a laboratory school for practice teaching by Normal.

In 1925, a campus laboratory school, Roosevelt High School, was completed. This building was planned to increase the capacity of the

Training School and to provide a suitable facility for the conduct of a relatively new concept in school organization, the junior high school.

McKenny had begun a campaign for a separate building for the high school in 1914. Two years later he revived the question, noting that the appearance of the high school in American public education had brought great changes and that the Normal must now prepare teachers not only for the common schools but also for the rapidly increasing number of high schools. He persisted in spite of the fact that a world war was in progress. After the war was over he pressed for acquisition of a site, which involved condemnation proceedings. And by 1925 the building stood ready for occupancy.

Use of the Roosevelt School did, however, cause a major headache. Once the war was over, student enrollments increased greatly and by 1926 had reached a high that would stand for many years. Space again was at a premium on the Normal campus, and to meet the threatening emergency it was proposed that the elementary training school be moved to the Roosevelt School building. To do this, McKenny advocated the abandonment of the senior high school, arguing that practice teaching could be provided adequately by the Lincoln Consolidated School. At once he was met by violent protest from Ypsilanti citizens whose children had attended or were attending Roosevelt. McKenny and the State Board capitulated.

A proud institution whose true status had been ignored, with a line of presidents of national stature, turned its attention to the national scene. Boone had been active with the National Education Association before coming to Ypsilanti and continued to play a role there; Jones had continued this relationship, and McKenny, working with a group of mid-west presidents of normal schools that had become colleges, was a pioneer in helping to establish an organization of teachers colleges that was national in scope. The story in brief is as follows:

Upon the initiative of President Homer H. Seerley of Iowa State Teachers College, five presidents of four-year degree-granting teachers colleges in the mid-west met informally in Chicago early in 1917. McKenny was present. Arrangement was made for a session to be held in February in Kansas City. This proved to be the first regular session of the American Association of Teachers Colleges. Two officers were elected at this session, a president and a secretary.

McKenny was elected president. At the second annual session, held at Atlantic City (1918), he was reelected. He was very active in this organization over a period of years. As chairman of its committee on a national educational honor society, he recommended that the existing society of Kappa Delta Pi[11] be recognized and approved by the AATC. In 1920, he served on a committee to investigate the possibility of acceptance of teachers colleges by the Association of Collegiate Alumnae on their approved lists. The report of this committee included an interesting assertion:

> This question (of recognition by the Alumnae Association) is of the same character as that of the admission of Teachers College Graduates to the graduate schools of the universities of this country . . . The Teachers Colleges do as good work, to say the least, in their four years' courses as the standard colleges and universities do in their four years' courses, and there is no good reason why their four-year graduates should not have the same recognition that is accorded the four-year graduates of standard colleges.

It should be noted in passing that this organization, under its later name of American Association of University Women, broke its taboo in 1930 by approving the Albany State Teachers' College of New York State. On May 25, 1933, at the Minneapolis meeting, the Michigan State Normal College was also approved.

When, in 1920, the AATC decided to become a member of the American Council on Education, McKenny was named chairman of the delegation to that important body. He served on the committee to investigate the question of amalgamation with another organization—the National Council of Normal School Presidents and Principals, whose report resulted ultimately in that body's decision to merge itself with the AATC. In 1922, as chairman of a committee on teachers colleges of the National Council of Education he presented a detailed and influential report on the scope of the teachers college movement in America and the standards therein. One of the recommendations of this report was that the teachers colleges "should address themselves to the task of standardization." Another asserted that the state legislatures, having created these colleges, should back them up financially.

For six years McKenny was chairman of the AATC's Committee on Accrediting and Classification of Teachers Colleges, concerned with the very heart of the Association's function. The work of this committee resulted in the adoption by the Association in 1926 of a basic statement of Standards for Accrediting Teachers Colleges.

The importance and influence of the AATC grew rapidly, and in 1925 it combined with the National Education Association as the Department of Teachers Colleges. In 1948, it achieved its ultimate triumph over the ancient prejudice held by universities towards teacher training institutions by reorganizing to include schools and colleges of education connected with universities. Appropriately, it modified its name to that of American Association of Colleges of Teacher Education.

It should be noted that long before the founding of the American Association of Teachers Colleges, McKenny had been an active participant in the National Society for the Scientific Study of Education. In 1908, he succeeded Stratton D. Brooks as president of this Society and was reelected for the year 1909–1910. He served on the executive committee from 1912 to 1914. During his terms as president, yearbooks were published on the Co-ordination of the Kindergarten and the Elementary School, Education with Reference to Sex, and Health Education.[12]

Charles McKenny possessed to an outstanding degree two characteristics that were noteworthy also in his immediate predecessor—a strong feeling for the responsibilities of the teacher and a warm human sympathy which extended both to colleagues and students. He was particularly gifted in ability to work with people at all levels, including the legislative. His was a spirit of fellowship, and to this was added a love of the aesthetic aspect of life, including the natural world of flowers and trees and birds, the endless variations of mood of sun and mist, of calm and storm, of the "crystalline beauty of the snow."

If, as an administrator, he possessed a weakness, it was the vice inherent in the virtue—a reluctance to exercise the authority that was vested in him.

The range of his interests was broad. His activities at the national level gave him valuable perspective on his own immediate area of concern. He once commented: "The great danger with normal schools is the tendency to live within themselves, and to measure themselves by themselves rather than by social conditions in the state at large."

He looked upon his own institution as strictly professional in character, pointing out that every student who entered Normal must sign a declaration that it was his intention to teach in the public schools of Michigan. In consequence, he held that Normal was in no sense in competition with any institution doing the traditional college work.[13]

He served as president of the Michigan Schoolmasters Club in 1920, was a president of the Michigan Authors Association and, as a citizen of Ypsilanti, helped organize the local Chamber of Commerce (and served as its first president). His death in September, 1933, caused widespread mourning. The resolution passed by the State Board of Education was more than a formality:

> The State Board valued most highly his counsel and advice. On every issue the Board looked eagerly to him for his opinion, and his attitude on educational matters was always sane, progressive, and constructive . . . President McKenny was a natural leader and a man of great initiative. He was a national figure in the educational world and in every association to which he belonged and in every enterprise he undertook he forged rapidly to the front and assumed a commanding position. Michigan was proud of President McKenny's prestige.

CHAPTER EIGHTEEN

JOHN MAURICE MUNSON

1933–1948

"Michigan is a great State, But neither because it is large nor rich is Michigan a great State. What then makes Michigan great? I will tell you . . . I see boys and girls ten hundred thousand of them, all different, all aspiring, all good. It is they that make Michigan great."

J. M.

The administration of John Munson was in stark contrast to that of Charles McKenny. At its inception the Great Depression was casting its rapidly darkening shadow over the land. The McKenny era saw a great war—but war provides a motive and stimulus, a reason accepted for self-denial, disappointment, suffering. What can one say, however, for a depression, whose destructiveness, material and moral, is more widespread than war, and for which there is no glorious purpose to be served? But the Munson era saw war, too, larger, far more destructive than the earlier war, far more demanding on the life of the College; and, in its closing years, the sudden overwhelming flood of returning veterans of that war.

John Munson's father fled from Sweden and came to America to escape the thralldom of a landlord who demanded implicit obedience from those who lived and worked on his estate. A letter from an older brother, Oliver, who was born in Sweden, describes the situation vividly:

Father's people lived in poverty under a tyrant landlord who was not satisfied because father hired a man to do the work for him. (Father was attempting to supplement his income by building up a business in herring) . . . One day father was out chopping wood when he shouted that Pino (the landlord) was coming and that he would split his head with an ax.

Mother took father's arm and led him into the house, put him in a bed covering him up, strictly forbidding him to enter into any dispute with Pino who was a three hundred pound giant with a long beard.[1]

Munson was born in Kane, Pennsylvania, where his father, after a few years, had brought some land and re-united his family. At age 13 he left home, joining the throngs who sought escape from the growing financial panic which reached its climax in 1893. He went to Michigan's Upper Peninsula where he worked as millhand and lumberjack on the Menominee River, printer and night school student, farmhand, and finally, teacher in the country and village schools. Munson explained how he came to be a teacher:

I came to Michigan in the early nineties. Shortly thereafter we had in this land what was known as hard times. The pinch of the city drove me to the woods. One day the other fellow on the cross-cut saw, a district school teacher, and an original ferrisinstitooter, said to me as we paused to drive the wedge: "Why don't you study up evenings and go with me to the teachers' examination in the spring? You don't want to stay in the woods all your life? And that is how, on the 19th of April in ninety-five, I passed the examination and was called to teach.

Learning of Ferris Institute at Big Rapids, Michigan, where one could prepare for college, he enrolled. It was here that he attracted the attention and admiration of the founder and head of the Institute, W. N. Ferris (later to be Governor of Michigan), and formed a close and lasting friendship with a fellow-student, Isaiah Bowman (later to become one of the world's most eminent geographers, and President of Johns Hopkins University).

From this humble beginning, Munson served successively as teacher in the public schools;[2] superintendent of schools;[3] Deputy Superintendent of Public Instruction for six years (appointed by Governor Ferris); Director of the Training School of the Central Michigan State Normal at Mount Pleasant (1919–1923); and President of the Northern Michigan State Normal School at Marquette (1923–1933). From this position he came to Ypsilanti.

Along the way he acquired a college education. A student at Michigan State Normal College (roommate, Isaiah Bowman), he received the BA degree in 1903. While superintendent of schools at Harbor Springs, with the aid of correspondence courses, he met the requirements for the PhB degree at the University of Chicago in 1911.

The high regard and strong support of Governor Ferris are noteworthy throughout these years. In 1931, in connection with Munson's unsuccessful candidacy on the Democratic ticket for State Superintendent of Public Instruction, Ferris wrote him:

> I suppose I am responsible for your nomination. You can rest assured that I am not ashamed of it. You are one of the men I have always admired and whether you are elected Superintendent of Public Instruction or not, I shall have no regret that I did what I thought was my duty. Sooner or later the better ways in politics are going to win.[4]

When the opening occurred at Marquette, Ferris wrote again:

> I have just learned that a President must be chosen for the Northern State Normal School. You are the man for that job. I am not at all sure that I will be able to accomplish anything, but I can have the very great pleasure of trying to accomplish something.[5]

The State Board of Education on May 8, 1933, named John Maurice Munson president of Michigan State Normal College, effective July 1. This was simply a transfer of one of its presidents, who had made an excellent record, from the smallest to the largest of the four State Teachers Colleges. Munson served in Ypsilanti for 15 years.

Munson's conservative approach to education was well indicated in a letter that he wrote to a fellow educator at about this time:

> I have said many times that we have been doing business educationally for several decades on the foundations laid by Angel, Pattengill, and Ferris. These men were the top-notchers in building up real educational sentiment. I believe that the modern quantitative movement in education has its place and is of value, but we still need some of the old-fashioned kind.[6]

At the State level, Munson's influence was broad and significant both as to State Board policy in meeting problems generated by the Great Depression, and on the curriculum of the four teachers colleges.

The appalling destructiveness of the Depression was felt deeply by the teaching profession in Michigan. In October, 1933, the State

Board called a conference of leading educators to consider constructive steps that might be taken. The conference adopted the following resolution:

> *Whereas,* we are facing the greatest crisis in the world's history and
>
> *Whereas,* education is a major means by which people can be brought to a realization of their responsibility in relieving the situation and preventing its recurrence and
>
> *Whereas,* to accomplish such results we need at all times highly capable and well trained teachers, to the end that the children of our commonwealth shall be assured a sound and dependable education (under the direction of the highest type of citizens possible to secure) which will perpetuate the ideals of citizenship and society in keeping with the ideals of our state and federal constitutional governments:
>
> *Therefore Be It Resolved:*
> 1. That the State Board of Education create an extra legal Planning Commission whose function shall be to act in an advisory capacity to the State Board in reference to teacher training problems.
> 2. That the certification of all teachers in the State be the exclusive responsibility of the State Board of Education.[7]

Within two days the State Board took action to implement the resolution as far as it could and passed another stating that it would undertake "*at once* the development of a uniform state program for the certification of teachers and for standards of training." It proceeded to set up an Extra-Legal Advisory Planning Commission, to be composed of representatives of the University of Michigan School of Education, Michigan State College, the teachers colleges, the Association of Private Colleges, municipal colleges, Catholic colleges, a superintendent of schools, and a county commissioner of schools. Munson was named to represent the teachers colleges.[8] The work of the Commission proved to be of outstanding and lasting importance to Michigan education. Munson's contributions consisted of a joint report with E. L. Austin of Michigan State College on the current supply and demand of teachers, especially in the elementary school ("The Present Teacher Employment Situation") and his report as chairman of a committee on teacher training ("Tentative Proposals for a State Program of Teacher Training").[9] The former, presented in April, 1934, called for a study which Munson himself undertook and published the following year, with important consequences.

The teacher training report contained proposals that, in time, became important in the Michigan pattern. They not only influenced the Certification Code, but also the teachers colleges in restating their curricular and degree requirements. Among these proposals, as embodied in the final report of the Extra-Legal Planning Commission, were some that would soon be implemented in a uniform Certification Code for the State (1936), and others that would ultimately appear in the new State Constitution, adopted some 30 years later (1963).

Recommendations adopted in the Certification Code were that four years of college work be required for a provisional certificate, five years for the permanent certificate at all levels of teaching in the public schools; and that there be strong emphasis on academic preparation. The statement on academic preparation read as follows:

> The preliminary years of college training . . . should be devoted to basic training concerned with the widening and deepening of cultural interests and with the control of subject matter. The basic courses . . . should emphasize fundamental principles in social, political, and economic fields. Pedagogical considerations should be delayed as late as may be feasible in each curriculum.

Recommendations incorporated in the Michigan Constitution of 1963 were that the State Superintendent of Public Instruction should be appointed by the State Board of Education, that the State Board should be a non-partisan body, and that there should be a state educational planning commission representing the several levels of the teaching professional as well as the employing authorities.

The legislature acted in 1935 to place sole authority for the certification of teachers in the State Board.[10] This placed on the Board the necessity for developing certification policies and procedures. It referred this problem to the Extra-Legal Advisory Planning Commission. The Commission, its basic policies resting on the recommendations of the above-mentioned report, proceeded to write a Certification Code for Michigan teachers.

Meanwhile, the heads of the teachers colleges had proceeded to draw up a recommendation affecting degree requirements and definations. In late 1933, the Normal Executive Council (composed of the four presidents) had authorized Munson and Paul Sangren,

Dean of Administration at Western State Teachers College, to draft a statement that might be included in identical form in the yearbooks of the four colleges. The resulting report, presented by Munson in 1934, was adopted verbatim by the Board, which took the occasion to add a statement that henceforth the teachers colleges would permit students to graduate with a degree only. Up to this time, the official requirement was that, to be granted a degree, a student must meet the requirements for a teachers certificate. This liberalization was particularly pertinent in a time when young people, unemployed, were making the decision to use their time by furthering their education.

The statement as adopted by the Board was faithfully reproduced in the yearbooks of the four Normals for more than twenty years; its essential elements are still basic policy. It included an extended statement of Purpose and Control which placed explicit emphasis on the fundamental importance of the liberal arts. A section was devoted to a grouping, under seven heads, of all subjects taught, accompanied by a statement of minimum requirements for all students, regardless of curriculum followed, which would insure a broad exposure to the liberal arts.[11] It also sharpened the distinction between the BA and the BS degrees.

The Munson study on the supply and demand of teachers was prompted by the publication in 1933 of a "Report of the Committee on Teacher Training," published by the Michigan Education Association and sponsored by the Michigan Conference of City Superintendents. This report purported to show a large oversupply of teachers in Michigan. The conclusion had a vicious effect in that it gave the Legislature an excuse for providing niggardly support for the teachers colleges, and even persuaded Governor William A. Comstock to propose, in the interest of economy, the closing of two of the four teacher training colleges. Furthermore, it discouraged young people from enrolling to become teachers.

Munson, writing to the Extra-Legal Planning Commission, called for a study to ascertain "the complete and accurate facts." He then went on to say that in its conclusion as to the number of new teachers produced in the year 1931–32, the report made an "overstatement" as to the teachers colleges of 137 per cent, and a similar overstatement as to the other teacher training institutions.

In the detailed, scholarly report that he presented the following year, replete with statistics and charts, Munson made a distinction between teachers who were "available and satisfactory" and those simply classed as teachers,[12] and showed that at all levels and in all specialized categories there would be a demand for every new teacher in 1935.

As mentioned above, the Governor was persuaded to recommend that two of the teachers colleges be closed as an economy. He did this in early January, 1935. The Senate thereupon appointed an investigating committee. Munson appeared at the hearing and was able to present a detailed and convincing report on the colleges. The committee voted unanimously to oppose the closing and the Senate unanimously adopted the report.

The chairman of this committee was Frank R. Mosier. In a letter to Munson on the occasion of the latter's retirement, he commented:

> . . . The way in which you stood up under the insinuating manner and grilling attack a certain Senator made upon you in the hearing on the investigation of closing a Normal College . . . I remember the unusual demonstration you gave as an educator in responding to the Senator's tirade in such a way that the committee voted to maintain the same Normal School . . . I am convinced, that had you not appeared before our committee, our college situation in Michigan would have been quite different.[13]

In 1938, the Extra-Legal Planning Commission recommended to the State Board that it approach the University of Michigan with a request that they appoint a committee to confer with the Board on the possibility of establishing a joint program of graduate work with the teachers colleges. Such a program, leading to a master's degree in education, to be conferred by the University of Michigan, was agreed upon. One consequence of this arrangement occurred the following year when the calendar of the teachers colleges was changed from the quarter plan, which had prevailed since 1899, to the two-semester plan because the U-M operated on this system.[14]

John Munson was in his mid-fifties when he arrived as Normal's President. He had presided over a much smaller institution at Marquette. His experience as Deputy Superintendent of Public Instruction, had, however, provided him with an overview of the State educational scene, and his earlier post as director of the laboratory school at Mount Pleasant Normal had contributed to his understanding of the teacher training program. No prior experience could, however, have given him or anyone a foretaste of the problems that lay ahead.

One can scarcely imagine a more inauspicious time for taking over the administration of a college. A man of average character or lacking the high esteem of fellow educators throughout the State could not have survived those first years. Because of the illness of President McKenny during the last months of his administration, the State Board had appointed an executive committee to administor the College. This was composed of Clyde Ford, head of the Department of Modern Languages, as chairman; Clemens Steimle, Registrar; and Charles Anspach, head of the Education Department. It was with this committee that Munson dealt as he prepared to take over.

The overriding problem was that of State financing. The State Legislature, faced with drastic cut in income, was reducing its appropriations to the University of Michigan and Michigan State College by 15 per cent. The four teachers colleges were anticipating a cut of 25 per cent. Munson proposed that these colleges be allowed to retain student fees instead of turning them over to the State. This would even out at about a 15 per cent cut. In May of 1933, Ford wrote to Munson as follows:

> I had the chagrin of seeing the salary (of the president) for our institution and for Western State Teachers College cut down, from $4,500 to $4,000, in spite of the fact that I made as valorous and violent a protest as I could. I spoke of Ypsilanti as the mother of teachers colleges, talked about standing and size and all the rest as arguments why the president's salary should be commensurate . . .

So Munson saw his salary cut after his appointment and before taking over the position.

As a matter of fact, the president's salary at Ypsilanti had, in 1929–30, reached a high of $9,000. At Northern, Munson had received $8,000. The $4,000 that he received at Ypsilanti remained at this level for four years, and proved to be the lowest reached during the Depression. During this time, department heads at Normal who had been earning a salary of $5,000 found their low at $3,192, and full professors were dropped from $4,500 to $2,400. It should be noted, in this connection, that a double standard as between men and women still obtained. For example, that exceptionally capable and valuable full professor, Estelle Downing, found her pitiful income of $3,200 cut to $1,884. Actually, the legislative cut in appropriations to the teachers colleges amounted to a disgraceful 33.5 per cent in that fateful year.

To a close personal friend in Aberdeen, South Dakota, Munson wrote: "Inasmuch as we have been cut 33.5 per cent, the job is not a pleasure entirely."

Doubtless the most difficult obligation that confronted Munson upon assuming his duties was that of reducing staff. The task had been begun by the executive committee. When it was completed, 23 members of the faculty had lost their jobs (two on the basis of leave without pay), and six others were placed on half-time. The same excruciating necessity was experienced by the other three teachers colleges. It was reported that when Normal's registrar was approached on the matter he shouted "That's the President's head-ache," and walked rapidly away.[15]

In the year before Munson arrived at Ypsilanti, the effect of the Depression on enrollment had been felt for the first time. From 1931-32 to 1934-35 it declined 28 per cent.[16] During the same peri-od, however, the legislative appropriations for general operation for Normal declined 40 per cent.[17] But this was only the start. In the period 1935-36 to 1940-41 enrollments took a turn contrary to the Depression, and climbed. The gain from the base year 1934-35 was 49 per cent. The increase in appropriations, however, was only 17 per cent.[19]

Then came war. This time the decline in enrollments was precipi-tous. The drop from 1940-41 to 1941-42 was 500, and from 1941-42 to 1942-43 was 550. The total decline caused by war over a period of four years (1941 to 1945) was a good 50 per cent of the pre-war enrollment.[20] Less than 50 men were left in the college dormitory. During this period, however, the legislature gradually increased the appropriations.

In the third period of drastic change, the post-war period, veter-ans flocked to the college campuses of the nation. In three short years 1,550 additional students came to Normal, a total increase of 130 per cent. The men definitely outnumbered the women. To meet this situation the legislature increased the appropriations from 1944-45 to 1947-48 by some 63 per cent. For the first time in Normal's history the budget reached the million dollar figure.

It should be noted, however, that the federal government (under the Fulbright Act) had undertaken to pay the actual cost of the veterans' education, a cost that was calculated in painstaking detail and set forth in the annual contract. This money went directly into the general fund of the State of Michigan. It was not available to Normal. Unlike the University of Michigan and Michigan State, who could retain the tuition money, the Normal College had to live strictly on its appropriations.

In the years beginning with 1955–56, when the College expanded from a student body of 2,800 to one of 8,500 in a decade, an important distinction from the earlier periods should be noted. The years of depression and war were years of crisis and uncertainty. No one could know how long the Depression would last or to what depths it would go; no one could predict the coming of the war, its length, or the extent of its demands. Conditions had to be met as they appeared. In the later, more happy, period, however, increasing enrollments could be and were foretold long before they appeared. Studies of the birth rates of the 1940's were made, culminating in specific estimates of the number of students the colleges might expect from year to year. It is true that enrollments exceeded estimates both in point of time and degree. But the legislative mind, the administrative mind and, to a degree, the public mind were prepared in advance. The result was that a very reluctant legislature was forced to realize that increased appropriations for operation (and also for capital outlay) would be necessary.

During a period in which money for higher education in any form was extremely hard to come by, Munson succeeded in procuring funds for 13 buildings.[21] More came as the result of two magnificent gifts to Normal, that of Walter Owen Briggs sr., which provided the outdoor athletic plant, and the Horace H. and Mary A. Rackham Fund, which provided a splendid facility for the work that Normal was doing in the training of teachers for handicapped children.

The gifts were an expression of confidence in Normal, and a recognition of important work being done there. The one originated in the desire of Briggs (Chairman of the Board, Briggs Manufacturing Co. of Detroit, owner and president of the Detroit Tiger Baseball Co.) to do something for the city in which he was born. Dean of Men James M. (Bingo) Brown served as guide when Briggs came to Ypsilanti to choose a site for an athletic stadium. After they looked the city over, the Dean led his guest to the Normal campus and stressed not only the importance of physical health for the coming generations but also the advantage that the College offered for permanent care and maintenance. Needless to say, no obstacle was encountered when Briggs made his offer to the State Board.[22]

The Rackham gift was a recognition of the pioneering work done at Normal by Charles M. Elliot in Special Education.

In addition to these benefactions, several highly important additions were made to the campus. It was the Munson era, for example, that saw the construction of the first dormitory. There were five by the time he retired.[23]

The barriers once crossed, other federally assisted projects followed. A most urgent need existed for a College hospital. Students were being cared for in a seriously inadquate "health residence," a frame dwelling on the edge of the campus that the College had acquired. A new fully-equipped, up-to-date and, for the needs of the time, commodious health service building was completed in 1939. The following year, the John W. Stevens Shop, a two-story structure suitably equipped, was completed. This shop made possible construction activities of considerable magnitude by Normal's maintenance staff.

In 1940, the Milton S. Hover Elementary Science Laboratory building was completed, a tribute to the beloved dean (also head of the Natural Science Department) who died in that year, and a monument to the work of an earlier head of the department, William Hittell Sherzer, who had introduced and established nature study as a vital part of the curriculum for teachers of the elementary grades.

The War Years

The sudden precipitation of the nation into the world war, on December 7, 1941, not only interrupted the building program but brought a train of events that profoundly affected the campuses of the nation. In no time at all, students who were the inheritors of many generations of carefree, uninhibited, unregimented campus life were in uniform, responding to the barked orders of "non-coms."

College administrators were faced with rapidly dwindling student enrollments, surplus faculty, severe budgetary problems, and all of the apprehension that accompanies an uncertain future. Some of the private colleges were forced to close their doors.

Faculty members had to wrestle with the question as to where their services would count for most in the great conflict, complicated by the responsibilities and ties of family. Many decided to enlist in the armed services.

Students were faced with the question of whether to enlist, and in what branch, or await the call of the draft board. Draft boards deferred the call for students who were doing well in their studies. The armed services organized college training programs for those who could qualify. But always there was the pressure to enter directly and immediately into the struggle—pressure from families whose sons were already in the service, from friends, from conscience.

The women students, too, were faced more and more with a decision as the armed services developed their women's auxiliary corps, and as war industry called for labor.

It is noteworthy that the Normal men of the 1940's went off to war quietly, in a spirit of grim determination. The war was an unwanted interruption of their plans, an extremely unpleasant task that must be performed, and the sooner and more thoroughly it was accomplished, the better. Quite absent was the frenzy of enthusiasm that characterized the Normal men of 1917–18.

Over the next years the thousand and more young men who left the campus to enter the armed services were joined by twenty-two members of the faculty. As time wore on, more and more accounts appeared in the student paper of Normal students whose lives had been taken, until a grim total of sixty-three was reached.[24] Leroy Grindle, former track captain, was the first to go—killed in a bomber crash near Pendleton, Oregon.

Enrollments at the College dropped in three years from somewhat over 1,900 to a low of less than 700. Faculty were now in surplus. The State Board acted promptly to retain all positions, and to implement this policy made off-campus ("extension") teaching, traditionally an extra assignment with extra remuneration, a part of the regular load. To meet the unabated need for teachers in the public schools, training time was shortened. Seniors who were within 10 credit hours of meeting the requirements for a teaching certificate were, upon request of an employing official, granted special certification. The spring semester was shortened by omitting the spring vacation week. The summer session, with an earlier start, was lengthened from the traditional six weeks to nine, thus providing opportunity for the earning of more credit in the calendar year.

Early in 1943, there developed a situation that threatened the very existence of Normal and came close to making her a casualty of the war. The great bomber plant at Willow Run, destined to play such a vital role in the winning of the war by its amazing production in volume of the B-25, was getting under way. Thousands of war workers were being brought to the Ypsilanti area, and these included large numbers of women. (Indeed, it was uncommon for a wife of a Normal professor to be found working in the great plant.) The problem of housing rapidly became acute. Plans were laid and construction begun on a large project of temporary, barrack-like housing in the Willow Run area, on the eastern limits of Ypsilanti. But it was argued that these facilities would not be adequate, or in time to meet the need. A demand was made for the use of the College facilities, not only the dormitories but classroom buildings remodeled to become dormitories. Col. George E. Strong, internal security officer of the Army Air Force central procurement district, stated with untroubled conviction:

> It's part of our job to do everything possible to attract more women workers to the bomber plant. Employees there eventually will be more than fifty per cent women. The army originally planned to establish a ground school for aviation cadets at the Ypsilanti institution. These plans have been abandoned partly because the Army feels the school buildings would be more valuable as quarters for bomber plant workers.[25]

Not a word was said about the numerous and large dormitories of nearby University of Michigan. The Normal alone was to sacrificed to the war effort, and no appeal to the popular mind could have carried greater weight—the winning of the war. The threat to the college was deadly.

Munson took prompt steps to meet the crisis, alerting Governor Kelly and the State Board, calling on a faculty committee to draw up a detailed brief in defense of the College, and calling upon the alumni to come to the rescue. The latter responded with hundreds of letters of protest. The student body sent a letter to the Governor citing Normal's sacrifices in the Civil War, the Spanish-American War, World War I and the present war. Kelly immediately took a public stand on the issue and referred it to the Defense Council, composed of the Governor, the Superintendent of Public Instruction

(Eugene B. Elliott), the State Director of the National Housing Authority (Raymond M. Foley), and the President of Michigan State College (John Hannah).

Kelly wrote to the *Ypsilanti Daily Press:*

> In the Normal College the state has not only a six million dollar invest-ment, but a college of which the people should be proud. It is one of the leading colleges in the United States. You can't just close a college of that kind and reopen it when you want to. It is too big a proposition to tem-porize with. We will employ all the weight of the Defense Council, and with the assistance of your paper and the community we shall not be los-ing time but will be progressing in the vital work of obtaining housing for workers. Those bombers are going to be kept going, but not at the sacri-fice of something as precious as the Normal College, unless it is absolutely necessary.

Foley took an immediate stand against the proposal, stating that at best the college facilities could house not more than 2,000 work-ers, that to close the school would ruin it for the next 20 years, and that great progress was being made by the government in construc-tion of 10,000 units near Willow Run. President Hannah was quot-ed, in a letter to the Normal alumni, as saying, "The Ypsilanti school is one of the finest and oldest teacher training institutions in the nation. To close it would be to cripple it for years." President Ruthven of neighboring University of Michigan proposed that a detailed survey be made of the area to discover available rooms, and this was carried out.

On March 22, the State Board passed a firm resolution which said in part:

> *Whereas,* the State Normal College has, since its establishment, enrolled 68,300 students, has, during the last 40 years, graduated 27,000 teachers, and has, during the last 12 years, graduated annually an average of 590 teachers, and

> *Whereas,* the need of teachers due to the war crisis is now the greatest in our history . . .

> *Be it therefore Resolved,* That it be the declared policy of the State Board of Education to continue the College in all its constitutional and legal functions as an educational institution, striving by all means to produce trained teachers for Michigan schools in the present emergency . . .

By the end of March the madness had subsided; the college was saved.

The campus still intact, recruiting teams continued to appear representing Army, Navy, Marine Corps. Then came the college training programs—the Army Enlisted Reserve Corps, the Army Air Corps Reserve, the Marine Corps Reserve, the Navy V-1, V-5, and V-7 programs. The question arose as to course credit for those forced to leave college before the semester was over. The administration decided to give full credit if more than half the semester had been completed. The Army Enlisted Reserve Corps received the largest number of enlistments, but by April of 1943 all had been called into active service. As these "E.R.C. boys" left, the student paper editorialized in youthful language:

> We, the students who stay on campus, want these boys to know that we don't like to see them leave . . . we are thinking about them—and, yes, praying for them too . . . Let us always remember that this war *will* end. This time of suffering *will* pass. He *will* return. We *will* be a vital part of the future world.

In February of 1943, preparations were made to receive several hundred aviation cadets who were assigned to Normal's campus for a period of training. Women were moved from King and Goodison dormitories to Munson Hall. Then, at the last moment, as the men were about to entrain for Ypsilanti, the order was countermanded.

In September of that year, however, a firm commitment was made with the newly-established Army Specialized Training Program. Company H of the 4651st Service Unit, 300 strong, arrived, under the direction of Capt. Charles F. Wetherbee, a genial but exacting giant from Texas. The women having been restored to their own dormitories, the new arrivals were housed on the upper floors of the men's dormitory (Munson Hall) with the ground floor assigned to the few civilian students left at school. A parallel unit was at the same time installed at the University of Michigan, under the tutelage of the College of Engineering.

These were described as engineering units. Their curriculum consisted of chemistry, physics, geography, mathematics, surveying, military science, American history and English composition. The object was to provide training for young men of superior ability such as would enhance their usefulness in a number of areas in the army.

Many colleges and universities over the nation, from 42 States, were represented in Company H.

A special plan of classes was arranged on a sequence of two twelve-week terms, additional instructors were secured where needed, and a highly intensive program ignored the traditional college vacation periods. The men were serious. From time to time their progress was tested by national examinations. Normal was inclined to take credit for teaching effectiveness when Company H consistently showed an edge over their counterparts in Ann Arbor, particularly in the areas of chemistry, mathematics, and physics.

Thus, for the better part of a year Normal conducted two colleges side by side. Relations between the civilian and military were good. Although the men of Company H were not permitted to engage in college athletics they loyally attended athletic contests. The football schedule for that fall consisted of just two games, both with Wayne University of Detroit. The army marched into the stands and cheered the Normal team to an unexpected victory. The victory was repeated, with an identical score, at the return engagement in Detroit. It was one of the few perfect football seasons in Normal's history.

When, in late March of 1944, Company H marched under the windows of the women's dormitories and down to the train that would take them away to Camp McCoy in Wisconsin, not a few were the tears that were shed. It was later reported that most of these boys were quickly shunted to the battle front in Europe and had scant opportunity to use their training. Many were pleased to be on active service to escape growing criticism from many whose sons were not so fortunate. Awareness of this attitude was expressed in a poem by one of the men, in part as follows:

> Maybe you think we aren't aware today of what is going on, that being here securely barricaded from the war by these scholastic bulwarks, we're content to sit and wait and let the others fight.

> And yet that lank, brown soldier, shaking New Guinea caterpillars from his clothes, burned, bony, brave, defying with a laugh the sticky swamp, mosquitoes, death, and Japs, happens to be my brother.

Perhaps some day this bookish bomb of mine will blast as big a hole in Hitler's fortress as Bill's grenade in Hirohito's palace.[26]

Nor was this feeling that college was not a good place to be in when others were fighting and dying confined to male civilian and A.S.T.P. students. The women, too, became increasingly restless. In November of this same year an editorial in the college paper, addressing "you (coeds) who feel your job in this emergency should not be 'putting in your time' at school but rather 'doing' something vital, perhaps in one of the services of the country," reminded that those preparing to teach were working for the future of America.

The Post-War Years

The war over, a different array of problems presented themselves. Veterans began to appear on the campus—at first a few at a time, then in a rapidly rising flood as the liberal assistance offered by the Fulbright Act (enacted in 1944) attracted the attention of those desiring a technical or college education. The precipitate nature of the demobilization of our armed services greatly complicated the situation in the colleges.

Veterans appeared on campus as soon as they received their discharge, and this meant that provision had to be made for enrollments, always lower than in the fall, now became the larger of the two. From fewer than 700 in the fall of 1943[27] the total jumped to more than 2,200 in the fall of 1946. In the spring semester of the latter year well over 300 additional veterans appeared and it became necessary to pressure Lansing for a deficiency appropriation to staff the classrooms. Applications of more than 200 veterans were held in abeyance until, at the very last moment, the Administrative Board voted the extra money. Telegrams were at once sent out to the 200 telling them to come. Enrollments continued to leap upwards in the ensuing years until, in 1949–50, the post-war high (as of that time an all-time high in the history of Normal) of 2,693 was reached.

Now the Normal had a housing problem. Additional beds were installed in the dormitories until their capacity was doubled, but this was not enough. Munson was unwilling to do what so many colleges were doing, erect temporary structures on the campus. They would, he felt, soon become an eyesore and a health menace. Hauling cinder blocks into the unused basement of the Union building (McKenny Hall), he created a new dormitory, four men to a room. But this was not enough. Two large barrack-like structures in the south side of Ypsilanti, war housing for colored labor, were purchased from the government. One of the buildings burned. And more and more veterans arrived.

The vast array of war-housing barracks at Willow Run (many of which, ironically, had never been occupied) became available for student housing. The University of Michigan contracted for a large portion of this facility but Normal secured enough to meet her needs. Bleak, draft quarters were rapidly transformed by enthusiastic young families into the paradise of home. Hardships and inconveniences were more or less cheerfully borne. A social and recreational center, a veterans' student union, was created by the U-M. Newcomers on the faculty who could not find housing in Ypsilanti went to Willow Village. The U-M bused its thousands to and from campus; Normal's hundreds were included.

To the classrooms the veterans brought a seriousness of purpose, awakened minds, a breadth of experience that stimulated and invigorated the entire school.

Many a former student who, before entering the service, had been on the scholastic ragged edge now stormed back to establish a commendable, sometimes a superior, record. A liberal policy of admission for those who had done poorly but had an honorable service record proved to be well-justified. If any instructor in any subject had fallen into the lazy routine of trivial questions and pat arbitrary answers, he soon found the new presence not altogether comfortable. This new breed of students was not content to be told, they had to be shown.

But scarcely had the College met these post-war problems and begun to settle down to a fairly calm existence when it became conscious of the imminence of a problem of a different nature. President Munson would soon reach the age of 70, the Munson era was coming to a close.

As his retirement drew near, concern for what the future might hold for the faculty became paramount. The present administration had been highly authoritarian. Would the next administration be similar? The thought was intolerable. Faculty thinking was in process of being conditioned for faculty participation in administration.

During the years that Munson had ruled conplacently in "splendid isolation," a ferment had been brewing over the nation. In 1915, a national organization had been formed whose main concern was academic freedom, spurred by arbitrary dismissals of faculty that were occurring all too frequently in the colleges of the nation. This organization was known as the American Association of University Professors.

A chapter of the Association existed at Normal. The spark caught on. A self-initiated organization of faculty led by members of the AAUP drew strong support. Efforts to persuade the State Board to permit faculty participation in the selection of the next president were made. Though the attempt was abortive, this organization did succeed in writing a constitution for an all-college faculty organization which provided for active faculty participation in college administration. With some modification the constitution was later accepted by the incoming president.

The campaign for faculty participation in the choice of the next president, and, for the future, faculty participation in the administration of the College generated considerable heat on the campus. Off-campus the inevitable occurred—newspaper interpretation that this was a revolt against Munson. The wire services carried to papers throughout the State and nation the assertion that "dissatisfaction with the administration of President John Munson led to a demand by members of the faculty of Michigan Normal College for sweeping administrative changes on his retirement, expected in June."[28] Shocked at this kind of publicity, the faculty committee wrote at once to Munson: "We were chagrined this morning to see the scurrilous article in the *Detroit Free Press* . . . At no time in our negotiations with the members of the State Board has there been voiced one word of criticism of the present regime."

As for Munson, he made no move. Once he commented, "If they wanted a change, why didn't they come and see me?"

Special attention to John Munson the person is warranted. Rugged, willing to absorb punishment for unpopular decisions, a man of high integrity, deeply committed to the role of the educator, with a lively sympathy for those in distress, a sense of humor that flashed unexpectedly and delightfully, his virtues were obscured, his effectiveness as an administrator blunted, by a certain gaucheness.

Certain idiosyncrasies and retroversions only aggravated the difficulty. For many years telephones were an expensive intrusion, even in administrative offices. Face-to-face encounters were much more satisfactory. Yet the President's outer office was much like the reception room of a doctor's office where the time of the patient was of no consequence. Manner of dress revealed a lack of attention to the on-moving world. Isaiah Bowman, his lifelong friend, wrote him once in these gently chiding words:

> From the photograph that you enclose I see first, that you survive; second, that you are in good physical condition; and third, that you wear high shoes. In the Baltimore climate, the last named are not essential, even in winter. I maintain that there are three marks of the conservative man: he wears a nightshirt, suspenders and high shoes.

But Munson represented values that were long upheld with pride as typical of the American character—forthrightness in dealing with others, an abhorrence of shame, thrift in public as well as private enterprise, a strong sense of responsibility in public trust. He believed that the reputation of the College should stand strictly on its performance and be revealed in the reputation earned by its alumni. He insisted that there was no money in the budget for advertising beyond the informative college bulletins. He believed that intercollegiate athletics should be amateur in the original sense of the term and refused to allow his coaches to go forth on recruiting missions to lure promising high school athletes to Ypsilanti. He placed great emphasis on the liberal arts as basic in the preparation of the teacher and insisted that the professional courses be limited to a minimum. He strongly and effectively supported a foreign language requirement for graduation.

Munson was adamant and unyielding in adhering to rules and standards. Once a regulation was established, it must be applied literally and equally to all. Every candidate for graduation must show every last required hour of physical training, regardless of age. Graduation lists were never posted until all the grades were in, and no one crossed the platform at commencement who had not met all requirements.

On the other hand, he was slow to dismiss students with substandard records, and kept a chart which showed clearly the number of students who, year by year, succeeded in raising their average to the minimum of "C" required for graduation. At the close of each semester he presided personally over an administrative session that reviewed the grades of every student. He signed congratulatory notes to the parents of those whose record was superior. He imposed restrictions on the class load carried by students, requiring that those who were earning their way through college by holding remunerative jobs and those who were faltering in their grades restrict themselves to a lighter academic load. The records in the registrar's office were reorganized in such a way that the current semester's grades and the overall grade average for every student could be seen at a glance.[29]

Fully aware of the economic status of most of Normal's students, he made every effort to keep the cost of an education to a minimum, both as to tuition and living expenses.

Munson accepted his presidential trust as a total personal responsibility and knew not how to delegate authority. Like the lord of a medieval manor, he took complete charge. No fact of any consequence should elude him, no question asked about his college should go without an informed personal answer. He did the hiring and, when necessary (which was rare), the firing. He drew up the complete budget. Maintenance, supplies, and new construction were within his direct province, and clerical personnel as well as faculty. When a position on the faculty was to be filled he usually would consult the department head, yet he might not. The librarian must submit her lists of proposed purchases to him that he might scan them for titles that might react against the College in the eyes of the legislature.[30]

Faculty standing committees were always appointive, and restricted to matters of routine administration. The time and energy of the faculty should be protected from dissipation in non-teaching duties.[31] Participation in community activities by his administrative staff was frowned on for the same reason, time and energy should be devoted to the job at hand. Attendance at conventions and conferences that kept faculty from meeting their classes, or administrative staff from their desks, was made difficult.

Having said all this, however, it is important to point out that Munson inspired respect and confidence. And he took considerable pride in having won from the State Legislature the appellation of "Honest John." Fred W. Green, as ex-Governor, in a letter to Normal's Dean of Men, James M. Brown, wrote:

> I recall he was the one head of an institution in Michigan whose requests did not have any looking over. When he asked for something it was always something that was really needed, and he never over-asked.

Recognition from his profession was well exemplified in a citation accompanying an honorary degree of Doctor of Arts in Education awarded him by Wayne State University, which read in part:

> He is recognized as an able college president, and as an authority in school law. Under his wise guidance much constructive educational legislation has been formulated for the State of Michigan. As an educator, administrator, and well-beloved counsellor he has contributed broad vision and sound direction to our state program of education.[32]

Munson retired in 1948, having reached the age of 70. His retirement brought many letters that contained much more than formal good wishes—from members of his faculty expressing appreciation for the sense of satisfaction and security which they had derived from confidence in his integrity, and gratitude for personal consideration shown in times of illness and distress. From associates, near and far, recent and past, appeared anecodotal letters expressing esteem and often gratitude. A large banquet was held in his honor, laudatory speeches were made, colleagues and friends from around the State were present.

The inauguration ceremony for the new president took place a year later, combined with the observance of Normal's centenary year. The president of the State Board presided, honored guests were on the program, Munson addressed a charge to his successor. No word in appreciation of the service of the retiring president was spoken.

Many have commented that if only Munson had married, his abrupt and arbitrary manner might well have been refined. He had three loves, history (especially American), the State of Michigan and the children of Michigan. His political hero was Grover Cleveland. His knowledge of the State of Michigan was so detailed that a student coming from the smallest hamlet would find a president who had been there and remembered the place.

Munson died in 1950, in Ypsilanti. In his will he assigned the bulk of his estate to the Michigan Historical Commission to organize and carry through a project for the writing and publishing of a history of Michigan, and a history of education in Michigan.[33]

CHAPTER NINETEEN

EUGENE BRADSHAW ELLIOTT

1948–1965

In contrast to the drastic and unpredictable adjustments demanded of the colleges and universities of the nation by the unstable economic and world situation of the previous two decades, the next two were characterized by a single irresistible pressure—the rapid, continuing increase in student enrollment.

The problems arising from this basic fact could, to a degree, be foreseen. In administrative circles of higher education, birth statistics and their implications were being studied and discussed. But the impact occurred earlier than was generally expected, and its force was greater. That intangible factor, the attitude of the public towards higher education, could only be known as it became explicit. That it would find expression first in the number of young people who would knock at the college gates and much later in the legislative halls, only complicated the matter.

It soon became evident that, in addition to stimulating returning veterans (aided by the G.I. Bill) to obtain a college education, the war had also strongly influenced the public mind in favor of more education. High schools that, before the war, did well to send a fourth of their graduates on to college saw the proportion raised to nearly half. These young people were about to merge with the veterans. And another war, that in Korea, as yet unanticipated, would in a very few years add an additional influx of ex-servicemen.

The more obvious and immediate problems that the new administration had to face, therefore, arose in the areas of staffing and plant expansion, and this, in turn, required a breakdown of the traditional legislative attitude of penury towards the teachers colleges.

205

The State Board of Education, meeting on March 23, 1948, accepted the resignation of John Munson (age 70) as of June 30, and appointed as his successor Eugene B. Elliott (age 52), effective July 1.

Eugene Bradshaw Elliott was a native of Michigan. He held degrees from Michigan State University and a doctorate from the University of Michigan. He was a Phi Beta Kappa from Albion College. Seven years of teaching and school administration had preceded his entrance into public office. He came to Normal from his elective position of State Superintendent of Public Instruction, a post in which he had made the remarkable record of serving, regardless of political party in power, for a period of 13 years, longer by far than any of his predecessors.[1]

At the State level he had served as Director of Research of the Michigan Education Association, Director of Research and Finance for the Department of Public Instruction, and chairman of the Michigan State Planning Commission from 1941 to 1947. As Director of Research and Planning he presented (in 1935) with exceptional effectiveness to the State Legislature the state-aid plan for the public schools that has since been in operation. When appointed to the position at the Normal College, he was serving as secretary to the Executive Committee of the American Council on Education.

Of fundamental importance to the president of a college or university is the confidence of his faculty, a consideration especially true in the post-war era when faculties began asserting with increasing insistence that they should play an important role in the decision-making process. This complicating factor is not present in the typical business organization.

At Normal, as we saw in the previous chapter, there had been serious discontent among the faculty. The State Board, by ignoring this factor, placed their appointee in a difficult position. They had summarily rejected the plea of a faculty committee to be permitted to submit a list of nominees, in which Elliott would be included. Consequently, Elliott came to Ypsilanti in the light of one foisted on those with whom and through whom he must work and achieve.

His pleasing personality, gracious manner and receptive attitude, however, bade fair to minimize in time the effects of this unfortunate decision. His family, wife Wilma and daughters Patricia and Ellen, met a long-felt campus-wide and community-wide desire and need. Upon Elliott's arrival in Ypsilanti, plans were in progress for the construction of a dwelling for the President. In his eagerness to establish prompt and intimate contact with the institution, he took temporary residence in a small campus apartment.

As for the administrative structure, his first step was to provide for a business manager. He created the office of Controller. This was long-overdue and was to prove essential to the orderly growth and development of the institution. Benjamin L. Klager was the first appointee. He functioned effectively until his retirement in December, 1961, when Lewis E. Profit became his successor. Under Klager the faculty experienced for the first time the specialized view and the restraining hand of a business executive.

When Elliott arrived in 1948, some 2,800 students were enrolled, an all-time high up to that time.[2] The campus comprised 107 acres and the buildings numbered 18, including five large dormitories. The legislative appropriation for operation and capital outlay for that year was $1,343,192.

When he retired in 1965, some 8,000 students were enrolled, and preparations for the coming fall were for 10,000 with the "G.I's." fairly out of the picture. The campus comprised 200 acres and options had been taken on 142 more. There were 37 buildings on the campus, including nine large dormitories, two large buildings in progress, others planned, and some 259 students apartments, with more in prospect. For the coming year the legislature had appropriated $7,038,000 to finance operation and capital outlay. To this would be added $2,331,000 from revenues, largely student tuition. Another $6.5 million was forthcoming from private bonds floated to finance self-liquidating projects (more dormitories, more student apartments, a doubling of the capacity of the Union building (McKenny Hall). A classroom addition was planned for the Quirk Theatre.

In brief, to meet the tripled size of the student body and the greatly increased costs of an inflationary era the legislature had, indeed, modified its attitude concerning the teachers colleges. It had increased its contribution nearly six times. Nor was the picture at Normal exceptional. The influx of students, need for additional buildings, rise in cost of operation were state-wide and nation-wide. To Elliott, however, must be given credit for anticipating the extent of this growth. In 1954 it became important to estimate the ultimate size of the institution. At the time, an ultimate figure of 5,000 students appeared high; he decided on 10,000, a figure which, though not proving to be ultimate, was reached upon his retirement.

For many years there had been a growing desire to drop "Normal" from the name of the College. The trend among teacher preparation colleges over the nation to do this had become so widespread that by 1956 the Ypsilanti institution was one of only three that still retained the designation. Normal's sister institutions in Michigan had taken the step in 1927.[3] (John Munson at the time was president at the Northern State Normal.) The feeling was that the name "Normal" belonged to an earlier era when teacher training institutions were two-year schools and not considered to be of college grade. At Ypsilanti the athletic department was particularly disturbed because—especially in track—the name was felt to be a barrier to inclusion in intercollegiate competition.

The major obstacle to a change of name for Normal had long been thought to lie in the State Constitution. The name "Michigan State Normal" was embodied in that document (whereas the three sister institutions were established by legislative action), and it was assumed that for Normal a change of name would require a constitutional amendment.

Elliott took steps to probe this matter. The State Board put the question to the Attorney General as to "whether it is within the authority of the Legislature to change the name of the Michigan State Normal College by statute." The opinion rendered was as follows:

> Answering your specific inquiry, it is the opinion of the Attorney General that the Constitution forbids changing the nature of the State Normal College but that the change in the name of the State Normal College is clearly within the power of the Legislature. The words "state normal college," as they appear in the Constitution of 1908, are not proper names but are descriptive of a specific type of educational institution.[4]

There ensued at Ypsilanti an eager search for a new name. A broad appeal was made for suggestions; many responded. Some suggested Michigan State College (the name recently abandoned by the East Lansing institution for Michigan State University); some, Michigan Eastern College. One proposal, Ypsilanti State College, received general disapproval, as connoting a regional or local institution. Normal had prided itself on drawing students from every county in the State, from many other states, and from several foreign countries. The discussion was conducted with skill by the president, and the outcome—Eastern Michigan College—was found generally acceptable. It was consistent with the names held at the time by the three sister institutions, and it recognized an unavoidable development: Normal had in fact become basically a regional college. The new name became effective July 1, 1956.

With scarcely a ripple, the name was again changed in 1959 from "College" to "University."[5] Normal was simply following the Michigan trend begun two years earlier by Western at Kalamazoo. The change was made at the same time by Central of Mt. Pleasant and in 1963 Northern of Marquette followed suit. At Normal, the college paper, *Eastern Echo,* merely commented:

> Monday morning, the college switchboard operators will begin greeting callers with "Eastern Michigan University" and college printing will began bearing the new EMU seal. . . . No special ceremonies have been planned. . . . The designation of Eastern as a state university, however, promises intellectual and physical expansion in the future.

The teaching load of the four teacher training institutions had traditionally been heavy. Large classes (often of 60 or more students) were taught, tested, and graded by the instructor without assistance. This was held to be the regular load of 15 class hours per week. In the science areas where laboratory work was involved the total was considerably higher. In addition, faculty were permitted to teach off-campus in the extension program—a voluntary decision but, though low in monetary compensation, a strong temptation in light of the meager salaries that were paid.

Meanwhile, in the universities throughout the land, the trend had been to provide more time for the professor to keep abreast of the literature in his field of learning, and for that element argued as essential to vital teaching—research. Candidates for graduate degrees were employed as assistants to grade papers and do some of the clerical work or, as teaching fellows, to conduct quiz and discussion sections. The class hours of teaching were set well below the load carried by the Normal faculties.

This matter of professional load was considered by an organization representative of the four teachers colleges, the Interfaculty Council of the Michigan Colleges of Education. At its March 1958, meeting, a Teacher Load Committee was appointed to study the problem and make recommendations. The work of this committee culminated in an extensive and detailed study, published and widely circulated in 1960.[6] Eastern promptly adopted its recommendation. On the initiative of the Vice-President for Instruction, Bruce K. Nelson, and with Elliott's support, a reduction in classroom teaching to 12 hours per week was approved for the instructional departments, most of which took advantage of the new policy.

The question of subsidizing athletes in intercollegiate competition became urgent as the athletic conference to which Eastern belonged leaned more and more to a policy of limited financial assistance and the consequent competition became more rugged. Eastern's traditional policy, strictly enforced under Munson, had been no subsidy and no recruiting. Under Elliott, a faculty committee was at length appointed to make a recommendation. The recommendation was for limited compensation, accompanied by a policy statement that required similar treatment for participants in other activities where the College was represented. The policy adopted was stated by the President as follows:

> We believe that a student participating in intercollegiate athletics must be admitted on the same basis and show the same level of academic achievement as the student who does not participate. We believe that a student participating in intercollegiate athletics should have the same opportunities, no more and no less, for loans, grants-in-aid or scholarships as all other students, and we further believe that the primary basis for granting such help is scholastic achievement. Our university is operated for the education of youth. That is our business.

The statement received wide publicity, was very unpopular in certain quarters and strongly supported in others. One superintendent of schools wrote:

> Secondary schools face the difficulty of keeping extra-curricular activities, particularly those that relate to athletics, in their proper perspective. Colleges and universities which have high pressure recruiting campaigns help to set up a false set of values, not only in the prospective athlete, but in his associates.[7]

The president of Wayne State University wrote: "I agree wholeheartedly with President Elliott's statement on the subsidization of athletics and would only add the qualification of financial need in providing such financial assistance."[8] Under this policy, Eastern felt obliged to resign from the Interstate Intercollegiate Athletic Conference (I.I.A.C.) in 1962. Later, Eastern joined one formed by Wayne State University and seven private colleges in four states, which purported to hold compatible views, called the Presidents' Athletic Conference (P.A.C.). But Wayne State shortly withdrew, alumni and coaches were not happy with the quality of competition, and in 1966 Eastern withdrew. As of Elliott's retirement, therefore, Eastern was a loner in the field of intercollegiate competition, forming season schedules catch-as-catch-can.

In the Munson chapter we saw how drastically and unfairly the salaries of Normal's faculty and administration had been cut during the Depression. The nadir was reached in 1933 just as Munson arrived in Ypsilanti. Nothing anywhere near comparable was done to the major institutions of higher education in the State. From this point on, the problem was how to start an upward trend. Some progress was made in the late thirities. By 1940, the President's salary had risen to $5,000, the department heads to $4,000, the full professors to $2,700. Restoration of the loss was still a distant and uncertain hope.

The Council of Presidents (presidents of the four teachers colleges) gave increasing attention to the problem. In 1942, they made a recommendation that was to have a major influence on salary planning and improvement. To replace the existing unorganized method, which produced many inconsistences, they developed an organization chart which defined the academic requirements for the several faculty ranks and prescribed minimum and maximum salaries for each, with biennial step increases. The State Board adopted the chart "because of increasing housing costs and adjustments of compensation in the faculties of the teachers colleges."

The new schedule became effective July 1, 1943—effective, that is, to the extent that the legislature would be willing to validate it. This proved to be a long and discouraging struggle. But a pattern had been set and it proved over the years to be helpful to all concerned in achieving flexibility, elimination of gross inequities, and an upward climb. Salaries were finally restored approximately to pre-Depression levels at just about the time of Munson's retirement in 1948.[9]

From this time, the objective was to obtain salaries comparable to those prevailing in other institutions of like character in the mid-

west, and to attempt to keep abrest of the increasing rise in the cost
of living.

A number of devices were employed to speed the process. Beginning with July, 1943, the salary year was shortened from 12 months
to 10, with no diminution in the rate, and extra compensation for
those fortunate enough to be needed for the summer session. Munson had for years been edging toward this step. In the budget request
for 1939–1940 he had begun to insert the phrase "for 12 months"
after each faculty name in the budget. Beginning with the following
year, he made an occasional 10-month appointment. By the summer
of 1943, all members of the summer staff were on additional salary.
(Prior to this time all faculty were required to teach two summers in
three as part of their academic year.) For the ensuing year the
biennial step increases were advanced by one year.

In 1944, a push from a faculty organization at Normal, Local 686
of the American Federation of Teachers, in the form of a report on
the salary schedule was submitted to Munson, presented by him to
the State Board, and filed by that body. In the same year, a first step
in basing requests for salary increases on the percentage decided
upon by the Civil Service Commission as to civil service employees
(teachers were not on civil service) was taken with regard to the
salary of the presidents. (The policy of following Civil Service decisions as to increases was applied to the faculty as a whole from
1951. A precedent having been established, it proved to be acceptable to the legislature as an effort to meet the increasing cost-of-
living factor.) In 1947, the schedule was revised to provide an additional step increase and to read "annual" rather than "biennial."

In August, 1947, Local 686 provided a second push for higher
salaries by presenting to the Council of Presidents a critique of the
salary schedule adopted in March, purporting to show that in actual
purchasing power the salaries shown fell seriously short of the prevailing salaries of 1939, and stating that public school districts were
paying higher maximums than were available to assistant professors.[10] In 1948, the Board requested the presidents to confer with
the State Budget Director concerning another over-all revision of the
schedule. Such a revision was adopted in 1950.

Elliott succeeded Munson as of July 1, 1948. In that year the State
Board requested the Council of Presidents to prepare a progressive
budget request that would achieve the full salary schedule for the
year 1951–1952. In 1950, the Board adopted a third revision of the

schedule, adding two increase steps, voting to make it effective as of December 1. At the same time, it requested a deficiency appropriation for the year 1950–1951.

However, an alarming attitude in the legislature developed in 1950 which affected all of the state-supported institutions of higher education, and brought about an unprecedented spirit of cooperation among the heads of the colleges and universities as far as budget requests were concerned. The rush of veterans to obtain an education under the G.I. Bill had slowed to a trickle. The impact of increasing birth rates during the late thirties and the forties had not yet been felt. Enrollments dipped. The legislature, in spite of the warning of educators that the flood of applications for admission to college would soon rise again, and to even greater heights, looked upon the immediate situation as an occasion for reducing appropriations. They threatened an across-the-board cut of 5 per cent.

Strenuous protests ensued. Articles revealing the plight of the universities, particularly the University of Michigan, appeared in the educational press. It was shown that other states had by this time recovered from the Depression cuts—but not Michigan; that post-war enrollments in Michigan institutions had exceeded those in some 20 other states; that state appropriations per student in those states had been four times that in Michigan; and that the current drop in enrollments had been less than half that in other states.[11]

For the teachers colleges, Elliott took up the cudgels. In one institution, he said, department heads were on the average nearly $1,400 below the prevailing salary schedule, professors nearly $1,100, associate professors more than $800, and assistant professors about $250. Many school districts, he said, were paying more than the ceiling for assistant professors.[12]

The legislature finally settled for a cut of 2-1/2 per cent below the appropriations for the previous year.

The rate of progress in salary improvement in the fifties and sixties was strongly prodded by the whip-lashes of creeping inflation. In the sixties, the newly-acquired status of University and the heightening intensity of competition for qualified faculty added their pressures. For a time the budgets provided for two factors—merit and promotion, and cost of living. But the latter came to be the all-consuming concern, and it prevailed. At one time, an across-the-board factor of 4 per cent was included; at another, 7 per cent. But it never seemed able quite to catch up with reality. Inflation came to rule the day and salaries reached heights that would have appeared fantastic in the forties. By 1965, the presidents were scheduled for $25,000, the maximum for department heads was $13,500, for professors $11,290, associate professors, $9,600, assistant professors, $8,200. And the ultimate was still in the laps of the gods.

That Eastern was moving forward with the times during these years is shown by projects undertaken, facilities acquired, and certain processes and emphases adopted. In 1960, closed-circuit television was installed and experimentation begun in instruction through this medium. In 1963, Eastern secured a place in the United States program for overseas educational projects. A grant was secured for the organization of teacher training facilities and the training of personnel for preparation of elementary teachers in the Republic of Somalia. R. Stanley Gex, at the time Dean of the College of Education, was granted a leave of absence to organize this project. In the Graduate School, the Specialist Degree (representing a year of graduate work beyond the Master's degree) was offered in 1964.

In the same year, an IBM Computer Center was established. This facility found many uses, one of the most helpful of which was the ability, through data processing, to pre-register and classify approximately seven-eights of the student body—thus saving much time at the beginning of a semester. An Office of University Public Relations and News Service was created, a revival on a much bigger scale of an attempt made during the McKenny era.

By far the most significant of all, however, was the decision to proceed with the enlargement of the library facilities. Plans were formulated for the abandonment of the old library building and construction of a new building which would stand as a model for college libraries everywhere. At the same time, the old policy, long stubbornly adhered to, of a seriously inadequate place in the budget for library operation and acquisitions was changed to permit an increase of 1 per cent per year until the appropriation should reach 6 per cent of the budget.

A matter of considerable debate was the threat to close Roosevelt Laboratory School, descendant of the original Model School that, throughout Normal's long history, had played such a vital role in the training of teachers. In the new era, the public schools were so ubiquitous and competently staffed that they could be used for this purpose, and this encouraged at the State level an economy move.

Again, as had been the case under President McKenny, local loyalties prevailed, and the evil day was postponed.

Such were a few of the more important developments.

One, of a minor nature, raised memories of a by-gone day, when the subject of women smoking caused a nation-wide furor. In January, 1960, Elliott received a letter from a student Protestant organization known as the Inter-Varsity Christian Fellowship, Eastern Michigan University Chapter, which objected to smoking in the religious affairs building on the campus, Starkweather Hall. It said in part:

> We oppose all smoking in Starkweather Hall, but it has been recommended by some to permit smoking in certain areas. . . . We do not believe in compromising principle. If even compromise smoking is permitted . . . it will be a sad day in the history of Eastern Michigan University. It will be a sad day because it will mean that Eastern Michigan University encourages its students to take up powerful, almost unbreakable habits by not providing at least one building—not even the building of religious affairs—in which a student does not have to smoke to be socially correct.[13]

The president turned the matter over to the Faculty Board of Starkweather. Smoking continues in Starkweather. Money was provided for the remodeling of Starkweather and today, under the able direction of Charles Minneman, it serves its purpose better than ever.

Note should be taken, too, of the expanded use of the College Union, McKenny Hall. Thanks to the initiative of Controller Benjamin Klager, the vast unused area of the basement was transformed into a recreational center where students and faculty could enjoy bowling and billiards. A portion was reserved for a college bookstore, where books and supplies could be sold at a saving to the customer. The ancient but fondly remembered establishments of Stanley's and Zwergel's faded gently from the campus scene.

No chief executive worthy of his position of responsibility can hope to avoid the conflicts of opinion, judgment, and interest (both group and personal) that are inherent in the operations of an institution, particularly a public-supported educational institution. In the case of Elliott, a series of developments occurred that were to make the going especially rough.

In 1952, he created a new position, Dean of Professional Education,[14] but did not specify its limits. The result was a free-for-all situation among his immediate subordinates. While stimulating in some quarters, it was depressing in others, and confusing throughout.

A turning-point in his relations with the faculty occurred two years later. Elliott's attitude toward the faculty organization had been amicable and cooperative. He had agreed to the existence of a faculty organization operating under a constitution, functioning through a representative council and working committees. But certain questions felt to be fundamental in the minds of the faculty remained unanswered. These went to the very foundation on which the organization rested. Was it considered to be a permanent feature of the decision-making process in operating the College, or did it exist merely at the pleasure of the incumbent president? If the latter, then its role might well vary with each incoming president—if, in fact, it continued to exist at all. Indeed, what degree of influence could it exert? Were there possible areas where it could be delegated authority equal to that of the president for example, curriculum development?

Because of the ready cooperation that the president had given over several years, the faculty had come to believe that he understood and supported their viewpoint. However, there came a time when he decided that his authority was being challenged and that he must act to protect it. In 1954, a confrontation took place over a question as to the nature of the position of department head. This he settled by imposing his will and, at the same time, ordering certain modifications to be made in the faculty constitution which clearly stated not only his position of authority but also his intent to influence the membership of the Faculty Council committees. While his was far from a denial of the principle of faculty participation in the decision-making process, the reaction of faculty leaders was bitter.

A year later, the president, in a move designed to develop a somewhat larger and more dynamic administrative staff to cope with the problems of a rapidly expanding institution, ordered a reorganization, effective January 1, 1956. Two new positions were created, and the office of Dean of Administration was replaced by that of Dean of Student Affairs.[15] With the Controller, the Dean of Professional Education and a representative of the Faculty Council, these constituted the president's "Policy Council." This administrative staff, by dint of unremitting effort and the determination to tackle head-on the challenges of a new era, soon won the president's complete confidence.

In the spring of 1962, a sequence of events began that led, through curious twists and turns, to a highly unpleasant climax. A group of alumni, convinced in their own minds (but entirely outside of and contrary to the sentiment of the Alumni Association) that all was not well with Eastern, undertook an inquiry among faculty and students which revealed numerous dissatisfactions. This led the group to ask the State Board for an investigation of administrative practices.[16] The State Board, on Elliott's suggestion, called on the North Central Association of Secondary Schools and Colleges to send an investigating team to the campus. The Association appointed a survey panel and instructed it "to assess the current status of this university with particular reference to certain allegations which have been made concerning student and faculty morale and the management of the University."

In June, 1963, the panel spent two and a half days on the campus interviewing all who wished to appear as well as members of the administrative staff. Some 50 to 60 per cent of the resident staff voluntarily appeared, more than could be adequately interviewed in the time available. Four months later, the panel made its report, indicated some things that appeared to require attention, and recommended that the next periodic visitation of the North Central accreditation commission be advanced from 1965 to 1964. It also recommended that Eastern undertake promptly a self-study in preparation for the visitation.[17]

The State Board, on its part, shocked the world of Eastern by requesting the president's resignation. When he refused, the Board ordered that his tenure terminate a year hence. At the same time it abolished one of the administrative positions that Elliott had created —that of Director of Planning and Development and Assistant to the President.

However, events were taking place in another area that would cause the demise of the State Board itself. The people of Michigan approved a new State Constitution, to be effective January 1, 1964. A provision in this Constitution abolished that venerable body, the State Board of Education, established in 1849 to locate, organize, and control a State Normal School.

The new Constitution provided for a separate board of control for each of the baccalaureate degree-granting institutions (not including the University of Michigan, Michigan State University and Wayne State University, whose boards were elective) to be composed of eight members, appointed by the governor with the advice and consent of the Senate.[18] The board for Eastern adopted the name Board of Regents of Eastern Michigan University. The governor acted promptly to appoint the new board. It met without delay and rescinded the action of its predecessor regarding Elliott.

Throughout this ordeal Elliott maintained an attitude of confidence and composure. His genial personality proved to be an invaluable asset, and he gave his utmost during the final trying two years that were left before retirement.

Elliott's services to education and to Eastern did not go unrecognized. In 1936, he had been granted an honorary LLD degree by Albion College; Hillsdale College conferred an honorary EdD degree the following year. During his tenure at Ypsilanti he served as president of the National Association of Colleges of Teacher Education (1956–1957) and president of the Association of State Colleges and Universities (1963–1964). In 1952, Wayne State University honored him with a Doctor of Laws degree, and in the citation said:

> Educators, government officials, legislators, and leaders in civic affairs in the State and in the nation have sought his scholarly analysis, wise counsel, and clearly conceived decisions regarding professional problems. Through war and depression, through a period of confusion regarding the objectives of public education, he has provided sound leadership toward the solution of many problems confronting schools and colleges in Michigan. To Wayne University he has given valuable assistance in the task of interpreting the relationships of this institution and its programs to the State and to the larger community it serves. . . . As the leader of a distinguished teacher training institution, he is eminently suited by experience, breadth of view, and philosophical temper to bring us nearer to realizing the goals we cherish for our system of free public education.

Elliott retired as of July 1, 1965, and made his home in Adrian, Michigan, from that time.

Adonijah Strong Welch (1851–1865)

David Porter Mayhew (1865–1870)

Charles FitzRoy Bellows (1870–1871)

Joseph Estabrook (1871–1880)

Malcolm Mac Vicar (1880–1881)

Daniel Putnam (1881–1883, 1885–1886)

Edwin Willits (1883–1885)

John Mahelm Berry Sill (1886–1893)

Richard Gause Boone (1893–1899)

Elmer Adelbert Lyman (1900–1902)

Albert Leonard (1900–1902)

Lewis Henry Jones (1902–1912)

Charles McKenny (1912–1933)

John Maurice Munson (1933–1948)

Eugene Bradshaw Elliott (1948–1965)

Harold E. Sponberg (1965–present)

CHAPTER TWENTY

AUTHORITY AND THE FACULTY

It will be remembered that the original intent of the State Board was to give the faculty a primary role in the internal conduct of the Normal. Suitable for a very small institution, in harmony with a fairly widespread but diminishing practice of the time, this concept of the role of a faculty met, as we have seen, varying fortunes in the century that followed, and ended under President Munson in being completely denied. The re-appearance, under vastly changed circumstances, of the belief that the faculty in an institution of higher education should play an important administrative role found especially vigorous and aggressive expression at the Normal under Munson and Eugene Elliott.

The tenure of Munson, second only in length to that of McKenny as of the time, drew to a close in 1948. The authoritarian character of his administration had become increasingly galling to the faculty. Not that academic freedom was threatened, not that the faculty were overburdened with administrative committee work (the exact opposite was, in fact, the case), not that the operation of the college was inefficient, not that the educational purpose and function of the institution were being poorly served. But times were changing rapidly; the administrative tone was paternalistic, the policies were extremely conservative. With the close of World War II the day had definitely passed in America when it could be said that "The faculty are employees; the trustees are employers; the president is the superintendent of the plant." The spirit of the times would no longer tolerate an Alston Ellis (President of Ohio University) "standing at his office window clocking professors as they arrived on the campus each morning."[1]

Perhaps as a microscosm of institutional travail accompanying birth of a different concept, the story is worth telling.

At the Normal, the initiation of a faculty movement for participation in the administration of the College was particularly difficult because faculty meetings were held once a year, and then only for the purpose of approving lists of graduates and conducting minor business of a routine nature. To the extent that there was backing for change by any organized group in the initial stages, it came from the local chapter of the American Association of University Professors. At the national level this Association had been studying the problem of faculty participation for 30 years. In 1917, it had set up its "Committee T" on the Place and Function of Faculties in College and University Government. Its detailed reports of 1920 and 1937 formed a solid platform on which a faculty might stand in an effort to gain recognition. Article IV of the latter report stated categorically:

> The faculty of the university at large or its authorized representatives, and the faculty of each college in the university, should have ultimate legislative power over educational policies within the jurisdiction of that faculty, and should control its own organization and its committees.[2]

Concern over the matter of faculty participation in college administration was manifested at the local AAUP chapter's first meeting of 1946–1947. Meetings for the year were scheduled as a series of discussions on specific areas of college administration and procedure. The national AAUP *Bulletin* had published articles on "What Makes a Good College President," "Ethical Argument for Democratic University Administration," "Choosing College Presidents," and "What Should be the Qualifications for the President of Utopia Teacher's College?" These articles were of particular interest to the local group as Munson's retirement approached. The faculty did not want a continuation of arbitrary rule; they were intent on insuring a more democratic type of administration by the proper choice of the next president. They strongly desired to have a voice in that selection.

In the spring of 1947 a faculty movement developed. It began by way of informal meetings of a few who were interested. The initiative came from a member of the local AAUP chapter, J. Henry Owens, chairman of the Foreign Languages Department. It was Owens who led the way through the next two years until, under the new president, a form of faculty government was established. The first approach, however, was an attempt to secure from the State Board consent to faculty participation in the selection of a president.

In May, 1947, a call was issued to all members of the faculty who might be interested in the question of faculty participation in the choice of the next president. A goodly number of the faculty responded. A dollar was solicited to defray expenses. It was readily contributed. An executive committee was chosen.[3] This committee proceeded to obtain interviews with individual members of the State Board. In June, in a frank letter to Munson, which included a copy of the petition that had been prepared requesting a voice in the selection of a new president and which had been submitted to members of the State Board, the committee said:

> This committee has met with the individual members of the Board and secured their approval of the steps taken. The committee would be delighted to meet with you any time at your convenience to discuss its operations and plans, and to receive any advice you may care to give.

Munson, who held that choice of a president was not a matter for faculty participation, did not arrange for such a meeting. The minutes of the State Board for June make no reference to this petition. In early August, however, a letter was received from the Secretary of the Board which said in part:

> This letter will acknowledge your letter concerning the selection of a president for Michigan State Normal College. The Board operates as a unit. In accordance with the best educational practice the members consider problems of policy as a board rather than as individuals. After careful consideration of your request it was decided to wait until President Munson officially resigns before going about the business of choosing a new president.

In February, 1948, the committee announced that it had met with the State Board and presented the petition formally, together with supporting petitions from alumni and a copy of a statement taken from the AAUP *Bulletin*. They were, they said, assured by the Board that it would take official action as soon as it had had time to

study the petition, and would communicate its decision to the committee.[4]

On March 23, 1948, the morning papers carried the announcement that Eugene B. Elliott had been selected by the Board as the
new president. The reaction of the faculty group was one of extreme
disappointment. The committee drew up a statement which they
gave to the press. It read:

> The faculty has never taken a position concerning Dr. Elliott. It has felt
> that the best interests of the State of Michigan would be served by can-
> vassing the whole United States for the best candidates. It has felt that the
> reputation of the College deserved that. The State Board of Education
> should conduct a thorough search for the best man even though the field
> be limited to the State of Michigan. The faculty offered its aid to the
> Board in such a quest. The Board did not see fit to follow these sugges-
> tions and did not consult further with the faculty.[5]

There is ample ground to assume that the Board held the view
that a college president, to be effective, must in no way be beholden
to his faculty. His decisions must, inevitably, meet at times with
disapproval if not outright opposition. His responsibility must be
directly and solely to the board that hired him, and he must feel
secure at all times in doing that which, in his view, would be in the
best interests of the institution. With this outlook, it was natural to
take the position that the faculty were meddling in a matter that was
none of their business.

Up to this time attention had been directed to securing a list of
candidates for the presidency which might in due time be presented
to the State Board. Now however, in light of the failure to obtain a
role in selection of a president, the committee concentrated on the
formulation of a faculty charter and constitution. In a series of news
letters, the faculty were kept informed. That of March 12, 1948,
began as follows:

> Your faculty committee has felt that the necessary corollary to its efforts to
> obtain a voice in the selection of the successor to the presidency of this
> college is the formulation of a plan of faculty organization . . . The hier-
> archial and authoritarian form of government that prevails in many of our
> colleges and universities is an anachronism altogether out of harmony
> with the aims and needs of a university designed to represent and serve a
> democratic society . . . The purpose is not to usurp any of the rightful

prerogatives of the executive . . . the object is to bring to bear the collective experience and intelligence of the faculty on every aspect of the activities of the university.

The code of principles drawn up and approved by the national AAUP was quoted: "There ought to be a close understanding between the faculty and the board of trustees . . . The general faculty should participate with the trustees in the nomination of a president, and the faculty of a school or division should have a voice in selecting the dean who presides over that school."

For the task of formulating a charter, the membership on the Faculty Committee was increased to ten.[6] By April 5, tentative proposals were presented for faculty reaction. In a statement of policy, the committee said:

It [the Committee] believes that, subject to the constitutional controls exercised over the college by the State Board of Education, the faculty can play a considerably greater role than it has in the past. It does not in any way contemplate removal of authority from the President, the deans, or other administrative officials . . .

As to the president, the statement is interesting in its revelation of the faculty concept of this position:

The role of the President in relation to such a constitution is not discussed, because his place should be apparent. He is the leader of the college, a symbol of the college to all outsiders, and the fountain of activity and encouragement to the faculty and students. He sets the tone of the college. He presents college affairs to the State Board of Education and, if need be, to the legislature. He talks with the alumni, keeps them conversant with faculty and student affairs, fires their enthusiasm for the college, encourages them to send excellent students, and inspires them to make financial and intellectual contributions to the institution. He speaks to town groups and others . . . supervises the budgetary matters of the college with the end of promoting economic management of the college and of getting all possible financial aid from the state and from private individuals . . . attends national and regional meetings . . . to keep abreast of what other colleges are doing and to widen his vision . . . from a broad perspective [he] harmonizes college and departmental activities to promote efficiency and good will . . . sits on important committees to lend encouragement and judgment . . . presides at general faculty meetings . . . supervises the problems of maintenance of college properties and plans for the physi-

cal growth of the college . . . supervises the problems of clerical and office
workers . . . initiates measures of all sorts for faculty consideration, and
in like ways aids and encourages the students. He is, indeed, the prime
figure of the college . . .

One is reminded of the statement made by Rutherford B. Hayes,
when a member of the Ohio State University Board, where he
enumerated the qualities of "fine appearance," "commanding presence," "fine speaker," "great scholar," "great teacher," "a preacher," "winning manners," "tact so that he can get along with and
govern the faculty," "popular with students," "trained in business,"
"a man of affairs," "a great administrator"—and ended by saying
"Gentlemen, there is no such man."

One proposal was to cause serious trouble at a later time, namely,
that departments of instruction of the college should be headed by a
chairman elected from the staff for a limited term by the members of
their respective departments. Such procedure would, it was felt by
many, tend to encourage faculty politiking. It was this extreme feature of the proposed constitution which raised serious doubts in some
minds where otherwise a generally favorable reaction might have
developed.

By May 10, the charter was ready for faculty approval. The
favorable vote required for passage was set at two-thirds. Ninety-
three per cent of the faculty voted; the charter was adopted but with
not a vote to spare.[7]

On May 26, representatives of the faculty met with the State
Board to seek approval of the document.[8] Gerald Sanders (head of
the English Department) made the opening statement for the faculty.
Charles Burns (president of the Board) spoke for the Board. The
session was a lengthy one. In its report of that meeting to the faculty
the committee said:

> After almost two hours of debate, the committee stated its case as follows:
> that it felt that the basic principles of the Charter were sound and neces-
> sary in the long run; that any power allotted to the Faculty must derive
> from the State Board of Education, the constitutional repository of power;
> and that the committee preferred no charter rather than to accept one via
> the President because of our belief that continuity of policy is imperative.

The faculty committee had, as we have seen in its communication
with the faculty, asserted that it did not "in any way contemplate

removal of authority from the President," but the Board gained a different impression. The minutes of that meeting read as follows:

> A delegation of faculty members of the Michigan State Normal College presented a proposed charter to the Board involving a faculty chairman who would have coordinate authority with the President of the institution.

The Board adopted the following resolution on the spot:

> This matter is referred to the President of the College. It is definitely understood by everyone concerned that the State Board of Education reposes administrative and executive responsibility solely in the President of the College and therefore matters relating to internal organization or procedure in the College are subject always to his determination or approval. This is affirming a policy which has prevailed in relation to each Michigan College of Education since its establishment.[9]

The resolution was read to the committee as the session ended, and induced bitter feeling.[10] Reporting their experience later to the faculty, the committee said:

> Inasmuch as the committee considered this meeting as merely an opportunity to expound the principles of faculty participation in college government, this action was astounding . . . The Board's decree disapproves this approach, and perpetuates the authoritarian tradition, whereby all power is delegated to the President of the College.

In October, after the new president had assumed his duties, the committee was ready to submit to the faculty a revised version of the constitution. In announcing this, the committee said:

> Your committee recommends this proposal to you as the best working agreement possible for the time being . . . The President has . . . signified his enthusiastic consent to the establishment of the organs specified in this constitutional draft . . . It should be made clear to the faculty that the machinery hereby set up will function only in an advisory capacity.

The "machinery" referred to was a General Faculty which would meet quarterly; a Faculty Council, to meet monthly; and committees to be elected by the General Faculty. In addition, the College and each of the Laboratory Schools were to be separately organized, hold monthly meetings, and organize committees. It is noteworthy that although specific disclaimer was made as to exercise of authority, and it was clearly advertised that the faculty government would function "only in an advisory capacity," there was written into the revised constitution, both at the General Faculty and the School Faculty levels, the statement that each "shall be a legislative body." At the all-campus level, this legislative body was to be "concerned with all matters that involve the general welfare of the Michigan State Normal College." At the college and school level, it would be "concerned with all matters that specifically involve their respective schools."

Use of the term "legislative" was unfortunate. The failure at any stage to define clearly a sphere of interest that could convincingly be argued to belong exclusively to the faculty led to future discord and an ultimate weakening of the faculty position.[11] However, the revised constitution was adopted and went into immediate effect. Bylaws were drawn up and approved, and standing committees established. Noteworthy was the fact that the list of committees was considerably enlarged over traditional lists, covering such novel areas as Integration of Curriculum, College Aims and Objectives, Budget, Health and Safety, Buildings and Grounds, Faculty Welfare, Faculty Social Activities and Faculty Fund, Personnel and Psychological Services, and Elections.

In the period from May, 1947, to September, 1948, (when a revised constitution was finally adopted and placed in operation) a tremendous amount of time and energy were expended by many members of the faculty in the effort to achieve a more satisfactory type of administration. Leaders of the movement appeared to give by far the major part of their time, energy, and thought to this project. One can only conjecture the price paid in terms of educational discipline and progress of the thousands of students (on and off-campus), and in professional improvement and contributions of staff which are part of the normal expectations from college professors. How many class sessions became routine, how many tests were not given, how much of the inspiration that is so catching in a professionally alive and dedicated teacher was lacking can only be surmised. Yet under the existing circumstances, there was no alternative means to the end sought.

For some years the faculty organization operated with vigor and enthusiasm, well-supported by the President. In his annual report for the year 1950–1951 the Dean of Administration could say:

The climate on the campus has been generally good. I believe I can say that as between the faculties and the administration there is a general spirit of confidence and good will.

By late 1953, however, the question of department chairman as opposed to department head became acute. A department chairman would be elected by his department and would serve a limited term. A department head would be appointed by the president for an indefinite term. There was strong faculty sentiment for the concept of department chairmen, and this had been embodied in the constitution. The issue became real in the English Department where a particularly difficult situation existed as to the naming of a head. It was known that the president favored the department head concept and would like to settle the problem by appointment. As the next meeting of the State Board was imminent, a special meeting of the General Faculty was called for via petition, as provided for in the constitution. The petition read:

. . . whereas doubts have been expressed publicly on the constitutionality and propriety of the vote in the English Department to terminate its chairmanship. Therefore, we the following members of the College Faculty petition for a special meeting of the College Faculty to be held prior to the date on which the President shall feel it is necessary to present any recommendation on the English Department to the Board of Education (other than postponement of the matter if it has already been communicated to the Board). etc.[12]

The meeting was promptly held (the president attending), the question was well threshed out on the floor, and the outcome was a recommendation favoring adherence to the constitutional provision for department chairman.

The fact that the faculty government possessed only an advisory function in relation to the president had, as we have noted, been clearly established and was generally understood. However, the constitution still retained a clause that, read by itself, would indicate a contrary intent. This statement read that the faculty organization was "a legislative body concerned with all matters that involve the general welfare of Eastern Michigan College." Perhaps because of this retention from the original constitution of the word "legislative," with its absolute connotation, perhaps because of the vigor of the discussion on the floor, the president chose to interpret the meeting as a challenge to his authority.

The next day he took the matter to the State Board and received not only explicit authority but direction to supervise the departments through an appointive department head. At its January meeting, the Board adopted the following resolution:

> On motion, the Board voted that each college department of the Michigan Colleges of Education shall be supervised by a department head recommended by the President of each institution. A person now holding the office of department chairman may complete the term for which he is named unless he resigns or the office is otherwise vacated. To be given immediate effect.

At the same meeting, the president settled the problem in the English Department by securing the Board's approval of John Sattler as head.

On February 3, he issued to the faculty a bulletin entitled, "President's Statement on Faculty Organization." In this statement he pointed out the obvious and well-understood fact that Normal operated under the authority of the State Board of Education and that this Board had delegated to him the administrative responsibility "as the single executive authority." Then, however, he proceeded to issue an edict: the present faculty constitution, except where it was inconsistent with the State Board's prescription as to the department head, could continue to exist only "until modified—but not beyond July 1."

This was severely damaging to faculty morale and to the relationship between faculty and administration. Henceforth, the faculty organization would be viewed as the president's organization, to be modified or even discarded at will. The strong faculty leadership that had pioneered the concept of faculty participation was antagonized and lost interest. Confidence in the president, who had approved the existing constitution, with its prescription for department chairmen, was undermined. The feeling grew that the College was being directed as a matter of expediency rather than of principle. The fear expressed by Sanders in the meeting with the State Board on the original charter had proved well-founded, that if the document were not approved by the Board, it could not be relied upon.

A new constitution was drafted in which the word "advisory" was written into the title. The committee structure was greatly reduced and membership brought within reach of presidential influence. It was approved in June by a reluctant faculty intent on retaining the principle of faculty participation. The statement of "Purpose and Control of the Michigan Colleges of Education," long a feature of the annual catalog, was dropped. This statement had been explicit both as to the source of control and the legislative purpose of the College. In its place appeared a brief paragraph entitled "Government of the College," which reminded its readers of the authority vested in the State Board of Education, and that the school was financed from tax monies.

In 1960, the Faculty Council, on its own initiative, was reorganized and enlarged to secure a representative from each instructional department and laboratory school in addition to the twelve elected at large. In 1963, as the result of unexpected reverses, the president changed his stand and gave the Council more than advisory status, though still without definition. The State Board showed a marked interest in securing the cooperation of the Council and prospects were more favorable for ultimate official recognition of a definite faculty role and responsibility in the administration of the, by now, University.

A footnote from two decades after the formation of the Faculty Council might here be appropriate. In their newly-found enthusiasm for democracy in administration the faculty extended the principle to include the students. A Student Council was encouraged and promptly became a reality. Student representation was provided for on certain faculty committees where student interests appeared to be directly involved, and occasional meetings between Faculty Council and Student Council were arranged. Transition from student participation to student domination was not envisioned. The phrase "Student Power" had not yet been coined.

CHAPTER TWENTY-ONE

LIBERAL ARTS AT
THE NORMAL

From the first the Normal served a dual function, provision for professional training in teaching and instruction in the subject matter areas. But its purpose was single, the preparation of teachers for the public schools. So strong was this commitment that, as we have seen, for many years the faculty tended to resent the subject matter courses as an intrusion on their proper sphere of activity. The Normal was a teacher training institution, a professional school.

In 1879, the University of Michigan established a Chair of the Science and the Art of Teaching (the first permanent chair in any college or university devoted exclusively to the preparation of teachers). This step was so strongly resented by the faculty of the Normal, who felt it an infringement on their area, that President Angell of the University felt impelled to say in his annual report:

> We desire it most clearly understood that we have no intention of invading the territory of our neighbors of the Normal school. The line between their work and ours is very distinct. We wish simply to aid our undergraduates, who come here for collegiate study to prepare themselves for the work of teaching, which they are certain to undertake, whether we have this new chair or not.

Mention of "collegiate study" and a "line between" was an adroit reminder that, so far as academic work was concerned, the Normal could be considered only as a glorified academy or school preparatory to work of collegiate grade. And, indeed, this was true. The demand met by the Normal was, frankly stated, the necessity that a teacher sent into the public schools should know as much about her subject as she was expected to impart to her pupils. As long as the major function was to prepare teachers for the elementary level, this requirement was not severe and certainly was not challenging to a professionally-oriented faculty.

The development of the Union School and of its successor, the High School whose spread was phenomenal, placed an increasingly heavy demand on the Normal for teachers adequately informed in their subject matter areas. The effect on the thinking of the faculty and the policy of the school is clearly seen in the ambitious brochure that was published in 1893 and distributed at the Columbian Exposition in Chicago. In this it was stated:

> The function of the Michigan Normal School is to prepare teachers, both academically and professionally, in the most thorough manner possible . . . And no teacher is so equipped unless his own culture and training have been carried considerably beyond the limit to which he may be called upon to conduct the pupils under his general supervision . . . In other words, he ought to pursue his own course of instruction considerably beyond the limit of the best High School courses of study.[1]

Proceeding to define the upper limits of high school instruction (based on the admission requirements of the University of Michigan), it said that the Normal was actually engaged in college-grade work in the areas of mathematics, history, English, physical science, natural science, Latin and Greek. "To the extent thus indicated," the brochure continued, "this school occupies the ground of higher education. Its advance into this field has been gradual, and it has been moved thereto by the steadily increasing demands of the Public Schools . . ."

Evidence that the broader view of the function of a teacher training institution was being accepted also by normal schools over the nation is seen in a statement by Normal's President Leonard in his annual report of 1900:

> There is a growing sentiment among the friends of Normal schools throughout the country that the courses in these schools can be materially strengthened on the scholastic and cultural sides without in any sense weakening the professional side of the work.

In 1917, agreement was reached with the University of Michigan for full recognition of credits transferred from the Normal, and admission to their graduate school of Normal graduates from the four-year bachelor's degree curriculum.[2]

Broad authority to grant diplomas had been given to the State Board by the legislature as early as 1889. Under this authority, the Normal offered a four-year degree called Bachelor of Pedagogics —conferred first in 1890.[3] In 1902, the four-year curriculum was arranged to lead to a Bachelor of Arts degree—called the Bachelor of Arts in Pedagogy or Education. In 1916, the degree of Bachelor of Science was adopted, known as Bachelor of Science in Education. By 1918, both BA and BS degrees were offered without inclusion of the term "Education." In 1934, the State Board ordered that notice be placed in the catalogs of all four of the teachers colleges stating that students could be granted a degree without at the same time having to qualify for a teaching certificate.

To the demands of the high schools, and the humiliation of a condescending attitude on the part of the University of Michigan, may be added other compelling reasons for the growth in emphasis at the Normal on the importance of academic work. We have seen the strong faculty pride stemming from a sense of mission, of high responsibility for meeting a fundamental need of the State. Dignity based on a sense of importance can become a force of consequence. Perhaps it was because of this sense that, from the mid-1880's, a number of exceptionally able faculty in the subject matter areas began to appear.

These men formed a stimulating group that set a scholarly pattern which received nationwide attention and created an enduring set of values for the institution. They were supported by successive presidents who were highly appreciative of scholarly endeavor— Richard G. Boone, author of the first comprehensive history of education in the United States; Albert Leonard, editor of an important educational journal; Elmer Lyman, author of many textbooks in mathematics; Lewis H. Jones, and Charles McKenny. And in 1897 came a powerful stimulus, the formal recognition of the Normal as a college.

English

Instruction in English took a three-way form (grammar, literature, public speaking) from the first. Principal Welch gave lectures on English grammar and elocution, and published a book on "The Sentence." At the same time the first Preceptress, Abigail Rogers, taught Botany and "Belles-Lettres." The first list of staff positions included an instructor in English Grammar and Elocution. Subsequent Principals Estabrook and Sill presented English as their major academic area. Sill, indeed, was originally brought to Normal to fill the post for English Grammar and Elocution.

Many years were to pass, however, before the subject was taught by specialists. In 1868, one teacher was assigned to English Literature and Elocution and another to English Grammar and Analysis. In subsequent years there were such teaching combinations as Geography, Drawing, History and English Literature (Anna M. Cutcheon); Geography, Rhetoric, and English Literature (Anna Cutcheon, Austin George); Director of the School of Observation and Practice, and English Language (George); English Literature and Civil Government (Cutcheon); along with an occasional instructor in English or English Literature.

By 1884, there appears to have been considerable dissatisfaction among the students with the work done in this area. An editorial in the *Normal News* for February of that year demanded an English Department, saying:

> . . . even the advocates of the classics grant the necessity of English . . . We can honestly say that the students in English Composition and Literature are not and have not been what they should be as trained teachers for the schools of the State.

Doubtless this represented a widespread feeling for in June of that year a new department of instruction, the Department of English Language and Literature, was announced and Theodore Nelson was employed to take charge. A year later Nelson was replaced by Florus A. Barbour.

It was during Barbour's long and able incumbency of 41 years (1885–1926) that the department grew and acquired its modern form and character. In 1928, Gerald Sanders became head. Sander's exacting demands on his staff, his judgments in staff selection, and his publications confirmed and enchanced a tradition that had placed the department on a high collegiate level of performance. John Sattler succeeded Sanders in 1953. Since work in English had always been a requirement of all students and most took at least a year in English literature as well as the required year in composition and a semester in public speaking, this department became the largest in the institution, and bore the full brunt of variations in student enrollment.

As to offerings, the record was one of evolution from the small beginning of a few lectures to a list of some 64 courses in the four areas of grammar, literature, drama, and speech. Glimpses are here and there available as to the nature of these courses. In 1874, for example, the work in English Literature was given in 20 lectures, covering a period from Caedman to the 19th century. In 1876, American literature was referred to with the hope expressed that now, with more time allotted, both English and American literature might be made more interesting. Later, the work in English and American literature was presented in two separate courses. In 1888, courses in Old English and Middle English were offered. At the same time 19th Century Novel and Shakespeare appeared. As to the Shakespeare course, the following explanation was given:

> It is hoped and somewhat confidently expected, that the daily discussions in class will not only constitute a preparation for teaching Shakespeare but will connect themselves more and more intimately with the student's study of psychology and pedagogy.[4]

In 1908, the course that had long been given under the title Principles of Criticism, and which obviously had evolved from the earlier lectures in English and American literature, was offered in two separate courses which became standard—American Poetry and American Prose. By 1819, the work in Shakespeare had become specialized in two distinct courses—Shakespearean Tragedy and Shakespearean Comedy. By this time, too, courses were offered on The Bible, The Short Story, and Children's Literature. Ten years later the course in the Bible had been expanded to two courses, Old Testament and New Testament, a course called Literature of World Good Will was offered, and a series of courses, later to become redefined and referred to as the "period courses," was added (Renaissance, 17th century, 18th century, Romantic Era).

Meanwhile, the work in public speaking had followed an irregular path. Originally provided for largely by extra-curricular activity nurtured by the campus-wide literary societies, more serious attention was given to it when Normal became a college. By 1898, formal courses were being regularly offered in Reading Orthoepy (pronunciation) and Elocution and Oratory.

In 1902, a department called Reading and Oratory was organized
headed by J. Stuart Lathers. This department was known by various
names in subsequent years. In 1915, it was the Department of
Expression and, from 1928, the Speech Department. Course offerings were expanded by 1918 to include Debating, Shakespearean
Reading, Victorian Poetry, Story Telling, Dramatization, and Play
Production. By 1928, major and minor areas of concentration were
offered, and the needs of the new Department of Special Education
were recognized in a course called Speech Correction. Service
courses for another department, that of physical education, also
made an appearance. Courses were offered in Public Speaking for
Men in Physical Education, and in Reading and Public Speaking for
Women in Physical Education. The description of the men's course
read:

> Its purpose is to qualify such men to present their work confidently and to
> represent their field creditably before student assemblies, teachers' groups,
> business men's clubs and community gatherings.

That for women was, alas "a study of the principles underlying
argumentation."

Lathers retired in 1940. In his 38 years at Normal he had developed the Department of Speech to its modern form and character.
He had also founded the all-campus honorary scholastic society, the
Stoics (1909), which continues to be the counterpart of Phi Beta
Kappa for Eastern Michigan University. He had the interesting
memory of having coached a young man by the name of John Munson (later to be his President) in debating. He had also coached in
oratory the young man who later was to join his staff and become
his successor as head of the department, Frederick B. McKay.

Upon McKay's retirement, in 1948, the Speech Department was
combined with the English Department under Sanders, and when
Sanders retired in 1953, a Speech man—John Sattler—became
head. In 1963, the two were again separated, the English Department being placed under Hoover Jordan, and the Speech Department under Sattler.

During these years the Departments of English and Speech
greatly expanded both course offerings and areas of specialization.
The areas of specialization multiplied from the simple major and
minor in Literature and in Speech to six major areas and seven

minor areas, some of which were designed for the student who did not plan to become a teacher. More attention was given in some of these areas to the history of the language, linguistics, and the dramatic arts.

In looking over those who labored in the English vineyard, certain names inevitably stand out. Some of these were noteworthy for their love of students and skill in teaching; others for their publications.

Barbour had prepared himself in Latin and Greek, with courses in English elected as a matter of interest.[5] His original intent had been to prepare for the study of theology, and in his later teens the Congregational Society had granted him a permit to preach. After graduation, however, his experience was in teaching of Latin, Greek and mathematics, and as principal and superintendent of schools.

The extensive development of the curriculum under his leadership and the splendid corps of teachers with which he surrounded himself attest to his scholarly interests and standards. When Barbour came to his position in 1885 there were three on the English staff, and the courses consisted of work in English Composition (Rhetoric and Orthoepy), English and some American Literature, and Universal Literature (Asia, Egypt, Ancient and Modern Europe) "with readings, reviews, and criticism as time may permit." The "universal" course disappeared promptly.

In his last year (1926), his staff had enlarged to fifteen, including a number of outstanding names: Esther Ballew, Alma Blount, Elizabeth Carey, Grace Cooper, Estelle Downing, Abigail Pearce and Estabrook Rankin. The offerings, now featuring areas of major and minor specialization, included the Essay, the Short Story, Fiction, Drama, and Poetry, a course in Exposition and Argument, and courses in Anglo-Saxon and Middle English.

As a teacher, Barbour was a magnet to students. One student explained it:

> His wholehearted enthusiasm in the study of Shakespeare with his students caused them to flock to his classes . . . When Professor Barbour took his Shakespeare book and read a passage to his class he would portray the characters so well that it was possible to see Hamlet acting, or King Lear in despair, or Othello bent on revenge.[6]

Mention was made of the strong, capable staff that Barbour assembled. The Normal College was beneficiary of a widespread prejudice in American higher education against women in faculty positions. No such prejudice prevailed in the teacher training institutions, and many able women found an opportunity there. The English staff at Normal was particularly fortunate in this respect.

Abigail Pearce came to the Normal as a supervising teacher in the elementary grades of the Training School.[7] Within three years, Barbour brought her into his department as an assistant. Along with her teaching, she studied at the University of Michigan, graduating as a Phi Beta Kappa, and later earning the master's degree there. Miss Pearce introduced a course in the English department, The Bible in the Making, which is still being offered under the title of The Bible as Literature. Her approach was historical and literary, and informed by the latest critical scholarship. As a citizen she was active at local, state and national levels.

Estelle Downing[8] was a contemporary of Abigail Pearce. In the classroom Miss Downing was an exacting but stimulating teacher. In youthful language, the college paper advised:

> You should take a course from Miss Downing and get yourself on the right track. She will give you a real workout but you will come away from her class with a healthier point of view, a fresh stock of new ideas, and a sincere desire to investigate worthwhile problems. She is a challenge to every student and professor on the campus.

It then quoted a student designated as "all-A":

> I got a "C" in her class and I earned it. I got more genuine stimulation while taking that course than I have from any other course I have taken on this campus. This is one of the differences that is not recorded by the marks in the office.

That Miss Downing was a woman of conviction cannot be denied. She was also a woman of action. Her interest was world peace and what women could do to promote it. She pursued this theme in her role as a teacher, stressing it in her English composition classes, to which she devoted much attention, and developing a course called Literature of World Good Will which she offered to in-service teachers in summer school.

She served as chairman of the International Relations Committee of the National Council of Teachers of English. This attention at the national level was well deserved. She had conceived the idea of what came to be known as the Itinerant Hope Chest, for use in the schools of Michigan. The name was not fanciful. It referred to an actual chest filled with posters, booklets and written proposals from many teachers for teaching international good will. The plan was that it should move from school to school on three-day loans. The demand was apparently lively, from both public and private schools. The chest was placed on exhibition both in Chicago and New York.

In the local community, Estelle Downing was also active. Before World War I she was an enthusiastic proponant of women's suffrage. In the early twenties she ran for the local city council and was successful, one of the first women in Michigan to achieve this distinction. At the first meeting of the council subsequent to the election the Mayor felt constrained to say:

> "I ask that councilmen and all persons in the audience kindly refrain from smoking during regular council meetings."

Miss Downing had informed him that she planned to attend all meetings.

Years after her death, friends among the faculty and alumni established a fund to build a collection in the college library in international relations. They called it the Estelle Downing Fund.

Among those who received attention from the academic world, three were preeminent: Alma Blount, Charles Frederick Harrold, and Gerald Saunders.

Miss Blount, a member of the staff for 35 years (1901–1936), was one of the early holders of the PhD degree. She did her work at Cornell University in English Philology and Medieval Romance. She had been a research student at the British Museum in London, the Bibliotheque Nationale and the Sorbonne in Paris, and at Harvard. She was widely known for her publications which included more than a half dozen textbooks.

Her major research project, however, was a dictionary of personal and place names in medieval Arthurian romances. Her sources were some 200 works in ten languages (French, Italian, Spanish, Greek, Latin, low and high German, Middle English, Icelandic, and Flemish). Her "Onomasticon Arthurianum" rests today, uncompleted, in the treasure room of Harvard's Widener Library.

Harrold was beyond question the outstanding scholar-teacher, known internationally for his work on Carlyle and on Cardinal

Newman. During his tenure at the Normal of 18 years (1925–1943) his interest was largely in Carlyle. In this connection he published five monographs, supplied the bibliography on Carlyle for the Cambridge Bibliography of English Literature, produced an edition of Carlyle's Sartor Resartus, and a volume on Carlyle and German Thought, 1819–1934. For this latter book he was elected to honorary membership in the Carlyle Society of Edinburgh, Scotland, and invited to lecture there.

From Carlyle, Harrold's attention turned to Cardinal Newman, and the remainder of his life (cut short by his untimely death at age 50) was devoted to this interest, on which he built a lasting reputation.

Sanders, though occupied as head of a large and growing department to which he gave close attention, published a number of articles and became nationally known through his textbooks, written for courses given by his department. He wrote one for each of the two courses, Poetry and Prose, and, assisted by younger members of his staff (Wallace Magoon, Hoover Jordan, Robert Limpus), produced a textbook in English composition for freshman classes that found wide and continuing acceptance throughout the nation. As a teacher, Sanders was both entertaining and exacting. He adopted the practice of requiring a daily written quiz, and willingly submitted himself to the killing task of grading. His students, in turn, were devoted to him and left his classes bearing a lasting imprint of his influence.

Foreign Languages

Instruction in foreign languages has always been offered. Normal's first principal, Adonijah Welch, was given the added title of Professor of Greek and Latin Languages. According to the catalog for 1853, instruction for the first term in the ancient languages was to consist of a review of Latin and Greek grammar, and study of Virgil's "Aeneid," Lucian's "Dialogues," Cicero's "Orations," Xenophon's "Anabasis." A professorship of modern languages was listed in the first catalog but not filled until the following year (1854) when Albert Miller was employed to teach German and Vocal Music (and gymnastics and fencing).

Miller was born in Thuringia, Germany. He had received a classical education at the gymnasium of Sondershausen and the University of Jena. He had come to Detroit in 1847, when he organized and conducted the Detroit Lyric Society, said to be the first successful musical organization in the city. At Normal he added French to the program (1859), and remained in his dual capacity of instructor in music and languages until 1866 when he resigned.

The inclusion of foreign languages in the curriculum of an institution which, on the academic side, was little more than a somewhat glorified academy may appear rather startling. Most of the students would go forth from the Normal to teach in the rural (district) schools of the State. There would be no occasion to teach a foreign language. For these, a curriculum was organized called the English Course. It contained no foreign languages.

But a new development was taking place in the public schools, known as the Union School, successor to the private academy and precursor of the High School. Here a growing need was being felt for teachers who could instruct in foreign languages, particularly Latin and Greek. For these, a program was offered at the Normal known as the Classical Course, and here the languages played a role. But besides the objective of meeting this need, a second was stated:

> . . . to secure for Normal students the benefit of a class of studies which, as instruments of mental discipline, have confessedly no superiors, if equals, to say nothing of the strong light which they (especially the Latin) reflect upon the etymology and structure of our own tongue, and upon many most interesting points of general literature.[9]

For a number of years instruction in foreign languages was at times combined with other areas, and such positions appeared as Greek, Latin and Geography, Latin and English Grammar, French and Geography, German and History.[10]

With the advent of Principal Estabrook, however, permanent departments of ancient and modern languages were established. In his first year (1871) be brought to Normal Joseph P. Vroman, who instructed in Latin and Greek for the next 15 years. In 1872, he secured August Lodeman for German and French. Lodeman presided over this department for the next 30 years.

Vroman's tenure was not altogether happy. A hint that not all might be well was provided by a visiting Englishman who spent some time visiting classes at the Normal around 1873, and wrote a delightful (and in general enthusiastic) account of what he found. Speaking of Vroman as "a gentleman eminently qualified to occupy the chair," he then said:

> . . . the whole lesson from beginning to end, was praise-worthy, stable and efficient; but I was not quite able to appreciate one thing, and this had no reference to the individual class, simply to the custom of the country. My whole enjoyment of the class . . . was spoiled by the American way of pronouncing the Latin. It was neither fish, flesh, fowl, nor good red herring. It was a hybrid—three parts continental and one mongrel.[11]

This was followed some three years later by the annual report of the Board of Visitors, two of whose three members were William H. Payne (shortly to be brought to the University of Michigan to occupy the first university chair in the nation in the Science and Art of Teaching), and Julia Anne King (within a few years to become a member of Normal's faculty). Their evaluation of Vroman's instruction was brief but pointed:

> In the department of Ancient Languages the instruction seemed to us to lack accuracy and thoroughness, and in this respect to form a noticeable exception to the general order of things.

In his report of the following year, Estabrook felt called upon to defend his professor, saying that the visit of the Board in that department had been extremely brief and asking for a special committee from the University of Michigan to make an inspection. Benjamin D'Ooge (of the Normal) and Henry Frieze (of the University of Michigan) were suggested. Whether such a visit was ever made is not clear. The Board of Visitors for 1878, however, found the deficiencies to be "of the external finish rather than of the essentials of scholarship." Vroman continued in his position until 1886 when he resigned and moved to Detroit. There he studied law and developed a successful practice.

His successor in ancient languages was D'Ooge.[12] His career at the Normal was the longest in its history (52 years), and his name among the brightest.

D'Ooge came to Ypsilanti at age 36, possessed of a master of arts degree and a Phi Beta Kappa key from the University of Michigan where his older brother, Martin Luther D'Ooge, was distinguishing himself as Professor of Greek Language and Literature.

At Normal, he gained a reputation with his textbooks in Latin, which were used in the high schools from one end of the nation to the other. He played an active role in the Michigan Schoolmasters Club, serving more than once as its president. He was a charter member and sixth president of the Classical Association of the Middle West and South.

In 1936, a grand all-day celebration was held in honor of his 50 years of service at Normal. The State Board of Education recognized the occasion by a formal resolution:

> Resolved, that the State Board of Education of the State of Michigan do hereby express their appreciation of the fact that the career of Professor D'Ooge has been one of signal distinction not only to himself and the Michigan State Normal College, but also to the whole cause of Classical education in America; and that he has exemplified in his long lifetime that the learning of the scholar and the graces of the teacher are in no wise incompatable . . .

Some twenty-one years after his death in 1940, it was reported that one of his former students, teaching Latin in Dallas, Texas, had secured the re-publication in lithograph form of D'Ooge's Elements of Latin for use in her classes, and that plans for a new high school building included a Benjamin L. D'Ooge Roman Theatre.

Turning now to the area of modern languages, Estabrook's choice of a head for that department proved fortunate. August Lodeman was born at Zeven, Hanover, Germany. His father, a lawyer, was attached to the King's court. For a time young Lodeman lived in France and in the French-speaking area of Switzerland. Coming to the United States at age 25, he settled in Kalamazoo, Michigan, where he conducted a private school in both ancient and modern languages, and mathematics. In 1869, he accepted a position as teacher of German and French in the Grand Rapids High School. (Edwin A. Strong, later to become an eminent member of Normal's faculty, was at the time the Superintendent of Schools). From there he came to Ypsilanti.[13]

Lodeman became an enthusiastic supporter of the normal school idea. He wrote and spoke frequently on this subject, publishing numerous essays and articles. It was said of him that he stood "as no other one person did" for the steady expansion of the library and for the presence of works of art in the corridors.

He formed a firm and lasting friendship with David Eugene

Smith, head of the Mathematics Department. Writing from Teachers College, Columbia University, at the time of his friend's death, Smith reminisced:

> We explored all the country round about Ypsilanti on our wheels, thrice we were in Europe together, and in four ocean voyages we were companions. His home was mine, and mine was his . . . what I most liked about him was his honesty, his unusual honesty. What he thought, he said . . . He was the Teuton professor; ever a scholar; ever a worker, ever modest in his labors. In our profession it is not easy to find such men.

Lodeman's successor was R. Clyde Ford. Coming to the Normal in 1903, at age 33, he spent the rest of his active life, a period of 37 years, as head of the Modern Languages Department, an able and worthy cohort of Benjamin D'Ooge. Ford's background included foreign study, teaching abroad, and public school and college positions at home. Like D'Ooge, Ford had studied in Germany, earning a PhD at the University of Munich. He had pursued research in Geneva, Paris, London, and Montpelier.[14]

On Normal's campus he represented the well-rounded, cultured gentleman of world-wide interest. His publications included a textbook translation, historical novels for young people, and a biography of Michigan's father of public education, John D. Pierce.

The story of R. Clyde Ford bears a certain fascination from the fact that he represented the transition period from the rough, arduous, limited life of the pioneer to the cultured gentleman of the automobile age. He was born in a log cabin in Calhoun County, Michigan. His grandfather came to Michigan in territorial days, knowing nothing but ox-team transportation. Reminiscing in later years, he wrote:

> I grew up in the horse age and learned the geography of ten miles around our house from horse-drawn vehicles . . . My father transported me bag and baggage to college in a farm wagon and though it was only a fifteen mile trip it was such a hardship to get back that I went home but once or twice a term . . . people lived a shut-in marooned kind of life . . . This [shut-in] attitude continued in my own case . . . till twenty years ago when the automobile suddenly annihilated space for me and pushed back my local horizons . . . . it was like being born again into a new world.

The Modern Language Department prospered under Ford's direction. Upon his arrival in 1903 he announced a series of informal lectures, open to all, which attracted wide interest. Such subjects were presented as "The Literary Martin Luther;" "Goethe and His Work;" "Heine and the Romantic School;" "The Grand Century of Louis XIV." In 1917, courses in Spanish were added, and in 1918 Ford inaugurated a series of "general" courses in Modern European Literature in English, open to all, concerned with Russia, Scandinavia, the Central Empires, France, and Spain. In 1936, with the adoption of a State Certification Code for teachers, language courses were developed and arranged to provide areas of concentration, major and minor.

With the retirement of D'Ooge in 1938, the Departments of Ancient and Modern Languages were combined under Ford.

Clyde Ford's presence in the classroom was well described by a statement in the college annual which read in part:

> Dr. Ford, although a Michigan product, bears a distinct mark of 'made in Germany' and 'patented in France'. His keen humor commands attention, his scholarly mind admiration . . . Always genial, in spite of a sometimes foreboding expression, he makes the most difficult work pleasure . . .

With his retirement in 1940, the Department of Foreign Languages was placed under the direction of a specialist in French, J. Henry Owens.[15] When Owens arrived he found a staff of four, and offerings in Latin, Greek, French, German, and Spanish.

During the subsequent years, experimentation as to effective instruction and changing demands from the public schools brought important changes. As of 1965, this department listed a staff of seven, and offered courses in French, German, Russian, and Spanish. With the exception of Russian, each of the areas offered a major concentration and a choice of three minors, with an appropriate methods course. An innovation which Owens pioneered was instruction in a modern foreign language (French) in the elementary grades, with an appropriate methods course.

The ancient languages fell victim to changing times and constraints of a budget-starved institution which found it difficult to justify extremely small classes to a non-classical-minded legislature. Latin, which once played so proud a role, found itself reduced by the year 1954–1955 to six students and one course. It did not appear thereafter and the associate professor in the classical languages began teaching courses in ancient history. Greek, facing a similar decline, was not taught from 1942 to 1946, was revived in 1946, dropped in 1948, tried once again and once only, in 1954. The department had become in fact a Department of Modern Languages.

On the other hand, the modern languages flourished. The newcomer, Russian, was first offered in 1951, dropped in 1954, revived in 1958, dropped, and temporarily revived in 1961.

Facilities for language instruction were greatly improved. The department responded to lessons learned from language instruction to meet war needs, and in 1954 a language laboratory was installed where recordings could be heard by the students in individual booths. This laboratory was greatly improved and enlarged in 1961, facilitating tape recording and dictation quizzes.

An outstanding project of the department was undertaken in 1948, called a Poetry Recital. This was held on the campus in the spring of the year. High school students were invited to hear and recite poems in French and Spanish. The project proved to be so successful that it soon adopted the name of Foreign Language Festival, included German, presented a variety show, and added elementary students to its invitation list. It has become a fixture and has proved to be a powerful stimulant to the study of foreign languages in the schools of the area.

History

Lectures in history were offered from the opening of Normal in 1853. The first area of interest was United States history, and the first course offered might fall under the category either of history or political science. It was called "Constitution of the United States." Who taught it is not revealed; there was no chair in either field.

By 1868, a course called "History" was included in the curriculum. This was doubtless a series of lectures in United States history. By 1870, it was a requirement in the Common School Course. In 1871, the subject was assigned to a specified member of the staff, Anna M. Cutcheon being designated to teach geography, drawing, history and English literature.

The emphasis in the teaching of this subject is revealed in the following official statement:

> In history, few dates are required; only those around which cluster important events, and which serve as milestones in the country's progress. We

aim to trace the connection between cause and effect, and to become
acquainted not only with the *facts,* but with the philosophy of history.

In general, it was felt that students should get their facts of history
in high school, and one of the requirements for admission to the
Normal department was a course in history. By 1875, however,
lectures were being given in the history of foreign countires. This
was accomplished by the cooperation of several members of the staff.
Principal Estabrook, for example, gave lectures on Jewish, Persian,
and Egyptian history; lectures on Greek and Roman history were
given by Professor Vroman of the Ancient Languages Department;
Professor Lodeman of Modern Languages lectured on German and
French history; Professor Putnam lectured on Spanish and Spanish-
American history; and Anna Cutcheon on English history.

As a department of instruction, however, history appeared first in
1888. The first department head was Julia Anne King. Called the
Department of History and Civil Government, it had a staff of three,
the other two being Annie A. Paton and Ella M. Hayes.

Miss King came to the Normal in 1881 as Preceptress and Professor of Botany and History.[16] Her career holds particular interest. In
later years, when asked for some biographical information, she
replied tersely, "Born and taught school." There was more meaning
here than one might expect. Born in a log cabin near Milan, Michigan, her formal education was limited to high school graduation
(Adrian) and three years at the Normal. She received Normal's Life
Certificate in teaching just five years after the Normal opened its
doors (1858).

In the course of time she became a highly educated woman
(though not in the formal sense), and strongly influential. Not only
was she responsible for organizing a Department of History at the
Normal, but she made a strong impression throughout the State as
an educator. An editorial in the *Detroit Free Press* at the time of her
death read in part:

> Miss King was unquestionably the greatest woman educator Michigan
> has ever had. She ranks, in fact, among the half dozen greatest educators
> the state has possessed.[17]

Her lack of formal education (she was 31 years of age when the
University of Michigan first admitted a women to its classes) was

compensated by constant reading, travel in Europe and, as one account stated, "unremitting habits of inquiry and interpretation." She was able to state in due time that she had taught every course at Normal excepting Greek, but that her preferences were history and physical sciences.

As Preceptress, Miss King made a strong impression on the young women, but her chief recognition derived from her work as a history teacher. Not content with history as an accumulation of fact, she sought to define it as a subject to be taught with a purpose. She came to the conclusion that history, rightly taught, has a social mission to perform. She explained:

> History is Society becoming conscious of itself . . . One could hope that social consciousness, understood in history, might become in time an idea in the individual sufficiently clear and strong to determine his thinking and conduct.

During Miss King's headship of the Department of History of 27 years, the offerings were expanded from four history courses (Greece, Rome, England, the United States) and one course in civil government to sixteen. Not only were the courses in history increased to include the constitutional history of both England and the United States, Medieval and Modern European History, and Industrial History, but the work in political science was expanded and a new area, sociology, appearing about 1908, was represented by two courses. Miss King was personally involved in the work in sociology, which she felt was closely allied to history, and in a course in the Philosophy of History. She was also deeply concerned with the teaching of history in the public schools, and taught the course in methods herself.

A worthy understudy and colleague was Bertha Buell,[18] whose particular area of concern was English history. Her formal training had been more extensive than that of Miss King. She, too, had earned a teaching certificate at the Normal (1893), but added to that a bachelor's degree from the University of Michigan in 1899 (the year that she came to the Normal). In the course of the next few years she earned a Master's degree in history at Radcliffe College. On occasion, in Miss King's absence, she served as acting head of the department.

As a member of the college community she organized a League of

Women Voters that proved to be a model for other campuses; promoted cooperative housing for students and strongly supported Dean Lydia Jones in her drive for student dormitories. As a citizen of the world, she, along with her colleague in the English Department, Estelle Downing, spoke and worked for world peace.

As for the students, their evaluation was expressed in a dedication of the college annual: "To Bertha G. Buell, in appreciation of her leadership, with gratitude for her high ideals of scholarship, and with admiration and respect for fostering the cause of peace."

Until 1913, the department had been staffed only by women. In that year, however, the first male intruder appeared in the form of Earl G. Fuller, a name that disappeared after a single year. The second was to prove enduring. Carl Pray succeeded Miss King as head of the department in January, 1914.

Pray's was a long and influential tenure, extending through 23 years. In that time the staff of the department doubled. Economics was added to the curriculum. The general courses were supplemented by a number of more intensive ones such as the French Revolution, American Colonial Institutions, Immigration and Americanization, and The West. A decided proliferation of courses occurred about 1928 when the social sciences were designated as a separate area, and subdivided formally into economics, political science, and sociology.

It was in 1928 that the State Board of Education provided for formal concentrations in the subject matter areas. In the History Department, this stimulated the initiation of the Honors Course—which actually meant individual attention to the exceptional student in the form of planned reading and discussion, freed from the formalities of class organization. Such, for example, were the courses in European Statesmen, 1848–1900 and the study of States Rights.

Pray took an active part in the Michigan Historical Society, serving as president and trustee. He published a number of articles in such periodicals as the *Bay View Magazine*, the *American Schoolmaster*, the *Teachers' History Magazine*. His particular interest was in the nature and influence of immigration in America, concerning which he developed a course.

But his chief contribution was as a teacher. His personal appeal was exceptional, he could tell a story with great charm, and he was successful in stimulating in his students a lasting attraction to history. Tributes to Pray as a teacher and friend of students were spontaneous and continuing. In 1915, the college annual said of him: "In his classes dead heroes come to life, ancient personalities speak to us, we live and fight the battles of long ago."

Twice the college annual was dedicated to him and in 1931 the graduating class presented a bronze bust of Pray to the College with the hope that this might be the beginning of a Hall of Fame for Normal. Concerning their choice of whom to honor, they said:

> From the lips of his colleagues one hears him called professor; but from the hearts of his students comes a more endearing title, one that connotes the simplicity and humanity at all times evident in his character. That fondest title of all—so representative of his genuine love for his fellow humanity is simply 'Daddy Pray'.

Pray retired in 1937 and from then until 1940 the department operated under the acting headship of a member of the staff, Anna Field, who without remuneration or relief in teaching load carried on the duties in a dedicated and efficient manner.

In 1940, the appointment was given to Simon E. Fagerstrom. Fagerstrom was a Swedish immigrant who, after coming to America, received inspiration and encouragement to get a college education which in turn led to graduate work and eventually the PhD from the University of Michigan.

During his regime, which extended 18 years, the staff again doubled (from 12 to 24) and offerings greatly increased. The areas of the social sciences were especially strengthened so that it became possible to offer a major concentration in economics, political science, and sociology.

In 1958, Donald Drummond, formerly on the history staff of the University of Michigan, became head. Again the staff was enlarged and an area added, that of philosophy. Manuel Bilsky was called from Roosevelt College in Chicago to establish this branch of learning, with the anticipation that in the course of time it might develop into a separate department.

CHAPTER TWENTY-TWO

SCIENCE AND MATHEMATICS

The purpose of the Normal School was prescribed in the statute which established the institution. In addition to the function of instructing "in the art of teaching, and in all the various branches that pertain to a good common school education," and in "the fundamental laws of the United States, and in what regards the rights and duties of citizens," the School was to "instruct in the arts of husbandry and agricultural chemistry." A subsequent section was more specific:

> Lectures on chemistry, comparative anatomy, astronomy, the mechanic arts, agricultural chemistry, and on any other science . . . shall be delivered to those attending said school by the professors of the University [of Michigan], provided the regents shall give their consent thereto.[1]

Interest in establishing schools for instruction in the practical arts first became manifest at about the time that Michigan became a state. An interest in agricultural instruction was evident from about 1838. Memorials for the establishment of colleges of "agriculture, mechanics, road making, and architecture" from several states had been presented to Congress in the 1840's. In 1847, a committee of the New York legislature had recommended that a school be established to teach "agriculture and the mechanic arts."[2]

In 1849, the Michigan State Agricultural Society was formed. This organization had a decisive influence on provision for instruction in agriculture. Indeed, one of the organizers of the Society, John C. Holmes, is felt to deserve major credit as founder of the Michigan Agricultural College (now Michigan State University). In December of this same year the Executive Committee of the Society resolved to ask the State Leiglsature to establish "as soon as practicable, an agricultural college." It will be noted that this took place subsequent to the passage of the Act establishing the Normal School.[3]

In the revised Michigan Constitution of 1850 provision for such a school was made, but with the suggestion that it be a branch of the University of Michigan. Here, then, was created a confusing situation. In the Normal School Act passed the preceding March, the Normal School had been authorized to instruct in agriculture. Now it was suggested that a school for this purpose might be organized as a branch of the University of Michigan.

That such a branch was not authorized by the legislature has been blamed on the rivalry that ensued between the U-M and the Normal School for the honor. In Ann Arbor, President Tappan insisted that this area was in his province. He had good reason for taking this stand. The organic act establishing U-M was revised in 1838 and modified to include the clause, "in one at least of the branches of the University, there shall be a department of agriculture . . .."

The U-M organized a course of lectures in agriculture, and the Rev. Charles Fox, an Episcopalain clergyman with BA and MA degrees from Oxford, gave some lectures on the subject without charge in the spring of 1853. The following year he was appointed by the Regents as Professor of Agriculture. Death prevented his serving.

In the same year (1853) the Normal School brought Lewis Ransom Fisk from the Wesleyan Seminary and Albion Female College (later to be known as Albion College) as professor. Fisk had been educated at Harvard, Dartmouth, and the University of Michigan.

In December of 1854, the Agricultural Society passed a resolution "that an Agricultural College should be separate from any other institution." In 1855, the legislature established a separate college, provided a site of nearly 700 acres, and appropriated $30,000 for buildings.[4]

Thus, neither of the two existing institutions won. Yet, in some respects, the Normal prevailed. The new agricultural college was placed under the authority of Normal's State Board of Education. And the new institution proceeded to secure Professor Fisk as its instructor in agriculture. Fisk (also spelled Fiske) was later elected by the faculty of the Agricultural College as Acting President, upon the resignation of President Williams in 1859.

It was thus, out of confusion of legislative intent and competition for possession of the area of instruction in agriculture, that science instruction at the Normal was born. Many years were to pass, however, before science instruction became specialized. Professor Jessie Phelps, for 41 years a member of the Natural Science Department (1898–1939), has given us this description:

> During the first three decades, from 1853 to 1883, the sciences taught here were not separated into distinct departments. They were all taught in one laboratory or suite of rooms on the first floor of the only college building. Physiology, Natural Philosophy (a potpourri of explanations of common phenomena such as gravitation, the formation of dew, etc.), Geology, and the physical sciences were presented by some one or two men of the faculty, while Botany was assigned to the preceptress.[5]

David Porter Mayhew (later to succeed Welch as Principal) replaced Fisk; botany was assigned to Ruth Hoppin, Preceptress; and, a decade later, psychology "theoretical and applied" was added.

In the 1870's courses in Structural Botany and Zoology were introduced, and a laboratory method employing a compound microscope ("a very up-to-date method") was in use.

By 1880, classes in zoology, physiology, hygiene, chemistry, astronomy, geology, and botany were being held. In 1882, Lucy Osband was added to the faculty as instructor in biology, assisting Professor McLouth. She was instrumental in bringing together the courses being offered in the natural sciences, and from 1883 headed a Department of Natural Sciences. In 1895, she retired and was succeeded by William Hittell Sherzer, who joined the Normal staff in 1892. Sherzer headed the department until his death in 1932.

At the same time physics and chemistry formed a department under McLouth, who had been teaching the sciences at the Normal since 1869. Two years later (1885) McLouth was persuaded to leave the Normal and take a position at the Michigan Agricultural College as Professor of Mechanics and Astronomy. His replacement, Edwin Atson Strong, became in time an outstanding member of the faculty. Strong remained with the Normal until his retirement in 1916, a period of 32 years.

Physics and Chemistry

The Department of Physics and Chemistry retained its identity until 1916 when the physical sciences were split into separate departments.

The separation elevated Bert W. Peet, who had been on the staff since 1899, to head of the new Chemistry Department. Peet served until his retirement in 1958, and was in turn succeeded by John A. Sellers. After Sellers' death in 1961, Marvin S. Carr served as acting head until 1962 when Clark J. Spike was named.

Turning to the Physics Department, Professor Strong's retirement in 1916 brought Frederick R. Gorton (who had been on the Normal staff since 1896) to the headship. Upon his retirement in 1941, Harry L. Smith became head. Smith retired in 1960 and was succeeded by James A. Barnes.

As for the Natural Science Department, Sherzer's death in 1932 brought Milton Hover as head. To his duties were added, in 1935, those of Dean of Administration. Hover served in both capacities until his death in 1940, when the departmental headship went to Clarence M. Loesell. Loesell died in 1958 and was replaced by Robert Belcher, whose department became designated in 1962 as the Biology Department. Belcher resigned to devote full time to teaching and research, and was succeeded by Richard Giles.

As of 1962, the offerings in science had developed from the few general lectures in agricultural chemistry in 1853 to offerings in four highly organized divisions, as follows: Biology—35 (Biology—10, Botany—11, Zoology—14); Chemistry—22; Geography—11; Physics and Astronomy—24 (23 in Physics).

Several of the names mentioned above are worthy of more attention. Lewis McLouth, of the Department of Physical Sciences, remained in this position only two years, leaving in 1885 to accept the chair of Mechanics and Astronomy at the Michigan Agricultural College. While at Normal, however, McLouth was instrumental in the construction of the astronomical observatory and of the ornate tower (a contribution of the citizens of Ypsilanti) on the Old Main Building. William McAndrew, an alumnus and one-time Superintendent of the Chicago Public Schools, reminisced as follows concerning McLouth:

Another strong and well beloved man we had was Professor Lewis
McLouth. I had him in natural philosophy, chemistry, geology and Bible
study. He was a living contradiction of Emerson's declaration that the
scientist is like the dried plants in his herbal, without sap and humor.
McLouth was one of the most lovably humorous and human teachers that
ever happened . . . He had a fad for fine looking glass-ware in chemical
demonstrations and an artistic arrangement of the air-pump and the electrical machine so that, as the art folks say, they would "compose" well on
the table before the class. He was as keen as a knife but he never hurt.[6]

Considerable resentment on the part of the students was expressed
against the authorities at East Lansing for taking him away from
Normal.

The Natural Science Department was placed under an exceptionally interesting and effective person, Lucy Aldrich Osband. Mrs.
Osband's educational experience had been varied. She had been
principal of the Sylvan Villa Seminary in Virginia; teacher at the
Northville, Michigan, high school; Preceptress and Professor of
Modern Languages at Albion College; teacher of Greek at Olivet
College.[7] In 1882, she was employed by Normal as instructor in
biology. Her contributions to Normal were impressive, and of
pioneering character. She developed good working collections in
geology and zoology. She originated the herbarium. With the aid of
her students she is said to have prepared one of the best osteological
collections in the State. Through personal friends she secured many
treasures for her department, among them a collection of fish gathered by Agassiz in South America.[8]

Through her classes in physiology she initiated work in physical
training which developed into a Department of Physical Education.
She can be credited with influencing the first head of that department, Wilbur P. Bowen, to leave his chosen field of mathematics
and devote himself to physical training. She was also given credit for
winning the State Legislature over to an appropriation for a gymnasium.

In her pre-Normal years, as a teacher in Methodist seminaries
and at Albion College, she was credited with having inspired many
young people to go as missionaries to Burma, China, Japan, India,
and Korea. Her zeal at the Normal in developing the new Department of Natural Science was unbounded.

Upon her retirement in June of 1895, the school paper made this comment:

> Mrs. Osband is a good example of what force of will can accomplish. Although hampered by a frail constitution, she had, nevertheless, by unfaltering resolution and careful use of her strength, accomplished a work which can be measured only by the lives of those who came under her influence.

The Osband daughter, Marna, writing about her mother at a later time, made this somewhat bitter comment: "Mrs. Osband never received any extra pay for all this special work. In fact, she never got but half of what the men professors did."—a statement all too true. Such were the times for women, and such they were to remain for decades to come.

Mrs. Osband's successor was William Hittell Sherzer who was at the moment temporary occupant of the chair of geology at the University of Michigan. After coming to Normal, Sherzer completed work for the PhD, and remained until he had served with distinction over a period of 40 years. Not only was he a superior teacher but he attained a national reputation in geology and anthropology.

At the national level he was engaged to make a special study in anthropology for the National Museum, was in charge of the Smithsonian Glacial Expedition to the Canadian Rockies and Selkirks (summers 1904, 1905), and made important field studies in the Hawaiian Islands, with special attention to the explosive eruptions of Mt. Kilauea (1920–1921). At the state level he assisted in the Michigan State Geological Survey (1896–1913). He contributed the Detroit Folio of the United States Geological Atlas and was consulting geologist for the City of Detroit in establishing a suitable location for the Detroit-Windsor tunnel under the Detroit River.

As head of the Natural Science Department he was the pioneer in Michigan in promoting the study of nature in the elementary curriculum. Here he developed a collection of material for use in teacher training that was probably unexcelled anywhere. His interest has been attributed to his theory that the child must recapitulate the experience of the race.

Sherzer was also active in organizing extensive field trips for summer school students. One announcement (that for 1924), advertising a tour of "about six weeks," read:

> . . . in the interest of teachers who feel the need of relaxation and who
> wish to see the choicest bits of scenery on the American continent, if not in
> the world.

There followed a list of places to be visited: Glacier National Park, Mount Rainier National Park, Seattle, Victoria, Vancouver, Alaskan and Canadian Rockies. One or two units of credit were offered, via the Extension Department. The announcement closed with a practical item:

> Pairs of close friends are desired who can occupy together a Pullman section, steamer cabin and hotel room.

In those years when teaching about evolution aroused strong antagonism, particularly in the area of public school education, Sherzer taught it. He insisted that there was no conflict between religion and science; that there is only one Truth. He commented that "nature is so beautiful—God and Mother Nature must be working together." Whenever sisters of the Catholic faith sat in his classes, however, he is said never to have asked them to recite.

In his teaching, Sherzer placed great emphasis on demonstrations. He developed a collection of minerals and rocks which in time was reported to be one of the best in the State. He acquired a valuable skull collection from a local dentist to show the evolution of vertebrate dentition. He organized the Nature Study Club, forerunner of the Natural Science Club (1898 or 1899) which still flourishes, and entertained students and colleagues extensively at his cottage, Fernwood, at Baseline Lake near Ann Arbor, where scientific topics were avidly discussed.

During his long tenure, Sherzer saw his staff increase from 2 to 8 (and 11 student assistants). New areas were developed, old areas expanded. The number of courses increased from 5 to 55, and included offerings in agriculture, heredity and evolution, nature study, as well as botany, geology, and physiology.

Two buildings stand on the campus as monuments to his interests: the old Science Building, re-named Sherzer Hall, which he helped to plan, and the Hover Laboratory Building, erected during World War II for the training of teachers in nature study for the elementary grades.

As a citizen of Ypsilanti, too, Sherzer made a lasting contribution.

It was he who brought the Boy Scouts to the community. He was president of the first Boy Scout Council, the camp at Peninsula Grove on the Huron River was named after him, and he was the proud host for a full week of the founder of the Boy Scout movement, Ernest Seton Thompson.

Sherzer's counterpart in the physical sciences, Edwin Atson Strong, also left a permanent impression on Normal. Strong came to be looked upon by his colleagues as the most learned man on the faculty.

He was brought to Ypsilanti from Grand Rapids in 1885 to head the new Department of Physical Sciences. In Grand Rapids, he had been principal and superintendent of public schools since 1861, and for 18 years was curator and promoter of the Kent Museum there.

Strong's professional contributions included publication of many pamphlets and articles on scientific and educational subjects, service on the Michigan Geological Survey, and publication of two numbers of the List of Fossils of the Lower Carboniferous of Kent County, Michigan. He was a member of the American Association for the Advancement of Science and a director of the National Educational Association (1892–1894). He was president at one time or another of the Michigan Academy of Science, Michigan Teachers Association, the Michigan Schoolmasters Club, and the Michigan Association of High School Principals.

Notwithstanding his role as scientist, he possessed a highly stimulating and attractive personality. W. N. Ferris, founder of Ferris Institute and one-time Governor of Michigan, is reported to have said that E. A. Strong was one of two men to whom he owed all the inspiration that made him what he was. The college paper, *Normal News,* paid him tribute in his late years, "not only as a teacher but as a man in whom rare intellectual attainments are combined with rarer and more precious qualities of a pure heart and a noble soul."

Sherzer once referred to him as "one of the few remaining naturalists of the old school, his mind encompassing the entire realm of scientific knowledge. But oddly, he was almost or quite as well informed in literature, art history, and matters pertaining."

The esteem in which his colleagues held him was strikingly illustrated at the time of his death by their preparation of a memorial booklet. In a prefatory note they said: "The loss of our distinguished colleague, Professor E. A. Strong—an inspiring teacher for over sixty years, a member of this faculty for thirty-five years, an eminent scholar of the broadest culture—is an event calling for more than passing notice."

Geography

The subject of geography was taught at the Normal almost from the first and was included in the first curricula, prescribed by the State Board as "geography, including the use of outline maps and instruction in map-making." It is probable that the example set by the European seminaries, which was influential in the existing normal schools in Massachusetts, New York and Connecticut, also influenced Michigan's State Board. Because of the map-making emphasis, the subject at Normal was long associated with drawing.[9]

The first course in geography and drawing was given by a student at Normal in his senior (second) year, John Goodison (1860). Upon graduating he was immediately added to the faculty where he taught both subjects regularly for years, and acquired assistants who at times added arithmetic, Virgil, and Greek.

Goodison was born in England. His father, an artist, at one time had an assignment as decorator of the interior of the British Museum. John, age 16, assisted him. The parents came to the United States in 1851, the son following a year later and in due course becoming a student at Normal. He taught at the Normal from 1861–1869, left to join the staff of D. Appleton and Co., publishers, and returned in 1885 to remain until his death in 1892.

In teaching, Goodison was said to have devised and made nearly all of the charts and illustrative appliances that he used. He was described as thorough, persevering, and patient in dealing with his students. "Let him once feel that a student was making an effort to advance," said his friend and colleague, Austin George, "and progress might be never so little or never so slow, he had for such student only words of cheer and encouragement."

Goodison was succeeded by Charles T. McFarlane, whose department continued to be known as Drawing and Geography. By this time instruction in geography had been organized and broadened to include courses in contour and relief of the earth's surface, hydrography, climate and distribution of vegetable and animal life, "anthropogeography" (man as dependent upon the physical condition of the earth's surface; the earth's surface as modified by the action of man), "special geography," and a course in the teaching of geography.

McFarlane, a native of New York and graduate of the New York State Normal School, came to the Normal at age 21. His enthusiasm for his subject was contagious, and spread also to those in attendance at the teachers institutes. On the campus at Ypsilanti, McFarlane guided a number of students into geography as a profession, among them H. H. Barrows (later to head the Geography Department at the University of Chicago) and D. H. Davis (later to become head of the Geography Department at the University of Minnesota). In 1901, he left to succeed David Eugene Smith, Principal of the Normal School at Brockport, New York, who had preceded him there from Normal.

McFarlane was succeeded by Mark Jefferson, strongly supported by W. M. Davis of Harvard. Jefferson remained until his retirement in 1939, and made a career that contributed greatly both to the teaching and the development of his field throughout the nation.

Jefferson had insisted that geography and drawing should be divorced. Upon his arrival in 1901, therefore, he became first head of the Geography Department. By the time he retired he had expanded the offerings to include all the continents of the world, and such specific areas as the British Isles, Switzerland, Africa, Egypt, and the Caribbean lands. From time to time courses expressive of a particular interest or novel inquiry would appear, such as Geography of Culture, Geography of Railways, Geography of Commerce, and Geography of Cities. Jefferson became known for his emphasis on a place for man in geography, and among the textbooks that he wrote were such titles as "Man in Europe," "Man in the United States," and "Exercises in Human Geography."

In the 38 years that he spent at the Normal he trained several of the future "greats" in the field of geography, served as Chief Cartographer of President Wilson's famous committee known as "The Inquiry," played an active role in the work of the Paris Peace Conference of 1919, and won three of the most cherished awards that the geographers of this country have to bestow: the Helen Culver Gold Medal of the Chicago Geographic Society, for original work in geography; the Cullum Geographical Gold Medal of the American Geographical Society; and the Distinguished Service Award of the National Council of Geography Teachers.

His influence as a teacher was profound. He started three men on their careers as geographers who later became presidents of the

Association of American Geographers—Isaiah Bowman, Charles C. Colby, and A. E. Parkins. Three recieved the Distinguished Service to Geography Award of the National Council of Geography Teachers—D. H. Davis, R. R. Platt and George J. Miller. The Annals of the Association of American Geographers made this comment at the time of his death:

> This disciple record is better than that of any other college. Indeed, few major universities with departments of geography and with large numbers of students, fine equipment, and graduate school opportunities have approached that record of starting in Geography as many men who subsequently rose high in the profession.

Many of his articles were directed towards the teaching of geography in the public schools. Many school teachers resorted to him for recommendation as to materials desirable for specific grade levels, for assistance in revising a syllabus, or for evaluation of their work.

Jefferson retired in 1939 at age 76 but not because his energies were waning. He was vigorous and brimming with ideas and plans. He retired reluctantly because he had to; a literal-minded Board had recently adopted a ruling that age 70 would henceforth be the arbitrary limit of faculty service.

His successor was James Glasgow, product of the University of Chicago, brought from Western Michigan Normal College (now Western Michigan University) at Kalamazoo. Glasgow remained as head of the department until 1956 when he resigned to take charge of the new Graduate Division of the Normal College (by then Eastern Michigan College). During the period of his administration of the Geography Department, courses in meteorology and geology and a course on Canada were added. The work done in meteorology proved to be particularly useful to a number of Normal's sons as they entered the military service of their country in World War II.

Glasgow was succeeded by Albert Brown, a product of Syracuse University. Brown left this position in 1961 to become dean of the new College of Arts and Sciences. He left this position in 1965 to accept the presidency of the College of the State University of New York at Brockport. Brown's replacement was John Lounsbury, brought from Antioch College in Ohio.

Mathematics

The first instructor in mathematics at the Normal was Orson Jackson. He was a member of the first faculty in 1853 and remained three years, followed in succession by John E. Clark, George S. Jewell, George E. Dudley, and E. L. Ripley. In 1867, Charles R. Bellows, a graduate in civil engineering from the University of Michigan, was employed. Bellows remained with the Normal 14 years, serving one year as Acting Principal (1870–1871), and resigning in 1891 to become the first principal of the Central Michigan Normal School at Mt. Pleasant.

The subject matter offered during this time concerned algebra (including "higher algebra"), geometry, trigonometry (plane and spherical), surveying, and bookkeeping A review course in arithmetic was given for those needing it. As for mathematical prerequisites for admission to the Normal, a notice in an early catalog read:

> It is earnestly recommended that all intending to become members of the Normal School acquire some knowledge of Elementary Algebra, before offering themselves as candidates for admission.

As with the other areas of the curriculum, mathematics was represented by one faculty member, referred to variously as professor of, holding the chair of, or head of the department of mathematics. As help was needed, assistants were brought in or particular courses farmed out to representatives of other areas. Ruth Hoppin, for example, although Preceptress and Professor of Botany, also taught arithmetic at times. Formal organization of a Department of Mathematics occurred only after an extended evolutionary period.

Bellows, although trained in civil engineering, became an outstanding enthusiast for the professional preparation of teachers. He, together with Professor McLouth in Natural Science, was an ardent promoter of the experiment, tried in 1879–1880, to make of the Normal a purely professional school. With its demise under Principal Mac Vicar (himself a mathematician of some note), Bellows continued his campaigning until he completely alientated the State Board and was asked to resign. Bellows' position in this matter was that all courses in the Normal should be professional in character, including the academic courses. Instruction should be planned in terms of teaching the subject rather than in terms of the subject matter itself. In defense of his position at the time of his dismissal, he wrote:

> I sought to give a professional cast to all my academic work. I aimed to have my students conscious all the time that they were studying to be teachers. It was my usual custom to address them as teachers. I sought to bring them day by day the freshest thought and the most recent approved views on matters under consideration.[10]

In a letter to Bellows from a committee sent by the State Board to evaluate his work, the chairman wrote:

> I call the work you were doing purely professional work. No lessons assigned, no recitations. All the work done by the teacher with now and then a drawing out question of the class . . . We desire to have the academic work the sharpest kind of a review of what is in arithmetic. Not original methods, devices or solutions.

With the arrival of David Eugene Smith in 1891, a Department of Mathematics came into existence and the work done represented the best standards of the field. Smith, born in Cortland, New York, was a product of the Cortland State Normal School. From there he had gone to Syracuse University where he earned the doctorate in mathematics, then had returned to the Cortland Normal as a member of the faculty. At age 31, he came to Ypsilanti and remained seven years, resigning in 1898 to become principal of the State Normal at Brockport, New York. Leaving Brockport after three years, he went to Teachers College, Columbia University, as Professor of Mathematics, where, through extensive publishing, he became an international figure in his field.

For Smith, the years at Ypsilanti were formative in that he developed and expressed an abiding interest not only in mathematics as a field of human achievement but also in the problems of teaching. The bibliography of his publications includes some 600 items.[11] He was the author or co-author of some 70 books. More than 40 of these were textbooks for all levels of instruction—elementary, high school, and college. His highly successful series of high school textbooks in collaboration with Professor Beman of the University of Michigan was begun while he was at the Normal.

His books on the history of mathematics became standard sourcebooks. His interest in this stemmed from his belief that the history of

mathematics revealed that which is most precious and most significant in our civilization. He began his excursion into this area while
a member of Normal's faculty, publishing his "History of Modern
Mathematics" in 1896. He published also several textbooks while at
Ypsilanti.

At the time of his death, in 1944, it was said of him: "His interests were unusually extensive but most of all he was an untiring
worker for the cause and improvement of the teaching of his favorite
subject, mathematics."

His successor at the Normal was Elmer Adelbert Lyman, brought
to the campus from the University of Michigan where he had been
teaching mathematics and had been in charge of the U-M's first
venture in organizing a summer school.

Lyman came to the Normal just as it was becoming a four-year
college. His arrival also coincided with the installation of the so-
called Normal School System whereby a president was appointed by
the State Board to be in charge of all of the normal schools of Michigan, and each school was headed by a principal. Lyman was the
principal of Michigan State Normal College during the period of
this experiment. As head of the Mathematics Department he served
under Presidents Jones, McKenny and Munson. From 1912 until
his death in1934 (at age 73), he was a trustee of Berea College, serving on two of the most important committees of the Board, the
Executive Committee and the Investment Committee. He was also a
trustee of Alma College. During this period he published nine textbooks in mathematics, some in collaboration with Albertus Darrell
(at a later date to become head of the Mathematics Department of
Wayne State University) and Edwin C. Goddard (later to achieve an
outstanding reputation as a member of the law faculty of the University of Michigan).

Lyman's death brought a member of his department of some years
standing, Theodore Lindquist, to the position of head. In 1946,
Lindquist, retiring, was replaced by Robert Pate, the present incumbent.

Additions to the mathematics offerings by the close of the Lyman
period were courses in Integral Calculus, Differential Calculus, and
Differential Equations. Further additions—some prompted by the
desire to strengthen a two-year curriculum called pre-engineering
that had evolved through offerings in the Industrial Arts, Mathematics, and Physics Departments—were courses in Statics, Vector Anal-

ysis, Fluid Mechanics, Digital Computing, Matrices, Functions of a Complex Variable, and some service courses for Education and Business.

Thus, from small beginnings there developed a well-rounded, extensive, competently administered and taught liberal arts program, worthy of a prominent place in a university. Along the way, the Normal (now Eastern Michigan University) was fortunate in its ability to attract faculty members who were both stimulating and a credit to their professional fields of learning. Particularly noteworthy is the fact that without exception these people were profoundly dedicated to the improvement of instruction in the schools of the land, to the preparation of competent teachers, and to the writing of competent textbooks.

CHAPTER TWENTY-THREE

OFF-CAMPUS SERVICES

The circuit riders of our day are the college teachers who leave the facilities and comforts of campus and home to brave the hazards of the modern highway, carrying the religion of education to every nook and corner of their expanded bailiwick.

Off-campus instruction is no novelty in our generation. Cambridge University, England, was a pioneer in this type of service, prompted by the desire to extend education to workers. This was undertaken first in 1867. On our own side of the Atlantic, at the University of Wisconsin, imbued with the "Wisconsin idea" that a state university should provide services for the whole state, the moving force was the urgent desire of Wisconsin farmers for vocational instruction. The University moved to meet this need in 1885.[1] At the University of Michigan off-campus lectures were held on Friday and Saturday evenings by members of the faculty given in response to public demand, probably as early as 1857. At the Michigan Agricultural College an extension division was organized in 1908 in response to the need of farmers.

For the teachers colleges, the need of teachers-in-service sparked the movement. Among the Normal Schools in Michigan the first to offer extension classes was Northern, at Marquette, in 1904. The report of the Principal to the State Board said:

In the spring of the present year, the normal school introduced a system of extension classes which has been quite successful. By this system, teachers who have taught at least six years successfully may avail themselves of work done in these classes under one of the professors of the normal school and gain full credit for the work done.

267

In the following year the Board accepted the recommendation of Principal Waldo, of the Western Michigan Normal at Kalamazoo, "that the policy of normal school extension now in operation at Marquette be made operative at the Western State Normal School under the same safeguards as prevail at the Northern Normal." With the Board's approval, Western thereupon developed a program leading to the Life Certificate that was based on a combination of residence and extension credit. The reasoning behind this move was explained by Waldo:

> Many of the older teachers having, through various causes, been deprived of professional training, it seemed desirable that the normal should make an effort to reach and benefit this class.

The program was made available only to those who (1) were high school graduates, and (2) had taught at least six years. These could earn the certificate by completing work under the direction of the Western State Normal School faculty as follows: (1) three summer terms in residence; (2) two years of non-residence work, either "class work at some center within range of the school, so that an instructor can meet the students once a week," or "carefully organized courses taken by correspondence."[2]

This program proved to be very successful, and in 1921 the State Board provided for an "Extension Life Certificate" to be granted by all four of the state teachers colleges and Detroit Teachers College, under the following conditions:

> (1) Applicants must be high school graduates and must have had *ten* years of successful teaching experience.
> (2) Completion of three summer terms in residence, and two years of non-residence work-class or correspondence.

In the following year, however, serious questioning of the quality of the extension work led to a State Board resolution putting an end to all registration for the Extension Life Certificate.

The Normal College at Ypsilanti was cautious, perhaps overly so, about adopting an extension program. In 1904, under President Jones, it was announced that the College stood ready, insofar as their regular work permitted, to offer services of its faculty as lecturers. The announcement read:

> The State Normal College hopes in the future to be helpful in developing
> and improving the educational work in city, village and rural communities
> by allowing its faculty members to give single lectures or courses of lec-
> tures at educational and social meetings.[3]

The cost to the community would be railroad fare and hotel accommodations, and it was noted that the most convenient dates were "of course, Friday evenings and Saturdays." A list of available lectures and lecturers was appended. Included were such names as Laird, Hoyt, Barbour, D'Ooge, Ford, Strong, Lyman, Jefferson, and even President Jones.

With the arrival of President McKenny in 1912, the first exten-sion course was offered in response to a request from the teachers of Bay City. Four years later, McKenny went to the Board with a request for a special appropriation. He said:

> One of the latest educational movements is extension work for teachers
> already in service . . . The work is growing by leaps and bounds. The
> expense of this extension work cannot well be met out of current expense
> and should be provided for by special appropriation.

The Legislature did not honor his request, nor did they two years later when he repeated it, nor have they, to this day (1968), accepted financial responsibility for this work. The extension program is still operated on the basis of being self-supporting; the faculty who par-ticipate do so on their own time, in addition to the regular on-cam-pus teaching load. The result has not been a refusal of faculty to participate, but a minimal compensation to them.

It was not until 1921 that a separate extension department, headed by Horace Z. Wilber, was organized. Under Wilber's guid-ing hand in the next fifteen years, it could be said that classes were being offered from Cheboygan to Monroe and from Traverse City to Port Huron—that is, over the entire Lower Peninsula of Michigan. At the same time correspondence courses found enrollees in 63 of the 82 counties of the State, and in 25 states and 4 foreign countries.[4]

The justification for this outward flow of courses and instructors from the Normal campus was stated and re-stated from time to time. The trend was toward ever more courses, more services, and the involvement of more instructors. The time came when, to conserve energy and avoid conflict and duplication, the State Board found it advisable to limit the geographical area served by each of the four colleges and to assign to each an exclusive territory. The Normal was given fourteen counties in Southeastern Michigan.[5] The time came also when the State Board found it advisable to remind the colleges that extension work existed primarily for in-service teachers.

A chronological review of formal statements of purpose will be instructive.

In 1904, as we have seen, the intent was simply the improvement in quality of teaching in rural, town, and city schools. McKenny, who encouraged at first a desultory sort of program, in asking the State Board for financial assistance in 1916, said "Not only is it necessary to train teachers for their profession, but it is necessary to keep them growing after they enter the profession.

The announcement of the new Extension Department (1921) said that it stood ready to serve "all teachers of the State and others interested in educational work." In 1923, Wilber explained its function thus:

> Our teacher training institutions have been founded on the assumption that the atmosphere in which one receives his training is a matter of importance. Efforts are made to surround the prospective teacher with all the influence essential to the make-up of a successful school. This would seem to indicate that instruction given to the teacher while engaged in her work, and in the midst of the usual school surroundings, has a value all its own . . . The teacher who receives instruction while engaged in teaching and who evaluates that instruction from the standpoint of her daily experience will gain more than is possible in other ways.[6]

Enthusiasm led quickly to a broader concept of the department's function. Suggested in the phrase contained in the original announcement as to the scope of its service, "and others interested in educational work," it became more explicit in 1924 with the published statement that the department would serve not only teachers in service but "others who wish college training but who feel they cannot spend the full time in residence . . . No young man or woman with ambition and a willingness to work need be without many of the advantages which come with a college education."

With time, programs grew and types of service multiplied. Wilber retired in 1944 and, after a short interval under an acting director (Professor Loesell), Carl Hood was appointed. The name of the department was changed to "Division of Field Services." The appeal to all who would seek a college education was dropped, but in its place came a newer movement called "adult education." The announcement now read as follows:

> Those interested in field services include not only in-service teachers but people interested in placement of teachers, adult education groups and agencies seeking speakers and consultants.

In 1952, with Carl Anderson in charge, and in light of a growing discussion of the true function of extension work, a renewal of emphasis on service to teachers was evident. Anderson said:

> All of the activities of the Division are predicated on the philosophy that our primary responsibility is the improvement of teachers in the field, so that the interests and welfare of the children of Michigan may be served to the greatest possible degree.[7]

In June, 1953, the discussion in the State Board as to the true function of field services came to a head with the adoption of a detailed recommendation from the Council of Presidents of the four teachers colleges. Its statement of objectives read:

> The Michigan Colleges of Education were established primarily for the education of teachers so that the interests and welfare of the children of Michigan may be served to the greatest possible degree. Because the campus of any college extends over the entire area served by that college, it becomes the responsibility of the Field Service Divisions in the four colleges of education in Michigan to make available those services listed in the areas designated.

The "services" were then indicated as follows: "the preparation and improvement of teachers, emphasizing the area of their in-service training;" "experimental and research projects relating to the needs of the field;" "adult education programs in cooperation with public school directors of adult education, deans of community organizations;" "to encourage improved alumni relations and recruitment of qualified prospective teachers."

This resolution, with its strong emphasis on service to the teaching profession, yet left the door open for the rendering of services of non-professional import by the inclusion of adult education and the improvement of alumni relations.

Standards

In a discussion of purposes one naturally raises the question: what quality of work has gone into the program? With what standards did Normal undertake extension work and how were they affected by the multiplication of demands both in number and variety and the increasing severity of competition for students among the colleges? What value, as compared with on-campus courses, was given to credits earned in Extension? What protection was afforded against the possibility that students might enroll in more work than one engaged in the full-time job of teaching could satisfactorily undertake?

During the early years of extension work the State Board laid down the restriction that not more than one-fourth of the credit hours leading to a degree could be taken in off-campus classes or by correspondence. To enroll, one must be a high school graduate. A student in residence at the college could not enroll. And no one could enroll in more than two courses at one time.

By 1922, at about the time that Normal organized an Extension Department, considerable discussion had arisen as to the quality of work being done, and the State Board felt obliged to take action. The following resolution was adopted:

> The best interests of the schools of Michigan require that all work done under the direction of the state normal schools shall be of a character that will be accepted without question by the University of Michigan and the other leading universities of the country. This fact is of special importance as affecting the character of the extension work carried on by the normal schools.

This was followed by a series of regulations which in their content and wording reveal the problems that had developed:

(a) After June 30, 1922, extension class courses shall conform to the same requirements, both as regards subject matter and recitation hours, as residence courses.

(b) Correspondence courses shall be equivalent in subject matter and work required by corresponding courses given in residence.

(c) After June 20, 1922, no more registrations for the Extension Life Certificate shall be accepted.

(d) Only members of the faculties of the various normal schools shall be permitted to give extension courses for credit.

In 1941, the question of residence credit for off-campus courses became pressing. The State Board met the issue in a series of resolutions which stipulated that, to qualify for residence credit (i.e., credit of the same value towards graduation as that given for courses taken on the campus), the following requirements must be met: (a) the course must require unique facilities inherent in the community and not available on the campus; (b) instructors must organize their courses so as to make use of these unique facilities; (c) the course must meet requirements as to prerequisites and time allotment for class sessions, and library facilities must be comparable to campus requirements. The Board also provided for the establishing of residence branch centers but stipulated that each one must receive its prior approval.

In 1951, the Board reiterated these requirements. They also stipulated that credit earned in off-campus instruction could be counted toward a degree only to a maximum of 30 hours (not more than 15 of these to be earned by correspondence work).

Meanwhile, beginning in 1948, the directors of the extension divisions of the four teachers colleges had undertaken, by holding joint periodic meetings, to place their own houses in order and to work for uniformity of standards.

The Association for the Accreditation of Colleges of Teacher Education created a subcommittee to study the practices of its member institutions. Carl Hood, then director at Normal, was a member of that committee. In 1953, the committee included in its report a new set of standards for the conduct of extension work. Standard X, "In-Service Education and Field Service Programs," was adopted by the Association in February, 1954. It stressed the exclusive function of meeting the needs of in-service teachers, and read as follows:

> The college for teacher education, in cooperation with responsible school authorities, should do whatever it can to help the school personnel of its service area to grow continuously and effectively as members of the profession and as useful members of the society. The initiating, planning, and developing of any program for in-service education of school personnel is a cooperative responsibility of local school systems, colleges for teacher education and state departments of education.[8]

Among the specific requirements that followed were two that paved the way for the placing of extension credit on the same footing as credit earned on campus. These were:

Require the same standards for admissions, the same amount of work and quality of teaching in off-campus credit courses as for similar courses in residence.

Prescribe as high qualifications for instructors and quality of teaching in off-campus credit courses as for similar courses in residence.

With this encouragement from the accrediting body, those in favor of recognizing credit earned by extension as of equal value to credit earned on campus gained complete victory. In January, 1954, the Council of Presidents was able to report that its recommendation "that all courses, with the exception of correspondence courses, should be considered of equal value whether given on or off campus, and would be considered as residence credit effective July 1, 1954," had been adopted by the State Board.

In the same year, Carl Anderson, then director at Normal, was able to describe the aims of his department in the following words:

This Department operates under the philosophy that all field work must be a reflection of the total campus program and all services so provided must be equal to, or superior to, the campus program because of the more mature and experienced clientele in the field.

The concept of "residence center" appears to have been accepted by the State Board as early as 1941. As originally understood and developed by the extension divisions of the four teachers colleges, a residence center was a location where courses were offered every year and for which credit was given. It was to be distinguished from locations where an occasional off-campus class might be offered, for which extension credit was given.

Four years later, a paragraph was added to the regulations providing that courses for residence credit might be conducted in any junior college where the available facilities were adequate.

Cooperative programs with the junior colleges of the State led rapidly to cooperation among the teachers colleges and with the other state-supported institutions. In 1952, a cooperative program was developed with the School for the Deaf in Flint. By 1954, it could be reported that the Normal had developed courses in cooperation with the Jackson and Flint Junior Colleges, the University of Michigan, Michigan State University and Wayne State University.

As we have noted, extension work was not subsidized by the State. This division thus had to be self-supporting. Hence it was permitted to retain its income, that is, it was not required to turn over to the State the monies it collected (as required of in-residence tuition money). To avoid the legal requirement that tuition money must be turned over to the State, the Division of Field Services, therefore, always used the term 'fees" rather than "tuition" for its charges. This was not always understood in certain quarters in Lansing. In January, 1953, the Board felt obliged to remind the Auditor General of "the authority of the State Board of Education to collect, administer, and deposit local fees."

For many years the income derived from credit courses in extension and by correspondence was used to pay the instructors and defray office and publicity expenses. A modification in policy was made, however, in 1948 when the State Board decreed that a stipulated portion of the fee (about one-fourth) should be retained by the division for its operation. By 1952, this was raised to two-thirds of the gross income of the division. Henceforth, the instructor's compensation did not rest, as heretofore, on the size of his class, but was standardized.

This new policy brought into existence a fund that was unrestricted, hence readily available for local projects and needs. It is probable that the division had been following such a policy informally for some years previous, for we find that as early as 1949, under Director Hood, two additional areas were placed under its supervision, each of which would require some subsidization—the Placement Office and the Office of Alumni Records; and the name of the division was changed to Division of Field Services.[9]

In 1950, a department called "Duplicating Services" was staffed, equipped and made available to the entire College for typing, duplicating, and printing services. This department undertook the publishing of an *Alumni News Letter*. In the summer of 1950, the division subsidized in part a Spanish Clinic, began to give financial help for holding conferences on the campus, and to subsidize faculty attendance at professional meetings elsewhere. Surveys and research were initiated. Cooperative programs with other state-supported institutions were undertaken. Requests for financial aid were evaluated in terms of benefit to the whole College.

The zeal for promoting new projects and areas of service outran basic policy, however, when in 1953 the State Board granted a request from the field services divisions of the four teachers colleges to conduct an "experimental" program called the "Retail Round Table." This was to be a service to businessmen in small communities and was an undertaking to be sponsored jointly by the colleges and the State Board in Control of Vocational Education. The persuasive argument was that these meetings would increase the effectiveness of the business enterprises in the community, and would thus result in increasing the tax base on which the local school must operate. The only tangible connection with school work was the stipulation that the Round Table must be set up through the local Superintendent of Schools.

Another project of this year was the funding of a research project for evaluating "Outdoor Programs" for teacher education. These programs involved a camping situation, in which teachers and students were brought together for a short time.[10]

In 1951, under Hood, the division had pioneered a highly important project, a program to provide for student practice teaching in the public schools "in the field" in addition to the on-campus program in the College's laboratory school. It was later evaluated by the division and found to be comparable in effectiveness to the work of the campus school.

This experiment helped prepare the way for the time (to arrive within the next five years) when it would become necessary for the College to expand its practice teaching program to provide for the rapidly increasing number of college students preparing for teaching. Approval of the State Department of Public Instruction was sought and (through one of its department heads) hesitatingly given. The phrasing of the consent is, perhaps, significant:

> For a long time I had certain convictions about these programs but I am beginning to think that at least it is an emergency measure and if adequate supervision could be given we should develop this possibility to the fullest logical extent. My reasoning on the thing is that we have such a fluid condition in the teaching profession and it is evident that real field experience is of superior value.[11]

The division found itself the object of an increasing number of requests for financial aid and thus in a position to be of increasing service to the College. If departmental travel funds were inadequate, Field Services could supplement them. If no funds were available through the College budget for the organizing and hosting of confer-

ences, Field Services could provide them. If a proposed experimental
program appeared promising and no departmental funds were available for its launching, Field Services could make this possible. A
history of the Normal, now well past her centennial, needed to be
written. Field Services supplied the funds.

A fringe benefit to the faculty in the form of a life insurance program was made possible through a plan whereby the College would
make a contribution to the premiums. Field Services was the "College." The organizing and advertising of special clinics was made
possible with Field Service funds. Travel courses became increasingly important, some extending as far as Europe, South America
and Japan. Field Services provided the initial costs of organizing and
advertising. A cooperative study by the several state-supported colleges and universities to lay the groundwork for an inter-institu-
tional permanent organization was set in motion. Normal's share of
the cost came from Field Services.

In short, it was not long before Field Services, in addition to its
essential function of providing off-campus and correspondence credit
courses and off-campus educational counseling for in-service teachers, was presenting a budget that included such items as Adult
Education (non-credit), Correspondence, Business and Trade Programs, Alumni Fund, Community Relations, Committees and Conferences, Insurance Program, Duplicating Service, Michigan Congress of Parents and Teachers, Rackham School of Special Education, Conservation Program and Out-door Education, Association
Development, and Curriculum Development.[12]

Thus, Field Services assumed a new and very important function
in relation to the College: it opened an avenue to experimentation,
research, and auxiliary services which previously had been unavail-
able. It became the searchlight of the College as the latter sought to
adapt its facilities to a society that grew ever more rapidly both in
size and in complexity, with attendant multiplying of problems.

A fascinating story could be told of the traveling faculty as they
carried their prescient, demanding messages to the towns and cities
and rural areas of the State. For the greater distances, trains and
hotels were the indispensable media. As road systems and automo-
biles improved, the auto became the universal transport—each, for
reasons of economy, arranged to carry several instructors to their
several classes. This huddling of teachers representing disparate
academic areas, in small groups over long miles of travel, promoted

conversation which inevitably covered the whole spectrum from the serious to the trivial, from the constructive thought to the petty gripe. Members of one department often gained new insight into areas other than their own.

Hazards of the road were faced together—a narrow escape from some reckless "other" driver; a vicious storm or blinding fog or snow; a hair-raising whirl out of control on an icy highway; speeding through the dark hours of the late night or early morning with a temperamental driver eager to return home. Similar experiences could doubtless be told by the students, some of whom drove over 200 miles to attend classes. Through all the years, the vicissitudes of a varied climate, the frailties of a machine, and the chance temperaments of the drivers, it is remarkable that very few accidents occurred, and that there was not a single fatality.

Out of it all came a stimulating and enlightening contact with teachers in service, new friendships, and a small but oh-so-needed added pittance to the modest it not quite inadequate salary. Out of it, too, came a subtle institution-wide formulation of a faculty opinion.

On December 11, 1941, Japan and the United States exchanged declarations of war. In the following months student enrollments declined rapidly and drastically. From an enrollment of 1,900, the figure descended to less than 900. This created a severe staff problem, alleviated only in part by the fact that many asked for leave of absence and joined the armed forces.

The answer to a suddenly overstaffed college was found in the Extension Division. Fortunately, neither depression nor war had materially affected enrollments in the field. To complete the normal load of the teacher, the extension class was included; the instructor no longer received a fee for his services. Instead he was given what was called an "energy increment," a mileage rate to compensate him for the extra time and energy demanded. Not until 1955 was the original policy revived whereby extension work was made additional to the regular on-campus teaching load of 15 hours.

Remuneration for teaching in Extension, either in class or by correspondence, varied from time to time. In 1915, it was $7.50 per credit hour plus, of course, expenses. In 1922, it was set at $10.00. By 1923, it had been raised to $12.50. In 1942, the "energy increment" was set at five cents per mile of travel, with minimums and maximums set at $5.00 and $14.00. By 1947, the rate had been doubled.

Because the instructor who undertook to give courses by correspondence had been held to no limit (the class instructor was limited to two classes in any one semester), it had been possible for a very few to derive a considerable income from giving work in extension. In 1951, the State Board felt moved to limit the amount an instructor could earn in an academic year in extension work to $900.00 plus expenses. This limit was raised in 1956 to $1,500.

Student enrollments have always been greater in the off-campus classes than in correspondence courses, and the rate of growth in the former much greater. A comparative statement covering a period of 30 years may be of interest. In 1923–24 the number of students enrolled in correspondence courses was 663; in off-campus classes, 1,460. The latter were distributed in 41 classes, taught in 25 class centers. In 1954–1955, there were 917 enrollments in correspondence courses, taught by 37 members of the faculty. In off-campus classes 2,911 students were enrolled, taught by 76 members of the faculty in 116 classes.

Administration

The Division of Field Services has been guided through its forty-odd years of existence by five division heads: Horace Z. Wilber (1922–1943); Clarence Loesell (1943–1946); Carl Hood (1946–1952); Carl R. Anderson (1952–1965); Earl Studt, 1965–on.

Horace Wilbur was an alumnus ('02) of Normal. His background included teaching in the public schools of Michigan and in Kansas State Teachers College. Added to Normal's faculty in 1907, he taught history of education, school administration, and philosophy. For ten years (1908–1918) he edited the periodical published by the Normal faculty, *The American Schoolmaster*. In 1918–1919, he was on leave of absence to serve as a Director of the Army Educational Work, where he assisted in organizing and supervising educational work in the Army of Occupation in France. From 1919 to 1921, he was Deputy Superintendent of Education in the Department of Public Instruction in Lansing.

Wilber's first move, upon receiving the appointment at Ypsilanti, was to visit two schools where extension work was being developed with marked success, the Iowa State Teachers College and the Teachers College at Emporia, Kansas. From this visit came a joint invitation to other schools known to be conducting extension work to gather to discuss mutual problems. They met at the annual meeting of the Department of Superintendence of the National Education Association at Chicago in 1922. The outcome of this discussion was the decision to form a permanent organization.[13] It was first known as the Teachers College Extension Association, later as the Teachers College Association for Extension and Field Services (1948–1954), and presently as the Association for Field Services in Teacher Education. At its first meeting (1923), the Association elected Wilber as secretary-treasurer, a position he retained until elected president (1939). Writing on the history of this organization in 1955, Irving H. Hart said: "For the permanence of the Association and the efficient planning of its programs, credit is due first of all to Horace Wilber of Ypsilanti . . ."

Wilber's contribution to extension work at Normal, extending over a score of years, was vital in the period of policy formulation, and decisive in the basic problem of effective organization.

Upon Wilber's retirement in 1943 (in the midst of the war), the duties of the department were added to those of the head of the Natural Science Department. President Munson appointed Clarence M. Loesell as acting head, and the extension work was carried on without interruption.

In 1946, Munson appointed a full-time director. He was Carl Hood, former head of the Henry Ford educational enterprises, in which position he not only directed the famous Edison Institute in Greenfield Village but also the Ford educational enterprises in many parts of the United States, Great Britain and South America. Hood's background had been somewhat similar to that of Wilber, teacher in a one-room rural school, alumnus of Normal ('24), high school teacher and principal (in Dearborn, Michigan, where his work brought him to the attention of Henry Ford).

Hood's tenure (1946–1952) was marked by an enlargement of jurisdiction, expansion of services, active promotion of cooperation with the other state-supported institutions of higher education. Hood, in temperament, personality, methodical habit of mind and background of experience was particularly well suited to move the department on to broader fields of service.

At the local level he expanded the course offerings by introducing the concept of the post-summer school institute, a highly intensive workshop type of course, held in the field, extending over a period of one of two weeks after the close of the regular six-week summer session on campus. He made a point of expediting course demands from the field to the several academic departments. With the encouragement and support of President Elliott, he assumed responsibility for the Office of Alumni Relations, providing it with staff and equipment to revive and develop the alumni file. He directed the Placement Bureau.

At the State level Hood very early was instrumental in establishing a pattern of periodic meetings of the directors of extension of the four teachers colleges, where they threshed out their common problems and developed uniform policies when possible. In recognition of the expansion of function and widening scope of activities the name of the Extension Department was changed in 1949 to Division of Field Services.

At the national level it should be noted that the Association for Field Services in Teacher Education had almost from the beginning maintained continuous relations with the American Association of Teachers Colleges, including cooperation on committees. In 1950, it became affiliated with the AATC (presently known as the American Association of Colleges of Teacher Education). The practical meaning of this affiliation was that the field services organization would henceforth be represented on the Coordinating Committee of the teachers college organization. In 1951, the latter authorized a study of the extension services offered by member institutions. Hood was one of three representatives from the field services who sat on this committee. The report was adopted by the teachers college organization in 1954. It stated that standards for admission to credit courses, quality of faculty and of instruction, and the meeting of accreditation requirements should be the same as for on-campus instruction.[14]

In recognition of his valuable services to the national organization Hood, as Horace Wilber had been before him, was made an honorary life member of the field services organization. He was only the fifth to be so honored. Upon his resignation as head of the Division of Field Services in 1952 to return to teaching, the Dean of Administration in his annual report commented: "Mr. Hood's decision to give up an administrative position for full-time teaching is in line with the best tradition of the college, which places classroom instruction always first in importance."

Hood's successor in 1952 was Carl R. Anderson, a member of the history and social sciences staff at Normal, with academic background in history and political science. In Anderson, there was the happy combination of vision and dynamic action. His administration was marked by a wholehearted acceptance of the goal defined in the standards set by the national teachers college organization. On the other hand, the services contributed by his division to the Normal were increased to a noteworthy extent, and in a number of instances have been of exceptional significance.

His office promoted and facilitated the holding of conferences on campus and, beginning with 1955, participated in a program of training for school bus drivers, set up by the four teachers colleges and the Department of Public Instruction. It subsidized evaluation studies, such as that which concerned the collaboration of the Normal with the Dearborn public schools in an outdoor education program. It made possible the initiation of a Summer School Session for High School Musicians, a Workshop for School Lunch Cooks and Managers, a Leadership Training Program for Parent Teacher Groups. It subsidized a study of college dropouts, the writing of a biography of Mark Jefferson. The list could be considerably expanded.

Experimental projects which might deserve State support but which were as yet untried and untested were given their trial by this division. Some proved their worth and were later included in the State budget. Such, for example, was the program of instruction by television. A similar instance was the original subscription by the Library to the invaluable *New York Times* microfilm series, later paid for by the State.

Naturally, such an expansion of activity brought an increase in income, which tripled from 1952 to 1962. In 1956, Earl Studt, from the biology staff of the Lincoln School, came to the division as Associate Director. The following year, Ralph Gessler, was added as Assistant Director. David Soule was made responsible for the School Bus Driver Training Program, and also charged with facilitating the holding of conferences on campus.

In the area of course instruction. Anderson worked consistently toward the raising of standards and the improvement of teaching facilities. His contributions to the College Library, for example, made possible the purchase of additional copies of books and instructional materials which instructors could take to their classes in the field. The purchase of duplicating equipment made possible the ready availability of articles and portions of books that could not be spared from the Library.

At the national level, Anderson was active with the Association for Field Services in Teacher Education, and in 1961 was elected its president.

In 1965, with the coming of a new president, Anderson was made Vice-President for Public Affairs. His assistant, Earl Studt, took over the reins of the Division of Field Services.

The story of the Division of Field Services reveals an institution that was particularly sensitive and responsive to the growing needs of a dynamic, growing society. Its mission was facilitated along the way by mechanical invention and improvements (the automobile, good roads, efficient copying machines), and in the future is certain to develop even greater impact as newer and better facilities appear. Beginning as an organization to improve teaching in the field, it not only established its place as an essential part of the teacher education program but in turn brought great benefit to the campus from which it emerged.

CHAPTER TWENTY-FOUR

THE GRADUATE PROGRAMS

Graduate instruction, in the sense of a program leading to a post-graduate degree, was provided for at Michigan Normal as early as 1889. In that year the State Legislature gave the State Board of Education authority to grant " . . . such diploma as it may deem best, and such diploma when granted shall carry with it such honors as the extent of the course for which the diploma is given may warrant and said board of education may direct."[1]

Under this authority the State Board established the degree of Master of Pedagogics, based primarily on a post-graduate thesis. The requirements for this degree were stated as follows:

> Any person holding the degree of Bachelor of Pedagogics (a four-year degree established at the same time) of the Michigan State Normal School, may upon application, receive the degree of Master of Pedagogics upon the following conditions:
>
> (a). He shall furnish evidence satisfactory to the Faculty that he has been engaged in teaching or in school supervision continuously and with pronounced success for five years since receiving the Bachelor's degree.
>
> (b). He shall prepare and present a thesis acceptable to the said Faculty, upon some subject connected with the History, Science, or Art of Education, the Faculty reserving the right to assign the subject of such thesis.

Unwittingly, the Normal (which had not yet reached the status of college) had taken the first step toward becoming a university (an institution characterized by work at the graduate level). The MPd was obviously used in some cases as an honorary degree. Early recipients included a number of members of Normal's faculty: J. M. B. Sill and Julia Ann King (1890); Charles F. R. Bellows and John

Goodison (1891); Austin George (1893); Charles R. Grawn (1897); David Eugene Smith (1898). Stratton D. Brooks, who was later to became a noted educator and university president, earned the BPd degree in 1893 and the MPd in 1899.

With the coming of President McKenny in 1912, the MPd as an earned degree was dropped. Henceforth, it was conferred strictly as an honorary degree and graduate work disappeared from the scene.

The next graduate undertaking was initiated in 1938 in the form of a joint program with the University of Michigan. In February of that year the Extra-Legal Planning Commission, a body created by the State Board of Education to study problems in public education and teacher training in Michigan, recommended to the State Board that it approach the University of Michigan with the proposal that a joint plan for a Master's degree in Education be developed as between the University and the four teachers colleges. The Board concurred, and by July a plan had been drawn that was acceptable to both parties.[2]

The program as developed at the Normal College was limited to three areas: Elementary Education, Special Education (the training of teachers of handicapped children), and Rural Education. The stated objectives were threefold: to improve the general effectiveness of the students, to add to their cultural and intellectual attainments, and to provide specific training. The supervision and control of the program was placed completely in the hands of the U-M. Courses offered on the teachers college campus were to be approved by it, members of its staff were to visit and evaluate courses conducted by teachers college staff, and members of the teachers college staff selected for the program were to be given the status of "graduate lecturer" by its Graduate School. The master's degree would be awarded by the U-M, but if as much as three quarters of the work leading to the degree were done on a teachers college campus, that fact would be indicated on the diploma. The fees charged were to be on the same basis as those charged by the U-M, would be collected by it, and only such portion of the fees would be returned to the teachers colleges as would represent "the amounts charged for University Health Service and other special privileges given University students."

The organization on Normal's campus was to be known as the Graduate Division of Michigan State Normal College in Cooperation with the University of Michigan. It was placed under the general supervision of a Graduate Advisory Council. Normal's first Council consisted of the Dean of Administration (Milton Hover), the chairman of the Education Department (Noble Lee Garrison), the chairmen of the Department of Special Education (Charles Elliot), and the chairman of two academic departments—English (Gerald Sanders), and Physics (Fred Gorton). Sanders served as chairman. The University of Michigan created the office of Graduate Advisor to the Michigan Colleges of Education, and appointed to this position Clifford Woody of its School of Education.

The calendar of the Normal College was, at this time, based on the quarter plan while the U-M operated on the semester plan. Significant because it proved to be a major factor in Normal's decision (in 1939) to adopt the semester plan was the following provision:

> It is proposed that all graduate courses offered in a Graduate Division be organized on the semester rather than the term basis, in order to facilitate the transfer of credit, to avoid misunderstanding about fees and to simplify the problem of cooperation of University staff members in course offerings.

It is obvious that the attitude of the U-M underlying this arrangement was one of jealous protection of its hegemony in the graduate area. Its connotation, as far as the teachers colleges were concerned, was of a relationship that involved only a one-sided kind of cooperation. It evinced distrust of the quality of instruction that a teachers college would, from its own sense of responsibility, provide. For Normal, with a proud and long record of eminent teachers on its staff, this was humiliating. In retrospect it would seem that the U-M would have been far wiser to have assumed the position of a tutor, interested in the pupil's development and planning his course to the point where he might participate in a truly cooperative situation.

As it was, however, the joint program continued for more than a decade before the colleges, one by one, broke away and established their own programs. The first to become independent was Western Michigan College. Finally, in October, 1951, the State Board granted the four teachers colleges authority to confer their own master's degree in education. The minutes of the Board read as follows:

> On motion, the colleges of education were authorized to offer graduate work leading to the master's degree with specialization in education, and

to grant such a degree beginning September 1, 1952. Also that the several colleges (1) request sufficient funds in the 1952–53 budgets to carry out these programs, and (2) to collect and utilize in part such tuition and fees as may be necessary to give support to the conduct of such programs.

In July, 1952, the Board approved a specific request to grant graduate credit for work done in a workshop conducted for those in attendance at the Ninth Annual Classroom Teachers National Conference which met on Normal's campus that summer. Those who received this credit were in fact the charter members of an alumni group that was soon to grow rapidly in numbers.

Normal continued for the time being on the joint program, however. Contact with the U-M had, through the years, been friendly and close. There was considerable reason to believe that an improved relationship could be achieved, and the geographical proximity of the two institutions (only six miles apart) provided the basis for feeling that facilities could be shared and that a continuing joint program would be desirable.

In December of 1952, however, the State Board authorized a separate graduate status for the Normal College. The announcement appeared, abruptly and without prior notice to the parties concerned, in the newspapers. From this time, therefore, Normal was engaged in planning, and in the fall of 1953 a specific program was approved.

To formulate a graduate program, President Elliott appointed a Study Committee, consisting of three representatives from the liberal arts area,[3] two from the area of professional education,[4] and the Dean of Administration, who served as chairman. A questionnaire was sent to public school officials in the area.[5] This survey was a move in the direction of developing a program with a practical, rather than theoretical, emphasis. It also had a political motive, an appeal for support to those in charge of the public schools, whose teachers would be the students.

Results of the questionnaire indicated enthusiasm for a new kind of program. The general tenor of the replies placed strong emphasis on the practical. The terms "internship" and "externship" were used. Reference was made to tying work to teaching situations. One frequent suggestion was that, before entering graduate work, the student should have some years of actual teaching experience. There was substantial support for "work in philosophy of education or education in the context of our particular society."

From a full year of deliberations by the Study Committee a program and set of standards emerged. The graduate curriculum was organized into five areas, and the student must satisfy requirements in all five. The areas were: (a) Individual and Group Learning; (b) The School and Community Foundations; (c) Contemporary Culture and Its Backgrounds; (d) Science and Scientific Method; (e) Contemporary Civilization and Its Backgrounds. The individual student's program was to be "tailor-made"—that is, drawn (with the assistance of a counselor) with the view to filling in deficiencies in the student's background as well as the furtherance of his professional training. The program must include a "Field Project Study," a research experience in which the student (who would be an in-service teacher) was expected to define and explore, with the help of his school authorities, some current educational problem.

Admission to the program would be open to anyone possessing a bachelor's degree from a college accredited by a regional accrediting association (such as the North Central Association or the American Association of Colleges for Teacher Education). Thirty hours of credit, quality "B" average, would be required for the degree. No one would be admitted to candidacy for the degree until he had earned at least six semester hours of "B" average credit at this institution, and had had at least one semester of teaching experience. The degree, a Master of Arts in Education, would be awarded only to those "who have had teaching experience or who hold a contract to teach."

Was this indeed a graduate program? Here was no emphasis on scholarly advancement of the frontiers of pure knowledge, an object derived largely from the German influence, and long adopted as a major function of graduate work in America. Rather, it was simply an additional step in the education and training of the teacher, with a nod in the direction of research for specific, practical ends. If the work done were to be of a higher grade than that done on the undergraduate level, it would be because the students had passed through the undergraduate mill with at least a modest degree of success, were better oriented as to their needs by virtue of having practiced to some extent their profession, and in general were more mature in their interests and attitudes. They would not represent a carefully selected group of promising scholars.

But graduate work in America had by the mid-20th century shown many variations. No restricted definition could possibly cover the scene. The one that was widely used and accepted was broad enough to cover not only the graduate schools of the great universities but even the program of a teachers college:

> Graduate Work—a term commonly used in America to indicate work done in the combined university-college institutions beyond the bachelor's degree; in other words, university work as opposed to collegiate work.[6]

Furthermore, the twentieth century had seen an increasing emphasis among the older graduate schools on the importance of tying graduate work closely with the needs of the living society. No better illustration of this fact could be found than that provided by one of Normal's own graduates and one-time instructor on its staff when, as president of perhaps the outstanding graduate institution in America, Johns Hopkins University, Isaiah Bowman said:

> Graduate work can not thrive on a philosophy of escape from the dominant social forces of the times. In learning and discovery, as in business and diplomacy, a good deal depends upon the prevailing wind. For example, science has flowered because of its obvious social use. If its benefits had not come to be shared and appreciated by the many, it might have starved underground.

Bowman then turned to the basic character of graduate instruction, the discipline through which the student should pass:

> . . . discipline is largely an inner, self-generating and difficult process. It is conditioned in students not only by hard work under Masters but also by intellectual integrity in both masters and students and by an unquenchable desire, in all fields of thought, to get nearer the truth.

Then he added a warning, one that was particularly pertinent to a situation where increases in teachers' salaries had been made to rest largely on the accumulation of additional college credit. He said:

> If it [graduate work] pretends to be something that is socially useful, and only fits a student to earn a better material living, it is a fraud. Nor is mere democratic amiability an acceptable substitute for intellectual enterprise. Between the everlastingly earnest and high and enterprising on the one hand, and the slack, the easy, and the conventional on the other, a choice must be made, and each institution engaged in graduate work is making it, consciously or unconsciously.[7]

The proposed program at Normal contained the essentials of a respectable graduate program in the best current sense.

Upon its initiation in the fall of 1953, enrollment leaped upward. Whereas in the fall semester of the last year of joint operation with the University of Michigan the enrollment was 89, a year later it was 158, and the following year 334. In 1962, it was 1,325. Summer enrollments took a similar direction. In 1953 (the last summer under the joint program), the enrollment was 126; in 1954, it was 342; by 1962, it had reached a 1,000, and in 1963 it was 1,775, with some 500 additional enrollments in pre- and post-summer school sessions.

The graduate program came to dominate the summer school enrollment. Naturally, this snowballing of numbers created a serious problem in staffing. The budget did not expand rapidly enough, and classes became large—particularly in the professional education area where a class of 60 or more was not unusual.

Almost from the first, off-campus courses were organized. Beginning in the fall of 1954, a special arrangement with the Flint Community School Program (a Mott Foundation project under the direction of an alumnus of Normal, Frank A. Manley) provided that a specified group of Flint teachers engaged in the program could take all the work necessary to earn the master's degree by way of off-campus courses held in Flint. A semester later, an off-campus course in reading was offered in Jackson. From this beginning, the offering of graduate courses off-campus became widespread.

It was not long before the requirement of teaching experience or a contract in hand was abandoned. Students needed the degree, it was argued, to secure a good teaching position. Furthermore, there was strong pressure from graduating seniors to continue on without break and complete their formal training. It would be more difficult later, as families were established and responsibilities, especially financial ones, increased.

Somewhat later, additional programs were approved. The way was opened when, in June, 1960, the State Board authorized Eastern to grant the master of arts degree in certain subject matter fields. In fairly rapid succession programs were authorized by the Graduate Council in French literature, biological science, industrial arts, physical education, geography, history, English literature, fine arts, and business administration, with others hovering in the offing.

In the spring of 1959, James Glasgow was made Director of the

Graduate Division and Dean of Instruction Bruce Nelson became chairman of the Council. With the change of status of the Normal College to University in 1959, the Graduate Division became the Graduate School. In October, 1960, Glasgow was given the title of Dean of the Graduate School. Holder of degrees from two of the outstanding graduate schools of the nation, Clark University and the University of Chicago, Glasgow was not only efficient in organizing the school but was meticulous in preserving personal contact with students at the counseling and classifying stages. In spite of the tidal wave of enrollments, he succeeded in preventing the Graduate School from becoming an educational mill.

In 1955, the North Central Association of Colleges and Secondary Schools visited the campus for the purpose of examining the program, and granted it accreditation.

In the spring of 1963, the program received the approval of the National Council for Accreditation of Teacher Education. In 1966, with the arrival of a visitation committee from the North Central Association, the graduate program received particular attention because of its proposal to install a six-year degree, that of Specialist in Education. Open discussion of the desirability of entending the graduate program still further, that is to the doctorate level, was taking place. Possession of adequate resources in staff, library holdings and equipment loomed as major problems for the immediate future. Admissions standards for the more advanced degree programs also were in process of being determined. And in the Faculty Council a move for a more representative Graduate Council which would also play a more decisive role in policy-making was under way. That there would be a pressing student demand for the advanced degrees no one doubted; it was already there.

CHAPTER TWENTY-FIVE

THE LIBRARY

The library is as old as the Normal. When the doors were first opened to students, in the spring of 1853, there was available to them "a select Library of Standard Works, amounting to one thousand volumes . . . "[1] This was just prior to the time when the University of Michigan employed its first paid librarian and developed a card catalog, described as one of the first in America, for their library. The American Library Association was not founded until a quarter of a century later.

"The books are intended mainly for reference, as the regular studies of the school leave little time for general reading." Such was the statement in the Normal catalog. But even this limited purpose was frustrated when, in 1859, the Normal building was destroyed by fire, along with all its contents. "We miss," said Acting Principal Sill, "perhaps more than anything else, our small but well selected library, which was totally destroyed." The State Board asked the legislature for $2,000 to replace it. The Legislature, however, did not lend a sympathetic ear.

The principal then resorted to an appeal to the students who unanimously agreed to pay one dollar over the regular tuition for two consecutive terms. Principal Welch reported:

> By the scheme referred to, we have already realized a sum sufficient, if judiciously invested, to supply our most pressing needs, and, as the Board of Education have taken steps for making the first purchase, we are looking forward gladly to the time when we shall no longer feel the pressure of a necessity which is second only to that of good instruction.

Subsequently, the Board added an annual fee to the tuition for the purchase of books. Thus was inaugurated a policy which proved to

293

be permanent and capable of great expansion, that of imposing a student fee in addition to the tuition charged by the State (and returned to it), the employment of which was entirely at the discretion of the school. As of 1962, this local fee amounted to 40 per cent of the total charge to the students, and was used to support (even to the point of constructing buildings) such student activities and services as the health service, student social center, student newspaper, and laboratory maintenance.

It is worthy of note that the State Board of this time was required to be "library-minded," as one of its legal responsibilities was the purchase of books for the district school libraries throughout the State.

The problems of building an adequate collection and making it accessible to student use were of a continuing nature, and often formidable. They involved such matters as administration and organization of the library, seating space for students, and policies as to the scope of materials to be purchased and degree of availability to students.

As to seating space, for example, as early as 1864 the Michigan Agricultural Society, in its proposal to construct a building for an agricultural museum on the campus, had agreed to provide a room for the Normal's library. This did not materialize. The attempt to solve the problem then took the form of shifting from one room to another in Old Main until, after nearly half a century of pressing the legislature, a separate library building was achieved.[2]

Organization and administration was also a matter of gradual development. In 1873, the Board of Visitors complained of the lack both of professional equipment and professional spirit. "The library," they said, "has given no indication that it is a part of the equipment of a Normal School. It has lacked, with insignificant exceptions, the professional treatises, sets of textbooks in the common school branches, etc., which seem necessary to its best use." The complaint brought results. The legislature made appropriations, the library room was improved, important accessions purchased, and the faculty turned its attention to the organization of the library. They chose Danial Putnam to be in charge, a responsibility that he exercised in addition to his teaching load until 1882 when he was named Acting Principal. During the summer of 1875 he, with members of the faculty and the Ypsilanti resident member of the State Board, devoted much time to devising a cataloging system, based on that

used at the University of Michigan.[3] The next visit by the Board of
Visitors brought commendation: " . . . the conveniences for using
and handling the books have been so multipled that the library has
come to be used very generally by the pupils, especially in the latter
part of their course."

Availability of books to the students involved questions of policy.
Just how freely should the students be permitted to use them? As
long as the collection consisted mainly of works of reference, these
could be made available without recourse to a charge-out slip, but
for use in the library only. Books for general reading, however, were
kept in alcoves behind railings and produced only on written
request. The report of the Board of Visitors for 1876 contained a
radical suggestion. Students should be encouraged to use books, even
to take books *from* the library! The report stated:

> . . . it seems to us, a far greater amount of reading would be done if
> pupils were allowed the privilege of taking books from the library. Every
> proper inducement should be offered to pupils for becoming acquainted
> with books and for acquiring a taste for library research.

The idea proved to be fruitful, but was very slow in germinating.
Some 20 years later, greater freedom was permitted at least within
the library room. The railed-in gallery of alcoves was thrown open
"somewhat freely" for the first time. Point was made that now one-
fourth of the entire library collection was made accessible to students
"without the formality of borrowing from the attendants." As a
result, there was better and greater use of the library by both students and faculty, and more of the library entered into the daily lessons.

Policy as to accessions gradually broadened. The transition from
the rather exclusive emphasis on general reference items and professional literature to the inclusion of items in the academic areas is
difficult to trace, but the trend in this direction must have been
greatly encouraged by the arrival of Principal Mac Vicar in 1880
and the consequent abandonment of the attempt begun in 1878 to
make the Normal a strictly professional training institution.

When Principal Willits arrived, in 1884, he gave first attention to
the library and reported that he found the collections especially rich
in literature, history and science. He noted that there had been
30,000 calls for books during the past year, "exclusive of teachers

and the departmental libraries." By 1893, reviewing his seven years as head of the Normal, Principal Sill could say that the library had increased by 70 per cent in number of volumes. Principal Boone, who certainly possessed a national view of higher education, made a rather lengthy statement in his first report (1894) to the State Board about the library. He said:

> From a considerable acquaintance with Normal Schools in the United States, I am persuaded that few of them are so well equipped with general and special library references as is our own. The Normal School library, both in its books and in its management, is something in which we may take legitimate pride.

He stated that the library possessed some 15,000 volumes and 63 periodicals; that all current reading matter plus about 300 volumes of general references were so placed as to give the students unrestricted access to them, and that the other books were "given out upon tickets." From the 800 students enrolled, daily loans aggregated not less than 650 volumes.

A similar statement was made some 42 years later by Edman Low in a survey which noted that as of 1938 the library possessed 90,000 volumes and was equalled by few teachers colleges in the entire country. He found particularly good collections in English literature and the Age of Chaucer, geography, American history, and children's literature. The periodical collection was unique among teachers colleges, containing over 100 complete files of magazines that had been published for a decade or more, some of which were no longer obtainable.[4]

In 1881 the State Board authorized a step that was to be continued until 1952, viz., the creation of libraries in the several departments of instruction in addition to the general library collection.[5] By 1894, nine departments were thus equipped, the books being listed in the regular library accessions book and transferred to the several departments, each of which maintained its own catalog. By 1929, the number had increased to twenty-two. At the dedication of the new library building in 1930, President McKenny indicated that, with the present expanded facilities, some of the departmental libraries were being discontinued and the books returned to the general library. The number diminished in the next few years to four. With the arrival of E. Walfred Erickson as Head Librarian in

1952, the last of these libraries were closed and the policy of a fully centralized library adopted.

Erickson's aversion to departmental libraries was based on considerations of economy, and also on the philosophy of a broad education which seeks to promote awareness in the student of the interrelations of subject matter and the need for their exploration.[6]

There was one type of special library, however, that could show ample and permanent justification, that for the Training School. The development of this library was gradual and natural, its time of origin uncertain. It originated in collections in the several grade rooms. In 1917, Head Librarian Walton described the library as having taken form "several years ago . . . from a miscellaneous group of books culled from the various grade room libraries, which had become too large to be handled easily." To these were added classroom libraries of books accumulated by teachers of the college course in Literature for the Grades.

The functions of the library were defined as (1) a reference library for the training of departmental teachers and student teachers; (2) a laboratory for the classes in literature for the grades; and (3) a lending library for children. The library was so organized that knowledge of how to use it would equip one to use the College library or any other library. Children were encouraged to find their books by using the card catalog, and any child was eligible to draw books who could either print or write his name, no matter how badly, so that it could be "translated."[7]

The modern era of the Normal library may be said to have begun with the coming of Genevieve M. Walton in 1892. Daniel Putnam, as first librarian, had organized the books by departments of instruction, and had been chiefly responsible for a card catalog. In 1881, he had been succeeded by August Lodeman, head of the Modern Languages Department. Lodeman was succeeded in 1884 by the Normal's first paid librarian, Miss Florence Goodison, who, in 1890, was succeeded by William S. Burns. Burns did not take his responsibilities too seriously and, after a year, left on vacation without completing a requested inventory. His vacation never ended, and Miss Walton was employed.

The name of Genevieve Walton represents one of Normal's cherished memories. Her 40 years of service alone is noteworthy. Her professional zeal, breadth of interest, concern for the training of teachers, positive character and personal charm made a lasting

impression on the library profession in Michigan and on the institution that she served.

In her day, professional training for libraries was very limited.
Her formal preparation consisted of attendance at a six-week summer institute at the Fletcher School in Amherst, Massachusetts. This
she supplemented through the meetings and journals of library associations and personal contacts with other librarians. Problems of
book selection, classification and cataloging she met with what limited tools were available, adapting them to her own special situation.
Some 13 years after joining the Normal staff, she obtained a master
of arts degree from St. Mary's College of South Bend, Indiana.

As to classification and cataloging, for some time the books were
grouped on the shelves according to extremely broad titles—history, general literature, classical languages, mathematics and science.
The books were marked for a particular shelf, and particular place
on the shelf, the newest book placed at the end of the group. Later,
the Dewey classification system was adopted, modified to meet the
need of the moment.

When the Cutter system of identifying authors came into vogue,
Miss Walton rejected it. She had a reason for this. The student
assistants must perform more than the mechanical task of securing
the book. They must become acquainted with the collection. Absence
of marking on the backs of the books forced the student to look
inside where he would find title and author as well as classification
number. Miss Walton also insisted that works must be identified
with their authors, authors with their works. Hence, biographies of
the authors were placed ahead of their respective works. Other liber-
ties with the Dewey classification system were taken. Frederick
Cleveringa, a student assistant after World War I and eventually the
Reference Librarian at the Normal, related:

> Miss Walton neglected the 400's completely, saying that there was no
> sense in talking about philology here—let's combine everything with the
> 800's on the score. With regard to the 914's which are the travel number
> in the Dewey system, she said, let's forget that and put travel and history
> together where they belong. If you are interested in a country, you are
> interested in its history also, and its scenery.[8]

As for book selection, purchases were based on requests from the
departments. Periodical lists consisted of important professional

journals and current literary magazines. There was very little money for expansion of the library; the acquisition of rare books was out of the question. Little or no initiative on the part of the librarian was possible until, beginning with the McKenny administration, the library had an annual budget.

The training of student assistants to work in the library was considered to be of particular importance as a part of their teacher training. On this matter Miss Walton said:

> The libraries of our four Normal schools, as they are still familiarly called, are interesting in our library development in having been among the earlier forces to accustom a large body of students to depend upon the intelligent use of books in teaching. A large percentage of these students have always come from the country, or from small towns with no libraries. They have returned as teachers to other small towns feeling the necessity of books in the schools, and have long been active in starting school libraries, which . . . have been a strong factor in the present school library movement.

She noted that the use of student assistants in the Ypsilanti Normal began in the early 1870's. They received no pay for years, but were given special privileges in the stacks. From the turn of the century, hourly rates were paid. Still later, a progressive system was installed whereby a student would be given the privilege of using the stacks for the first term or two, if proficient, he would be hired at an hourly rate.

Systematic instruction of student assistants began under Miss Walton in 1894, this taking the form of Saturday morning lectures, open to all who were interested in learning about libraries. These lectures were the forerunner of the present course known as "Use of Books and Library," which all student assistants must take.

As an aid to her administration Miss Walton prepared a Library Staff Manual which was revised and reprinted from time to time. In this she defined her staff, and assumed that the full-time members were members of the faculty. One of her instructions read:

> All full members of the Library Staff are required to attend Faculty meetings. The spirit of the Normal College assumes that all its members will attend the professional meetings of the several departments, and a strong effort should be made to attend Library and Educational meetings.[9]

The culmination of Miss Walton's career was, of course, the acquisition of a separate library building. She worked indefatigably on plans, procuring them from all over the country. She finally adopted as a model the plan of the McGregor Public Library of Highland Park, Michigan. In October of 1928, the State Board, noting that the plans had been approved by Governor Green and Budget Director Thompson, moved for the advertising for bids.

On Sunday, January 30, 1930, the formal opening took place. The building had cost a quarter of a million dollars and was, for the time, sumptuous. Seating facilities were provided for 400 students; shelving for 150,000 volumes. Special features included a reading room "for special study," special chairs and tables "for short people," tables and chairs placed throughout the bookstacks for faculty, a study room for student assistants, and a "fire-proof room for books of special value."

Completion of the building came at a fortunate time for Genevieve Walton. Two years later she died. Her influence had extended beyond the campus, throughout the State. She was a co-founder of the Michigan Library Association and became its first woman president. Known for her love of books, she was described as "a woman who can discuss books so that you can hardly wait to read the ones she talks about." In a paper she read at a meeting of the American Library Association at Kaaterskill, New York, in 1913, she commented, using a strong word for those times, as to Fitzgerald, "I am sorry so many people know Fitzgerald only because of the 'Rubaiyat.' I confess myself to be rather likeminded with

> That certain old person of Ham,
> Who grew weary of Omar Khayyam,
>   Fitzgerald, said he,
>   Is as right as can be,
> But this cult, and these versions,
> O, Damn!"

For the 50th Anniversary of the American Library Association, in 1926, she wrote a "History of Michigan Libraries." Her home in Ypsilanti was a center for visiting librarians, and it was later said that in this home were planned those first round-table meetings that meant so much to the State. The State Association issued a special number of the Michigan Library Bulletin in her honor on the occasion of the dedication of the new library building.

Genevieve Walton's influence was strongly felt by Normal's students. She often took a student home with her for lunch, and one in later years stated that the very fine art library which she had acquired in her home inspired in him a life-long interest in art collecting.[10] An ancedote is told of scenes in the library on a winter's night:

> Often during the winter during a snow storm, she would prepare a big camp coffee pot at home, hire a cab, and come up to the library in the evening. Along about 8:30 you could see the students in the reading room sniffing and wondering what was going on. When the smell became too tantalizing, she would go out and announce that coffee was ready, and each one was served.

Perhaps the most revealing statement of the character of her impact on students is that of Francis Goodrich, who said:

> I owe a great deal to her. Not that the training was formal or systematic, but she encouraged us to read—and, in fact we *had* to read. She would inquire what we were reading and she wanted her staff members to be up to date, not so much with current events but with current literature. That was quite insisted upon. She made me learn to catalog. I didn't want to do that and I didn't have to catalog, but she said I had to learn, so I did . . . When I went to library school, I found that I knew so much more about library practice than my associates in the class that I did a great deal of personal instructing.[11]

Miss Walton left as her successor in 1932 Miss Elsie Andrews who had been a faithful assistant for many years and who also had an artistic interest as an accomplished pianist. The Andrews period of 20 years felt the full brunt of retrenchment forced by depression and war. The library staff was severely cut, and annual budgets became more and more slender. It was not a good time to serve as college librarian. Miss Andrews inherited, however, an able staff.[12] Two events are noteworthy—a Carnegie grant of $20,000, which looked large in 1939, and, on the arrival of President Elliott in 1948, confirmation of the professional staff as members of the faculty.

In 1952, Miss Andrews resigned and was replaced by Erickson. A graduate of a teachers college, former head of the library of a teachers college, and engaged at the time in writing a doctoral dissertation concerned with teachers college libraries, Erickson possessed an exceptional sympathy with and understanding of the needs of that type of institution.

Faced with the problems of a rapidly growing institution and at the same time with an administration that lacked appreciation, he persisted year after year in the effort to increase the library budget from its place at the bottom of the list of comparative libraries in the country. Finally, in 1965, he succeeded in getting the adoption of a progressive program that would lead to a standing share of 6 per cent of the University budget.

Faced with a classification and cataloging situation that derived from earlier years and simpler circumstances but was seriously inadequate for the present, he added the Cutter classification system to the Dewey system, and undertook to reclassify the entire collection.

Faced with an institution that soon began to leap forward in size and scope, increasing from an enrollment of about 2,800 to more than 10,000 in 12 years, he was successful in his quest for a new library building which would meet the increased and more varied demands of what was no longer a teachers college but a developing university.

Meanwhile the accessions policy was expanded to include microfilm acquisitions, particularly in the area of newspapers, which underwent rapid and extensive development.[13] A policy of acquisition of current periodicals to satisfy the Periodical Index was undertaken. And, as resources were available, the library not only encouraged but prodded for departmental requests and assumed considerable initiative itself.

The new building, dedicated in the spring of 1967, was planned to provide seating space for 1,800 students, shelving for 300,000 volumes. Climaxing the tortuously slow, century-long development of the policy of free access to the books, the new arrangement shelves virtually all of the collection in the open so that students can go directly to the books. The library is arranged on a subject divisional basis, each division having its own collection of materials and a staff of subject specialists to serve students and faculty.

Each division features a smoking room (shades of the McKenny era!), a faculty study, a seminar room, and a microfilm reading room. There is a map library and cartography workroom, and a spacious modern Instructional Materials Center to house the latest materials used in instruction. The Audio-Visual Center has been greatly enlarged and provides facilities for film projection, preview and conference, production of visuals, recording, equipment repair, and record listening facilities whereby taped programs of music or literature can be heard by merely dialing a number. Classrooms and offices for the Library Science division (program for the training of school librarians) are provided. There is provision for a University archives. The cost was nearly eleven times that of the structure that it replaced;[14] the services made possible infinitely greater.

The mind, heart, and soul of an institution of learning is its faculty; the chief and indispensable instrument in its effectiveness is the library. Assurance and great promise for Eastern Michigan University lie in the story of its library. The tempo of increasing demands at the present time is so rapid that within a very few years, it is estimated, library facilities will have to be doubled again and plans have been laid to make this feasible at minimum cost. However that may be, a pattern has been achieved that will serve the institution and society well.

CHAPTER TWENTY-SIX

PRECEPTRESSES AND DEANS
OF WOMEN

Coeducation on the American campus, inaugurated in 1837 by Oberlin College, brought in time an institutional sense of special responsibility. The land-grant colleges and state universities of the mid-west followed suit from 1855, and by the 1870's faculty positions for women to look after the health, social relationships, and moral standards of coeds began to appear. The University of Wisconsin, opening its doors to women in 1863, created the position of Dean of Women in the 1890's; the University of Michigan, admitting women in 1870, established the position in 1896.

Probably because the title "Preceptress" was widely employed in female seminaries and in high schools at the time, carrying with it special responsibility for deportment and character development, it was included from the very first in the organization of Normal. The need for such a position in a teacher training institution was greatly enhanced by the general assumption that the teacher must be a model of upright Christian character.

But the title also had an academic connotation. The Preceptress was, in fact, first a teacher, then a counselor. The history of the term reveals its traditional significance, that of an older or superior practitioner who undertakes the tutoring of the neophyte. In the area of medical training the Preceptor was the practicing physician who accepted the young student as an assistant and gave him personal training. In the area of higher education, he was the faculty member who undertook to direct the reading and study of a small group of students in his field. The emphasis on rules and regulations, discipline, and social counseling was to come much later, and with it a change in title from Preceptress to Dean of Women.

At Normal the period of the Preceptress extended to the close of
the century. Then, after an interval, with the coming of President
McKenny in 1912, the office reappeared in its modern dress and
character and title.

In 1853, the position of Preceptress and Teacher of Botany and
Belles-Lettres was filled by Abigail Rogers. It stood next to the
Principal in importance.

Miss Rogers, coming from New York State, had been in charge of
a seminary for girls in Canada, preceptress in a seminary in White
Plains, New York, head of the Female Department of the Genesee
Wesleyan Seminary at Lima, New York, and a teacher in the Albion
and Ypsilanti schools. Putnam, writing in 1900, said of her: "She
was a lady of 'the old school' and the ceremonious courtesies of old-
time forms had their last exponent in her." He added:

> I well remember how, at the close of the session each day, in the 'old
> Seminary,' as the young ladies passed, in a long, decorous line from the
> school room, each one turned at the door and 'made a curtsy' which was
> so graciously and kindly returned by her stately figure standing at the
> desk. The work of Miss Rogers, as first Preceptress of the Normal School,
> set the high standard which has always continued to mark this position.
> The exalted aims and large success which so many young women have
> shown, who have been trained here, had their beginnings in the founda-
> tion which she laid in the first years of the school.

But Abigail Rogers was not content with social forms, nor with a
co-educational Normal School that was, academically speaking, as
yet but a glorified academy. She believed strongly in higher education for women—so strongly, in fact, that she decided to devote the
rest of her life to the establishment of a state-supported college for
women. Discouraged over the failure of efforts to open the University of Michigan to women, she resigned her position at Normal in
1855 and moved to the new state capital at Lansing where, with her
older sister Delia, she founded the Michigan Female College. This
school lasted until her death 14 years later.

Miss Rogers' place at Normal was filled by Sarah Allen, recently
graduated from Oberlin College. Miss Allen held the position of
Assistant Principal of the Ladies Department of Oberlin at the time.
She remained at Normal four years, then married James Lawrence
Patton, a Congregational minister. Writing in later years, Mrs.
Patton said:

> I entered upon my work with a good deal of trembling, and the trembling never entirely ceased during my four-year stay. It was a very responsible position and I never for a moment got out from under the load. I tried to do good work in the classroom and in this I was, perhaps, fairly successful, but my great anxiety was to do what one in my position ought to do for the young ladies, and be to them what one ought to be . . .

She must have made a strong impression on the students, one of whom was to follow in her footsteps and become an outstanding influence in the institution, Julia Anne King. Commenting some thirty-six years later, Miss King said:

> I cannot forbear confessing my debt to Miss Allen, a debt which every woman owes to that one who is both her ideal and her inspiration. Miss Allen's influence was far-reaching and permanent. She made a difference in my whole life.[1]

To replace Mrs. Patton, Normal went again to Oberlin College and again brought to the school one who had been Assistant Principal in the Ladies Department, Mrs. A. D. Aldrich, a young widow. Mrs. Aldrich served as Preceptress and Professor of Botany and Mathematics, and remained at the Normal from 1859 to 1867 when she married the professor of mathematics, E. L. Ripley, and went with him to the normal school at Columbia, Missouri.

Mrs. Ripley was succeeded by still another Oberlin graduate, Ruth Hoppin, who came as Preceptress and Professor of Botany and History. Miss Hoppin had been Preceptress in the Three Rivers (Michigan) High School where she taught under Principal William H. Payne, who was later to hold the first permanent chair in any American university devoted exclusively to the professional training of teachers (Chair of the Science and Art of Teaching, University of Michigan, 1879). During the three years prior to coming to Normal, Miss Hoppin taught in the Ann Arbor High School. Her background was that of the southwestern Michigan pioneer. Of her early life she said:

> Before the era of rag carpets was the notable one of the scrub brooms; those well remembered homemade splint brooms. The rule for cleaning was to dash on and sweep off water till the floor was clean enough to 'eat off' and rinsed until the water was clear as drinking water. My mother spun, wove, colored and made up the wearing apparel for her whole fam-

ily until the incoming railroad changed everything and made home manufacture unprofitable.

She described her early schooling with just a touch of wistfulness:

> Much of the time until fifteen years of age my only schooling was obtained
> by walking two miles and a quarter through the dust of summer, and the
> drifting snows of winter. The teaching in the country schools then might
> not have been as scientific as now, but those schools had an element that
> the district school of today [cir. 1900] has nearly lost, namely, the stimu-
> lus, moral and intellectual of all the best minds in the district. I look back
> to this portion of my life with pleasure, as one of real value in fitting me
> for my life work.

Preceptress-Professor Hoppin remained with Normal for 14
years, resigning in 1881 to accept the offer of the chair of botany at
Smith College.

The last of the Preceptresses was Julia Anne King, of Puritan
stock and Puritan inclination. Lacking the formal academic training
of her predecessors, she nevertheless was strongly attracted to the
fields of history and government and gave her attention increasingly
to teaching. In 1888, she organized the Department of History and
Civics which she continued to head until her retirement in 1915.
Meanwhile, in 1899, the position of Preceptress was dropped.

Miss King was a graduate of Normal, receiving her life certificate
with the class of 1858. Her formal training was concluded with an
additional year but her ability as an organizer was early recognized.
State Superintendent John M. Gregory requested her assistance in
organizing a graded school (including high school) at St. Clair,
Michigan, and made her the principal of the high school. She
became high school principal at Lansing, then was put in charge of
the Lansing schools. From there she went to Kalamazoo College as
head of the Ladies Department under Gregory who was then president of the college. The honorary degree of Master of Arts was later
conferred on her by Kalamazoo. Here she taught modern languages,
history, and literature. Later she was principal of the Charlotte high
school, then superintendent of the Charlotte schools.

Thus her experience, when she returned to her alma mater, had
been essentially administrative, yet tempered with an experience in
teaching that covered a broad range of subject matter. Later in her

career at Normal she commented that she had taught everything in the curriculum except Greek, and that her preferences were history and the physical sciences.

Miss King made a strong impression on all the students, male as well as female, perhaps as a teacher even more than as a preceptress. We have, for example, the awe-inspired question of a young man just entering Normal:

> Who is that woman with her hair combed straight back and dressed in plain black? Why, was the answer, that is Miss King, teacher of History. They say that she makes her classes work awful hard, and then there are lots of them who don't pass; and I wouldn't wonder if it were so, too, judging by the looks of her.[2]

But, as of a later time he added: "So remarks a student who is not yet acquainted with one of the grandest, noblest hearted women that ever lived."

A young woman student of the late 1890's, commenting some sixty years later, said of Miss King:

> Julia Anne King was a beautiful woman as well as a very strict disciplinarian. She could hold a study hall of 150 giggly girls in complete silence by one well aimed remark. She was feared but much respected.[3]

The concept of Miss King's duties as Preceptress was described broadly by her superior, President Willits:

> The preceptress has the special charge of the ladies, as regards their deportment, etc., which makes it advisable that at least once a day she may see them all at one time alone. Matters which have to be repeated in three or more different rooms lose much of their force, and the effect is to distribute that personality which ought to be a unit.

These meetings evolved into Miss King's famous weekly sessions known as her "Conversations," and referred to by her colleague in the History Department, Bertha M. Buell, as the precursor of the weekly "Faculty Chat" which later and for many years brought students and faculty together in weekly discussion of some topic of broad interest. These Friday meetings, held in the study hall of Old Main, dealt with matters of conduct, social forms, and religious ideals. As Miss Buell later stated, they inspired "a feeling that one's life among neighbors shapes the world community." It was not unusual for Ypsilanti women also to attend.

This social emphasis carried over strongly into Miss King's teaching, creating a unity in what otherwise might have been two distinct and disparate positions.

Julia Anne King's role as Preceptress, and the position itself, came to an end with the administrative reorganization of 1899 in which President Boone resigned, and the three Normal Schools of Michigan were placed under a statewide presidency (President Leonard), with the Ypsilanti institution presided over by Principal Elmer A. Lyman. For a period of 10 years there was no preceptress. Instead, a Standing Committee on Student Affairs, consisting of three or more members of the faculty, was organized to assume this function. Miss King served on this committee, which was chaired by a male member of the faculty. Much later she was made chairman.

The committee system did not prove to be satisfactory. Although the student enrollment remained through these years fairly stable at 1,500, with a great preponderance of women, there was dissatisfaction. In 1909, President Jones established the office of Dean of Women by adding its duties to those of the head of the Department of Household Arts.

Grace Fuller thus became the first to hold this title. When President McKenny arrived in 1912, the following paragraph was inserted in the College catalog:

> The College authorities appreciate the solicitude which parents feel when they send their sons and daughters away from home to school and they also appreciate the great responsibility which a college assumes . . . No subject is given more serious consideration by the faculty of the Normal College than the physical and moral welfare of its students.

The new title, "Dean," implied a modification of concept, a shift from emphasis on personal guidance and counseling to one of administration of rules and regulations, of regularization and discipline. Indeed, rules and regulations in regard to rooming and boarding houses were a matter of first concern for the Dean of Women and were listed in the catalog for all to become familiar with. A "Women's Council" was organized under the chairmanship of Dean Fuller which included some matrons from the community.[4]

The function of the office could, then, be better described as enlarged rather than altered. Where the emphasis would lie might vary with the incumbent; where it might eventually rest, only the future could disclose. But the essential psychological conflict between the function of policeman and that of counselor would remain to plague and puzzle all future deans.

Miss Fuller had been with the College as head of the Department of Household Arts since 1905. She had won the hearts of her students as a teacher; she now extended her following to the entire campus. In 1910, at the close of her first year as Dean, the college annual was dedicated to her.

Edwin A. Strong, in a tribute to her which appeared in the same volume, said:

> It is as the wise and efficient Dean of Women that she is best known among us. In this capacity her home has come to be a social center of great attraction for the girls of the school, who find in her a faithful friend and judicious adviser, and, through her influence, an introduction to a wider circle of interests than they could otherwise have known.

After five years the heavy load proved to be more than Miss Fuller's strength would bear, and she resigned.

She was replaced in 1915 by Marion B. White, who came to Normal from an associate professorship at the University of Kansas. While at Normal she founded a faculty women's organization known as "The Contemporary Club." She quickly acquired a reputation for upholding high academic standards, womanly behavior, and the college regulations on housing. In other words, her emphasis in dealing with students appears to have been on the side of enforcement. A brief statement in the student paper at the time is revealing:

> Possibly her Scotch and Puritan ancestry did not incline her to great sympathy with purposeless, selfish or lazy girls, yet many such girls she has helped.[5]

Miss White resigned after three years to take a teaching position at Carleton College in Minnesota, and was replaced by Bessie Leach Priddy.

Mrs. Priddy continued the tradition of combining the deanship with teaching in an academic field. She had come to Normal in 1915 as assistant professor of history, and while in that position pursued her doctorate, which she received in 1917 at the University of Michigan.

A year later she received high praise from G. Stanley Hall, at that time president of Clark University, for an article she had published on teaching the war.[6] In a letter to her, he said:

> I have been trying to keep tab . . . for some time on the effect of the war on education in this country . . . and I find that most of the articles on the subject . . . are utterly inadequate; nor do I get much that is really valuable in English or French literature, while from Germany we have quite a number of excellent articles. The spirit and method of your own work seems to me the best I have seen in English anywhere.[7]

Mrs. Priddy assumed the additional responsibility of Dean of Women in the fall of 1918. For the first years, her path as dean was relatively smooth. In 1921 the senior class dedicated its yearbook to her with the following inscription: "To Bessie Leach Priddy, Dean of Women and mother of us all, this volume is lovingly dedicated."

It was not to be thus much longer, however. Indeed, the story from early 1922 could well be headed "Hazards of Administering a State-Supported Teachers College," and involved President McKenny as well as Dean Priddy. Upon his return to the campus in Mid-April from a week's absence at a national educational meeting, McKenny found that the press had picked up an item and broadcast over the country the news that seventeen coeds had been dismissed from the Michigan State Normal College for smoking. Great excitement ensued. The president promptly drew up a lengthy statement of explanation and correction, the Governor of the State talked to the State Superintendent of Public Instruction, and newspapers headlined that a probe of the Normal was about to be made. One of the students dismissed insisted that the president and the dean had no authority to deny her readmission, appealed her case to the State Board, then went to the Circuit Court for Washtenaw County, and from there appealed to the Michigan Supreme Court.

Meanwhile, the newspapers were having a gala day. A good example was *The Kansas City Post* which sent a reporter to the campus, printed pictures of the president, the dean, the irate coed and the Governor of the State—and such quotations as the following:

Miss Tanton: It's the fault of my landlady. She did find two cigarette stubs in my wastebasket. She told Mrs. Priddy. Mrs. Priddy charged me with being an inveterate smoker. In reality, I used those two burned cigarettes as punk to burn the edges of a poster I put on my wall. I have smoked cigarettes . . . Once last fall several of us girls smoked in a dark street just to be devilish. But I never smoked in my room or in the presence of a man . . . the regulations and constant surveillance over us by school authorities tend to make us all sneaks.

Dean Priddy: The action taken by the school was right. We had the interest both of the girl and of the teaching profession at heart.

President McKenny: The Normal does not wish to pass on whether women should smoke. But it has reason to believe the people of Michigan do not want as teachers women who smoke.

Governor Groesbeck: It makes no difference whether teachers bob their hair or wear short skirts. But teachers or girls preparing to be teachers should not smoke.[8]

The president did not misinterpret the sentiment of his time. Resolutions of support came from the women students' organization, the Women's League; the Student Council; the Ypsilanti Matrons' Association. The leading ladies' club of Ypsilanti, the Ladies' Literary Club, published a strong resolution in defense of Dean Priddy.[9] The State Board met and supported the president. There was no probe of the College. Miss Tanton's suit in the Circuit Court for Washtenaw County failed and was appealed. Two years later, the State Supreme Court rejected her plea for a writ of certiorari. In explaining the rejection, Justice Fellows took occasion to commend Dean Priddy "for upholding some oldfashioned ideas of young womanhood." The official attitude of the teaching profession on problems of this nature was stated in item 12 of the Code of Ethics published by the Michigan State Teachers' Association:

Since teachers are rightly regarded as examples to pupils, a teacher should so conduct himself that no just reproach may be brought against him. When liberty of conscience is not concerned, a teacher should stand ready to make a personal sacrifice, because of the prejudices of a community.

One can agree with McKenny when, in the course of his ordeal, he said: "Unquestionably the position of Dean of Women, in an institution enrolling 1800 girls, and where there are no dormitories, is in many respects the most difficult one on the campus."[10]

He thought very highly of Dean Priddy and when, in the summer of 1923, she resigned to take a similar position at the University of Missouri, he wrote:

> All in all she is the most capable woman with whom I have been associated. She has scholarship, teaching power and signal administrative ability . . . She has leadership both with the faculty and with the students and she has the confidence and respect of the young women of the college.[11]

The College did not forget her and, in June, 1935, under another administration, voted her the honorary degree of Master of Education. It was awarded posthumously. She had died a month earlier.

Her successor, Lydia I. Jones, arrived in the fall of 1924. In the interim, the post had been filled by Acting Dean Fannie Beal, who became Assistant Dean under Miss Jones.

The new dean had a Master of Arts degree from Teachers College, Columbia University, had taken undergraduate work at Harvard University, Oxford University and the University of Chicago, and had held the position of Dean of Women and head of the English Department at the State Teachers College at Geneseo, New York. She came to the Normal College from the State Teachers College at San Jose, California, where she was Dean of Women and associate professor of English. She was the first at Normal to devote full time to the office of Dean of Women, qualified by the fact that from time to time she taught a course in Shakespeare.

In her fifteen-year tenure at the Normal College, Dean Jones played an active role in the national organization of her field, the National Association of Deans of Women (now known as the National Association of Women Deans and Counselors). For instance, at the 17th Annual Meeting of the Association, held at St. Paul, Minnesota, in 1933, she addressed a luncheon of the state presidents on "A New Co-operation in Changing Times." At the same meeting she addressed the general session on "Experiments in Creating Morale in Student Groups." At the meeting of 1939, held at Cleveland, she was cited by the Association for completion of 25 years of service.

Her work at the Normal College was characterized by an emphasis on good taste, courtesy, and the importance of self-discipline. The student must be educated for self-direction toward the goal of the common good. To facilitate this educational aim, the College should house its students.

Throughout her years at Normal she persisted in urging dormitories for women. Indeed, the policy of housing students on campus at all four of the teachers colleges of Michigan owes much to Dean Jones' pioneering fervor and effort. From the time of her arrival at Normal in 1924 she avidly collected stacks of pictures and information about dormitories on other campuses. She found an active supporter in a State Board member, Edna Wilson.

In September of 1933, the Board recommended that each teachers college be provided with a dormitory to be financed by that depression-fathered federal agency, the Public Works Administration. In December, Mrs. Wilson presented a proposal. The Board thereupon asked her to survey the conditions in the four colleges and to call a conference of the deans of women to formulate a uniform plan of action. At this conference the deans were constituted a committee to cooperate in the survey and Dean Jones was named chairman. A year later the survey was presented to the Board, whereupon Mrs. Wilson was authorized to confer with the state representative of the Public Works Administration (Mortimer E. Cooley, Dean of the Engineering College, University of Michigan) concerning the possibility of federal assistance.

Two years later (1937), both Normal and Western were authorized to proceed with plans. In another two years (1939) the first dormitory for Normal was completed (Julia Anne King Residence Hall), financed 45 per cent by the Public Works Administration, the rest by a bonded loan from the Ann Arbor Trust Company.[12] Thus began not only the dormitory program at Normal but also the concept of the self-liquidating project.[13]

In her contact with students, Dean Jones stimulated them to think about their problems, and encouraged them to keep their goals ever in mind. At the same time she tried to make the students feel that rules and regulations were not ends in themselves.

We wish [she said] to make the regulations of the college seem not as obstacles, but as aids to the achievement of the three fundamental things in college life—namely, studies, health, and emotional balance. We want

you to attain these things that you may enjoy life more, both while you
are attending college and after you have finished.

She was skillful in encouraging self-restraint and reflection. The
student paper reported a talk that Dean Jones made to entering
students:

> Miss Jones sympathizes with the students who are revolting against out-
> worn traditions and hypocrisies of another day. They should carry the
> revolt still further lest they become the victims of the machine age and lose
> their appreciation of beauty. Youth unconsciously are developing new
> fallacies and modern prejudices in spite of their fight for freedom of
> thought.[14]

She resigned in 1939 for reasons of health.

Today, two women's dormitories stand in honor of her
memory—one at the Geneseo State University in New York, where
she had served as first Dean of Women; the other on the campus of
Eastern.

Dean Jones' successor was Susan Burch Hill, who came to the
Normal College from the position of Assistant Dean of Women at
Iowa State Teachers College. At that institution she had been in
charge of dormitories. At the Normal College she initiated dormitory
self-government and programs. The first women's dormitories, Julia
Anne King and Bertha Goodison Halls, were placed in operation
that fall.

Dean Hill was a product of Milwaukee-Downer College of Milwaukee, Wisconsin, the University of Minnesota, and Teachers
College, Columbia University, where she received her master's
degree. She had taught in high schools at Ironwood, Michigan, and
Des Moines, Iowa.

She was the second Dean of Women at the Normal College to
devote full time to her position, and the first to come with professional training for it. It was well that this type of person was chosen,
not only because it meant keeping in step with the times but because
of the immensely greater responsibilities being assumed by the College with the advent of dormitory life. Henceforth, the College
would assume responsibility for the physical, social and cultural life
of the student twenty-four hours a day. Programs in student self-
government, cultural growth, social development would receive

strong emphasis; problems moral, ethical, family, academic would be laid at the dean's door. The parallel development of professional health services and psychiatric care would in time provide her with greatly improved facilities for effective work.

The annual reports from her office revealed the extent and variety of the areas of concern. There was, first, the operation of the dormitories, in which self-government was adopted as a fundamental policy. Dean Hill described it as follows:

> The social life of the women and social regulation are conducted on the principle of democratic self-government. Each residence hall has its council, whicn in turn is in close contact with the executive board of the Women's League (representing *all* women students both in and outside of dormitories). The women make and enforce their own regulations.[15]

There was the organization known as the Women's League, with its many ramifications; the Panhellenic League, representing the sororities and the major problems attendant on rushing and bidding; jobs for women working their way through college; academic counseling for those in need; psychiatric and health counseling and treatment, not infrequently under the pressure of emergency. Lengthy studies were made in the area of academic difficulties, student employment, the evaluation of students by employers, the desirability of separate houses for sororities, psychiatric and personnel services, the function and role of the dormitory Head Resident and the Assistant Head Resident.

A student-counselor program, initiated in 1940, saw a senior student selected in each corridor to interpret rules and regulations, and to be concerned with the general welfare and happiness of the girls. A record system consisting of a folder for each student was maintained. Special projects were initiated, encouraged, conducted, such as a leadership clinic, a picture rental program, an extensive program of social service in the community.

But always of chief importance were the personal interviews in the office of the dean. Every student reported as doing unsatisfactory work was interviewed by Dean Hill personally, as well as many, many others who appeared on their own initiative, totaling a minimum of 600 in the year 1950–1951 and increasing as the student body increased through the years.

The Community Service program, developed and carried on for

many years under the initiative and direction of Professor Frances
Gates, was of particular significance. It encouraged the girls to contribute to the community life, and provided opportunities for them in
recreation, community activity centers, with handicapped children,
the Red Cross, Girl Scouts, nursery school, and other activities. At
the same time, those young people planning to be teachers were
provided with opportunity to gain experience with children at an
early time in their college careers, an opportunity that often helped
them decide whether they were really temperamentally equipped to
work with children. Dean Hill herself set a personal example of
community service by serving for two terms on the Ypsilanti City
Council.

Dormitory life and a greatly expanded student body added tre-
mendously to the responsibilities of the office of Dean of Women.
Social problems, arising with the advent of the automobile, changing
attitudes towards the use of alcoholic beverages, and a general confusion in society about social standards, multiplied. At the same time,
growth of the counseling concept and closer attention nationally to
the functioning of the personnel dean had raised her to a professional status which meant not only informed attention to many more
areas of concern, but impact on a far larger percentage of the student
body. Fortunately for Normal, the personal touch and deep concern
for the individual student, so characteristic of the Preceptress, had
not been lost.

The two women's dormitories of 1939 multiplied to ten by 1969.
Student apartments, first constructed in 1955, totaled more than 250
and more were under construction. At the same time, there were six
dormitories for men and one which housed men and women in separate areas.

In 1963, Dean Hill found herself in a position of responsibility for
all students. Following the trend in the larger universities, the offices
of Dean of Women and Dean of Men were consolidated under a
Dean of Students. Miss Hill occupied this position until she retired
early in 1969.

CHAPTER TWENTY-SEVEN

THE STUDENTS

Campus life during the early years was strikingly different from that of our own time. The admission age was 16 for boys, 18 for girls. The faculty assumed a high degree of responsibility for their conduct. The college catalog contained a detailed list of regulations to be observed, and there was apparently just one penalty for disobedience—dismissal.

Perhaps the story of early student life at the Normal is best told by the students themselves. Following is an excerpt from a letter written in 1860, when Adonijah Welch was principal:

> The new building is much superior to the old one [destroyed the year previous by fire]. . . . The Normal is very much the same as it was when you were here and the students similar, though this is a progressive age, and they are somewhat *faster,* an adjective of much signification in late years. The young ladies, as a class, are better looking, I think, than when you were here (Miss Fisher always excepted).[1]

Later in the same year a letter from a student to his cousin who was thinking of attending the Normal provided a more detailed picture. Asserting that if he could persuade her to come he would feel that he had accomplished "some good in this world," he continued:

> I suppose there are nearly three hundred students in the Normal School and over two thirds of these are ladies. . . . There are many things required of students who attend the Normal School. As the school is pretty much free, being only three dollars a year, they lay down many rules which we have to obey, or we can go home, just as we please. . . . All recitations are conducted in the fore-noon, so we have to go to the building but once in a day; and that is at twenty minutes after eight, and holds four hours. We have to stay in our rooms two hours during the afternoon

except Saturdays or Sundays, also after seven o'clock in the evening except the two days above mentioned when we can stay out till ten in the evening. The students room all over town just where they can get rooms and board. If you should go out of your room during study hours . . . perhaps you would not be seen, but if one of the teachers should happen to see you, he would probably report you to the Principal; and after you have been reported twice you are expelled from school. We are not allowed to whisper at all in the school room except during two short recesses. We have to tell them . . . what church we attend while here for they say that they do not want students who do not attend church. . . . The teachers are very particular about our having good lessons. . . . You will please excuse some of my mistakes, as I have acquired a rather careless habit in writing.[2]

Normal in the Civil War

Within a year the students were to become involved in the tragedy of civil war. Thanks to the records left by a member of the faculty, Austin George, a fairly intimate view is afforded of its impact upon Normal.[3]

The Normal community was shocked at the outbreak of war. None had believed the worst would happen. The excited students met constantly as war talk reached fever pitch. When Governor Austin Blair answered President Lincoln's call of April 15, 1861, for a regiment of infantry, he asked for ten companies of militia. Two companies from Washtenaw County, one from Ypsilanti (Company H), succeeded in getting into Michigan's original Civil War regiment (the 1st infantry). A few of the Normal students signed up to go at this time. The 1st Michigan Infantry reached Washington on May 16, arriving before any other troops from the west. Three more infantry regiments were formed in Michigan by June 20. Within a year the State had raised a total of twelve infantry and four cavalry regiments.

The recruits in Ypsilanti were housed in the newly erected Thompson Block on the northeast corner of River and Cross Streets, a building long after referred to as "the barracks." Of the men drilling on the site of Gilbert Park and Woodruff School, the Rev. Harvey C. Colburn, historian of Ypsilanti, wrote: "Interested crowds gathered to watch the painful evolutions and halting manual of arms of the raw soldiers."

Many patriotic rallies were held in Ypsilanti. The singing at these affairs was led by Professor Ezra Mead Foote, head of the Normal School's Music Department. Long after the war Normal graduates told Colburn how Foote would appeal to his students to "Wake up, boys, wake up!" whenever they were singing "We are coming, Father Abraham."

Before the end of Normal's 1862 summer term the students decided to organize a Normal Company, the State Board of Education promising leaves of absence to any enrollees. The students were disappointed when, on July 18, school closed before the signing up could take place. One person, however, took the initiative and saved the day. He was Austin George, a student living in Ypsilanti. George took it upon himself to complete the recruiting. In his history of the Normal Company, he wrote, ". . . I assumed responsibility to hang out the flag and open a recruiting office at Kinne and Smith's Book Store on the north side of Congress Street. A circular letter was prepared and mailed to the boys all over the state. Responses came quickly, in person."

The company was soon full, with complements from Jackson and Washtenaw Counties joining the Normal students. Gabriel Campbell ('61), then a graduate student at the U-M, was elected captain. Of 83 privates, 19 were from the Normal, which, however, did not furnish any of the specialities—fifer, drummer, and wagoner. All commissioned officers were Normalites, and of the non-commissioned officers only one sergeant and four corporals were not.[4]

Austin George, the real hero of the outfit, the one whose talent and drive organized Company E, had only one arm and could not regularly enlist. Notwithstanding, he did accompany the organization as company clerk and remained in service four months, doing duty at the front as regimental postmaster and clerk at brigade and division headquarters.

Professor John M. B. Sill declined the offer of company commander, feeling that it was more properly a student unit. He induced the business and professional men of Ypsilanti to contribute money which was used for the purchase of a sword, belt, and sash for Captain Campbell. These gifts were presented by Sill in what George, who was present, called "a handsome speech" at Hewitt (later Light Guard) Hall. The ladies of the city gave to each recruit a special gift. George received a pocket edition of the Testament and Psalms, with the name of "Louise Loveridge" written inside the cover. On the last Sunday in Ypsilanti the young soldiers went in a body to the Methodist church and heard the pastor, Dr. F. B. Cocker, preach what George called "an eloquent and appropriate sermon."

The company was mustered in at Detroit on August 19 and was designated as Company E of the 17th Infantry Regiment. The regiment went on to Washington, where company E guarded the Navy Yard bridge, from which point the men could hear the guns of Second Bull Run. When Generals Lee and Jackson invaded Maryland in 1862, the 17th saw its first action at South Mountain. As a result of a successful charge against the enemy entrenched behind stone fences, the 17th acquired the name of "Stonewall Regiment."

South Mountain took place on September 14. Three days later two Normal youths, John Marvin and Webster Ruckman, were killed and Fred Webb mortally wounded at Antietam. After this battle the regiment was present in a review of the army by President Lincoln.

In November, the regiment was moving into northern Virginia and, at Waterloo, Principal Welch visited Company E. An amusing incident, of which a student soldier wrote George, occurred:

> I remember we were stopping for three or four days, and he was disappointed at not witnessing some fighting, and expressed a wish to take a gun and go in with the boys, if such an occasion occurred while he was there. The evening before he was to leave we had a 'spread,' with singing and speeches. Morgan gave me his horse and I went out three or four miles and 'found' some potatoes and chickens. Other boys also foraged. Rubber blankets were spread on the ground for tables, around which we sat like Turks and had our banquet, while an outside rim of spectators were interested admirers of the occasion. The Professor again spoke of his desire to be with the company in actual fighting, and had hardly more than finished speaking when the long roll beat, as we heard some picket-firing. Everyone sprang for his gun, and the Professor soon rigged himself up in the accouterments of a soldier who had that day gone away sick. I well remember how comical he looked, so little, with a silk hat on, and a belt, and a gun! He turned in with the company, and was as good as his word. Fortunately, it proved to be only a scare, and no further test of valor was required.

The Normal Company fought at Fredericksburg, Knoxville and in the West. The Wilderness, Spottsylvania Court House and Petersburg were battles taking their toll of men of the 17th. Finally, Lee's surrender on April 9, 1865, brought the war to an end. The return trip home was delayed long enough for the regiment to be a part of the grand review of the Union armies in Washington on May 23. On June 3, the regiment was mustered out and on June 7 it reached Detroit where the men were paid and discharged.

In the course of its fighting the 17th (consisting of ten companies) had lost 89 men killed in battle. Mute testimony to courage and aggressiveness is the fact that 13 were Company E. men.

The history of the Normal Company does not, of course, constitute the whole story of Normal men participating in the war. Indeed, the honor roll of Normalites who lost their lives lists more than twice the number lost by Company E. The record compiled by George reveals a total of 160 Normal men enlisting in the course of the war.[5]

According to George, the war did have one noticeable effect on most of the men (and this observation reflects a striking difference from later generations). George wrote, "After leaving the army, comparatively few of the boys returned to scholastic pursuits, and fewer still took up the work of teaching. The current of their lives had been turned from its old channel, and their purpose changed."

As one could anticipate, the impact of the Civil War on the Normal campus was somewhat different from that on those campuses where only men were enrolled. The University of Wisconsin, for example, introduced a Normal Department during the war largely as a device for restoring enrollments. They thereby brought women on their campus for the first time. This was an innovation which caused no little disturbance, and which raised the question of admitting women to higher education, an issue which finally had to be settled by the state legislature.

Admission to the halls of Ypsilanti Normal never presented such an issue. At the opening of her portals, some 47 per cent of the students were men. During the first year and a half of the war (1861 and spring 1862), the proportion of men remained about the same. But from the opening of the fall term of 1862 the proportion dropped markedly, and during the next three years hovered between 20 and 30 per cent.

As an indication of student reaction to the war, the Normal Lyceum's minutes of April 19, 1861, following the firing on Fort Sumter and the call for troops, read:

On motion the special order of the evening was then taken up. The house resolved itself into a committee of the whole to discuss the question (selected the week before), 'Resolved, That the North would be better off morally, socially and politically without the South.' The discussion was of much interest; gentleman on the affirmative producing unanswerable statistics, which were nevertheless overborne by patriotic enthusiasm and Union sentiment. The question on being referred to the house was lost. Then followed the magnificent Marseillaise Hymn, stirring deeper depths than the discussion had agitated. Miscellaneous business being taken up, this question was selected for the next discussion: 'Resolved, That the South has no right to secede.' A quartet, the Red, White and Blue, was then sung, and after a chorus of real live cheers, the society adjourned.

Religion

In common with the prevailing spirit of the day on campuses everywhere, religion played an important role in the life of the campus from the first. The fact that this was a normal school, training teachers of the young, only served to enhance the importance of the religious spirit. Mrs. S. A. Allen Patton, an early Preceptress at Normal, wrote in later years:

I went to Ypsilanti in the fall of 1855. . . . I found the Students' Prayer Meeting one of the institutions of the school, and, so far as I know, its beginning was contemporaneous with that of the School. It seemed to fit into its place and be so thoroughly alive and efficient to meet as real a want as the recitation hours, the Lyceum, or anything else that was an essential to the life of the school.

Ruth Hoppin, Preceptress a few years later, wrote in a similar vein:

It was a joy to see all those noble young people so seriously in earnest in the great work to which they were called, and I was sure that when the schools of the State should go into such hands our educational interests would be safe. Very few of the teachers attended in those days, but no evening passed that did not bring noble President Mayhew [1865–1870] into our midst.

Principal Estabrook (1871–1879), at the request of the students, took charge of the weekly religious meeting. A member of the faculty at the time, Mrs. Mary L. Rice Fairbanks, later wrote:

He was a grand leader and had the rare power of securing expression from others. There was a spiritual baptism, decisions were made that have moulded lives. That old chapel was a sacred place in which were formed some of memory's best pictures. A crowd of young people in the benches, the leader standing in front of the desk, what expostulations fell from his lips, what songs, what prayers, what confessions, what resolves responded!

Daniel Putnam, contemporaneous with these times as a faculty member, recorded that the reorganization of student societies brought about by Principal Mac Vicar in 1881 involved the prayer meetings. A room was fitted out on the second floor of the conservatory building where the Wednesday evening prayer meetings were held. A student of 1890 made the following appraisal of a prayer meeting:

He feels better for having gone than he would if he had stayed at home. He accomplishes more in the two hours that are left than he would in four if he had not gone. There is something in a prayer meeting composed of students, all of whom are young, energetic, active workers, that inspires one. Whether a person takes part or not, there is something in the genuineness of the enthusiasm that wakes one up. Of all the influences with which I was thrown in contact during the first year of my student life at Normal, none were so potent for the time being, or so lasting in its effects, as that exercised by the Students' Christian Association.[6]

In 1891, because of growth of the school and particularly of the Conservatory of Music, the room had to be relinquished. From that time, the Students' Christian Association became active in raising money for a building of their own. To their great joy, in 1895 Mrs. Mary Ann Starkweather, a wealthy and public-spirited citizen of Ypsilanti, added to the hard-won but too meager student fund of a thousand dollars the generous gift of $10,000, and the building was assured. The State Board of Education provided the site; the Association, to enable it to own the property, became incorporated; and on March 26, 1897, a beautiful building was dedicated in the presence of its donor with pomp and ceremony. The building committee through its chairman, Professor Putnam, in presenting the building said:

While the State is wisely prohibited from making direct provision for religious education and culture, it can well afford to permit and to encourage

private individuals to furnish means and facilities for such education at
their own expense. Indeed, by so doing the State is only fulfilling the obligation imposed upon it by the provisions of the famous ordinance of 1787
. . . that 'Religion, morality, and knowledge being necessary to good
government and the happiness of mankind, schools and the means of
education shall be forever encouraged.'

Starkweather Hall has been the center for student religious groups
to the present time, broadening the scope of religious enterprise from
the Protestant only to an inclusion of Catholic, Christian Science
and Jewish, but still exclusive of non-Western faiths. At various
times, these groups have collaborated in all-campus projects through
a Students' Religious Counsel or, as in the past few years, a Council
of Student Religious Organizations. A Faculty Board for Religious
Affairs stood ready with advice. Thanks to a grant from the Dan-
forth Foundation, a permanent staff was provided. Gladys Eriksen
and Margaret Menzi, both faculty wives, gracious and deeply concerned about students, jointly carried on an active program.

More recently, Charles Minneman was employed as head of an
Office of Religious Affairs, which has carried on its work under the
aegis of the Vice-President for Student Affairs. The responsibilities
of this office were rather ponderously described as "coordination of
university and religious concerns through the structures of communication . . ., administration of Starkweather Hall, student counseling
and referral, religious representation of the University, and provision of direction and resources for university-level, campus-wide,
inter-religious programs."

"In short," ran the statement, "it is the hope that the religious
program at Eastern will serve as a resource for bringing the given
religious situation at Eastern to that level of theological intelligibility
and ethical sensibility as befits the stature of a university framework
of action."[7]

Student Health

Concern for the health of college students has, in America, manifested itself in the outdoor gymnastic phase of the 1820's, soon to
disappear, and the indoor gymnastic craze sparked in the late 1840's
and early 1850's by the German Turnverein, supplemented from

about 1900 by increasingly meticulous medical examinations.

The story at the Normal roughly paralleled the national trends. Student health became a problem of major importance within the first few years of Normal's founding. The Board of Visitors for 1859, urging that the Normal be equipped with a gymnasium, said:

> If we mistake not, there is a decided want of appropriate physical exercise among the pupils, and we would call your attention particularly to the question whether the frequent cases of mortality among students soon after graduating, may not arise from a like cause . . .

Principal Welch, renewing the request in 1860 and 1861, asserted that

> . . . from a fourth to a third of our entire number were compelled, on account of sickness, to leave before the close of the term, while those who remained showed in the pallor of their faces, the exhaustion that follows protracted study without muscular exercise.

Meanwhile, Professors Sill and Miller, and Principal Welch himself, led the men students in open air exercises, and Preceptress Aldrich did the same indoors for the women as they stood beside their desks.

Reluctance on the part of the legislature to respond to the repeated appeals for a gymnasium was somewhat offset by private contributions and help from the State Board of Education. A modest building was erected. Instruction in this building was, for lack of a special teacher, "necessarily irregular and intermittent." It was destroyed by fire in 1873, and was not replaced until the substantial structure of 1894 was completed.

The practice of requiring activity classes in physical education of all students began with the opening of the new gymnasium. At the same time, a medical examination of all students was required, a blank for this purpose being provided for the family physician. The stated purpose of this examination was to determine "the strengths and needs" of the student, and to insure against injury. Women were given a special medical examination.

Julia Anne King, preceptress from 1881 until 1899, is credited with the creation of a faculty committee on student affairs in 1897. It was this committee that first placed a medical emphasis on student health, securing the employment of a registered nurse. This led in time to the establishment of a health clinic.

Upon the arrival of Charles McKenny as president in 1912, increased attention was given to the problem of student health. In his report for that year he drew the attention of the State Board to a situation that he considered alarming, namely, that an epidemic could easily break out among the students and the city of Ypsilanti had no hospital.

From this point a health service began to take shape. In 1913, a room was set aside in the Training School Building (now Welch Hall) as headquarters for the nurse. In 1915, a house on Perrin Street was acquired and equipped as a "Health Cottage." "Student doctors" from the University of Michigan were used to service it, one a young woman named Glenadine Snow. In 1916, Dr. Snow was employed full-time as "Medical Inspector" for the girls' gymnasium (also to conduct advanced work in physical education); and the following year she was made Director of the Health Service.

The tenure of Dr. Snow, which extended until her retirement in 1947, was a notable one. Vivacious and full of energy, deeply interested in students, she was at the same time a leader in her chosen field of student health. In addition to her duties as Director of the Health Service she was instrumental in organizing an instructional department in Health Education which she headed, drawing her staff from the departments of Physical Education, Home Economics, and Biology.[8]

At about the same time, she published an article advocating the direct teaching of health in the secondary schools. Her thesis was that the foundation courses in science (biology, chemistry, bacteriology, anatomy) should be offered only after the student (the prospective teacher) had been motivated by courses dealing with health problems. This was the exact reverse of common practice at the time. Dr. Snow's departmental offerings included such courses as Personal Health, Nutrition of School Children, Health Education in the Elementary Grades, Health Education for Rural Schools, and Health Examinations.

It was doubtless because of her pioneering work in this area that, in 1930, the Children's Fund of Michigan (created by the Couzens Foundation) offered to employ her to complete work begun by a study committee on the framing of a program of health instruction for teachers in the four teachers colleges of Michigan. At the same time the Foundation undertook to subsidize a health instructor in each of these colleges, and also a health supervisor in the Department of Public Instruction. The State Board accepted the offer. Dr. Snow was given a leave of absence to do the job. Although the positions subsidized by the Foundation were not included in the college budgets after the trial period of three years had elapsed, the State Board did press for the development of a uniform and adequate health service program in the four colleges from this time.

The subsequent story of the Department of Health Education was one of gradual abandonment of cooperation among Health Service, Biology, Home Economics, and Physical Education Departments, and its ultimate merger with Physical Education, controlled and staffed entirely by that department. The merger took place in 1947–1948 (the year following the retirement of Dr. Snow); the year 1955–1956 saw the last course taught by a medical doctor; and beginning with 1957–1958 a minor field of concentration in Health was offered by the Physical Education staff.

As for the Health Service, its work continued to expand. In 1939, a hospital building was erected. Planned by Dr. Snow, this facility, with its eight beds for in-patients (capable of being doubled in an emergency), its consulting rooms, its provision for keeping records, its cheerful and ample receiving room, was furnished with the most up-to-date equipment and stood as a model hospital for a college that might number as many as 3,500 students. In 1954, it was dedicated as a memorial to Dr. Snow and henceforth as the Glenadine C. Snow Health Center.

In November, 1959, after 20 years of service, and in anticipation of an ultimate student body of 8,000, this building was given to the Music Department and replaced by a much larger and truly resplendent facility, financed with federal assistance and student fees. Thirty beds, with a possible emergency capacity of eighty, an ample number of consulting and examining rooms, a conference room, contagious rooms, nurse station and suite, air conditioning, elevators, a solarium area, and again the most modern equipment featured the new Glenadine C. Snow Health Center.

Since Dr. Snow was the true founder as well as the first director of this vital service to students, let us examine her contribution.

In 1920, the American Student Health Association was organized in Chicago. At the fourth annual meeting of this Association Dr. Snow brought the Normal into membership. In 1934, a Michigan branch of the Association was organized. The Normal College was a charter member. From this contact, at both the national and state levels, Dr. Snow gained much of her perspective and emphasis. In a brief history of the Health Service at Normal, she said:

> The purpose of a college health service is not to offer to a group of doctors a chance to practice medicine, but it is an educational agency closely cooperating with every other department of the college. Its purpose is to discover and correct early symptoms of any difficulties which will keep students away from their classes and to teach them the proper attitude toward scientific medicine and health.

This emphasis on the preventive and on the educational aspects of medicine characterized Dr. Snow's entire administration. As a practitioner of preventive medicine, she carried on a continuing program of personal conferences, an immunization program for polio, influenza, smallpox and typhoid fever, and, of major importance, an annual physical examination for every student. In 1944, the chest X-ray was added to the physical examination.

Upon her retirement in 1947, Dr. Snow was replaced by Dr. Verne Van Duzen. Dr. Van Duzen carried through the policies of the service, gave close attention to follow-up on continuing problems, to special physical examinations for athletes in intercollegiate competition, and to graduating seniors in need of a health statement in connection with securing a position. He drew particular attention to psychiatric cases, and established a referral arrangement with the Ypsilanti State Hospital and the Neuropsychiatric Institute at the University of Michigan. He left the Normal after four years to accept an offer from the Ypsilanti State Hospital, and was replaced by Dr. Olga Sirola.

Dr. Sirola came to the Normal from a similar position at Western Illinois Normal. Her professional training was obtained at the University of California. She brought to Normal a dedicated attitude of concern for student health, a keen awareness of the importance of psychological and emotional health, and a willingness to employ unlimited time and energy. Her administration at Normal was a continuation of, and enlargement upon, the Snow period, actively maintaining national and state contacts, emphasizing preventive medicine in particular, carrying on an instructional program of movies, exhibits, lectures, and at the same time taking up where Dr.

Van Duzen left off with regard to psychological problems of students.

The Normal College was ready, therefore, when, in January of 1951, Dr. Walter Obenauf, Assistant Medical Director of the Ypsilanti State Hospital, (with the active support of his superior, Dr. Ray Yoder) offered a continuing psychiatric service, with a program of regular hours on campus for consultation between student and psychiatrist. This service continues.

Student Organizations

If all the formal student organizations that have existed on Normal's campus could be identified, the number would probably reach nearly 300. Available records reveal a total of 274, distributed over more than a century, and amenable to some 15 categories.[9] Not one spans the entire life of the school but three can show a continuous existence through the several phases from Normal School to University: the Athletic Association (1887); Arm of Honor fraternity (1894); and Sigma Nu Phi sorority (1897). Two others have had an intermittent existence through this span of time—the Christian Association (in various forms from 1881) and the German Club (1895).

In the first decade of Normal's existence just one society was formed, but every decade since has seen a number of new ones, the high point being reached during the first ten years of the McKenny regime when there were 57. Nor has the trend abated in recent times. During the 1940's and 1950's, 61 new groups were organized.

To understand organized student life at Normal, one must look to the winds that brought tidings from the prestigious colleges and universities of the East. The Yale Report of 1828 had firmly and, for the time, convincingly upheld the traditional humanistic curriculum as against demands for one more broad, more practical. Accompanying this philosophy of education was a classroom method of formal recitation and rigid memorization. In his "History of the American College and University," Rudolph says: "The classroom, while officially dedicated to disciplining and furnishing the mind, was in reality far better at molding character and at denying intellect rather than refining it."

He then points out that the reaction of the students, those "now unknown and forgotten hosts of undergraduates," accomplished what the liberal educational leaders of the time were unable to do, a revolution which resulted in a fundamental reform of the American college, an escape and freeing from the narrow limitations of tradition. This revolution was expressed in those student-initiated, student-conducted activities that today we refer to as extracurricular.

By the time that Normal arrived on the stage, the literary society, or Lyceum, had long flourished in the East. Its emphasis was on freedom of discussion, the challenging of stereotypes, and the importance of reason.

At Normal a Lyceum was organized in the very first term and it continued to be the only student organization for nearly twenty years. Obviously it could not have been student inspired; rather, it would appear to represent the intent that this institution should travel the way of the colleges of the country. But it very definitely represented the intent that the informal life of the campus should emphasize the intellectual, and be kept under control. Of this society, Putnam said:

> It is noteworthy that the teachers of the institution entered into the matter of organization and management in common with the student body. The same thing is observable to a considerable extent during the subsequent history of the Lyceum. Some members of the Faculty habitually attended the weekly meetings, frequently delivered lectures, and, at times, participated freely in debates.

Principal Welch was elected the first president of the society and Professor J. M. B. Sill was made corresponding secretary. In 1876, the society was incorporated and the membership limited to 400. The unwieldiness of a large membership, as the school grew, led in time to formation of several other societies.

As might be expected of a mixed faculty-student organization, the topics debated remained well within the limits of propriety. However, they did represent serious attention to problems of the day. A few of the propositions were: "That men engaged in manual labor act a greater part in the formation of the character of a community than men of scientific research;" "That the aims and tendencies of the so-called 'Know-nothing' party are detrimental to the institutions of our government;" "That the discovery of the California mines has been detrimental to mankind;" "That the ladies ought to be allowed to debate; that the interest of the society and its existence depend upon their debating" (1870); "That the acquisition of Cuba is an object much to be desired by the government of the United States;" "That the Bible should be retained in the public schools." This last resulted in a protracted and animated debate, participated in by several members of the faculty, and extending over three evenings. The Lyceum finally adopted a resolution stating that "we believe the Bible should not be excluded from our public schools and that such exclusion would not, in our opinion, render them more acceptable to any class of our citizens."

Besides its value as an intellectual stimulus, the old Lyceum served as a center for social life and was active in bringing lecturers to Ypsilanti and the campus. Through the years, too, in pursuance of its debating and literary programs it developed a sizable library. In 1888, its collection of more than a thousand volumes was absorbed by the general library.

A number of smaller literary societies sprang up in the 1870's: The Normal Zealots (men only), The Pleiades (ladies only), The Riceonian (after Miss Mary Rice, teacher of English), The R. H. Society (for Preceptress Ruth Hoppin), and The Independent Lyceum (for students in the Training School). Viewing this development as undesirable, the faculty, through Principal Mac Vicar, in 1880–1881, arbitrarily abolished them, and re-shaped the "Old Lyceum" into the "New Lyceum," a four-way subdivision into societies known as Olympic, Atheneum, Adelphic, and Crescent.

In 1881, the Christian Association was formed. In 1888, a Mock Congress (organized at first under the name of Political Debating Society) appeared, apparently inspired by Principal Willits, who also taught the work in government at Normal. In 1887, the Athletic Association was born "to promote and foster all legitimate sports and athletic exercises, and to afford facilities to its members for participating therein."

In the 1890's appeared the Shakespeare, Webster, Debating, and Child Study Clubs; the Oratorical Association, the YM and YWCA, the Kamera Klub, the Washington Toastmasters' Club ("dedicated to genuine, genial, goodfellowship"), the Arm of Honor ("to foster in its members the ability to think and to speak extemporaneously"), the Philosophic Society.

During this decade, too, appeared the first of a kind of social organization known as the regional club, made up of students from the same county or area. This type of organization grew and flourished through the next two decades, numbering in all about 40, and representing areas throughout the State as well as one for the area "outside of Ohio and Michigan." These organizations served to preserve local loyalties and at the same time to stimulate hometown interest in the Normal.

But of greater and lasting importance to the life of the Normal was the appearance in the 1880's of another type, the departmental club. As with the literary society, this was an organization initiated by faculty for students, participated in by both. The character of these clubs was that of the specialist in a particular area of learning on practice. Composed of students who had developed an interest in the subject matter of the department of instruction, they held discussion meetings, presented papers, brought in speakers. Many held an annual dinner to which alumni returned.

The idea first found expression in the formation of the Scientific Society in 1884 to promote interest in scientific reading, study and investigation among seniors in the science courses. In the decade of the '90's appeared the Mathematical Society (1891), the Pease Musical Art Club (1894), the German Club, the Physical Science Society (1895), the Shakespearean Club (1896), and the Nature Study Club (1898). In all, some 46 departmental clubs were formed. Twenty are still active (1968), including seven which, under one name or another, can trace their lineage back to the early 1900's (Biology, Chemistry, English, German, Mathematics, Men's and Women's Physical Education).

The next step was the appearance of the honor society. Beginning with Alpha Delta Sigma in 1912 (Household Arts), some 14 departmental or professional honor societies were formed, about half appearing in the 'teens and the twenties.

At the all-campus level, Adahi, an honor society for senior women based on scholarship and evidence of qualities of leadership, was formed in 1957.

Oldest of all, however, was the all-campus Stoic Society. Informal in origin, it began on the initiative of a member of the faculty, J. Stuart Lathers, who invited a select group of faculty and students into his home for fellowship and serious discussion in 1909. Out of these meetings grew the society that has represented Normal's high regard for scholarship. In due course the name "Stoic" was adopted, perhaps because it sought out students who took little part in the social activities of the school. Because at this time, and for many years after, the Life Certificate could be earned two years in college, admission to the Society was set at the sophomore level. It has remained so. In its first year it started a scholarship fund to encourage promising students to return for a third year of study. This has been a continuing major project of the Society. Since it was founded in a teacher training institution, the factor of "character," that is, the type of person generally acceptable in the public schools as a teacher, entered into its selection of members. This had the unfortunate effect at times of eliminating a promising candidate who did not conform to the mores of the time—for some years, for example, those who smoked. Since scholarship was the basic consideration, however, its membership consistently held the respect of the campus and contributed in a vital sense to its tone.

By honoring outstanding faculty of the past in the form of scholarships and annual attention to their lives, the Stoics serve to perpetuate valuable traditions of the school. Its faculty sponsors have been teachers of exceptional ability in their respective areas, and outstanding in their interest in students. By seeking the advice of the current faculty on nominations for membership, the selective policy involves more than a bare perusal of the scholastic record. The tone and character of its annual dinners represent the student body at its best. It is Normal's version of Phi Beta Kappa.

As the literary societies declined, fraternal life grew. The last of the old all-campus literary societies were formed in the Mac Vicar reorganization of 1881. From 1894 to 1902, some eleven Greek letter societies appeared; from 1903–1912 nine more; from 1913–1922 another nine. Each succeeding decade added to the number. Looking back, we can count more than 40 fraternities and sororities.

The fact that, at the national level, sororities had by the '90's passed through the early stage of being looked upon as imitative of fraternities and were accepted on their own merits probably accounts for their appearance on the Normal campus at the same time as the fraternities. Through the years the number of societies remained fairly even as between the men and the women.

Two fraternities claim a continuous existence from this first decade: Arm of Honor (1895) and Kappa Phi Alpha (1902). Two sororities make a similar claim: Sigma Kappa (originating as Pi Kappa Sigma in 1894) and Alpha Sigma Tau (1899).

One new aspect of fraternity life should be noted. After World War II, the question of discrimination on the basis of color became increasingly agitated. Four fraternal groups that were predominatly colored (two fraternities and two sororities) came into existence. These were not, however, based on a principal of color exclusion.

National leadership on this question of discrimination was both reluctant and evasive. After noting a number of court decisions that dealt with college regulation of this problem, the following statement appeared in the official manual for fraternities and sororities:

> It would, therefore, appear that the courts of the country have recognized that a 'voluntary association' has the right to be selective in the choice of new members and that in the exercise of this *private* right, the action does not violate any constitutional amendments. If this right should be connected with governmental control and supervision, then there is a different question.[10]

The National Interfraternity Conference passed an evasive resolution "reaffirming belief in the right of each fraternity to establish its own criteria for membership, applicable to all its chapters, determined by the chapters in convention."

What was the nature of these Greek letter societies? Why did they appear on the college scene? What qualities accounted for the fact that they replaced the old literary society, once supported with such great enthusiasm by the entire student body? Why, although sponsored by members of the faculty, did the Greek letter society develop an independent life of its own?

For answers to questions such as these, one must turn to the national background. Fraternity life in America developed in the first half to the nineteenth century. By 1840, it existed in most of the New England colleges and in New York. Wherever it appeared, the older literary society faded.

But the fraternity did not arise without opposition. The University of Michigan, for example, experienced the appearance of the Greek letter fraternity in the first years of its existence (the early 1840's). The faculty resisted it, expelled it from the campus in 1849, but were forced by outside and student pressures to reverse their stand in 1850. This conflict between university administration and students, won by the students, caused such a sharp reaction against the apparent weakness of the administrative pattern that one result was a move to secure election of the board of regents rather than their appointment by the governor. Since appointment was provided for in the State Constitution, a constitutional amendment was necessary. One authority on education has said that the call for the Constitutional Convention of 1850 was a direct result.[11]

This negative attitude toward fraternities at Ann Arbor had had its precedents in the East. Mark Hopkins, at Williams College, found sympathetic support when he said:

> The influence [of fraternities] have been evil. They create class and factions, and put men socially in regard to each other into an artificial and false position. . . . The alienation of feeling and want of cordiality thus created are not favorable to a right moral and religious state.

Anti-secret societies and movements developed in the colleges. But boards in control, college presidents, even student opposition were all to no avail. The fraternity movement grew and flourished. Rudolph explains the phenomenon in terms of purpose, "to fill an emotional and social rather than a curricular vacuum;" in substitution "they filled the vacuum of home and community life." He goes on to say that they were an escape" from the monotony, dreariness, and unpleasantness of the collegiate regimen which began with prayers before dawn and ended with prayers after dark."

The fraternity movement at Normal fitted largely into this image, although the extremes reached on the more sophisticated campuses were never approached. The secrecy, the not-to-be restrained disciplines of "hell week" programs for the neophytes, the off-campus parties (not infrequently without the full knowledge of the faculty sponsor), the kind of judgment in selection of pledges, the on-campus air of pride and superiority, the annual dinners which drew alumni like a magnet year after year back to the fellowship—all gave evidence of a kind of rebellion against the restraints of traditional values and of institutional authority and a strong attraction to the mystic but secular bonds of "brotherhood." (Today all students are demanding these freedoms.) The students, by their reaction, contributed a broadening, if not intellectual, influence on the curriculum. The artistic and intellectual life at Normal could be carried on by other groups (the departmental club, the honor society) but here was centered a social, emotional, semi-rebellious way of life of the here-and-now.

General problems of fraternal conduct, problems arising out of inter-society competition, and the pressures of nation-wide criticism brought about some degree of fraternal self-regulation in the Panhellenic Council and the Interfraternity Council in the ensuing years. The former was organized at Normal in 1919; the latter in 1922. Both served primarily to regulate competition for new members and eligibility for membership. In the course of time, objectives were stated in terms of intellectual and cultural growth of the individual, promotion of democratic principles, encouragement of commendable behavior, development of managerial responsibility, provision of a "beneficial" living environment.

Student Self-Government

At Normal, which for more than half a century had been the home of faculty-inspired student activities, the student self-government idea arrived in the second decade of the present century. Its first expression took the form of a Student Council.

The move for a Student Council came not from the students but from President McKenny. In November, 1912, the following information appeared in the student paper: "A plan has been worked out through the faculty whereby the students of the college may have a definite part in studying the needs of the college and in making suggestions for the betterment of student life in general."[12]

Two months later a news item appeared: "The first meeting of the student council is called for next Monday evening in the president's office. . . . Developments will be eagerly watched about the campus, as there has been no end of guessing as to what the new organization will do and the amount of power it will be given."

At the first meeting of the Council, McKenny gave the following explanation for its creation:

> It is easy for an administrator to know what the faculty thinks, but there is no way of knowing what the students themselves think about college affairs. They are the more important factor; it is for them that the State of Michigan has created this and other like institutions.

A student editorial commented: "The president has presented the students of this institution with a splendid opportunity for self-expression; he has asked them to speak frankly and thoughtfully concerning any student interest whatever . . ."

The Council appears to have been active through the year 1928, then it faded from sight. Nearly a decade later, in 1936, some student agitation appeared for its revival. A constitution was drawn the following year and presented to President Munson for his approval. The students themselves failed to rally behind the project. The president did not approve. Instead, he appointed what was called a "Mediating Board," to be composed of three elected representatives each from the two all-campus organizations, the Women's League and the Men's Union. No duties or powers were defined. Representatives were elected but there is no evidence that the Board ever functioned. It is noteworthy that no student protest occurred.

After World War II a Council again came into existence, this time with vigor (1949). It is still functioning as the Student Senate. The initiative came from the students, encouraged by the faculty. Its formation was facilitated by the support of the Women's League and the Men's Union. The Dean of Administration, in his annual report for 1949–1950, commented that "this organization has great potentialities both as an educative activity for the students and as a channel to bring student interests and opinions to the notice of faculty and administration."

Along with the Council, a Student Court was established. This functioned effectively in the handling of the more serious problems of student conduct, and in general had the support of the administration.

In the spring of 1913, an editorial in the student paper made a plea for a new type of organization.

> It is time [the editor said] that the men stood closer together and labored more earnestly to bring more men of the right type to Ypsi, and then, after they get here, to see to it that a healthy class spirit is maintained. What would be the matter with an organization for that very purpose, a Men's Union that would see to it that 'the rights of the minority' are fully protected, and that Ypsi is a good place for young men to come to?

A year and a half later (October, 1914), such an organization was formed. While its prototype had existed for some years at neighboring University of Michigan, the scope of its interest was considerable narrower. The situation at the Normal was quite the opposite of that in Ann Arbor, namely, the numerical inferiority of men to women. There were, in 1914, seven women to one man on campus.

At the mass meeting when the Union was formed, four-fifths of all the men attended.

President McKenny supported it, saying that it was the best thing that had come to the men in the Normal for twenty-five years.

Its voice was always important in campus affairs. Identified for many years with its faculty sponsor, Dean James M. Brown, and his magnetic personality, its interests broadened to include fraterinty life and intercollegiate athletics. It sponsored the outstanding social event of the Christmas season, the Yule Log Drag. It organized mass meetings for football games. It worked intimately with the fraternities, informally through personal contacts with its sponsor, formally through its membership on the Interfraternity Council. It was always represented on the Student Council. It held annual dinners where it awarded a recognition pin to the captains and managers of the athletic teams. Its contribution toward placing the Normal on the map as a school for men as well as women was large.

With no fanfare at all, the women of Normal organized at the same time the Women's Self-Government Association. The college annual for that year contained the following statement.

> For some time it has been felt among the women students of this college that there should be some organization among them, not only to increase their spirit of unity and sense of responsibility toward one another, but also to deal with such questions concerning student life as do not come under the supervision of the faculty.[13]

A year later, the women of Normal were, at the beginning of a term, meeting incoming girls at the trains, helping them enroll for classes, and giving them a reception in the evening. They felt that there was need for training in etiquette and organized classes "in social form." At the close of their first year, they expressed their enthusiasm.

> A spirit of unity is developing among the women of the College [they said] through the efforts of this organization. It is our sincere hope to establish a precedent among colleges because of the wholesome way in which our students respond to the responsibilities of self-government.[14]

In the fall of 1919, the Women's Self-Government Association was replaced by the Women's League. The membership of this organization was broader, including also faculty women.

Worth noting at this point is the fact that although the men were a small minority on campus during these years, they certainly controlled the press. Not more than passing notice was given in the college paper either to the organization of the Women's Self-Government Association or the Women's League.

The Women's League was the vigorous counterpart of the Men's Union. Through the years it was more effectively and more extensively organized than the Union, and undertook a much wider variety of activities. It organized clubs and societies for women at the several class levels, a League of Women Voters for all interested women, the Campus Sisters to assist new students arriving on campus, and the Community Service Club designed to give women experience both in community service and in working with children. It provided a special organization for women living off campus. And, as dormitories came into the picture, it sponsored dormitory self-government organizations.

In 1955–1956, the League became a member of the National Intercollegiate Association of Women Students. In 1960, it changed its name from Women's League to Associated Women Students Organization, consistent with the modern trend from the personal to the formal.

Conclusion

The extracurriculum as constituted by the student organizations at Normal represented not only a rebellion against the traditions and values of their elders but also an awareness on the part of the faculty of the limitations of the formal curriculum. From the first, the Normal faculty was, to an unusual extent, sensitive to the needs of youth and the limitations of the classroom, and attempted to meet these needs through the informal association of student-faculty organizations.

Student initiative brought about organization of another type. The fraternities and sororities were a phenomenon that not infrequently defied the authorities and insisted on a degree of off-campus freedom, yet proclaimed undying loyalty to their alma mater. Today this spirit has spread to non-fraternity students as well, and they are demanding the same types of "freedom" that the "Greeks" have traditionally exercised. The Men's Union and Women's League represented to a considerable degree the character of student pressure that found ready acceptance by the faculty.

CHAPTER TWENTY-EIGHT

ATHLETICS

After the Civil War, an interest in athletic competition and team sports developed throughout the nation. This phenomenon has been attributed largely to the industrial revolution. Professor Ralph Gabriel expressed it graphically:

> Forests of chimneys arose above cities sprawling beyond their former bounds. City streets became canyons and men, like jungle trees, struggled upward for light. Americans went indoors to serve machines, stand behind counters, or sit at desks . . . The reaction of an out-of-door people herded in a single generation into overgrown cities was the rise of sport and the appearance of an out-of-door movement. Athletic development was as swift as that of industry . . .[1]

In 1868, the New York Athletic Club was organized; in 1876, the National Baseball League. A convention at Springfield, Massachusetts, in 1880, saw the beginning of American football, under the leadership of Walter Camp. A year later, the American Lawn Tennis Association was formed.

At Normal's near neighbor, the University of Michigan, baseball games between the U-M and city teams from Ann Arbor, Jackson, and Detroit were played as early as 1862. Their first intercollegiate football game was played in 1878. In 1893, a Board in Control of Athletics was formed, and track and tennis were recognized as intercollegiate sports. In 1896 the Western Conference, popularly known as the "Big Ten," came into being. In the same year, amateur athletics were greatly stimulated by the revival of the Olympic games.

At Normal, track and field events and baseball attracted student attention at least as early as 1880. The local paper in that year reported that "Normal boasts a student who can clear twelve feet standing jump," and also that "baseball fever" had arrived and "a crack nine" was to be formed.[2] A year later, the following item appeared:

> The Normal students talk of going to Ann Arbor on Saturday. In their unprepared condition we would advise them not to go. A nine, in this stage of ball playing, that will appear on a campus without uniforms and without practice will not reflect credit on the school they represent. Experience has proven the unfitness of Normalites for baseball. Better give it up.[3]

Baseball continued to be plagued by inadequate facilities and some lack of student support.

> The boys are cramped to play baseball, and so we never have anything but muffin games. There are a class of fellows who frequent baseball grounds who never play, who never contribute toward the ball, but who spend their time in ribaldry, coarse jokes, and in swearing at the efforts of the younger players. Lacking physical vigor, they sit on the ground and hawk and spit, lacking mental judgment, they are unable to distinguish between a good or bad play, and between their senseless remarks and obscenity they make themselves thoroughly odious to all who love a good game.[4]

However, not only did baseball survive this uncertain beginning, but track and field became very popular. In 1887, through the initiative of a member of the faculty and a student,[5] a Normal Athletic Association and Council were formed to govern and promote the several sports. This was some six years before the Board in Control of Athletics was formed at the University of Michigan.

The competition in track and field took the form of "Field Days," extending over a period of three days. The first one was held on the campus in 1888. So great was the interest of the town, however, that thenceforth for some years they were held at the fair grounds. An item of 1890 in the Ypsilanti paper read:

> The first annual fall games of the Normal Athletic Association will be held at the Ypsilanti Fair Ground tomorrow (Saturday) afternoon. The rivalry between the Normal and the Business College (the local Cleary College) is more spirited than ever this fall, and we may expect exciting contests. The Normal has, in the person of J. R. Jenkins, one of the best known amateur athletes in the West.

A typical program showed the dashes (100 yards; 220 yards); the "440," half-mile, and mile runs; the jumps (standing broad, running broad, high jump, and hop, step and jump); bicycle races of a quarter, a half, and five miles, and the one-mile tandem; the high kick, shot put, hammer throw, and pole vault; wrestling, horizontal bar, and class drill with Indian clubs; the "allaround," and relay.

Records of times and distances achieved in events were a far cry from present-day achievements, supported as they are by highly developed tracks to run on, special shoes to run or jump in, scientifically developed menus for nourishing the body, and rigorous training schedules supervised by professional coaches. Winning time for the half-mile run, for example, was 2:25 (Normal's George Mason ran it in 1964 in 1:52.9); winning distance for the 16-pound shot was 31 feet, 8-1/2 inches (James Allen, in 1957, pushed it 52 feet, 5/8 of an inch.)

Football probably appeared at Normal at about the same time, possibly earlier. So-called "scientific," or Rugby, football, an intercollegiate sport at neighboring University of Michigan since 1878, soon involved the Normal, whose teams contested with class teams of the U-M. The first discoverable newspaper mention, however, appeared in 1891 with the following item:

> The football team got their new football Wednesday. They have a game arranged with the Albion College team for the last of the month.[6]

Tennis and basketball were played by Normal teams in the 1890's. Soccer, swimming, cross-country running, golf, and wrestling all belong to the 20th century.

A distinguishing feature of competitive sports at Normal was the very early development of an underlying philosophy. For this, the institution was indebted to its first head of the Physical Education Department, Wilbur Pardon Bowen. While still a member of the mathematics staff, he had been a party to the formation of the Normal Athletic Council in 1887. Over this Council he presided for many years. Fortunately for his school, and for the profession to which he contributed so much, his interest was both scientific and concerned with student health rather than competition.

Bowen was critical of the general athletic policy of the time regarding competition. He said that it was a mistake to allow all men to compete regardless of differences in ability. Contests should be graded so as to bring men of fairly equal ability together. This simple rule, he commented, had long since been adopted in horse racing and in bicycle racing. The existing policy only served to crowd the less talented out of the picture. It was also a mistake to judge a man's performance by whom he happened to compete against, Bowen felt. His opponent might be mediocre—hence, a victory of little significance. Performance should be judged by objective standards, such as a system of percentages based on amateur records. Bowen thought it unfortunate that recognition in these contests went only to the winners. A school should also receive recognition for the *number* of men competing.

This emphasis on bodily health was maintained in the years to follow and led to the development of athletic programs that provided opportunities for every student, female as well as male. Half a century later, when it was no longer a novelty for a Normal athlete to tie or break a national record, a strong intramural program, based on voluntary participation, was at the same time being vigorously pushed.

When, in 1925, the women organized their extensive athletic activities under the Women's Athletic Association, they gave evidence that they, too, were intent on fulfilling this college-wide objective. Their purpose was stated as follows:

> To offer a sports program so varied as to interest every girl on campus, encouraging each one to take an active part in the sports program and offering individual and team sports that have a definite carry-over value to the participants.[7]

In 1961, Eastern Michigan University withdrew from a very fine conference rather than accede to the present-day trend toward subsidization of athletes. She was adhering to her traditional and oft-repeated philosophy. This policy was followed through the administration of President Elliott.

The emphasis on athletics for everyone did not, however, preclude or diminish the interest in varsity competition. In 1892, Normal joined the MIAA (Michigan Intercollegiate Athletic Association), a body that had been organized four years earlier, composed of Albion, Olivet, Hillsdale, and Michigan Agricultural Colleges. Annual field days were the main feature of the Association program. Within a few years, Bowen urged that a full-time trainer be employed by Normal to supervise systematic training of the athletes. He said:

A very noticeable defect in our athletic practice at Normal consists in the apparent lack of perseverance and serious purpose on the part of the men. While a few practice faithfully, and get good from it, and succeed, the tendency of a greater number is merely to dabble in athletics. If they have nothing else to do, and feel like it, they practice; otherwise not. I do not see any way to prevent this but to place the work under a regular instructor or trainer, and then to hold those entering to faithful performance of the work undertaken. This is the ideal way, in my opinion, to conduct athletics.[8]

At the same time, he complained that the regulations of the MIAA were being violated. The professional athletic clubs, he said, from which the field day was borrowed, had set a bad example, and the MIAA had become "tainted with questionable practices." In the early 1900's, the Normal College resigned.

Not until 1920 did Normal take the step to rejoin. This time the period of membership was relatively short. In the spring of 1926, President McKenny announced withdrawal. The decision appears to have been prompted by a strong feeling among the members that they would prefer a conference consisting exclusively of private colleges. Furthermore, aided by growing enrollments and by the fact that more and more students were enrolling in the four-year curricula, Normal's athletic prowess had been growing.

In December, 1926, a new conference was formed. Called the Michigan Collegiate Conference, it was composed of the Central State Normal School at Mt. Pleasant, Detroit City College (now Wayne State University), Western State Normal School at Kalamazoo, and Ypsilanti Normal. The college paper opined that this was "one of the most forward steps that Ypsi had taken in the field of athletics in the history of the school." Among the first regulations adopted by this conference was a three-year eligibility rule whereby freshmen were made ineligible to compete, a policy based on consideration of academic success for the new student. In 1931, Detroit City College withdrew, causing the collapse of the conference.

Disagreement developed at the same time between the Normal and Western State Normal. From nearly the beginning of Western's existence (1903), the two colleges had maintained athletic relations. In 1915, a break had occurred in football relations but competition in this sport was resumed with the formation of the MCC. Now, however, the breach was complete and permanent. The local announcement read:

Athletic relations between two of the bitterest 'natural' rivals in Michigan
collegiate circles appeared severed again today when news dispatches from
Kalamazoo indicated that Western State authorities will cancel the game
scheduled with Michigan Normal at the Celery City on October 31.

Football rivalry had indeed been bitter. The record showed a total
of ten meetings, with five victories for the Normal and one tie.

When World War II hit the Normal campus, athletic competition
paused, came to a complete stop, then gradually revived. In 1942,
the Board in Control of Athletics abandoned the "freshmen rule"
which prohibited freshmen from competing on varsity teams. The
action came as a result of war-time decline in enrollment. Normal
was the last of the teachers colleges in Michigan to take this step
and, among all of the colleges and universities of the State, only the
University of Michigan, Michigan State College, and Michigan
College of Mines (now Michigan Technological University) retained
the rule.

In 1943, there were only about 400 men enrolled in the College.
In 1944, the number became so reduced that football, cross-country
and track were abandoned. Basketball remained the sole active fall
and winter sport; only baseball in the spring.

After the war, there was again agitation for membership in a
conference. In 1950, Normal accepted an invitation to join one to be
known as the Interstate Intercollegiate Athletic Conference. This
conference dated back to 1908. Originally, it consisted of seven Illinois colleges. Here was an organization of long standing and a successful history. It was well organized, and controlled by a full-time
commissioner as executive officer. Prospects for a long and satisfactory relationship were excellent.

Ten years later, on December 14, 1960, President Elliott of what
was now Eastern Michigan University posted a letter to the Commissioner announcing intent to withdraw. His published statement
read: "Due to the incompatibility of the athletic philosophies held by
Eastern Michigan and the other schools in the Conference, we feel it
is best for both Eastern Michigan and for the Conference that we
leave the league."[9]

Earlier, in a statement to the college paper, he had said:

Our university is operated for the education of youth. That is our business. We like to win games as much as anyone else but we are not willing
to compromise our educational values as a price for winning games.[10]

The difficulty had arisen over the proposal to subsidize athletes. Normal had never engaged in subsidization, and its policy with regard to coaches going forth to high schools to persuade athletes to come to Ypsilanti had been conservative. Under President Munson the practice had been forbidden. Assistance in securing or providing jobs for athletes while in school had been very limited.

But the trend over the nation had set in strongly against this conservative policy. First openly adopted by the colleges and universities of the south, the policy of remunerating college athletes brought strong reverberations and heated argument from the north. The North Central Association of Colleges and Secondary Schools, a powerful accrediting agency of the mid-west, had attempted to restore the old order. It had been forced to compromise, consenting finally to the payment ("reimbursement" it was called) of board and room, books and tuition, and $15 per month for laundry services, provided none of this money was paid directly to the athlete.

The battle had been fought in the meetings of the Executive Committee of the IIAC and had finally, in December, 1958, been resolved in favor of the North Central position. The vote was five to two (Eastern and Eastern Illinois forming the minority).

Discussion at Ypsilanti had begun some two years earlier (in 1956) when it became evident that some of the member schools were securing athletes by financial inducements and Eastern's teams were beginning to lose. In 1958, the coaching staff voted unanimously to recommend withdrawal from the conference, but the Board in Control refused to concur. As late as 1959 the Board advocated the following policy for the athletic department: (1) special consideration for loans and grants, (2) permission for the coaching staff to promise jobs to prospective athletes, (3) reimbursement to coaches for travel expenses incurred in contacting prospective athletes, (4) more campus jobs for athletes.

Matters were finally brought to a head when the 1960 football season produced a loss of eight players through injuries which included several broken bones. The Board in Control changed its position, and the President's letter was sent.

Withdrawal from the IIAC, effective in 1962, was followed by membership in the recently-formed Presidents' Athletic Conference. This conference, formed by the presidents of eight colleges in four States,[11] had as its objective a return to the traditional amateur code which, in terms of current widespread practice, meant restraint as to subsidies paid to athletes, and "de-emphasis" of athletic competition. Ultimate control was vested in the presidents of the respective institutions.

However, Normal had hardly become an active member when Wayne State University announced its intention to withdraw. This encouraged dissatisfaction among those of Normal's followers who felt that the PAC did not provide competition of recognized quality. In consequence, Normal's new Board of Regents approved, in May, 1964, a resolution of the Board of Control to withdraw from the PAC, effective at the close of 1965–1966. The college paper commented:

> The move by the Board of Regents is considered to be a step in the right direction and should put Eastern on the path toward attaining intercollegiate respectability.[12]

The Major Sports

From the beginning, baseball, football, and track were the major sports, with track and baseball in the ascendancy in the early years and again from the early 1920's.

Baseball, as we have noted, was one of the earliest organized sports at normal. The team of 1893 appears to have been the first of several outstanding nines. It "defeated even the mighty Albions and the Junior Laws."[13]

With the coming of the new gymnasium in 1894 some indoor practice was possible. An interesting item in the yearbook of 1899 read:

> For the past month or so, several batteries have been twirling the sphere up and down in the gymnasium, and, except for a few broken windows and steam pipes, besides a dent in the piano, which resulted in the suspension of operations for a time, until the Faculty could decide whether or not that was in the game—except for these little accidents our baseball material is developing rapidly.

In 1901, the professionals formed the American Baseball Association and the Detroit Tigers held spring training on Normal's campus, practicing with the college talent. In 1903, a coach was secured who had been in the older National Association for many years, Sam

Thompson. The season stimulated considerable enthusiasm, eliciting the following comment in the college annual: "Our baseball team, of which we are very proud and which has always been the strongest factor in Normal athletics, is in the midst of a very successful season."

In 1907, under Coach "Indian" Schulte, not a game was lost and the team claimed the championship of Michigan. It was a long wait thereafter, but in 1924, 1925, and 1926 the Normal team held the MIAA Championship. The coach was Elton Rynearson. In 1926, Charlie Zahn pitched a no-hit, no-run game against Hillsdale, and in the final game Albion was downed in the fifteenth inning. In 1949, the team won 15 games and lost three. As a member later of the strong IIAC, while not winning a championship, it took a second place under the coaching of Bill Crouch (a former big league player) in 1953.

Basketball was introduced at Normal in 1894, just three years after its invention by Dr. Naismith of the Y.M.C.A. College at Springfield, Massachusetts. It was used as an intramural game, a regular feature of class work in the new Department of Physical Education. Modifications were introduced to make the game more open, and more safe. The so-called "Ypsilanti Rules" were widely adopted in the public schools of the State. In 1910, under Coach Clare Hunter, the Normal team was particularly successful, winning 10 out of 12 games. In 1917, under Elmer Mitchell, the wins were 17 in 18 starts, and the state title was held jointly with Kalamazoo College. In 1918, under Rynearson, the record was 12 won, 1 lost. Rynearson coached teams which achieved outstanding records also in the three ensuing years.[14]

Several more successful seasons led to an insistent complaint that the gymnasium was not large enough to contain the fans. To meet this situation in 1926, students were limited to attendance at three games in the season.

The next 35 years saw only an occasional successful season.

Football, too, climbed mountain peaks and descended into deep valleys. The team of 1896 touted as the best in the history of the school to that time. The University of Michigan was the only opponent to score on the Normal (winning 18–0). The team boasted the title of Intercollegiate Champions of Michigan.[15] In 1899, the game with the U-M left quite a different taste and a reporter lamented: "Instead of merely the defeat by a score of 21–0 they did us up for the season." Three members of the team were out with injuries for six weeks.

The team of 1906, very light and not expected to accomplish much, created great excitement. It went through the season with one tie and no defeats (the University of Michigan was not on its schedule), and wound up with a hair-raising defeat of an old rival, Hillsdale College. Three thousand people witnessed the battle. "Indian" Schulte was the coach, and was given great credit for molding a light team into such an effective instrument for victory. The headline employed a name since translated as "Huron." It read: "Schulte's Indians have scalped all their foes." The celebration featured a bonfire, Roman candles, speeches, an impromptu band, and a thousand students on the march.

The team of 1913 was sufficiently impressive in the early part of its season to lead Coach Yost of the University of Michigan to ask for a game. The letter read in part:

> At the suggestion of Coach Yost I am writing you to secure a game between the Normal team and the Varsity . . . We hope that you may consider this proposition favorably. Coach Yost is greatly pleased with the work of Normal's team this fall, and now that Michigan has reinstated herself by defeating Vanderbilt, should be able to offer the Normals a good class of football. We notice that your men play a little rough, as in the game with U. of D. Saturday, where they laid so many of Lawton's men on the shelf, but we believe that husky handling like this is just what Michigan needs, and are willing to take the risk of escaping without a large hospital bill.
>
> Signed, T. G. Bartelme
> Director of Michigan Athletics[16]

Actually, Normal played the U-M freshmen and lost 26–0.

In 1925, under Rynearson (who remained as head coach through 1949), the team was undefeated and won the MIAA championship. Indeed, it was scored upon only once, a touchdown by Kalamazoo College in the final game.

The teams of 1927 and 1928 won the Michigan Collegiate Conference championship, losing only one game in the two seasons and none at all to a Michigan opponent. In 1929, Normal tied with Western State Teachers College for the crown.

The banner year was 1930. Not only was the MCC title won

handily, but Normal held Harry Kipke's University of Michigan team to a 7–0 score. Guard Andy Vanyo was the star of this rugged contest. Knute Rockne, in making up his all-western teams for the season, placed Vanyo on his second eleven, saying:

> To those who may lift an eyebrow at the mention of Michigan State Normal, may I mention that these embryonic teachers had a great season and lost only to Michigan 7–0 after a stern struggle. The outstanding player on the team was Vanyo at guard.

Reviewing Rynearson's record, the student paper reported:

> In his six years as football mentor, Elton J. Rynearson's teams have piled up 1069 points to 111 for opponents. Normal has won 40 games, tied two and lost four in that period . . .

The forthcoming years were not to maintain this record. Normal again played the University of Michigan in 1932 but lost 32–0. As late as 1938, Coach Rynearson could say, however, that he had never lost more than two games in a season. But in 1939 his team lost three and in 1940 it was only one victory in seven starts. Student comment in 1941 told a still sadder story:

> The law of averages thumbed its nose at Michigan Normal's 1941 football team and turned a deaf ear to the Huron pleas for a single opposition scalp. Normal's twenty-first Rynearson-coached team . . . hit a new low for points scored with 12 as against 65 for the foe.[17]

During World War II, the football schedule was first reduced and then, with less than 50 men on campus, eliminated entirely. In 1945, bolstered by returning service men, the game was revived and a very successful season ensued, five wins and one tie.

Thereafter, football fortunes declined. Rynearson, now Director of Athletics, stepped aside and his erstwhile star, Harry Ockerman, was brought in as head coach in 1949. The season was a disaster. For the first time in their football history, the Hurons lost every game (8) on their schedule.

In the years that followed, football fortunes varied from a conference championship in 1957 to 8 defeats and 1 tie in 1960. In 1968, Eastern was ranked seventh in the nation in the Associated Press small college poll.

Track and field differs from most sports in that it rests on individual prowess rather than cooperative performance. Hence, great emphasis is placed on the records of individual performers. Comparative records have meaning as long as conditions are standard. The seasons for this sport are winter and spring—winter for indoor competition, spring for outdoor. One other season provides the occasion for a particular type of track event, cross-country running. Here the distances are long and the course traverses hill and dale, amidst the brilliant colors and bracing air of fall. Distances vary and standard conditions are out of the question.

Standard conditions can, however, be fairly well achieved indoors, where great attention is given to the quality and condition of the running track, and standard apparatus and careful measurement accompany the field events. In outdoor track, the same precautions are taken but weather conditions must also be considered and, to establish running records, wind velocity is carefully measured.

Track and field competition, as with baseball and tennis, originated at the Normal as an intramural interest. Students were practicing their favorite events as early as 1882. Upon the organization of the Normal Athletic Association in 1887, the era of organized competition began. Field Days became the great sporting events of the year. After Normal joined the MIAA in 1892, they became a regular feature of intercollegiate competition.

In 1915, under Director Beyerman, the team won the indoor Western Michigan Intercollegiate Championship, led by its star, Captain Deyo Leland, in the dashes. The team repeated in the outdoor meet. Said the student yearbook:

> According to those who know the history of Normal's track team, the team representing the college this year is the strongest ever turned out. It is a remarkably well balanced team, especially in dashes and long distance men, hurdlers, pole vaulters, jump and weight performers.[18]

But the truly outstanding history of track and field at Normal began with the arrival of Coach Lloyd Olds, a Normal graduate, in 1921. His drive, organizing ability and vision carried Normal athletes to great heights, and gave Normal the reputation of being a "track school." Student comment upon his return to his alma mater[19] was that "the return of Lloyd Olds to the Normal College to take charge of track athletics insures the success of our future track squads and at once makes us strong contenders for the MIAA Championship in this sport."[20]

Olds was a disciple of Wilbur Bowen and this influence remained strong throughout his tenure, in the course of which he continued his studies at the University of Michigan and earned the degree of Doctor of Public Health. At Normal, he built a career that attracted national attention, holding important positions with the national AAU and the American Oympic Committee. He assisted in coaching American athletes for the Olympic Games, managed tours of American athletes in the Near and Far East (after World War II), managed the Pan-American Games in Mexico, and served as lecturer and consultant for the State Department in European universities and elsewhere.

As coach at Normal, he built teams which quickly made their presence felt in college competition. Titles were won in state-wide collegiate meets in the years 1923–1926 inclusive, 1931–1933 inclusive, 1936, and 1940. Normal's relay teams were even more impressive, meeting competition from the entire mid-west. In 1926, the medley relay team was victorious in the Drake Relays at Iowa City. In 1927, they were outstanding in the Ohio Relays at Columbus. In 1940, a Normal team broke the American college record, and broke its own record the following year.

During World War II, Olds served the Navy in its physical training program in the Pacific coast area, holding the rank of Commander. Upon his return to Normal he asked to be relieved of coaching and devoted his full time to teaching and the development of the intramural athletic program—a move that continued Normal's early emphasis on athletics for all.

He was succeeded by his asssitant, George Marshall, who added lustre to Normal's track tradition. In 1947 and 1948, Marshall's teams won state titles, and his relay teams dominated the Relays held at the Illinois Institute of Technology. In 1947, the *New York Times* rated Normal as the best college team in the nation and did so again in 1951. During the period of membership in the IIAC, Normal's team won the annual track meet in the years 1952–1955, inclusive.

Individual Stars

Track athletes of national stature appeared at Normal from the 1930's. The first was Eugene Beatty who won the National 400-meter low hurdles title three consecutive years (1931, 1932, 1933).[21] In 1939, distance star Tommy Quinn won the National Junior AAU title in the 5000-meter run. In 1949, Garion Campbell set a world's indoor record in the 75-yard dash. In 1957, 1958 and 1959, Hayes Jones developed into an almost unbeatable competitor in the hurdles, winning in meet after meet regardless of the quality of competition. In 1960, he became the first man in the history of Normal to win a birth on the Olympic team and took third place in the 110-meter high hurdles event. In 1964, he again placed on the team—and this time won the coveted gold medal.[22]

Cross-country running, engaged in sporadically at least as early as 1911, was revived and consistently promoted with the arrival of Olds. Its story from this time (1921) is one of oustanding performances, not only within the conference that Normal was a member of at the time, but also in national AAU competition. The MIAA championship was won in 1924; the National AAU in 1929 (against such opponents as the Universities of Indiana, Ohio State and Pittsburgh, and Pennsylvania State). In 1931, Normal was second in the National Junior AAU run (held this time, in Ypsilanti). In 1940, led by two outstanding stars, Tom Quinn and Duane Zemper, the team placed second to Indiana in the Third Annual National Intercollegiates; second in the National AAU behind the New York Athletic Club, and first in the Fifteenth Annual Central Collegiate Conference Run. In 1942, Normal tied with Bowling Green University for second place in the National Junior AAU meet.[23]

George Marshall, succeeding Olds in 1945, maintained the outstanding record that he had inherited. In 1946, his cross-country team placed third in the Central Collegiate Conference meet behind Drake and Notre Dame, and second in the College Division of the National Collegiate meet. In 1954, it won the National AAU championship. By 1956, Marshall had won the IIAC championship for seven successive years. The last of these outstanding performances occurred in 1958 when Normal (now Eastern Michigan College) ran second in the IIAC and also second in the National Junior AAU meets.

Tennis teams have represented the school since 1911. In 1912, a soccer team was placed in competition against the University of Michigan. In 1915, there were matches with the U-M, Battle Creek and a Detroit team. In 1916, six games were scheduled, including matches with Walkerville and Ford of Canada. Swimming was initiated in 1919. From 1932 to 1947 no varsity competition was scheduled, but since that time Normal has been represented by both men's and women's teams. Gymnastics was initiated in 1921. In this sport, exhibition performances prevailed rather than intercollegiate competition. In the 1920's and early 1930's it was customary for the team to present exhibitions in a number of cities. In 1931, some twenty cities were included in the itinerary of the Normal College gymnastic team. Golf, for both men and women, has been scheduled since 1931. An outstanding performance was that of Shirley Spork who, in 1947, became the National Women's Collegiate Champion. Wrestling was initiated in 1937, bowling and billiards in 1952.

Intramural Sports

Bowen's emphasis on sports for all found early expression, and the "for all" included women as well as men. Activities for the women featured various types of ball games, tennis, hockey, swimming, and dancing.

For many years basketball was featured. Until 1910, a women's basketball team engaged in intercollegiate competition. In that year, however, the Director of Women's Athletics, Fannie Burton, announced withdrawal and greater emphasis on the intramural program. The time given to coaching six or eight girls, she said, could more profitably be devoted to a greater number, and the saving could be used for permanent athletic improvements that all the women could enjoy. Furthermore, she felt that in intercollegiate competition there was a tendency to over-exert. She added that the type of audience experienced on foreign floors involved some risk.

By 1915, some 100 women were involved in tennis competition, another 100 in "games for pleasure" (hockey and swimming), and some 500 juniors and seniors in a variety of contests in the Annual Girls Meet. In the 1920's there was strong competition also between the freshman and sophomore classes. In the "General Girls' All College Indoor Meet" those enrolled in the kindergarten, primary, and rural education curricula combined to oppose those in the intermediate and high school curricula. Track events, tumbling, "national" dancing, field ball, basketball, and volleyball made up the program. By 1939 the activities had been broadened to include horseback riding, badminton, bowling, fencing, ping-pong and archery.

Activities on the men's side were less well recorded, but it is clear that inter-class football contests were dominant in the earlier years.

With the arrival of Olds, a broad program for men was developed under the Men's Intramural Program. Four years later the women's activities were organized and promoted by Doris Ewing under the name of WAA (Women's Athletic Association), changed in the 1950's to the present WRA (Women's Recreation Association).

During World War II, the Men's Intramural Program was dropped but resumed in 1947 with the return of Olds from his assignment in the Navy. Giving his entire attention to teaching and the intramural program, Olds developed a wide range of sports designated as inter-fraternity, inter-dormitory, and all-campus contests.

Conclusion

As one views the history of sports at Normal it becomes evident that here is an institution of higher education that has adhered with exceptional fidelity to two principles that were adopted almost from the beginning of organized athletics—the benefits of athletics for all and, in intercollegiate competition, the acceptance of standards and regulations that required self-restraint and not infrequently lead to defeat.

The acceptance of standards and regulations involved a policy requiring acceptable academic performance for membership on varsity teams, and the concept of amateur standing. The concept of the amateur in sports has been carefully defined by the Amateur Athletic Union. It reads: "An amateur sportsman is one who engages in sports solely for the pleasure and physical, mental, and social benefits he derives therefrom."

Eastern was among the last of the colleges and universities of the nation to relax this rule and adopt a policy of offering athletic scholarships. Indeed, not until 1965 was a step taken in this direction. In football, it has paid at times a severe penalty for adherance to the original concept. But no football coach has been fired for losing games.

Faculty have, for the most part, been interested and active in supporting and promoting intercollegiate competition. Faculty were instrumental in organizing the athletic program in the first place. Bowen left the mathematics staff to devote his life to physical education and the sports program. Charles McKenny was outstanding among the school's presidents in his enthusiasm for athletic contests. Registrar Clemens Steimle, formerly on the mathematics staff, an old Normal athlete himself, was an avid supporter, and on every occasion of a cross-country run would be found in front of a blackboard in the fieldhouse, calculating the complicated scoring. Dean of Men James M. ("Bingo") Brown was the idol of athletes in all sports and, through the Men's Union, provided the annual awards banquet. These men were symbolic of widespread faculty interest and support.

The interest and respect so widely accorded the athletic program at Eastern have been based on more than the fact that sports are a pleasant and often thrilling diversion. In a culture which, through its emphasis on individualism, places competitive success in all areas of life on an inordinately high pedestal, there comes a feeling of relief and satisfaction that, in one area of life at least, competition of a most strenuous, exhausting, and exacting character can be conducted according to limitations and regulations that the competitors accept.

CHAPTER TWENTY-NINE

INSTITUTIONAL PURPOSE

The original purpose for which an institution of higher education has been established may be found carefully phrased in some formal document or legislative act. The effective purpose, however, can only be discerned after years of operation. It is to be found in the minds and hearts and conduct of several generations of those entrusted with the direction of the enterprise, and it often provides that sense of high importance and dignity which powers its members through all the years to heights of achievement and a profound sense of personal satisfaction.

Sometimes the original intent is so broad that the practice never quite catches up. The University of Michigan of today is probably still somewhat short of Judge Woodward's concept of a "University of Michigania," which was truly universal in scope. On the other hand, and this is more usual, an institution may outgrow its original purpose. Michigan State University, for example, legally established just six years after the Normal as an agricultural college, has grown far beyond its original function. The role of the University of Wisconsin found expression some 40 years after its founding when President Bascom said that "the University of Wisconsin will be permanently great in the degree in which it understands the conditions of the prosperity and peace of the people, and helps to provide them." Of Cornell University's original concept, "the idea of an institution freed from obligation to religious or political or social prejudice, and devoted to the advancement of knowledge in all fruitful fields of inquiry," its historian, Carl Becker, could say after 75 years that "there is nothing we could wish to add to it, or anything we could wish to take away."

Normal's experience was that of possessing a well-defined, limited, powerfully-motivating concept that guided its thought and purpose, and roused its enthusiasm for a full century. Then, under the impact of social forces that pulled in opposing directions, its purpose became dulled and diffused. A committee of the North Central Association of Colleges and Secondary Schools, assigned in 1963 to make a special report on the institution, said:

> As the first institution of its kind west of the Alleghenies, the Ypsilanti State Normal School had a long and distinguished record in the field and had attained some national distinction as a teacher-training institution . . . Its graduates, the faculty and its supporters in the State took justifiable pride in its accomplishments, and in its position of local and regional prestige in its special field. Beginning with its conversion to a multipurpose institution but more especially since it assumed the title of Eastern Michigan University, this pride in its past accomplishments and status as a teacher-training institution became less secure.[1]

Under the Michigan Constitution of 1835, which instructed the legislature to provide for a system of common schools, the Legislature of 1849 passed "An Act to establish a State Normal School."[2] Its threefold purpose, the major one of instruction in the art of teaching, and the minor ones of instruction in the mechanic arts and the arts of husbandry and agricultural chemistry, and in the legal basis of citizenship, was reduced to two when, in 1855, the legislature established the Michigan Agricultural College.[3]

For more than a century Normal operated under this legal directive, its administrations and faculties accepting their mission with enthusiasm and a sense of high importance. Meanwhile, three other normal schools were established—at Mt. Pleasant (1895), Marquette (1899), and Kalamazoo (1903). Then, in 1927, their desire to abandon the name "Normal" as connoting an institution inferior to a college brought legislative action. Henceforth, they were known as teachers colleges.

The institution at Ypsilanti, however, which had long since achieved college status, proud of its pioneering past under a name that had become nationally known and respected, clung to "Normal College."

In 1941, the three "Teachers Colleges" persuaded the legislature to change their names again, this time to "College of Education." Normal retained its designation.

By 1955, the pressure of the post-war avalanche of G.I.'s, who sought not only a college education but preparation for admission to a wide range of professional programs and schools, broadened the curriculum still more, and the legislature was persuaded to drop the term "Education" and designate the three schools simply as "College." With the elimination of this term, and no accompanying legislative definition of function, the colleges could now avoid to some degree the emphasis on teacher preparation. One must reluctantly observe that the move was dictated by a prestige factor that reflected under-valuation of the teaching profession by the society that supported it.

This time Normal, too, was caught up in the change. Its time-honored and nationally respected name was abandoned, and in its place came a faceless title referring to geographical location only—Eastern Michigan College. The geographical reference itself was a denial of a long and proudly-held belief, doggedly clung to long after the necessity for sharing the territory with three similar schools arose, that Normal was not a regional institution but served the entire State. Unlike its three sister institutions, which were created by legislative enactment, Normal had been established by the State Constitution and its purpose was therein defined.[4] To satisfy the Constitution, therefore, in changing Normal's name, the legislature of 1955 re-stated the constitutional purpose. Thus, the statute read:

> The state board of education shall continue the normal college at Ypsilanti . . . under the name of Eastern Michigan College after July 1, 1956. The purpose of the normal college shall be the instruction of persons in liberal arts, the art of teaching, and in all the various branches pertaining to the public schools of the State of Michigan.[5]

Four years later the final step was taken. Eastern Michigan College, along with two of its sister institutions, was designated as a university. Again the legislature referred to function and purpose. The statement of 1955 was repeated.[6]

In the revised Michigan Constitution of 1963 the only specific reference to Eastern Michigan University is in the section requiring the legislature to "appropriate moneys to maintain" the several state-supported institutions of higher education. The only reference to purpose is general, applying alike to all levels of public education, expressed by repeating that oft-quoted assertion in the Northwest Ordinance of 1789:

> Religion, morality and knowledge being necessary to good government
> and the happiness of mankind, schools and the means of education shall
> forever be encouraged.

A legislative provision may well be compared to a theory that has
not been put to the test of application. It may or may not work. But
in the present instance the legislation expressed so well the deeply-
felt need of the commonwealth that it found ready support, particularly in the minds and hearts of those who were to conduct the enterprise. Adonijah Welch, the first to head the school, spoke with feeling at the dedicatory exercises in 1852 when he said:

> I receive with deference this commission and these symbols of authority
> which you have presented . . . It may savor somewhat of enthusiasm, yet
> in my humble judgment, this day's work will form a prominent item in
> the history of western progress. This side the Empire State it is the first
> experiment of similar character made under the auspices of legislative
> enactment. Who will venture to predict the influence which its success will
> exert upon the educational interests of the entire Northwest?

A first step, taken as the school opened, was the requirement that
every student admitted to the Normal must sign a Statement of
Intent.

> We, the subscribers, do hereby declare that it is our intention to devote
> ourselves to the business of teaching in the schools of this State, and that
> our sole object in resorting to the normal school is the better to prepare
> ourselves for the discharge of this imperative duty.

Not until 1934, during the Munson administration, was the
requirement dropped that, in order to receive the bachelor of arts
degree, one must also meet the requirements for teacher certification.

As we have seen, the question as to how much academic work or
whether any at all, should be given in a normal school troubled
many minds for many years. For a period beginning in 1878, a policy prevailed of cutting academic instruction to a minimum.[7] Instruction in the academic areas was to be left to the better academies,
union and high schools.

The ensuing years completely upset this restrictive interpretation
of Normal's function. The rapid increase in the number of high
schools (promoted by the famous "Kalamazoo" decision of 1872 in

which the high school was legally acknowledged to be a part of the free public school system of Michigan) and the general improvement of their quality eliminated the need for an academic program of high school level at the Normal. At the same time, these factors gave rise to a pressing demand for competent high school teachers, necessitating an academic program beyond the high school level—in other words, of college grade.

In 1893, on the occasion of the World's Fair in Chicago, Normal published a brochure entitled, "The State Normal School of Michigan, its Plan and Purpose." It was issued "in order that the friends of education in America may be informed concerning what Michigan is doing in the professional training of her teachers," and "to aid educators from other countries in gaining an acquaintance with the present condition of progress in American normal schools." A list of specific courses in mathematics, history, English, physical science, natural science, Latin and Greek, French and German was given.

This trend toward collegiate-grade instruction continued. In 1900, President Leonard observed a growing sentiment among the friends of normal schools throughout the country "that the courses in these schools can be materially strengthened on the scholastic and cultural sides without in any sense weakening the professional side of the work. It is becoming more clearly recognized every year that pedagogical training is not a substitute for scholarship and culture, and that the most serious lack of the teaching profession in schools below the high school grades is found in the meager educational qualifications of the teachers in these schools."

In 1916, President McKenny told the State Board that "the growth in the number and the development in scope of the high schools is one of the most outstanding facts in education in the last twenty-five years."

Even as he spoke, he was presiding over a faculty that, on the liberal arts side of the curriculum, boasted men of national repute.

In 1934, the State Board adopted a new statement of purpose. Headed "Purpose and Control of the Michigan State Teachers Colleges," it was drawn by the presidents of the four colleges and printed in identical form in all catalogs. After directing attention to the repeated strictures of the legislature that the purpose of these colleges "shall be the instruction of persons in the art of teaching and in all the various branches pertaining to the public schools of the State of Michigan," the statement continued:

The public school system, less than a century old, has developed from the meager rudiments which satisfied the frontier settlements to the enlarged and complex organization which attempts to meet the needs of today—a day which faces the solution of social, political, and economic problems of fundamental significance. Only honest, intelligent, and well-informed citizens can cope with such problems. Such citizens it is the first duty of our public schools to produce. Only honest, intelligent, well-educated and devoted teachers are adequate to meet these enlarged duties and responsibilities—the day of the mere school-keeper is gone . . . The Michigan State Teachers Colleges, therefore, have always stood and do now stand for two things paramount and inseparable in an institution for the training of teachers.

    1. A thorough grounding in such fields of study as may lead to the intellectual growth of the student.

    2. A thorough grounding in the science and art of teaching under direction.

Presented at the same time was a detailed statement of the requirements for the bachelor of arts degree. In this program, professional courses in education occupied one-fifth of the total credit prescribed for the degree, the academic areas the rest. Two years later (1936) a Certification Code for teachers was adopted that confirmed this relative emphasis. "Teacher training" had come a long way since 1878; indeed, the term itself no longer suited. The process had become one of "teacher education and training." But the State Board had decreed earlier "that persons may qualify for graduation with a degree without meeting requirements for a life certificate."[9] The gates were flung wide at the normal schools for all who wanted a college education and could meet admission standards, whether or not they intended to teach.

The College maintained its uninterrupted existence during World War II and, from 1945, experienced a flood of veteran enrollments. The anticipated impact of unprecedented birth rates of the late '30's and the early '40's, due to be felt beginning with the late '50's, was preceded by a great swell of national sentiment in favor of higher education. Veterans returning from the war who, at an earlier time, would not have considered going to college even with financial support provided by the "G. I. Bill," now thronged the campuses. Nor were their objectives limited. Many wished to become engineers or be trained for business.

At the Normal College, the statement on "Purpose and Control of the Michigan State Teachers Colleges" appeared for the last time in the catalog for 1953–1954. No statement whatever appeared the year following. In 1955–1956 there was a new one, "Educational Aims and Objectives." Following a brief history of the College, it read as follows:

> As indicated above, Eastern Michigan College was originally founded to educate teachers. This is still one of its basic functions. To this it has added, over the last half century, programs of instruction in the liberal arts and sciences, and a wide range of specialized and pre-professional programs . . . It is the judgment of the staff and faculty of Eastern Michigan College that the College has not changed its function in its century-old history, but has expanded and broadened it. The additional professional education necessary for the teacher has its counterpart in the other specialized areas for those planning to enter other professions.

Perhaps the most noteworthy aspect of this statement was the blurring of the original function of Normal; perhaps equally important was the dropping from sight of legislative prescription and State Board direction. In any event, it represented the pressures of a new age, carried to Normal's doors (as to the doors of colleges everywhere) by an undreamed-of hoard of young people who demanded to be let in regardless of their objectives.

No wonder that when, in 1963, the accrediting agency, North Central Association of Schools and Colleges, sent an investigating panel to Eastern's campus, it found that "a major source of tension in the total situation at Eastern Michigan University is the present indeterminate status of the institution," and recommended that "the Board of Education or other appropriate board or boards of control of higher education in Michigan should clearly define the functional role of Eastern Michigan University in the 'System' of public education of the State . . ."[10]

From the time when the curriculum developed to the college level, it was inevitable that many of the courses offered in the liberal arts would lend themselves to ends other than teaching. Such, for example, was the work in mathematics and the sciences. Students intending to become medical doctors could take their pre-medical work at Normal, then, without remaining to earn a degree, transfer to a medical school. Those planning to enter engineering school could get the first two years of work at Normal. After 1934, permission at Normal to earn a degree without a teaching certificate encouraged the trend and met the tendency of some of the professional schools (particularly law and medicine) to favor a college degree for admission. Other pre-professional programs developed with demand: pre-forestry, pre-pharmacy, pre-social work. And it was only a step from a pre-business administration program for teachers of business education to a full non-teaching program in business administration and one in secretarial work. From the pre-medical program, it was only a step to a full medical technology curriculum. From the curriculum preparing teachers of handicapped children, it was not difficult to develop a full curriculum in occupational therapy. Thus, by mid-century the school was offering a number of courses that had no relation to her essential function, inviting students who had no interest in teaching.

The demand of the North Central Association panel that Eastern define its purpose could not be easily met. For, although offering a variety of non-teaching curricula, and known by the name of "university," it was at the same time still essentially a teacher training institution. Between 70 and 80 per cent of its students still graduated with a teaching certificate. Any new definition must still recognize that fact and, along with it, the fact that the need of the State of Michigan for adequately prepared teachers was far from being adequately met.

In any event, one thing was clear—Eastern had in the processes of change lost something that once held great meaning, roused intense enthusiasm and devotion, and gave it a past of greatness. It was the sense of what one might well describe as sacred mission that had inspired one who would later become her president to exclaim, in the course of the first world war:

> Why is it, when all the world is warring, Uncle Sam is so calm and patient and unafraid? . . . It is because from Ocean to Ocean, from Lakes to Gulf, he hears the tramp, tramp, tramp of twenty million boys and girls who every morning, rain or shine, set out for the American Public School to conquer the knowledge of the World. That is the largest, the most invincible host that ever marched in any country in all history. The whole globe sways under its footstep.[11]

Whatever direction the new formulation of purpose might take, it would need above all to possess a quality that would grip the imagination and stir the soul of the generations to come if it would adequately replace the old.

In 1964, the Board of Regents asked President Elliot to draw up a statement of objectives, The resulting document represented the thought of faculty, administration and regents. It was approved unanimously by the Faculty Council and formally adopted by the Board. It read in part:

> Eastern Michigan University, even in its earliest years as a normal school, had some of the characteristics of a multi-purpose institution, and over the years it has steadily acquired more. In the future, mounting enrollments which bring to this institution even more students in search of university education rather than teacher preparation will force the University to diversify and expand its offerings still further. At the same time, however, teacher education will continue to be a main concern. These goals are never fixed but evolve with time and with such increase of wisdom as the faculty, administration and governing board may acquire.[12]

The basic philosophy of the University, as approved by the Board of Regents and as it appears in the current catalog, is outlined in these words:

—to provide the quality of intellectual experience that will add meaning, scope, richness, and interest to all undergraduates no matter where they make their careers.

—to provide for undergraduates an education which will equip them to make important cultural, social, and economic contributions to their community.

—to provide for undergraduates education of a quality and scope that will qualify them to enter graduate and professional schools.

—to provide specific education and training to qualify students for careers in business, education, and some technological or specialized fields where the basis for such training traditionally exists or grows naturally from a strong program in the liberal arts and sciences and where there is a need for such training.

—to provide graduate work at the fifth-year level (master's degree) and the sixth-year level (specialist's degree), and further graduate work as the demand arises.

—to cooperate with other institutions of higher learning in meeting needs of adult and continuing education.

—to extend and diversify present programs, including more support for research, as circumstances require and as financial support becomes available, provided that the expansion enriches the instructional program.

CHAPTER THIRTY

THE ALUMNI

A major influence on the life and growth of a college or university can be and at times is its alumni. Indeed, they are the bread cast upon the waters which in due time will return to bless or plague its maker. A college that has performed its function well will forever be blessed with successful alumni whose hearts are filled with gratitude and enthusiasm and tender memories of their alma mater, and who wish, in return, to make a contribution. There are, as might be expected, times when their zeal may be excessive or their judgment somewhat perverted. They may, for example, place an emphasis on intercollegiate athletic competition which is out of proportion to the function of the institution. Or, their feeling of interest may be so strong that it may lead to a desire to run the place.

The experience of the American college has, however, been so overwhelmingly favorable that the continuing interest and support of its alumni, both as individuals and through organization, has been zealously sought by the college administration. The creed drawn up for the University of Michigan by President Ruthven in 1932 expresses a widespread sentiment:

> We believe that the student should be trained as an alumnus from matriculation. He enrolls in the University for life and for better or worse he will always remain an integral part of the institution.

In its long history, Normal had, as of June 30, 1968, issued 16,088 provisional teaching certificates, 21,130 life certificates and 5,093 others. As of the same date, it had conferred 25,837 bachelors degrees. It is worthy of note, however, than even as early as 1873 the records show that of those who did complete the full Normal curriculum and were entitled to be called graduates, only 59 per cent actually made education their career—this in spite of the fact that all who enrolled at the Normal were required to sign a statement of intention to teach in Michigan schools. Most of these doubtless did do some teaching. But 10 per cent of them eventually became lawyers, and others found their life work in medicine, business, farming, the ministry and missions, and a number of other lines of endeavor.

Eastern has been fortunate from the first in the spirit of loyalty and continuing interest of her graduates. Because of the economic status of the teaching profession, the major gifts (Starkweather Hall [the religious center], the Briggs athletic plant, the Rackham building for the Department of Special Education) have not come from wealthy alumni. But these gifts from outside private sources have been equaled, if not surpassed, by the contributions of approximately 15,000 alumni.

Hence, the support given to Normal by her graduates has been much more through the activities of organized groups than by individuals. The fraternities, sororities and societies have consistently held their annual get-togethers with their alumni in the form of dinners and receptions, and thus have served to promote the sentiments that cling to college days and friendships. Some of the department clubs—the Chemistry Club is a prime example—have done the same. The Conservatory of Music formed, in 1897, a Conservatory Alumni Association which for many years held an annual reception. In 1938, an Alumni Track Club was formed.

The oldest, most consistent, and by far most important in terms of direct contribution has been the Alumni Association.

Early references to an association of alumni are fragmentary. Minutes of meetings were not preserved prior to 1922. However, there is evidence of the existence of such an organization in 1872. Typical of the history of alumni associations everywhere, this one has run an uneven course—now appearing, when some project captivated attention—now disappearing entirely—now reorganizing, and from time to time reorganizing again.

Normal was, from the beginning, solicitous to publish the names of its graduates. Every catalog, from the first graduating class (1854) through the class of 1893–1894, carried a cumulative list, shown by year of graduation. The alumni began the practice of gathering at Commencement sometime in the 1860's. In 1872, a "Mr. X," probably a member of the faculty, made a list "from memory, aided only by a catalogue of the Normal School," of names and positions of

Normal graduates, 1854 to 1872 inclusive, and published it in Normal's periodical, *The School*. The administrative positions shown were numerous and impressive. Three years later (1875) this periodical included an alumni directory, listing graduates and positions held, from the class of 1854 to 1875 inclusive.

The Association appears to have had a continuous existence from 1881 to 1899. Daniel Putnam, writing in 1899, said:

> An Alumni Association was formed quite a number of years ago, but the organization has had somewhat of an intermittent life. Recently, however, it has held its annual meetings with a good degree of regularity, and several local societies have been formed in the larger cities of the State.

Putnam was able to list the presidents of the Association from 1881 to 1899 inclusive. Included were such later well-known names as C. T. Grawn, W. S. Perry, C. F. R. Bellows, J. M. B. Sill, Austin George, W. P. Bowen, Fred L. Ingraham. He also presented in full a song by Austin George, written to the tune of "Michigan, my Michigan," for the alumni meeting held in Lansing in December, 1895. Following is one of the stanzas:

> The student life in Ypsi. town
> Michigan, my Michigan!
> Through all thy realm holds high renown,
> Michigan, my Michigan!
> Lyceum, S. C. A.'s fond spell,
> The rush, the club, the dinner bell
> The Normal girl! The Normal Yell!!
> Michigan, my Michigan.

The meeting of the Alumni Association in 1881 was noteworthy for launching a project that would become a permanent feature of the Normal. The report of that meeting contains the following cryptic sentence: "At the business meeting of the Alumni speeches were made and it was decided to publish the Normal News."

The editorial page in the first issue indicated that the new monthly was to be published by the students, but three functions were listed as follows:

> 1. As a medium of publication for the students. Experience has demonstrated the advantage to young people of preparing articles for the press . . .

2. As a means of communication between the schools and those temporarily absent . . .

3. As the organ of the Alumni—making known all matters of interest
to the Association, and conveying to its members such individual items
as are always of interest to old friends and classmates . . . the Alumni
are requested to keep us informed of their location and to let us know
when changes in position occur, that we may make our files a complete
Alumni directory.

At first a monthly, it combined the features of a literary and a
news magazine. Student compositions, addresses and papers by faculty members, and articles on serious topics were mingled with news
items, obituaries, and personals. In October of 1903, a change in
policy led to the publishing of a weekly, the first three issues of each
month to be devoted to news items, under the title *Normal News
Letter,* and the fourth to be a magazine issue devoted to literary and
cultural interests. This issue appeared under the title of *Normal
College News* (recognizing belatedly that Normal had become a full-
fledged college). The year 1904–1905 saw another change in policy
which made of the *Normal College News* a professional magazine
for the in-service teacher. Beginning with the following year (1906),
it was separated from the *News Letter* and published under the
name *Western Journal of Education.* Under this title it appeared
until 1913 when the name was changed to *The American Schoolmaster.* In 1933, succumbing to the economic pressures of the
depression, it creased to exist.

Meanwhile, upon the separation that occurred in 1904, the
Normal News Letter adopted the name *Normal College News* and
was published under this name until the issue of October 25, 1951.
The immediately preceding issue observed the 70th anniversary of
the paper. In this issue a facsimile of the first page of the first issue
was reproduced, showing the original name to have been *The
Normal News.* Apparently influenced by this, subsequent issues
reverted to this name. In 1954, coincident with the name change to
Eastern Michigan College, the current name of *Eastern Echo* was
adopted.

The 1880's saw no new Alumni projects, and the continuing one
of maintaining an up-to-date register of graduates and their positions degenerated into miscellaneous news items. Friendships and
contact with the school were, however, kept alive by annual meet-

ings. The 1890's witnessed a decided increase in activity. Two re-
unions were held, one at the time of the meeting of the Michigan
State Teachers' Association at Lansing; the other at Commencement time in Ypsilanti. The mid-nineties saw a decided revival, due
in part to the interest that Principal Boone took in the alumni and
in the history of the school.

The big project of the 1890's was the establishment of "Foundation Day," to be an annual event honoring those who founded Normal and instructing the student body in its history. This observance, later to be known as "Founders' Day," appears to have been
held more or less regularly in November, over a period of 33 years,
culminating in the celebration of Normal's Seventy-Fifth Anniversary in January of 1928.

No subsequent observance could, however, have equaled the first
one, held March 28, 1895. The day was declared a holiday from
classes. The afternoon and evening programs featured alumni and
others who in their person represented the early days: C. F. R. Bellows, now principal of the new Normal at Mt. Pleasant, had attended the dedicatory exercises, enrolled as a student in the first
Normal class, and later served as professor and acting principal of
Normal; Dr. F. K. Rexford, an Ypsilanti citizen, had subscribed to
the original fund offered to meet the requirement of the State Board
for financial assistance in establishing a Normal School; Ruth Hoppin, now retired, was an early Preceptress at the Normal. There
were letters from E. M. Foote, first music professor at Normal, living in Ypsilanti but now too feeble to attend the exercises; Mrs. D.
P. Mayhew, widow of Normal's second principal, David Porter
Mayhew; Mary B. Welch, from California, widow of the first principal, Adonijah Strong Welch; and Malcolm Mac Vicar, from Ra-
leigh, North Carolina, a former principal. Bellows recalled that his
first child, born in Ypsilanti, was christened by Welch and thus was
the first Normal baby. In addition, there were current dignitaries of
the day: Perry F. Powers, president of the State Board of Education;
H. R. Pattengill, Superintendent of Public Instruction, and Governor John T. Rich.

In the following year (1896) interest in organizing additional
alumni clubs led to the formation of a University of Michigan-
Normal School Alumni Association, composed of Normal graduates
attending the University; and a Normal School Graduate Club in
Ypsilanti composed of Normal graduates taking post-graduate work

and faculty. At about the same time, clubs were organized in Detroit, Jackson and Grand Rapids.

The annual meeting of the Association in June of 1905 was of particular importance. The position of "resident secretary" was added to the responsibilities of the general manager of *The Normal News*. At the same time a membership fee of $1 per year was approved, which would include a subscription to the college paper. A life-membership fee of $25 was also approved.

Continuing alumni activity was climaxed in 1916 by the purchase of land for an athletic field. This land, known as the Beal property, consisted of about 10 acres and lay within five minutes walk of the gymnasium, along the north side of Cross Street. The price was $5,000 and the Alumni undertook to pay for it "little by little" from an Alumni Fund, the Athletic Council to make the necessary improvements so that it could be used for football, baseball and soccer. It was named Alumni Field.

In 1921, the Association discussed the need for an alumni office, where records could be kept and promotional activities centered. The executive committee was authorized in 1922 to appoint a permanent secretary, organize an alumni group in each State Teachers Association district and in the principal cities, devise a plan to improve the finances of the Association, and promote a proper observance of Founders' Day. At the same time, President McKenny was authorized to purchase a life-sized portrait of John D. Pierce for the price of $500. This portrait was formally presented to the College at the 1923 Commencement and now hangs near the south entrance to Pierce Hall.

A committee was formed in 1923 to recommend reorganization of the Association. Their report proposed incorporation and a board of directors of nine members with three-year staggered terms. The Association was incorporated November 23, 1925. Annual dues of $1 were set. The grand project, already well under way, of an "Alumni Building" to serve as a student union and a home for the Alumni Association was approved.

The story of this project actually began in 1924 when McKenny persuaded the executive committee of the Association to initiate the move. The building was to be "a general social center for student life . . . a home for alumni returning to the college, serving a purpose similar to that of the Michigan Union at the University of Michigan." The Flint alumni immediately responded to the proposal by turning over to the Association the balance of funds in their treasury. The students were galvanized into action. In 1925, the Student Council secured pledges amounting to $55,000. The faculty at the same time pledged $10,000. By the time formal action of approval was taken by the Association, the steamroller had already begun to roll.

In 1926, a contract was signed with a professional fund-raising company (Tamblyn & Brown of New York City); preliminary plans for the building were drawn (Fry & Kasurin); an architectural firm was employed (Burrows & Burich). The plans called for a building costing about $500,000.

A full-scale alumni drive was launched in April of 1927 with a dinner at the Masonic Temple in Detroit. Twelve hundred Normal graduates attended. A hundred thousand dollars had already been pledged from various sources. Governor Fred Green, a Normal graduate, spoke. An honorary committee was formed, headed by alumnus Frank Cody, Superintendent of the Detroit Public Schools. It was hoped that the drive could be completed in time for the formal celebration of Normal's seventy-fifth anniversary, scheduled for the Mid-Winter Conference in January. Alumni dinners were held over the State. The office of field secretary was created and Edwin Stahl appointed to it.

Indeed, as far as pledges were concerned, the prospects for a successful campaign were excellent. But enthusiasm and campaign pressure proved to be somewhat more than the traffic would bear. Payment of pledges lagged. Instead of a triumphant presentation at the Diamond Jubilee of a $500,000 building fund, there was a quiet special meeting of some eighteen district representatives to promote the idea of organizing a new alumni club wherever 25 or more alumni could be found resident in one area.

Later in the year, a finance committee was created under the chairmanship of Daniel L. Quirk to pursue the collection problem. A discount of 5 per cent was offered for all pledges paid in full. A request to the legislature for an appropriation of $160,000 was considered but abandoned. By the middle of 1929 somewhat more than $50,000 had been collected from 7,000 pledges. The excellent record of the students in honoring their commitments was held before delinquent alumni. A year later, the Alumni Association had garnered $133,000, a noteworthy achievement in view of the fact that by this time the depression had struck America.

The State Board had given its consent to the start of construction when $175,000 was in hand. This was lowered to $150,000. A bond issue was proposed, at first for $150,000, soon thereafter for $190,000, and this was arranged, at 6 per cent interest for a period of 16 years, with the First Detroit (Bond & Mortgage) Company. The bid of general contractors Lovering and Longbottom was accepted and, on November 8, 1930, the ground-breaking ceremony took place on a site provided by the State Board. Some 2,000 students, alumni and townspeople were present on this occasion. Speeches were made by the president of the Association, Norman Arthur, by President McKenny, the State Superintendent of Public Instruction (Webster Pearce, an alumnus), and by the Mayor of Ypsilanti ("Mat" Max) who presented the keys of the city to the Alumni Association. On January 17, 1931, the cornerstone was laid, and the formal dedication took place in the new ballroom Saturday morning, October 24.

Nearly a year later, at the annual alumni meeting for 1932, an enthusiastic report on the operation of the building revealed that an average of 700 people a day had entered its portals and some eleven conventions had been held, including the 28th Annual Meeting of the American Geographical Society—a signal recognition of Normal's geographer, Mark Jefferson.

But the financial problem hovered like a dark cloud over all. In November of 1932, the bondholders were asked to waive their sinking fund rights for two years so that equipment obligations could be met. A year later, short-term notes were issued to pay interest on the bonds and the question of re-financing the $190,000 issue was raised. Finally, the State Board was persuaded to take over the building and equipment. The Board purchased the bonds at par value. To make the purchase, it issued 20-year certificates of indebtedness at 4 per cent interest. These were funded by a student membership fee plus the net profits from the operation of the building. Thus was the long-standing problem finally resolved.

The grand project had occupied the minds and hearts of many people for a dozen years. It had required qualities of initiative, daring, dogged determination. It had run head-on into the greatest economic depression of all time. It had shrunk from a half-million dollar facility to one substantially more modest (equipped, it was valued at $375,000). Normal's most prominent alumni had given freely of their time and thought.

To one in particular, a special tribute was felt to be due. On the death of Clarence E. Gittens, legislator and Detroit lawyer, in 1935, the Alumni Association passed a resolution which read in part as follows:

> . . . it was largely through the efforts of Mr. Gittens that it was possible to promote a program of enlarged service and carry it to a successful completion. Much of the success in financing Charles McKenny Hall and putting it on a working basis was due to the wisdom of his counsel and to the personal service which he gave freely and generously.

Today its collegiate-gothic form stands as a monument to a loyal and devoted alumni body.

No stronger testimony as to the usefulness of this building could be asked than the action of the State Board of Education (March, 1963) approving plans for a $2,000,000 renovation and enlargement.

Meanwhile, the Alumni Association had also been active with smaller projects. Founders Day was revived (1925), and observed annually. An annual Homecoming Day was initiated (October, 1928). An alumni paper was published from time to time. An Alumni Office was established (1928), an Alumni Song Book printed and sold (1929), the sale of a book of poems by President McKenny, published posthumously, was undertaken. Formal tributes were paid to outstanding faculty and alumni at time of death. Portraits of Professor Sherzer (1930) and Professor D'Ooge (1931), and a plaque of Dimon H. Roberts (1937) were presented to the College. The lovely ballroom in McKenny Hall was named after Fred W. Green (1937).

But the ensuing years witnessed a decline in alumni interest. Perhaps it was a reaction to the insistent demands of the McKenny Hall period; perhaps it was influenced by the continuing economic depression, or by the outbreak of World War II in 1939. Or perhaps it was due to a lack of interest on the part of the college administration.

By 1944 the Board of Directors felt a need to stimulate alumni activity and to make the Association a more positive factor in the affairs of the College. Ironically, one of the requests was for an alumni headquarters on campus. Special meetings were called, which evoked a number of suggestions that made the past seem very dead indeed, such as an annual alumni membership fee, bringing alumni files up to date, an alumni publication, the encouragement of alumni clubs throughout the State, and alumni "homecomings" at times other than Commencement.

The story from this point is one of increased activity and increasing momentum. Encouragement soon came from the new president of the College, Eugene B. Elliott, who, in 1948, solicited alumni support and interest, and provided room for a headquarters and equipment, and assigned the function of Alumni relations to the Extension Division of the College. The board of directors was increased in 1946 to sixteen, including the President of the College *ex officio*. In 1951, two men, successful in the business world and prominent among the older alumni, were elected to the Board who were to exercise a strong influence—R. C. Runciman, '11, and Clarke Davis, '12.

A consistent record of activity and worthwhile contributions to the College was the result. In 1947, an Emeritus Club was formed for alumni of 50 years or more standing. In 1950, a Chimes Memorial Committee was created, under the chairmanship of Runciman, whose activities resulted in the dedication, on October 24, 1953, of a set of chimes in the Pierce Hall tower to the veterans of World War II. Money began flowing into the treasury from membership fees and drives for special projects, and the directors began to consider investment of surplus funds.

At the same time, there was greatly increased emphasis on the promoting of alumni clubs outside of Michigan. In 1958, it was Pasadena. In 1959, President and Mrs. Elliott visited clubs in Arcadia, San Diego, and Sacramento, California; in Corvallis, Oregon; and in Seattle, Washington. A plan for honoring alumni for outstanding loyalty to the College was inaugurated in 1957 with the recognition of Federal Judge Arthur Lederle.

The importance of a loyal, enthusiastic, and active alumni association to a college has been well demonstrated in the history of Eastern.

NOTES

Chapter One

1. Quoted in Michigan Legislative Manual, 1903, p. 78, from H. R. Pattengill: "Primer of Michigan History."

2. Quoted by Charles Hoyt and Clyde Ford, "John D. Pierce," (Ypsilanti, 1905) frontispiece.

3. Oliver C. Comstock, State Superintendent Report, 1843, Legislature 1844, Joint Doc. No. 6, p. 7.

4. Report of Board of Visitors for the University of Michigan, August 2, 1847. Legislature 1848, Joint Doc. No. 5, pp. 19–20.

5. Quoted by George L. Jackson, "The Development of State Control of Public Instruction in Michigan," (Lansing, 1926) p. 156.

6. Public Acts 1849, No. 178. See also State Superintendent Report 1880, p. 393ff.

7. Public Acts 1850, No. 139.

8. See the following statutes conferring corporate powers on the controlling board throughout Normal's history: Public Acts 1849, No. 138, 178 (control over revenue derived from salt spring lands; authority to procure site and erect buildings); Public Acts 1850, No. 139, sec. 19 ("body politic and corporate"); Public Acts 1889, No. 194, sec. 1 ("body corporate"); Public Acts 1963, No. 48, ("to provide for the organization, powers and duties of their boards of control") (re the four teachers colleges, by now universities).

9. John C. Springman, "Growth of Public Education in Michigan," (Ypsilanti 1952) pp. 134–135, quoting Superintendent Shearman's annual report for 1850. Legislature 1851, Joint Doc. No. 14, p. 6. Springman gives the detailed offers from Ypsilanti's rivals at 133–134.

10. Report of the Board of Education, Legislature 1853, Joint Doc. No. 6, p. 53.

Chapter Two

1. Barnard, *The American Journal of Education* (vol. 8, June 1860), XVII, "Teachers' Institute," at p. 673.

2. State Board Report 1853, pp. 109–110.

3. Normal Catalog, 1853.

4. Normal Catalog, 1853.

5. State Board Report 1861, p. 107.

6. Supt. Pub. Inst'n Rpt, 1861, p. 103. The courses that constituted the professional training at this time were methods of teaching spelling, reading, and penmanship; arithmetic; geography; grammar; chemistry; object lessons and objective training; lectures on schoolroom duties; lectures on primary education and on means of teaching the virtues; practice teaching under supervision of the principal of the Experimental Department (the Model School); and lectures on the philosophy of education.

7. State Board Report 1863, pp. 129–130. Rpt. Supt. Pub. Instr'n. 1861, p. 103. The report notes that some instruction in Pestalozzian method had been given during the past three years; it now approved the incorporation of this method in the course of study for all students. In chapter one, *supra*, we mentioned that interest in this country in the Pestallozian method dated back at least to 1839, with the Report on Education in Europe of Alexander Dallas Bache, president of Girard College.

8. State Board Report 1863, p. 132.

9. State Board Report 1868, p. 213.

10. State Board Report 1865, pp. 20–21.

11. State Board Report 1867, pp. 152–153.

12. State Board Report 1867, p. 152.

13. Address, "What Constitutes the True Teacher," by A. S. Welch at the Teachers' Institute held at the Normal School on the occasion of its opening. See Supt. Rpt. 1853, p. 128.

Chapter Three

1. Laws of the Territory of Michigan, vol. 2: An act to provide for and regulate Common Schools, 1929, sec. 28, p. 774.

2. Act 194, P.A. 1889, sec. 6.

3. State Supt. Rpt. 1878, p. 35 (Gower).

4. State Supt. Rpt. 1892, pp. 119, 120 (Fitch).

5. Putnam, Hist. MSNS, p. 131.

6. The list of charter members included four Michigan institutions—University of Michigan, Albion College, Grand Rapids and Detroit High Schools, and the Military Academy at Orchard Lake. It also included two normal schools—Oshkosh of Wisconsin and Cedar Falls of Iowa. See *N.C.A. Proceedings,* 1905.

7. In 1905, 1910 and 1912. See *N.C.A. Proceedings.*

8. "The State Normal School of Michigan, its Plan and Purpose." Grand Rapids: Dean Publishing and Printing, 1893.

9. See *North Central Association Quarterly,* vol. III, no. 1 (June, 1928) pp. 68, 73.

10. Boone was preoccupied at the moment with a project that he hoped would contribute to the usefulness and prestige of Normal, viz., the anniversary observance of the founding of the institution. It so happened this day fell on the 28th of March. The program was ambitious, including Governor John T. Rich, State Superintendent H. R. Pattengill, and State Board Chairman Perry F. Powers. It also included President Angell but he was unable to be present, having gone to the Evanston

meeting. "Founders Day," Boone hoped, would became an annual affair—and did indeed over many years.

Chapter Four

1. For the early history of The Model (variously referred to as *The Model,* the *Experimental School, School of Observation and Practice,* and the *Training School,* since 1931 as the *Laboratory School*) see Putnam, pp. 86–113, who carries the story to the late '90's.

2. Putnam, p. 89.

3. See Putnam, p. 90, quoting the Principal's Report for 1860.

4. State Supt. Rpt. 1871, pp. 12–18.

5. Putnam, p. 99.

6. Quoted by Putnam, p. 106.

7. Putnam, pp. 108–109.

8. State Supt. Rpt. 1894, pp. 349–50.

9. State Board Report of 1894–1896, p. 19.

10. The building was first occupied on Monday, March 29, 1897.

11. State Bd. Rpt. 1908, p. 21.

12. *Aurora* 1925, p. 22.

13. State Bd. Rpt. 1927–1928, p. 57.

14. Catalog, 1900–1901, p. 92.

15. See brief Ms. History by a member of the Training School staff, Jane Matteson, in EMU Archives.

16. See Cubberly, pp. 554–5

17. The Owen property, lying on the north side of the campus, was purchased as the site.

18. The school paper, *The Parrot,* vol. 2, p. 10 (June 1927).

19. *Rough Rider,* November 19, 1928.

20. State Bd. Rpt., December 31, 1929. The citizens committee consisted of George H. Millage, George Handy (editor-owner of the *Ypsilanti Press*), C. V. Brown, Harry Shaefer, and State Representative Joe Warner.

21. *Rough Rider,* January 14, 1930, p. 2.

22. The citizens' committee consisted of Dr. Olin Cox, chairman, Mrs. Beth Milford, Bert Harrison, Dr. Robert Belcher, Miss Virginia Cooper, Miss Margaret Gotts, Carroll Caldwell, David Goodell, Allister MacDonald, David Gauntlett, and Orlan Wilde. This list included members of both the Roosevelt and college faculties.

23. The members of this committee were Roy E. Robinson, Paul E. Emerich, Robert W. Cranmer, Beth W. Milford, Olin J. Cox, La Verne W. Weber, M. Ethel O'Conner, Charles J. Alexander, Allister MacDonald, Scott W. Street, Lloyd W. Olds, Elizabeth Warren, Bert M. Johnson, Louis P. Porretta, Robert J. Fisher, R. Stanley Gex, and Lucille M. Kirchoff.

24. As of this time, the Roosevelt capacity could take only about 20 per cent of the students who needed to be accommodated. Prior to World War II, and for a time thereafter, the college facilities had been adequate (in the later years through seriously overloading the supervising teachers) to take all.

Chapter Five

1. Cubberly, "Public Education in the United States," rev. ed. 1934, p. 385 ff.

2. Based on Wayland's "Intellectual Philosophy" which treated such matters as order of development of the several "faculties," a corresponding order of observation and reflection, cultivating the "sensibilities," and religious instruction. See Putnam, pp. 49–50, and M.S.N.S. Catalog 1868–69, pp. 26, 29.

3. Topics and problems treated were what education; principles of testing; selection of materials; relation of materials to culture; classifying the sensibilities; the will—how to strengthen and guide it; culture and conscience. See M.S.N.S. Catalog 1868–69, p. 29.

4. MSNS Catalog 1868–69, p. 27.

5. MSNS Catalog 1888–89, p. 23.

Chapter Six

1. Act 261, PA 1895, sec. 1.

2. Act 51, PA 1899, sec. 1.

3. Act 156, PA 1903, sec. 1.

4. MSNC Catalog 1902–03, p. 45.

5. MSNC Catalog 1918–19, p. 70.

6. The one and two-room schools used by the Normal College for practice teaching were: Stone (1919–1927), Denton (1923–1952), Begole (1924–1931), Spencer (1933–1942). See Clara Smith, *infra,* p. 271.

7. *Aurora* 1922, p. 209. See M. S. Pittman, "The Ypsilanti Kiwanis Club and the Country Schools," *American Schoolmaster* (December 1923), pp. 134ff., for a description of the strategy employed.

8. The 13 district schools that thus gave up their identity were Allen, Biship, Brick, Centennial, Childs, Hardy, Island, Lowden, Model, Morgan, Ridner, Tuttle and Vedder.

9. See Clara May Freeman Smith (doctoral dissertation, University of Michigan): "A History of the Lincoln School and its Contributions to the Improvement of Rural Education" (1962), p. 192. The original contract is shown at pp. 187–8.

10. In the school year 1967–68 the Senior High School enrolled 554 pupils; the Junior High School, 290; the Elementary School, 1094—a total of 1938.

Chapter Seven

1. Catalog 1868–69, p. 30.

2. See chapter 23, Jefferson, and "Mark Jefferson: Geographer," EMU Press.

3. Catalog, 1913–1914, p. 125.

4. Catalog, 1929–1930, p. 189.

5. State Board Minutes, February 21, 1938.

6. Catalog, 1949–50, p. 77.

7. Cleary Business College not only played for many years an important role in Normal's curricular offerings, but flourishes today as one of the outstanding institutions of its kind in the country. It offers the degree of Bachelor of Business Administration, boasts many outstanding alumni, and is at the present time located on a new campus on the edge of the city of Ypsilanti.

8. Catalog, 1903–04, p. 122.

9. Catalog, 1901–02, p. 165.

10. Putnam, p. 251.

11. Putnam, p. 252.

12. Harvey C. Colburn, "The Story of Ypsilanti" (1923), p. 143.

13. Quoted in Catalog 1921–22, p. 242.

14. *Conservatory of Music Bulletin*, 1932–33, pp. 9–10.

15. Though not directly connected with the Conservatory, the name of John Challis, known the world over as a maker of 18th century keyboard instruments (clavichord, virginal, harpischord) is intimately associated with that of Frederick Alexander. In 1926, Professor Alexander introduced a young and promising student in the Conservatory to Arnold Dolmetsch of Haslemere, England, pioneer in the recovery of early instrumental music, and maker of clavichords, harpsichords, and recorders. Challis made a strong impresson and was granted the first scholarship to be offered by the Dolmetsch Foundation. In due time he returned to Ypsilanti where he built his instruments until 1946 when, enlarging his operation, he removed to Detroit. See Grove's "Dictionary of Music and Musicians" (1955 ed); Una L. Allen, "A Dolmetsch of the Middle-West," *The Musician* (Nov. 1932).

16. Judge Breakey recalled with satisfaction his role in initiating a move for a bachelor's degree program in music. It culminated in the adoption of a curriculum in Public School Piano, was first offered in 1928–29, and was the first four-year degree program in music offered at Normal.

17. A member of the faculty from 1927, Miss James earned international recognition as a composer. She wrote for the theatre, for orchestra, for chorus, and chamber music. Among the better known of her works are incidental music for *Paola and Francisca*, an opera in three acts; *Three Pastorals*, for clarinet solo, strings and harp; a cantata, *The Jumblies* (presented at the May Festival of the University of Michigan in 1934); a cantata, *Paul Bunyan* (presented at the May Festival of 1937); *Four Preludes from the Chinese*, for contralto and piano quintet; *Rhapsody*, for violin, cello and piano. She retired from the faculty in June, 1968.

Chapter Eight

1. Supt. Rpt. 1863, p. 128.

2. See EMU Archives, Osband.

3. See Governors' Papers, Box 535, Folder No. 11 (May 30, 1893), State Archives.

4. See chapter 28, Athletics.

5. *American Physical Education Review*, vol. 33, p. 557 (Oct. 1928).

Chapter Nine

1. Frampton and Rowell: Education of the Handicapped (1940), vol. 1, p. 141.

2. "Normal College Hymn," with C. Lavatee; "The Hills of Washtenaw," with George P. Becker; and "Green and White," with Richard L. Owen.

3. See MSNC Catalog, 1923–24, pp. 103–104. See also the Ms. history of the Special Education Department by Paul F. Thams (assisted by Francis E. Lord), in the EMU Archives.

4. The method used was that of the German, Karl Bruckmann, whose writings were translated by Professor Reighard. See Thams-Lord Ms. history of the Special Education Department, p. 5, EMU Archives.

5. A gift of $5,000 annually was accepted by the State Board, January, 1927. In September of the same year it acknowledged receipt of $15,000, and closed the arrangement with a vote of thanks and appreciation. State Board Reports, January 29, 1927; September 24, 1927.

6. Such, for example, were Carl M. Badgeley, M.D., head of Bone and Joint Surgery, University of Michigan; F. Bruce Fralick, M.D., chairman of the Department of Ophthalmology, University of Michigan; Harry Jay Baker, Psychologist of the Detroit Public Schools; Dr. Leo Kanner, Director of Child Psychiatric Service, Johns Hopkins University; Dr. Samuel Laycock, Dean, School of Education, University of Saskatchewan (Parent Education); and Dr. Berthold Loewenfeld, Director of Educational Research, American Foundation for the Blind.

Chapter Ten

1. He received an MA in 1852, and the honorary degree of LLD from the University of Iowa (1873) and the University of Michigan (1878).

2. Supt. Public Instruction Rpt., 1853, p. 130.

3. The former published in two editions: 1855, 1862; the latter, in 1862.

4. C. F. R. Bellows, "The Early Days of the Normal School." Anniversary Day Exercises, March 28, 1895. In Archives.

5. *The Normal News,* Feb., 1894, p. 7.

6. Mary Beaumont Dudley of Jonesville was the second wife of Adonijah Welch. His first wife, Eunice P. Buckingham, of Mt. Vernon, Ohio, died in 1867 at Jacksonville, Florida.

7. *The Normal News,* Feb., 1894, p. 7.

Chapter Eleven

1. The Reverend Porter had been pastor of the Congregational Church in Spencertown, New York; and later of the Presbyterian Church at Catskill, New York, where he conducted a classical school.

2. The Columbus school system in 1854 consisted of three grammar schools,

eight secondary schools, nine primary schools, three German schools, four Negro schools, a high school, and a night school.

3. *The Normal News,* v. XIII, March, 1894, p. 9.

4. See his extended defense in *The Michigan School Moderator,* June 18, 1891, pp. 622 ff.

5. The Pedagogical Society was organized in 1885, during the administration of Principal Willits. It appears to have had a continuous existence until about the close of the century. Composed of members of the faculty, its purpose was stated in its constitution to be "the investigation and discussion of principles of education and methods of teaching, and the consideration of such other professional subjects as may conduce to the success of our united efforts as teachers." Meetings were held on the third Tuesday of each month during the school year. A committee selected the topics to be discussed, usually planning a program of discussions for the entire year. Great care was taken in the preparation of formal papers, many of which were subsequently published. Putnam was a most active participant and commented: "The Society has done much to improve the professional spirit of the school." See Putnam, pp. 234–235.

6. Act 261, P. A. 1895.

7. See Chapter Four, *supra.*

8. Bernard Bigsby, "The Michigan State Normal School." Extract from "A Roving Englishman's Notes in America," written for *Cassell's Magazine.* (Ypsilanti, 1873).

Chapter Twelve

1. State Supt. Rpt. 1880, p. 87. The Normal was at the time trying an experiment in curriculum, viz., the offering of professional courses in education to the practical exclusion of academic work.

2. See *Dictionary of American Biography.*

3. State Supt. Rpt. 1881, p. 67.

4. *Handbook of the Mac Vicar Tellurian Globe for the Use of Teachers, Schools, and Families.* A. H. Andrews. Chicago, 1878.

5. Putnam's experience appears to have been similar to that of Mac Vicar in Leavenworth, Kansas. He submitted a detailed plan for the organization of the schools in Kalamazoo which was adopted, whereupon he was asked by the trustees to serve as superintendent and principal of the high school. One part of the plan was the establishment of a school exclusively for the colored population. (Correspondence, Russell Davey, Director of Research and Pupil Personnel, Kalamazoo Public Schools. Aug. 19, 1958).

6. Putnam: "Twenty-Five Years with the Insane." John McFarland. Detroit, 1885.

7. See manuscript in EMU Archives, eulogy of Putnam by Miss King at the end of thirty years at Normal.

8. Report, Superintendent of Public Instruction, 1883, p. 69 (annual report of State Board of Education).

9. *Normal News,* November, 1882, pp. 8–9.

10. Act 188, P. A. 1861.

11. Allen S. Whitney, "Training of Teachers at Michigan," p. 48. The request of the U-M was ultimately granted during the Sill administration in 1891 (Public Acts, 1891, No. 144). Two years later it was removed from both institutions and given to the State Board of Education (Public Acts, 1893, No. 136).

12. See *National Encyclopedia of American Biography,* Vol. 11, p. 259.

Chapter Thirteen

1. *Ypsilanti Commercial,* September 16, 1887.

2. For a good sketch of Sill's career, see Leslie L. Hanawalt, "A Place of Light; The History of Wayne State University" (Detroit, 1968), pp. 109–110.

3. *Detroit Board of Education Minutes,* March 24, 1881 (Wayne State University Archives).

4. Sill served for three years, 1867–1870.

5. Act 194, P. A. 1889.

6. State Supt. Rpt. 1891, p. 111. The academic areas claimed as offering college-grade courses were English Literature, History, Latin, Greek, French, German, Mathematics, Botany, Zoology, Geology, Physics, Chemistry, Astronomy. See "The State Normal School of Michigan: Its Plan and Purpose." (Grand Rapids, Dean, 1893), p. 19.

7. State Supt. Rpt. 1893, pp. 272–273.

8. See State Supt. Rpt. 1887, p. 151, and MSNS Catalog 1892–93.

9. For some reason, unexplained, the State Board desired a change. In his final report Sill alluded to this when, in his "Account of Stewardship" he said:

> Especially is this (account of stewardship) proper because of the fact (of which I was made aware with marked kindness and courtesy) that you deemed it best to place the executive charge of the school in other hands, which was the immediate cause of my declination of reappointment.

10. *Michigan School Moderator,* vol. xiii, No. 20 (June 15, 1893), p. 626.

11. The Prismatic Club, Nursery Rhymes, January 8, 1872 (Archives, Wayne State University).

12. "Synthesis of the English Sentence, or an Elementary Grammar on the Synthetic Method." New York, Ivison, 1856. "Practical Lessons in English." New York, Barnes, 1880.

13. "Since that date he has engaged in missionary work whenever other duties permitted." National Cyclopoedia of American Biography, Vol. 10, p. 353.

14. *The Normal College News,* April, 1901, p. 203.

Chapter Fourteen

1. 1883 and 1889, respectively.

2. See Editor's Preface, p. v., in Richard G. Boone, "Education in the United States, Its History from the Earliest Settlements." New York, D. Appleton. 1890.

This is Volume XI of the International Education Series, edited by William T. Harris. Boone's other work was "A History of Education in Indiana." New York. D. Appleton, 1892.

3. It has been asserted that the Normal School at Livingston, Alabama, became a State Teachers College in 1882, and that the institution at Bluefield, West Virginia, became a State College in 1895. See Edgar B. Wesley, "NEA: The First Hundred Years." New York, Harper, 1957, pp. 88, 89. The Livingston school was organized as a Normal School in 1883, and became a State Teachers College in 1929. The Bluefield school was founded in 1895 as Bluefield Colored Institute, first gave instruction at the college level in 1919, and acquired the name of Bluefield State Teachers College in 1929. See Allan M. Cartter, ed., "American Universities and Colleges," 9th ed., 1964, at pp. 159, 1199.

4. A decade later Lord Acton, in a lecture of enduring fame delivered at Cambridge University, would make a similar assertion, but expressed in the broadest terms: "the knowledge of the Past, the record of truths revealed by experience, is eminently practical, as an instrument of action, and a power that goes to the making of the future." Lord Acton, "A Lecture on the Study of History." London, Macmillan, 1896.

5. The expressions of his educational views are taken from a paper that he read in December, 1893, before Normal's Pedagogical Society titled "Education as a Dialectic Process" See Normal Papers, Richard G. Boone, "Education as a Dialectic Process" (EMU Archives), pp. 3, 4, 8. It was published in the *Inter-State School Review,* April and May, 1894.

6. *A Study in Unification of School Work,* being a Series of Papers read before the Normal Pedagogical Society (Ypsilanti, 1893-4). The papers were, in order of presentation: Richard Gause Boone, "Education as a Dialectic Process" (December, 1893); August Lodeman, "Languages as a Center of Instruction" (January, 1894); Julia Anne King, "History a Unifying Element in a Course of Study" (February, 1894); Daniel Putnam, "Selection of Subject Matter of Instruction" (April, 1894); Edwin A. Strong, "Concentration of Studies with Science as a Base" (April, 1894).

7. Governors' Papers, State Archives; copy in EMU Archives.

8. Act 261, PA 1895, "An act to establish a normal school in central Michigan." Approved, immediate effect, June 3.

9. Act 175, PA 1897, "An act to fix the relatives of the existing normal schools of the State." Approved May 29.

10. Act 51, PA 1899. Approved, immediate effect, April 28.

11. Act 52, PA 1899, "An Act to change the name of the Michigan State Normal School to Michigan State Normal College." Approved, immediate effect, April 28.

12. State Bd. Rpt. 1896–1898, pp. 18, 19.

13. See the *Detroit Free Press,* May 22, 25, 26, 28; *Detroit Evening News,* May 25, 26, June 23; *Detroit Tribune,* May 25, 26; *Ypsilantian,* Oct. 5, *Ypsilanti Commercial,* May 25; *Ann Arbor Daily Argus,* June 30 (all of 1899).

14. *Detroit Evening News,* May 25, 1899.

15. *Detroit Free Press,* May 28, 1899.

16. *Detroit Free Press, Detroit Evening News,* May 26.

17. The *Ann Arbor Daily Argus* ran a long pro-Boone article, asserting that Boone was given $2,000 to resign.

18. I am indebted to Professor Leslie L. Hanawalt, author of the history of Wayne State University ("A Place of Light." Wayne State University Press, 1968), for part of the story; to the *Ann Arbor Daily Argus* for the Ypsilanti aspect.

19. I am indebted to Miller R. Collings, Research Assistant, Department of Research, Statistics and Information, Cincinnati Public Schools, for this quotation from the *Cincinnati Times-Star,* Centennial Edition, April 25, 1940, p. 14.

20. *The American Schoolmaster,* vol. 16 (May 1923), pp. 184–185.

Chapter Fifteen

1. *Michigan Legislative Manual,* 1903, p. 78.

2. See State Supt. Rpt. 1899, p. 10. The resolution was adopted by the State Board June 23, 1899.

3. A quarterly, published at various times from Syracuse, New York, for two years from Ypsilanti; and from New Rochelle, New York.

4. *Journal of Pedagogy,* October, 1900, p. 74. No mention of the plan appeared in any subsequent issue of the Journal.

5. State Bd. Rpt. 1902, p. 7.

6. *Ibid.,* p. 7. The "Michigan System" was discontinued as of July 1, 1902.

Chapter Sixteen

1. James M. Greenwood, "Some Educators I have Known," *Educational Review,* vol. 25 (April 1903), pp. 409 ff. at pp. 410, 410–11, 412.

2. Now in the possession of his daughter Edith (Mrs. Harry Shaefer of Ypsilanti).

3. "Impressive Service Held in Memory of Dr. Jones," *Normal College News,* Dec. 14, 1917, p. 1–2 at p. 2.

4. State Bd. Rpt. 1910, p. 23. This refers to the activity of an organization, composed of citizens and faculty, called the Normal Park Association. See State Bd. Rpt. 1906, pp. 9–10, for membership list and initial gift to Normal.

5. State Bd. Rpt. 1912, p. 18.

6. State Bd. Rpt. 1904, pp. 20–21.

7. Act 202, P. A. 1903.

8. Florus Barbour and Alma Blount (English Literature), Bertha Buell (History), Fannie Cheever Burton (Women's Physical Education, Bertha Goodison (Art), Frederick Gorton (Physics), Julia Anne King (Preceptress, History), Stuart Lathers (Speech), Jessie Phelps (Natural Science), Daniel Putnam (Pedagogy and History of Education), Dimon H. Roberts (Teacher Training), Genevieve M. Walton (Library) and Margaret E. Wise (Teacher Training).

9. State Bd. Rpt. 1908, p. 26.

10. Senior student Jessie Clark's tribute to President L. H. Jones in *Aurora* 1903.

11. Dr. Davis (Life Certificate '08, B.Pd. '09, A.B. '12) received the Ph.D. in

Chemistry from Columbia University ('15); taught at Utah State College and at Columbia, and achieved a highly successful career in industry.

12. See the *Daily Ypsilantian-Press,* Aug. 13, 1917.

13. *Ypsilanti Daily Press,* Sept. 1, 1958.

14. "The Jones Reader" (5 vols.) Boston, Ginn, 1903; "Education as Growth, or The Culture of Character—a book for Teachers' Reading Circles." (Boston, Ginn, 1911.

15. Harvey C. Colburn: "The Story of Ypsilanti." (Ypsilanti, 1923.) p. 286.

16. It is of interest to note, in passing, that the pre-eminent position of Normal in relation to the three other State Normals ended during the Jones era. The title of Principal for the heads of these institutions was changed to President (signifying their recognition as colleges) on October 30, 1908 (State Bd. Rpt. 1908, p. 7). The first to hold this new title in each of these college were Charles T. Grawn (at Central), James H. G. Kaye (at Northern), and Dwight B. Waldo (at Western).

Chapter Seventeen

1. State Bd. Rpt. 1914, p. 21.

2. *Daily Ypsilantian Press,* May 14, 1913, quoted by *Ypsilanti Press,* May 14, 1963.

3. Charles McKenny, "The Teachers' College," *The American Schoolmaster,* vol. 18, (March 1925), p. 102.

4. Among others were President Henry Churchill King of Oberlin College; President Lotus D. Coffman of the University of Minnesota; Dean Percy Boynton of the University of Chicago; Dean Shailer Mathews of the Divinity School of the University of Chicago; President Bruce Payne of Peabody; Dr. Alexander Meicklejohn, then of the University of Wisconsin; Everett Dean Martin, Director of the Cooper Union Forum of New York.

5. State Bd. Rpt. 1914, p. 22.

6. Charles McKenny, "The Sabbatical," *The American Schoolmaster,* vol. 18, no. 2 (Feb. 1925), p. 51.

7. Tanton v. McKenney (sic), 226 Mich. 245 (March 5, 1924) at pp. 247, 248, 253.

8. *The Normal College News,* April 21, 1922, p. 1.

9. *Baltimore Sun,* Feb. 26, 1931.

10. *Ypsilanti Press,* May 3, 1927.

11. Kappa Delta Pi had been organized at the University of Illinois in 1911 by William C. Bagley.

12. *National Society for the Scientific Study of Education,* 7th, 8th, and 9th Yearbooks (1908, 1909, 1910).

13. Just when the practice of requiring this commitment to teach was actually abandoned is not clear, but the year 1936 witnessed the abandonment of the requirement that certification for teaching was necessary for graduation with a degree. The announcement in the 1935–1936 catalog (p. 37) reads as follows:

> The primary function of the Michigan State Normal College is the preparation of teachers for the public schools of Michigan. The State Board of Education, realizing that all students are not

fitted by ability and interest for the teaching profession, has made it possible for students to
graduate with a degree without a certificate.

Chapter Eighteen

1. Brother Oliver to John Munson, Dec. 25, 1943. Munson papers, Michigan
Historical Collections, Ann Arbor.

2. At Ingalls, Michigan.

3. Clarkston (1903–1905); Harbor Springs (1905–1913).

4. Ferris to Munson, Feb. 20, 1913. Munson paper, note 1, *supra.*

5. Ferris to Munson, Feb. 5, 1923. Munson papers, note 1, *supra*

6. Munson to F. W. Arbury, May 17, 1933. Munson papers, note 1, *supra.*

7. See State Bd. Minutes, 1933–34 (Oct. 28, 1933), p. 30. The resolution was
signed by Fred T. Mitchell, G. L. Jenner, Eugene B. Elliott, L. N. Lamb and
Arthur B. Moehlman.

8. Leslie A. Butler, a Normal alumnus, superintendent of the Grand Rapids
Public Schools, was made chairman of the Commission. Years later Butler was to
come to Normal as Director of Laboratory Schools and Head of Placement. Here he
played a highly important role, too, in helping to plan the strategy and in securing
alumni support during the war-housing crisis of 1943.

9. See E. L. Austin, "A Summary Report of the Extra-Legal Advisory Planning
Commission for the Period of November 8, 1933 to July 1, 1935," at pp. 36–38 and
46–49. Austin was secretary of the Commission. The members of Munson's committee were Father Carroll F. Deady of the Detroit Catholic Schools, and W. E.
Lessenger, Dean of the School of Education, Wayne University of Detroit.

10. Act 55, P. A. 1935 (approved May 13, 1935); under the Constitution of
1963 by Act 287, P. A. 1964, effective July 1, 1967.

11. Thus at long last the teachers colleges of Michigan were brought in line with
a national movement in colleges and universities. This grouping of subjects and
degree requirements of a minimum course credit in specified groups was in answer
to certain evils that had developed under the free-elective policy, sponsored at an
earlier time by Harvard University to break through the rigid traditional limitations
of college curricula and open the way for recognition of newer areas of knowledge,
especially in the sciences.

12. Prior to 1935, when the State Board was given sole authority for the certification of teachers in Michigan, there were some 15 certifying agencies of various
types issuing various kinds of certificates. This had resulted in the certifying of
many who would not, according to the standards of the teachers colleges and the
University of Michigan, have been considered qualified.

13. Frank R. Mosier to Munson, March 10, 1948. *A Book of Letters Presented
to John M. Munson,* June 1, 1948.

14. State Bd. Minutes, 1938–39 (Dec. 13, 1938), p. 50. The plan to be implemented in the fall of 1939 "if possible."

15. *Normal College News,* July 13, 1933 (vol. 30, no. 28).

16. The reported figures are 1931–32—2,262; 1932–33—2,121; 1933–34—
1,833; 1934–35—1,628. These statistics are head-count for the regular on-campus
enrollments for the fall term of each year.

17. From $887,050 in 1931–32 to $529,262 in 1934–35.

18. From a low of 1,628 in 1934–35 to a high of 2,423 in 1940–41.

19. From $557,635 in 1935–36 to $652,213 in 1940–41.

20. From 2,423 to 1,199.

21. North football stands (1938); Glenadine Snow Health Residence (1939); Goodison and King Residence Halls for women (1939); Munson Residence Hall for men (1940); John W. Stevens Shop (1940); the J. Milton Hover Elementary Science Laboratories (1941); Greenhouse (1942); Jones Residence Hall for Women (1948); an administration and classroom building to replace Pierce Hall (1948); and two that were completed early in the succeeding administration—Brown Residence Hall for men (1949) and a power plant (1951).

22. The Briggs gift built a baseball stadium (in the image of the Detroit Tigers'), a small fieldhouse (much later transformed into a classroom building for the Mathematics Department), and the south stands for the football field (1937). The whole was designated as Walter O. Briggs Field.

23. They were known as Residence Halls, and named for outstanding members of faculty and staff. In order of dedication they were as follows: 1938—two for women students: Julia Anne King, former Preceptress, and first head of the Department of History and Social Sciences; Bertha Goodison, former head of the Art Department. 1939—one for men students: John M. Munson, President of Normal. (A surprise action taken by the State Board, somewhat embarrassing to Munson.) 1948—for women students: Lydia Jones, former Dean of Women. 1949—for men students: James M. Brown, Dean of Men (named at the request of the student body).

24. See "Michigan State Normal College—Veterans of World War II." Insofar as it was possible to obtain the information, this volume includes the names and nature of service of all who participated. EMU Archives.

25. *Ypsilanti Daily Press,* March 2, 1943, p. 1.

26. Sergeant Keith Cox, *Normal College News,* March 2, 1944 (vol. 21, no. 12), p. 2.

27. Women—612; men—83. Registrar records.

28. *The Detroit Free Press,* Feb. 3, 1948.

29. Known as "Summation Sheets." It has required much mechanical genius and expensive apparatus to provide this constantly up-to-date information in institutions of very large enrollments. For some years, during the period of rapid growth after the Munson administration, this record lapsed. The development and use of I. B. M. equipment corrected this.

30. Professor Willard Reninger of the English Department protested that, while the book in question might, indeed, prove embarrassing to a state-supported institution, yet it was "a pity that mature students should be denied an introduction to so good a book (Wolfe's 'Look Homeward Angel')." He added, "But let it join the other pities of the world."

31. An example is provided by his policy as to control of enrollment in classes. Aware of the inter-departmental competition for students that had prevailed prior to his administration, Munson took authority to open and close class enrollments away from the department heads and, on the very evening of the day in which registration was completed, would personally scrutinize the results, calling in the heads for consultation as deemed necessary.

32. Conferred in 1942. Munson had previously been the recipient of the honorary degree of MPd from Normal (1913), and an LLD degree from Ashland College, Ohio (1939).

33. The history of Michigan was written by Frederick Clever Bald: "Michigan in Four Centuries." New York. Harper, 1954. 2nd ed. 1961. The history of education in Michigan will appear in four volumes.

Chapter Nineteen

1. From 1935 until his appointment at the Normal in 1948. In 1935 he was appointed to fill the vacancy left by Maurice R. Keyworth who was killed in an automobile accident before taking office. Thereafter, tenure rested on the biennial elections.

2. In round numbers the enrollment immediately preceding the war was 1,900.

3. Act 163, P.A. 1927, effective May 12, 1927, changed the name of the other three Normals to "State Teachers College."

4. Quoted by Clair L. Taylor, State Superintendent of Public Instruction, in a letter to Elliott, April 20, 1955. (Not included in the Biennial Report of the Attorney General). EMU Archives.

5. Act 3, P. A. 1959, effective June 1, 1959.

6 Michigan Interfaculty Council, "Faculty Reactions to Professional Loads of Instructors in the Four Michigan Institutions of Higher Education under the Michigan State Board of Education, 1958–1959," Report of the Professional Load Committee adopted by the Interfaculty Council on March 12, 1960. (Ishpeming, 1960).

7. Ray W. Barber, Superintendent of Area Schools, Holly, Mich. to Elliott, Feb. 29, 1960. EMU Archives.

8. Clarence Hilberry, President of Wayne State University, to Margaret R. Kelly, student at EMU, Jan. 21, 1960. EMU Archives.

9. McCalla files, EMU Business Office.

10. See A.F.T. letter to the faculty, Mar. 15, 1948. EMU Archives.

11. Robert R. Williams (Assistant to the Provost, University of Michigan), "The Need for Increased Appropriations in the State-Supported Institutions of Higher Education in Michigan," *Mich. Ed. Jl.,* vol XXVII (March 1950), p. 400, "State Support for Higher Education in Michigan," vol. XXVIII (March 1951), p. 383.

12. Eugene B. Elliott (President, Michigan State Normal College), "Financial and Educational Problems of Higher Education," *Mich. Ed. Jl.,* vol XXVIII (Feb. 1951), p. 335.

13. James L. Stutesman (student president of Inter-Varsity Christian Fellowship, EMU chapter) to Elliott, Jan. 18, 1960. EMU Archives.

14. Elliott chose Earl E. Mosier for this position. Mosier was a member of Elliott's staff when the latter was State Superintendent of Public Education.

15. See letter to faculty, Oct. 19, 1955, and accompanying description of positions. EMU Archives. Two new positions were created: Dean of Instruction and Director of College Planning and Development and Assistant to the President. The area of student affairs was assigned to the Dean of Administration. The new

appointees were in the age bracket of the early forties: Bruce Nelson, Superinten-dent of the Lincoln Consolidated School, as Dean of Instruction; James E. Green, Librarian and Assistant to the President, as Director of College Planning and Development and Assistant to the President; and William C. Lawrence, associate professor of special education (psychology), as Dean of Student Affairs.

16. The group was led by James G. Matthews jr., M.D. ('37). Their letterhead bore the inscription, "Organization for Eastern Michigan University Action—Alumni—Faculty—Students—Friends." A questionnaire was mailed and a monetary contribution solicited. Beginning as an anonymous group, they soon felt it desirable to identify themselves. Besides the chairman, the members were Olin J. Cox, D.D.S. (student in the early forties), John S. Ecclestone ('36), William E. Foy ('28), Alan E. Hutchins ('43), Dean Rockwell ('35), Jerry R. Steele ('62) and Raymond L. Stites ('30).

17. See *Ypsilanti Press,* June 19, 1963, for the full report. A faculty Steering Committee was elected by the Faculty Council to conduct the self-study and write the report. This committee was composed of the following: Earl Roth, Dean of the College of Business, chairman; George Brower, Professor of Education; Kenneth Cleeton, Acting Dean, College of Education; Richard Giles, Professor of Biology; Egbert Isbell, Professor of History; Edgar Waugh, Professor of Political Science. The first draft was published in June, 1965.

18. Constitution of the State of Michigan of 1963, Article 8 *(Education),* sec's e, 6.

Chapter Twenty

1. See Frederick Rudolph: "The American College and University, a History." New York. Knopf, 1962, p. 420.

2. Quoting the 1937 Report of Committee T. See *AAUP Bulletin,* Spring 1948, for the 1948 report and a review of the history of the study.

3. The committee consisted of a representative each from four faculty organiza-tions: the American Federation of Teachers—Howard Blackenburg of the History Department; the Faculty Women's Club—Eleanor Meston of the Roosevelt Ele-mentary School: AAUP—Charles Walcutt of the English Department; Faculty Men's Club—J. Henry Owens, head of the Foreign Language Department.

4. The meeting was held in Lansing. The AAUP statement came from the 1937 Report of Committee T of the AAUP on "The Place and Function of Faculties in University and College Government," *AAUP Bulletin,* vol. 24 (Feb. 1938), pp. 141 ff. Owens recalls that at this meeting he explained to the Board that the faculty wished a nationwide search to be made for the very best candidate that might be found. He also states that in late February or early March the president of the Board, Steven Nisbet, invited him to dinner and informed him that Elliott would be appointed. It was this information that caused the committee to turn its attention to a charter for a faculty organization.

5. *Ypsilanti Daily Press,* March 24, 1948, p. 1.

6. The members were J. Henry Owens (Foreign Language Department Head), chairman; Howard Blackenburg (history); William J. Brownrigg (manager, student

union); Lawrence Dunning (Lincoln laboratory school); Fred J. Ericson (History); Hoover H. Jordan (English); Eleanor Meston (Roosevelt laboratory school); Lloyd Olds (physical education); Gerald D. Sanders (English department head); Elizabeth Warren (history).

7. *Faculty News Letter* #8, May 10, 1948.

8. The representatives were Gerald Sanders, Howard Blackenburg, Fred Ericson, Hoover Jordan, J. Henry Owens, and Edgar Waugh.

9. See State Board Minutes, May 26, 1948, p. 61.

10. The resolution had obviously been prepared in advance, President Charles Burns drawing it from his pocket at the close of the two-hour discussion.

11. The word "legislative" was later said to mean simply the "will of the faculty;" not in a legal sense.

12. Petition dated January 18, 1954.

Chapter Twenty-One

1. "The State Normal School of Michigan, its Plan and Purpose" (1893), p. 21.

2. See *Normal College News,* May 18, 1917, for the announcement, and details.

3. Putnam writes that, in working out the requirements for the B.Pd. degree, it was the intention to "indicate scholarship equal to that required for the degree of B.A. from a reputable college." Putnam, p. 131.

4. Catalog 1897–98, p. 83. See also the Ms. History of the English Department by Grace Cooper (written for the centennial celebration, 1949). EMU Archives.

5. He received his A.B. degree from the University of Michigan in 1878, graduating with a Phi Beta Kappa key.

6. *Normal College News,* December 9, 1926 (editorial).

7. She served the Normal for nearly half a century (1885–1930). She was born in Ingersoll, Ontario, but received her education at the Michigan State Normal College (1878), and the University of Michigan (1898).

8. Born in 1869 near Romulus, Michigan, she was a graduate of Michigan State Normal College (1898), of the University of Michigan (1902), and received an M.A. from the University of California at Berkeley. Her period of service at the Normal was from 1898 to 1938.

9. Catalog 1857–58, p. 32.

10. Of interest is Joseph F. Carey who taught Latin and Greek in the 1860's, whose grand-daughter was Elizabeth Carey, vivacious and energetic member of the English Department, 1913–1956.

11. Bernard Bigsby, "The Michigan State Normal School," an extract from "A Roving Englishman's Notes in America," written for *Cassell's Magazine.* Ypsilanti, 1873, p. 17.

12. Benjamin Leonard D'Ooge's career at the Normal extended from 1886 to 1938 when, at age 78, he retired just before the mandatory retirement age of 70 became effective (a step taken by the State Board in 1938, effective July 1, 1939).

13. August Lodeman remained with the Normal from 1872 until his death in 1902.

14. Teacher in the Anglo-Chinese school at Singapore, 1891–1892; country school teacher and village superintendent; assistant professor of French and German, Albion College, 1894–1899; professor of modern languages at the Northern State Normal School, 1901–1903. He was at the Normal from 1903 to 1940, retiring at age 70.

15. PhD, University of Minnesota. Owens came to the Normal College from the State Teachers College, River Falls, Wisconsin, where he headed the foreign language department.

16. She remained at the Normal from 1881 until her retirement in 1915.

17. *Detroit Free Press,* May 12, 1919.

18. Miss Buell served the Normal from 1889 until her retirement in 1936.

Chapter Twenty-two

1. Act 138, P. A. 1849. See sections 1 and 13. The provision that the lectures should be given by the professors of the University of Michigan was dropped in the act of 1850 to consolidate the laws relative to the establishment of a State Normal School. Act 139, P. A. 1850, section 13.

2. See Cubberley, "Public Education in the United States," pp. 278–279 (1934).

3. The Act was effective March 28.

4. Act 130, P. A. 1855.

5. Jessie Phelps ms. history of the Natural Science Department. EMU Archives.

6. *Normal College News,* October 7, 1909.

7. Mrs. Osband's husband, Professor William M. Osband, had been a classmate at Genesee College, Lima, N. Y. The Osbands had taught together for some fourteen years before coming to Ypsilanti in 1878. Osband bought a controlling interest in the local paper, *The Ypsilantian,* and both Osbands contributed to the editorial page. Harvey Colburn, historian of the city, wrote: "The writing of both Professor and Mrs. Osband had marked influence upon the life of the city. Their wide circle of friends brought to the paper correspondence from all parts of the world." See Colburn, "Story of Ypsilanti," p. 252.

8. Professor Harman, curator of the Museum of Comparative Zoology at Harvard University (known as the Agassiz museum) was a friend of William Osband, husband of Lucy. Harman offered Osband a collection of fishes for any school he was connected with that would furnish the jars and alcohol to preserve them. Mrs. Osband inquired if the offer included her, was reassured, received Principal Willit's cooperation, and secured for the Normal "a priceless collection of the fish the great Agassiz himself collected on his last trip to South American waters." See ms. history of the Natural Science Department by Harold O. Hansen. EMU Archives.

9. MSNS Catalog 1853. See also Putnam, pp. 34–35.

10. C. F. R. Bellows, "The True Reason," *The Michigan School Moderator* (June 18, 1891), p. 624.

11. See *School and Science,* vol. 44 (December, 1944), pp. 338–339. It should be noted, in passing, that under the pen name of David Dunham he wrote imaginative plays and essays.

Chapter Twenty-three

1. Merle Curti and Vernon Carstensen, "The University of Wisconsin," 1949, vol. 2, p. 552.
2. State Board Report, 1909–1910, pp. 55–56.
3. Catalog 1904–1905, p. 31.
4. See Miriam O. Barton, "Extension Work at the M.S.N.C.," p. 8 (cir. 1935), EMU Archives.
5. Circa 1941.
6. Horace Wilber, "Teachers College Extension," *The American Schoolmaster,* vol. 16. May, 1923. pp. 162–163.
7. Annual Report of Dean of Administration, 1952–1953, p. 49.
8. See bulletin, "Historical Information Relating to the Association for Field Services in Teacher Education," pp. 9–11, (Office of Field Services).
9. Annual Report of Dean of Administration, 1949–1950, p. 37.
10. See correspondence, Anderson to Elliott, June 18, 1953. (Office of Field Services).
11. Correspondence, Hood with State Department, May 18, 1951. (Office of Field Services).
12. Correspondence, Anderson to Elliott, June 6, 1955. (Office of Field Services).
13. See the 1922 Constitution. (Office of Field Services).
14. "Historical Information Relative to the Association for Field Services in Teacher Education," 1956, pp. 11–12.

Chapter Twenty-four

1. "The State Normal Schools," Mich. Com. L., 1897, c. 66, p. 630.
2. State Board Minutes, February 21, 1938 and July 29, 1938.
3. Chemistry: Perry Brundage, head of the department; Geography: James Glasgow, head of the department; and Hoover Jordan of the English Department.
4. Noble Lee Harrison, head of the department; and Earl Mosier, Dean of Professional Education.
5. Annual Report of the Dean of Administration, 1951–1952, p. 69.
6. Goode, "Cyclopedia of Education."
7. See the Annual Report for 1937 of President Isaiah Bowman to the Trustees of the Johns Hopkins University. Quoted in part in *School and Society,* vol. 49, pp. 28–30 (January 7, 1939).

Chapter Twenty-five

1. Catalog 1853.
2. Prior to the fire of 1859 the library appears to have been located on the second floor, and remained in a similar location in the new building. In 1878 it was moved from a "small" room to a "large" room on the same floor, over the principal's

office. In 1887 it was removed to the recently-constructed north wing of the building, where it was given most of the first floor. Here it remained until, in 1930, it
was provided with its own separate building, which it occupied until 1966. Thus, a
request that had been made to the legislature as early as 1887 by the State Board
and repeatedly renewed both by the State Board and the Board of Visitors was
finally achieved. See State Board minutes, July 29, 1887.

3. The features of the system were (1) a journal catalog or inventory arranged
alphabetically by author, containing information as to cost, and a brief description
of the contents of the item, (2) an author catalog on cards, (3) a catalog of subjects.

4. Edman Low: "A Survey of the Teachers College Libraries of Michigan,"
1938. It is a matter of interest that on occasion the selection by the faculty of books
to be purchased was participated in by the resident (in Ypsilanti) of the State
Board, and that the Board requested a complete list of books in use. See State Board
Minutes, Nov. 9, 1880 and Sept. 1, 1881 (in office of Superintendent of Public
Instruction, Lansing). Also, the resident member participated in drawing up rules
for the use of the library. State Board Minutes, September 17, 1888.

5. The report added: "Here are kept cyclopedias, technical dictionaries, standard
authorities, and such books as are more often needed for consultation in the recitation rooms than in the general reading-room."

6. See EMU Archives for Erickson statement of viewpoint.

7. A paper read by Miss Walton before the Ann Arbor Library Club in 1917.
EMU Archives.

8. Recollections of Frederick Cleveringa. EMU Archives.

9. Library Staff Manual in EMU Archives.

10. Miss Walton was especially interested in painting, and at one time had taken
lessons from the landscape painter, George Inness.

11. Recollections of Francis L. D. Goodrich. EMU Archives.

12. Including such long-standing members as Frederick Cleveringa, Reference
Librarian; Martha Rosentreter, Cataloger; Wanda Bates, Order Department, and
the Milliman sisters.

13. Files of the *New York Times,* for example, are now nearly complete. A project which was of great assistance in the writing of the Normal's history, the micro-
filming of the local newspaper was initiated by the library and accomplished with
the collaboration of the local press. The number of miscellaneous items, periodicals
and newspapers is growing constantly.

14. $2,680,000.

Chapter Twenty-six

1. *Normal News,* September, 1895, p. 8.

2. "Sketch from a Student's Notebook—A Student's Experience." *Ypsilanti
Commercial,* September 5, 1890.

3. Correspondence, Mrs. Cora Ann Ballore to Donald M. Currie, March 6,
1957.

4. For instance, Mrs. Elizabeth Fletcher, Mrs. Sarah W. George, Mrs. E. M.
Newton, Mrs. D. L. Quirk.

5. *Normal College News,* September 27, 1918.

6. Bessie Leach Priddy, "Teaching the World War," *The American Schoolmaster,* vol. 10, p. 354 (1917).

7. Correspondence, G. Stanley Hall to Bessie Leach Priddy, January 25, 1918. EMU Archives.

8. *The Kansas City Post,* April 26, 1922.

9. *Daily Ypsilantian-Press,* April 28, 1922.

10. Article by Charles McKenny, *Normal College News,* August 2, 1923.

11. Correspondence, Charles McKenny to President Kinley of the University of Illinois, June 27, 1923.

12. The plan of the dormitory rooms excited considerable interest on other campuses. Students were housed in two-room suites, one room for study and one for sleep. Two students were assigned to a suite, and "midnight oil" for one need not disturb the other. The plan proved to be financially practical, and ideal for promoting serious study. Unfortunately, post-war and later years brought crowded conditions and arrangements meant for two became sleeping quarters for four—with a corresponding de-emphasis on study conditions.

13. Architects were engaged at Normal and at Western State Teachers College at Kalamazoo within a month of each other in 1937, and at Central State Teachers College at Mt. Pleasant a year later. Approval for a union-dormitory project at Northern State Teachers College was given in September of 1938 "if and when desirable." See State Board Minutes for July 30 and August 26, 1937; and June 21 and September 8, 1938. Western (with the initial aid of a loan from their alumni association) moved a little faster and completed their building in the fall of 1938. See Knauss, "The First Fifty Years," p. 38.

14. *Normal College News,* February 4, 1932.

15. Annual Report of Dean of Women to Dean of Administration, 1949–1950.

Chapter Twenty-seven

1. E. P. Flanders to "Old Chum," April 13, 1860. Folder 3391, Michigan Historical Collections.

2. J. O. Beal to Almira Beale, Oct. 20, 1860. EMU Archives.

3. For this account I am greatly indebted to Professor Donald W. Disbrow of the History Department who collaborated in its writing. Austin George's account of the fortunes of Co. E constitute chapter XIV of Putnam's "History of the Michigan State Normal School."

4. See Putnam, pp. 280–294, for complete listing, including those who gave their lives.

5. By years, 129 can be accounted for, as follows: 1861, 32; 1862, 67; 1863, 12; 1864, 12; 1865, 6.

6. Bristol, "A Student's Experience," *Ypsilanti Commercial,* October 10, 1890.

7. Bulletin of Office of Religious Affairs, May, 1961.

8. Initiated in 1926.

9. I am greatly indebted to Dr. Adelyn Hollis, Associate Dean of Women at the Normal College from 1947 to 1958 who, upon resigning to become Dean of Women

at Eau Claire State College in Wisconsin, left with me the extensive notes from her inquiry into the names and origins of student organizations at the Normal.

10. Baird Manual, 1963, p. 767.

11. Joseph Bursley in "The University of Michigan," p. 1800. While probably not a major reason for the call for the convention, it may have influenced the inclusion in the Constitution of 1850 of Article XIII, sec. 6, which provided for election of the regents.

12. *Normal College News,* Nov. 8, 1912.

13. *Aurora* 1915, p. 139

14. *Aurora* 1916, p. 118.

Chapter Twenty-eight

1. Ralph Henry Gabriel, ed., "The Pageant of America," vol. XV, p. 4.

2. *Ypsilanti Commercial,* April 10, 1880.

3. *Ibid.,* June 11, 1881.

4. *Ibid.,* April 22, 1882.

5. George Key, assistant in mathematics, and Joseph Jenkins, a second-year student.

6. *Ypsilanti Commercial,* October 9, 1891.

7. Constitution, Women's Athletic Association.

8. *Normal College News,* March 9, 1898, p. 245.

9. *Ann Arbor News,* Dec. 14, 1960.

10. *Eastern Echo,* Oct. 15, 1959.

11. The colleges and universities were in Michigan, Wayne State University; in Ohio, John Carrol, Case Technical and Western Reserve University; in Pennsylvania, Thiel, Allegheny, and Washington and Jefferson; in West Virginia, Bethany. Eastern Michigan University became the ninth member.

12. *Eastern Echo,* May 7, 1964, p. 7.

13. *Aurora,* 1893, p. 85.

14. In 1919, 10 victories in 14 games; 1920, 13 in 15 games; 1921, 13 in 17 games.

15. *Normal News,* Dec., 1896, p. 64.

16. EMU Archives.

17. *Aurora,* 1942, p. 122.

18. *Aurora,* 1915, p. 123.

19. Olds was a graduate of '16; had captained the Normal team of '14.

20. *Aurora,* 1922, p. 146.

21. Beatty was eliminated in the final trials for the 1932 Olympic team when he overturned the last hurdle and was helped to his feet by an overzealous official (an assist that violated the rules).

22. Both black, Campbell and Jones starred in a time before black athletes held the dominant position they have now attained.

23. Team scoring in cross-country, unlike track meets, is based on the position of the man when he finishes. Thus, the winning runner scores 1, the second 2, and so on down the line. The sum of the scores of the first five men of a school to finish is

considered the team score. The team with the lowest score is the winner. The problem of accurately scoring large numbers of runners as they crossed the finish line was solved by Olds by running the boys through a chute which forced them into single file, thus preserving their position until the judges could record their order.

Chapter Twenty-nine

1. *Ypsilanti Press,* June 19, 1963, p. 17.

2. Michigan Statutes, 1849, P. A. 131, sec. 1.

3. Michigan Statutes, 1885, P. A. 130.

4. Michigan Constitution of 1850, art. XIII, sec. 9; Constitution of 1908, Art. XI, sec's 6 and 10.

5. Michigan Statutes, 1955, P. A. 100, sec. 3.

6. Michigan Statutes, 1959, P. A. 3, sec. 3.

7. See Chapter Four, pp. 77ff.

8. Catalogs 1934 and following.

9. State Board Minutes, April 27, 1934.

10. See *Ypsilanti Press,* June 19, 1963 for the panel's report.

11. John Munson, "Why Michigan is Great." EMU Archives.

12. Eastern Michigan University 1964–65 Institutional Self-Study, June 1965, p. 240. See pp. 240–244 for the full statement.

INDEX